1971

1971

A GLOBAL HISTORY OF THE CREATION OF BANGLADESH

Srinath Raghavan

Harvard University Press

Cambridge, Massachusetts
London, England
2013

Library of Congress Cataloging-in-Publication Data

Raghavan, Srinath.
1971 : a global history of the creation of Bangladesh / Srinath Raghavan.
pages cm
Includes bibliographical references and index.
ISBN 978-0-674-72864-6 (alk. paper)
1. Bangladesh—History—Revolution, 1971.   2. India-Pakistan Conflict, 1971.
3. South Asia—Politics and government.   I. Title.   II. Title: Global history
of the creation of Bangladesh.
DS395.5.R199 2013
954.9205'1—dc23   2013012267

To my parents

CONTENTS

1971

PROLOGUE:
THE CHRONICLE OF A BIRTH FORETOLD?

"It is very bad with your prime minister," blurted the burly Russian guard to the private secretary, "It is very bad." By the time the secretary rushed to the bedroom the prime minister of India, Lal Bahadur Shastri, was dead. It was a little past midnight in Tashkent on 11 January 1966. Less than twelve hours ago, Prime Minister Shastri and President Ayub Khan of Pakistan had agreed on a declaration restoring status quo ante between their countries after the war of 1965. The declaration had formally been inked in the presence of Premier Alexei Kosygin of the Soviet Union. Now it was Kosygin's turn to sign the condolence book placed near the deceased prime minister.

Later that morning, the casket mounted on a gun carriage and ringed with wreaths began moving toward the airport. The seventeen-kilometer route was lined by the city's mourning residents and flanked by Indian, Pakistani, and Soviet flags flying at half-mast, draped in black. At the airport, Ayub Khan joined the Soviet leaders in paying final homage to Shastri. As the casket was lowered from the carriage, Ayub and Kosygin stepped forward and became the lead pallbearers. When the coffin was placed on the gangway of the aircraft, the Red Army band sounded the funeral dirge, and Soviet soldiers reversed their arms. At 11 AM, the aircraft took off for New Delhi.[1]

None witnessing this tragic yet remarkable scene on that icy morning would have contemplated the possibility of another India-Pakistan war any time soon. The 1965 war was not, of course, the first conflict between the two countries. India and Pakistan had been rivals from the moment of partition and independence in August 1947. A few months later, the two neighbors were at war over the princely state of Jammu and Kashmir. The ceasefire agreement of January 1949 left the state divided between

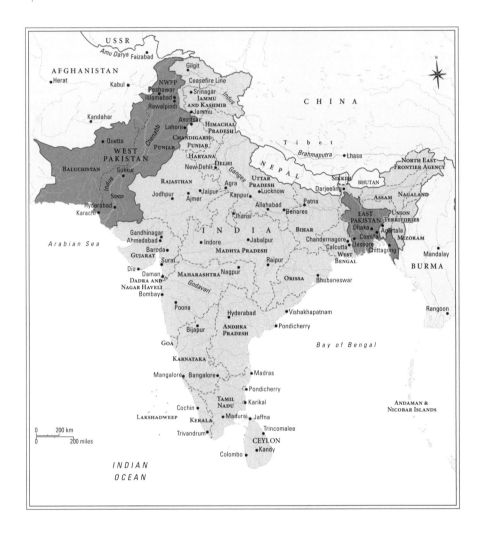

the belligerents. Although the dispute continued to simmer, the ceasefire held for sixteen years. India sought no more than to cement the status quo. Given the asymmetry of power between the two countries as well as India's willingness to flex its military muscle, Pakistan refrained from using force to wrest Kashmir.[2]

This prudent policy was jettisoned by the Pakistani leadership following a standoff with India over the Rann of Kutch in early 1965. Emboldened by India's tepid response to this crisis, Ayub Khan authorized a covert invasion of Kashmir that escalated into all-out war.[3] When the ceasefire was brokered, Indian forces were in control of territory ahead of India's western borders with Pakistan. The Tashkent agreement not only restored the territorial status quo but also stipulated against the use of force in resolving outstanding disputes. In consequence, the negotiators at Tashkent could look forward to another long spell of armed peace.

The conclusion of this agreement in Tashkent underscored the interest of the superpowers in preserving peace in the subcontinent. Indeed, superpower encroachment had been an endemic feature of postcolonial South Asia. In the early years after decolonization, the United States preferred to follow Britain's lead on subcontinental affairs. In the wake of the Korean War, the United States—fearing a Soviet thrust into the Middle East and desirous of tapping into Pakistan's military potential—concluded a defense pact with Pakistan in 1954. By the end of his term in office, President Dwight Eisenhower was ruing the damage wrought on US-India relations by his decision to arm Pakistan.[4] His successor, John F. Kennedy, undertook a drive to shore up ties with India. The outbreak of war between China and India in late 1962 afforded him an opening. Trounced by China, India desperately sought military assistance from Washington. Pakistan, however, lobbied to stem the flow of American matériel to India. President Kennedy responded by coaxing India to negotiate with Pakistan on Kashmir. The failure of these talks left all parties disenchanted.[5] When war broke out between India and Pakistan in August 1965, the Johnson administration—knee-deep in the bog of Vietnam—adopted a plague-on-both-your-houses attitude, imposing an arms embargo on the antagonists and allowing the Soviet Union to forge a postwar settlement.

The Soviet Union was a relatively late entrant to the geopolitics of South Asia. Not until the advent of Nikita Khrushchev in 1953, with his emphasis on peaceful coexistence to woo the postcolonial states, did South Asia acquire importance in Moscow's eyes. This led to an upswing in relations with India, which coincided with a downturn in Moscow's relations with Pakistan owing to the latter's entry into US-led alliances.[6] By the end of the 1950s, the Soviet Union was the one great power that supported India in the Kashmir dispute.

From late 1964 onward, there was a gradual shift in the Soviet outlook toward Pakistan. The backdrop to this was the rift between the Soviet Union and China. Moscow watched with concern as China drew close to Pakistan after the Sino-Indian war of 1962. The emerging Sino-Pakistan entente prompted the Russians to invite Ayub Khan to visit Moscow—the first visit at this level. Ayub's trip in April 1965 led to a thaw in Soviet-Pakistan relations. When Prime Minister Shastri visited Moscow seeking Soviet support on the Rann of Kutch, General Secretary Leonid Brezhnev observed that "every question like a medal has two sides to it."[7] After war broke out later that year, the Soviet Union urged both sides to cease hostilities. Even before the ceasefire was announced, Kosygin offered his good offices for mediation. In so doing, Moscow sought primarily to forestall American intervention.[8] An ancillary aim was to prevent China from deepening its relationship with Pakistan.[9] After the Tashkent Conference, the Russians were understandably sanguine that they had paved the way to a settlement of the Kashmir dispute and to peace in the subcontinent.[10]

I

And yet India and Pakistan were at war inside of six years. More intriguingly, the war was fought not over Kashmir but over the eastern wing of Pakistan. The West Pakistani military regime's use of force to suppress a popular movement for independence in East Pakistan led to a massive exodus of refugees to India and eventually to an Indian military intervention. The war of 1971 was the most significant geopolitical event in the subcontinent since its partition in 1947. Few contemporary conflicts have been so brief and localized but had such protracted and global ramifications. At one swoop, it led to the creation of the large and populous state of Bangladesh, and tilted the balance of power between India and Pakistan steeply in favor of the former. The consequences of the conflict continue to stalk the subcontinent. The Line of Control in Kashmir, the nuclearization of India and Pakistan, the conflicts on the Siachen Glacier and in Kargil, the insurgency in Kashmir, the political travails of Bangladesh: all can be traced back to nine intense months in 1971.

For the peoples of South Asia, the conflict has not really finished. For historians, it has barely begun. To be sure, the guns had hardly fallen silent when the first accounts by journalists and analysts began to be published. Hundreds more have been written in the four decades since. Although this body of writing remains important, there are remarkably few books that provide a *historical* account and explanation of the crisis and war of 1971. Most existing accounts lack the detachment and distance as well as the sources that make for good contemporary history. A superb exception to this trend is Richard Sisson and Leo Rose's *War and Secession*.[11] Drawing on interviews with key participants in Bangladesh,

Pakistan, and India, the authors presented an excellent and scholarly account that rose above the partisanship of the literature.

In the twenty years since Sisson and Rose wrote their book, there has been a deluge of documentary sources, but no single account has yet emerged that makes full use of this trove of materials to revisit the 1971 crisis. This is partly because professional historians of South Asia remain reluctant to venture beyond the boundary of 1947. Further, over the past two decades cultural and social history have occupied the center ground of South Asian history, evacuating political and diplomatic history to distant suburbs that are rarely visited and are increasingly uninhabited. It is not surprising that to the extent the emergence of Bangladesh attracts scholarly interest the subject tends to be viewed from the perspective of memory, violence, and identity.[12] This emerging literature has already expanded our horizons of inquiry and will no doubt enrich our understanding of the period. It would be a pity, however, if these themes detracted from a serious engagement with the staid but ineluctable questions on the causes, course, and consequences of the conflict.

This is all the more important because this emerging body of work leaves undisturbed some key parameters and assumptions of the older literature. The existing historiography on the creation of Bangladesh is beset by two dominating characteristics: insularity and determinism. Most of the books are written from the standpoint of one of the subcontinental protagonists and are often inflected by their nationalism. Thus, accounts from a Pakistani perspective tend to portray the conflict as a war of secession in which the Bengalis—a mistreated group in some accounts, benighted in others—betrayed the idea of Pakistan as the homeland for the Muslims of South Asia. These accounts invariably blame India for instigating Bengali separatism and for using the ensuing crisis to vivisect Pakistan—arguments that were originally advanced by the Pakistan government in a white paper published at the height of the crisis.[13]

By contrast, books from a Bangladeshi standpoint present the conflict as a war of national liberation: the story of the rise and realization of Bengali nationalism.[14] In most Indian accounts, the conflict of 1971 is the third India-Pakistan war: a continuation and decisive resolution of the long-standing military rivalry between the two countries as well as the contest between India's secular nationalism and Pakistan's "two-nation theory" that posited Hindus and Muslims as separate nations. Indian victory, these accounts argue, not only cut Pakistan to size but also shattered the ideological underpinnings of the Pakistani nation-state.[15]

The problem with these narratives is not simply one of bias. Rather, it is their shared assumption that the crisis was primarily a subcontinental affair—the world beyond playing only a bit part, if that. In thrall to their chosen national narratives, the authors of these accounts have rarely considered the impact of the wider global context in which the crisis began and played out to its denouement. Even the best accounts, such as the one by Sisson and Rose, tend to relegate the international dimensions of the crisis to the margins.

For all the differences of perspective, these narratives also tend to assume or argue that the breakup of Pakistan and the emergence of an independent Bangladesh were inevitable. This determinism is nicely captured in Salman Rushdie's mordant image of united Pakistan—in his novel *Shame*—as "that fantastic bird of a place, two Wings without a body, sundered by the land-mass of its greatest foe, joined by nothing but God." The historian Badruddin Umar, to take but one example, writes that "from the beginning Pakistan was an unstable state. The physical distance between the two wings of Pakistan . . . and the very considerable differences in the social, cultural and political life and traditions . . . differences in the economic conditions of the two parts and the imbalance in the structure of power. All these factors, *from the very beginning,* decided the course of political developments which *logically and inevitably* led to the disintegration and partition of Pakistan."[16] Similarly, Anatol Lieven argues that "no freak of history like united Pakistan with its two ethnically and culturally very different wings separated by 1,000 miles of hostile India, could possibly have lasted for long."[17] Even those scholars who shy away from such a strongly teleological and determinist position tend to argue that united Pakistan was structurally predisposed to fragmentation.[18] The history of the emergence of Bangladesh, then, is no more than the chronicle of a birth foretold.

Indeed, apart from the geographic separation of the two wings there was a widening gulf between them along two axes. First, there was the question of language. From the outset, the central leadership of Pakistan made it clear that Urdu would be the sole official language of the state. This triggered protests by Bengali students in East Pakistan, who feared that this policy would undermine their career prospects and demanded that Bengali be recognized as an official language. During his visit to Dhaka in March 1948, the founding father of Pakistan, Mohammed Ali

Jinnah, brusquely turned down their demand. The reiteration of Jinnah's stance by Prime Minister Khwaja Nazimuddin—himself an East Pakistani—in February 1952 led to widespread agitation in the province. The government's ham-handed response resulted in police shootings and deaths of student protesters. Thereafter, the language movement continued at a lower ebb until the Constituent Assembly's decision in 1956 to accept both Bengali and Urdu as state languages. It is argued that the events of 1952 "marked a sharp psychological rupture. For many in the Bengal delta it signified the shattering of the dream of Pakistan."[19]

The second axis of conflict was economic. The partition of India had sundered the trade and transportation links between East Pakistan and other parts of Bengal and Assam; the few industrialized areas of undivided Bengal remained in India. These problems were compounded by the economic policies adopted by successive governments of Pakistan. Thus, the foreign exchange earnings from the export of jute grown in East Pakistan—the principal export of Pakistan—were used to procure imports for the industrialization of West Pakistan. Moreover, the foreign aid received by Pakistan was largely diverted to projects in the western wing. Even when allocation of public funds to East Pakistan was increased in the late 1950s, the economic disparity between the wings remained stark. Although East Pakistan's annual growth rate increased from 1.7 percent for the years 1954–55 to 1959–60 to 5.2 percent for the period 1959–60 to 1964–65, the corresponding figures for West Pakistan shot up from 3.2 percent to 7.2 percent.[20]

Nevertheless these differences did not of themselves make an independent Bangladesh inevitable. How do we account for the fact that the language movement peaked in the early 1950s but the nationalist struggle for Bangladesh began only late in the next decade? Similarly, why did it take almost twenty-five years for the economic "contradictions"— present from the outset—to come to a head?

More persuasive are explanations that link these axes of conflict to the nature of the Pakistani state.[21] In this account, the move from linguistic regionalism to nationalism occurred only because of the tightly centralized character of the Pakistani polity. This system stemmed from the viceregal tradition bequeathed by the British Raj and reflected the domestic and foreign interests of the West Pakistani ruling elites. In particular, the bureaucratic-military oligarchy that ran the state from the early 1950s felt threatened by the political demands voiced by the Bengalis and sought continually to derail them. For a start, they sought to whittle down the political significance of East Pakistan's demographic and electoral majority by insisting on "parity" between the two wings—a move aimed at blunting the Bengalis' legislative and political influence. The East Pakistan government's continued prostration before the central leadership upended it in the first provincial assembly elections of 1954. These elections ushered into office a United Front government that had campaigned on the basis of a twenty-one-point program. This charter called for a greater role for East Pakistan in national affairs and sought "complete autonomy" for the province. Unsurprisingly, this proved uncongenial to the West Pakistanis, and the United Front was swiftly dismissed by the governor-general. The imposition of martial law in 1958 and the abrogation of representative democracy under General Ayub Khan sealed the political hopes of the Bengalis and turned them toward independence.

The argument that the breakup of Pakistan was in the cards from at least the late 1950s still does not explain why the inevitable took over a decade to come about. This is because it underestimates the willingness of the Bengali political elites to reach an accommodation with the central leadership and to work within the framework of a united Pakistan. Given the numerical preponderance of their province, Bengali politicians were always enticed by the glittering prize of high office at the national level as were Bengali civil servants and diplomats. This entailed a dilution of their quest for maximum autonomy for East Pakistan. When and why the Bengalis chose to exit Pakistan cannot be explained solely by recourse to the nature of the polity. In any case, an explanation for why this option was chosen does not tell us why the move to exit was bound to succeed. In short, the inevitability thesis—whether in its strong or milder formulations—does not really wash.

II

Against the grain of received wisdom, this book contends that there was nothing inevitable about the emergence of an independent Bangladesh in 1971. Far from being a predestined event, the creation of Bangladesh was the product of conjuncture and contingency, choice and chance. To understand why united Pakistan ceased to remain a viable political entity, we need to focus on a much shorter period starting in the late 1960s. It was then that the politics of Pakistan took a turn that made regional autonomy a non-negotiable demand of the Bengali political leadership. The military regime's unwillingness to countenance this set the stage for a rupture in March 1971. However, this *breakdown* of the political or-der of Pakistan did not automatically imply its *breakup*. The story told here is not of inevitable victory and forward march, but rather of nar-row squeaks and unanticipated twists. The book argues that the break-down and breakup of Pakistan can only be understood by situating these events in a wider global context and by examining the interplay between the domestic, regional, and international dimensions, for much of the contingency stressed in this account flowed from the global con-text of the time.

Owing to the marginalization of this dimension in the existing litera-ture, our understanding of its impact remains rudimentary. Most books continue to purvey a picture of the Cold War's imperatives leading to a lineup of the United States and China on Pakistan's side and the Soviet Union on India's—a caricature that has etched itself into the popular imagination. This grossly simplifies both the complicated context of the period and its multifarious impact on the events in South Asia.

The global context of the late 1960s and early 1970s was shaped by three large historical processes, each of which was at an interesting junc-ture. The decolonization of the European empires, which had begun in the aftermath of World War II, gathered pace in the late 1950s: a little over a decade on, scores of new nation-states swelled the ranks of the international system. The rise of the Third World altered the political topography of the globe and turned the spotlight on the divide between the developed North and the backward South.[22] It also put paid to at-tempts by the former colonial powers to devise new groupings—such as the modified British Commonwealth—that would perpetuate their influ-ence in Asia and Africa. More importantly, it was possible by the early 1970s to discern a general crisis in the postcolonial world. Wrought by the frequently ill-conceived drive toward decolonization, by the baleful authoritarian legacy of colonialism, and by the rapacity and ineptitude of the new governing elites, this crisis saw a series of nationalist govern-ments in Asia and Africa succumb to military or authoritarian rule.

Then there was the Cold War, which had begun in Europe as an ideo-logical and security competition between the United States and the Soviet Union, backed by their allies. By the mid-1960s, the rivalry in Europe had stabilized, but the Cold War had gone global, and its hottest locales were in the Third World.[23] By this time, the Cold War had also ceased to be a simple bipolar contest. The spectacular postwar economic recovery of Western Europe and Japan had loosened the ties that hand-cuffed them to the United States. Cracks had also opened up in the

Socialist bloc—the most dramatic manifestation of these dissensions being the uprising in Czechoslovakia in 1968, which was put down by the Red Army, and the Sino-Soviet military clashes of 1969.

The third, and incipient, historical current that swirled through this period was globalization. Spurred by unprecedented improvements in transportation, communications, and information technology, various parts of the world were being pulled into an increasingly integrated global market for goods and money. The unfolding process of globalization was not, however, restricted to the economic domain. The rise of multinational corporations and financial institutions that straddled the globe was impressive, but so was the rapid increase in the number of transnational nongovernmental organizations focused on development and relief in the Third World.[24] Equally important was the surge in movement of people, particularly of skilled labor, from the developing world to the advanced industrial economies of Western Europe and North America.[25] The existence of these diasporas was as crucial to the emergence of a transnational public sphere as the development of satellite telephones and television. Terms such as "global village" and "spaceship earth," which came into circulation in the 1960s, captured this emerging consciousness of a global whole. The upshot of this was the global diffusion of standards in various spheres that ranged from accounting practices to sartorial style, from language to political action.[26]

The confluence of these three processes shaped the origins, course, and outcome of the Bangladesh crisis. Viewing the conflict in this larger global perspective is not merely the conceit of a historian. The subcontinental protagonists in the drama themselves realized the importance of the international and transnational dimensions. By turns, the Bangladeshis, the Indians, and the Pakistanis sought to inform and mobilize international opinion—not just governmental support—behind their own causes. Winning this contest for world opinion, they felt, was at least as important as winning the conflict on the ground. Moreover, individuals and groups far removed from the scene of action consciously worked to influence the unfolding crisis.

III

In recovering the global dimension of the crisis, I have drawn on the work of international historians who have reminded us that there was much more to this period than the deep freeze of the Cold War.[27] But this book would have been impossible without the tremendous expansion over the past decade in archival sources relating to the Bangladesh crisis. The documentary foundations of this study are based on materials from the United States, Canada, Britain, Germany, Russia, and Australia as well as the United Nations and the World Bank. In India, I have used the mass of private and official papers available at the Nehru Memorial Museum and Library, which throw considerable light on Indian decision-making at the highest level. The Indian ministry of external affairs has begun to transfer its materials to the National Archives. More are available in the ministry's in-house archive—though only for a privileged few. I have proceeded on the premise that the book that awaits all evidence is unlikely to be written. Archives in Pakistan remain firmly shut on this controversial episode in the country's history. And there are no official archives relating to 1971 remaining in Bangladesh, as most of the documents were destroyed by the Pakistanis before they surrendered to the Indian forces. However, I was able to conduct a series of oral history interviews in Dhaka to supplement the memoirs and other accounts.

The book follows a broadly chronological approach, with individual chapters analyzing events and decisions in particular countries or institutions. As the story moves from one country to the next, there is also an unfolding logical sequence of knock-on events and decisions. The book opens with the downfall of Ayub Khan in early 1969, which I argue was the critical turning point that led toward the road to Bangladesh. Chapter 1 also examines the subsequent developments up to the mammoth victory of Mujibur Rahman's Awami League in the general election of December 1970. Chapter 2 considers why the negotiations for transfer of power failed and why the military brass led by General Yahya Khan decided to crack down on the Bengalis. Chapter 3 looks at India's response to this turn of events; in particular, it asks why India took a cautious tack and refrained from an early military intervention to curb the flow of refugees from East Pakistan.

The next five chapters focus on the international response to the crisis. Chapter 4 looks at the approach of the Nixon administration in the United States to the developing situation in South Asia. It examines the reasons behind Washington's reluctance to lean on Pakistan and asks whether alternative courses were open to the US leadership. In any event, that administration's stance played an important role in elbowing India toward the Soviet Union, resulting in the Indo-Soviet treaty of August 1971. Chapter 5 analyzes Moscow's position on the crisis and argues that the Soviet Union and Indian stances on the crisis were not in sync until late in the crisis. Chapter 6 and Chapter 7 ask why the South Asian crisis caught the global imagination and whether trends in the transnational public sphere had any impact on the major powers and the United Nations. Chapter 8 considers China's response to the crisis and suggests that its support for Pakistan was at best ambivalent.

Chapter 9 returns to the subcontinent, examining why the crisis escalated into all-out war toward the end of November 1971. Chapter 10 considers why the war ended with a Pakistani surrender on the eastern front and the creation of an independent Bangladesh. Both these chapters challenge conventional accounts and underline the importance of the international dimension for satisfactory explanations of these events. The conclusion argues that things did not have to turn out the way they did: at various points, there were alternative choices open to the various actors and forks on the road that were not taken. These are not hypothetical choices conjured up in the comforting light of hindsight, but options that were actively weighed and discarded by the protagonists themselves. The conclusion also considers the longer-term consequences of some key choices made during the crisis.

The analytical focus of this book unavoidably leaves out swaths of issues related to a conflict that was played out at multiple levels: between combatants and noncombatants (especially women), between non-Bengalis and Bengalis, between West Pakistanis and East Pakistanis, and between Pakistan and India. I also avoid adjudicating on the controversy over the total number of casualties and victims. Bangladeshi accounts tend to put the figure at 3 million; Pakistani official figures claim no more than 26,000. A recent study claims that "at least 50,000–100,000 people perished in the conflict" but that anything above this figure is speculative.[28] The fact, however, remains that we cannot know with any degree of certainty the total number of victims. In the first place, the crisis and war occurred in the immediate aftermath of the worst natural disaster to strike the Bengal delta in the twentieth century. Disentangling the numbers of fatalities caused by these natural and man-made crises is likely to be impossible. In the second place, the Pakistan army left behind no record of civil casualties during the crisis—if it maintained any at all. In principle, it should be possible to arrive at an approximation of the number of "missing" people by a demographic analysis comparing the census data of 1961 and 1972. In practice, the reliability of the result would depend on the quality of data collection during these censuses and the availability of age-specific and gender-differentiated mortality rates. There is the additional problem of accounting for the number of Bengali refugees who stayed back in India after 1971—another politically charged minefield. At any rate, my spirit quailed before this task. However, my approach and focus are aimed not at downplaying the agency of those who struggled against a murderous military regime, but rather at placing their struggle in the broader context in which it occurred and by which it was so decisively shaped. People, as Marx famously observed, make their own history but not in circumstances of their own choosing.

A final reason for privileging such a broad treatment is the contemporary resonance of the Bangladesh crisis. Today, similar crises and their attendant international debates continue to occur against different regional and political backdrops. In exploring the 1971 example, therefore, I hope to open a window to the nature of international humanitarian crises and their management. In particular, I wish to underscore the complex mixture of motives that drives such crises and the manner in which strategic interaction in such situations can produce unintended outcomes. This story is unlikely to provide nostrums for our current predicaments or answers to contemporary debates, but it can perhaps prompt us to consider whether we are even asking the right questions.

1

THE TURNING POINT

The morning of 25 March 1969 was unseasonably cloudy in Islamabad. Dressed in a light gray suit, his hands deep in his pockets, Field Marshal Ayub Khan paced the presidential lawns, which were ringed yellow with brilliant lilies. He was waiting for General Yahya Khan, the commander in chief. When the latter arrived, they retired to his study wherein Ayub recorded his last speech to the people of Pakistan. Explaining his abdication, Ayub declared, "It is impossible for me to preside over the destruction of our country." "The whole nation demands," he lamely observed, "that General Yahya . . . should fulfil his constitutional responsibilities." By the time Ayub was finished, the presidential residence seemed funereally sedate. The two military men parted after a bluff handshake. As the speech was broadcast that evening, a curtain of rain swept the president's house and hammered the roof.[1] His public life at an end, Ayub Khan withdrew into an embittered seclusion, insisting that "democratic methods are foreign to our people."[2]

Ayub's departure was not merely the result of another military takeover. Yet the erosion of his authority had been remarkably swift. A little over a decade earlier, Ayub had seized power in a coup d'état. Stability and growth were the watchwords of his regime. He dispensed with Pakistan's parliamentary democracy and introduced a presidential system based on indirect elections. For this achievement, he was hailed by a prominent American political scientist, Samuel Huntington, as a leader akin to "a Solon or Lycurgus or 'Great Legislator' on the Platonic or Rousseauian model."[3] Over these years, Pakistan emerged as the first of the Asian tigers. For the first ten years of Ayub's rule, annual economic growth rates had averaged 5.5 percent. Pakistan also began rapidly to

14

industrialize: large-scale manufacturing grew over the same period at nearly 17 percent a year.[4]

Starting in late 1968, however, a series of protests racked the regime and eventually brought down the field marshal. The uprising that shook the regime of Ayub Khan was, of course, fired by the specific social, economic, and political context of Pakistan. But it had been touched off by a rash of revolts that had erupted across the world, and its aftershocks would shift the tectonic plates that underlay united Pakistan. The crisis of 1971 had a global dimension from the outset.

I

Nineteen sixty-eight was a year of global tumult triggered by student protests. The US Central Intelligence Agency (CIA) observed that "youthful dissidence, involving students and non-students alike, is a world-wide phenomenon. It is shaped in every instance by local conditions, but nonetheless there are striking similarities." It went on to note, "Student protest is visible, highly vocal, increasingly militant and feared by many to be interconnected world-wide . . . Student Power is no longer a chimera."[5]

Indeed, more than twenty countries across the globe pulsated with protests. North America and Western Europe, China and Eastern Europe, East and West Asia, Africa and Latin America—none were immune to the contagion of youthful dissidence. Yet the hefty literature on the Sixties remains entranced by the events in Western Europe and the United States.[6] Even the emerging scholarly work that attempts to view 1968 in a wider framework barely acknowledges the significance of the year for South Asia in general and Pakistan in particular.[7] This is especially regrettable because the uprising in Pakistan was arguably the most successful of all the revolts in that momentous year.

The upheavals of 1968 at once reflected and accentuated the incipient process of globalization, but they were also shaped by the other historical currents washing through the Sixties: the Cold War and decolonization. The uprising in Pakistan mirrored, in many respects, the movements in other parts of the world. First, in Pakistan as elsewhere, the roots of the student movement lay in the expansion of higher education over the past two decades. The number of colleges affiliated with these universities also rapidly increased. Dhaka University, for example, had over 50,000 students in 1968, of whom over 7,000 resided on campus.[8]

Second, the student movement had gathered steam from earlier protests over educational issues. The Education Commission constituted by Ayub Khan had decided in 1962 to extend undergraduate education from two to three years, to tighten the grading criteria, and to provide only one opportunity for failed students to make good. The students felt that these steps would not only delay their entry into the employment market but also undermine their career prospects. This led to widespread protests in both the eastern and western wings, especially in East Pakistan.[9] Since the mid-1960s, students had also been chafing at the government's interference in the functioning of universities and the servile acquiescence of the university authorities. By 1968, reform of the university was as important to Pakistani students as to their counterparts elsewhere.

Third, there was an economic dimension to the events of 1968. The postwar economic performance of Western Europe, Japan, and the United States had both benefited the Sixties generation and drawn their ire. As the West German student icon Rudi Dutschke observed, "Not until 1964–65 when the growth of industry suddenly sank from 6–8% per annum to 2.5–4% per annum did we begin to realise that capitalism had not eliminated its inherent contradictions."[10] Pakistan, too, had experienced an economic boom under Ayub Khan. Much of this impressive growth, however, benefited Pakistan's small private sector. This was not an unintended consequence: Ayub's economic policies—designed and implemented with Western assistance—were aimed at fostering the bourgeoisie. Between 1963 and 1968, the absolute number of impoverished people rose from 8.65 million to 9.33 million.[11] Consciousness of this disparity grew after the revelation by the chief economist of the planning commission that a mere twenty-two families owned or controlled 66 percent of the country's industrial wealth and 87 percent of banking and insurance. Among the student protesters, "22 families" became a favored slogan. The regime's attempt to celebrate the "Decade of Development" under Ayub in late 1968 provided another target for the students.[12]

Fourth, the movement in Pakistan, much like elsewhere, had a generational dimension. Access to a university education in an urban setting made the students self-conscious about their difference from their parents—many of whom had limited education, if at all, and lived in the villages—and so weakened traditional family hierarchies. Further, the students did not share their elders' unstinting admiration for the Pakistani state. Their parents belonged to the generation that had struggled to bring Pakistan into existence, but the students had come of age after the authoritarian turn taken under Ayub. Nowhere was this truer than in East Pakistan, where the students were increasingly impatient with their elders' willingness to work with the central authorities.

Fifth, this generational divide was widened by new cultural mores influencing the youth of Pakistan. The counterculture of the Sixties found a fertile bed among Pakistani youngsters—even if all the movement's flowers could not bloom in this cultural context. In the finest memoir of that decade, Sheila Rowbotham noted that for her generation "music was the barometer of consciousness."[13] Indeed, rock 'n' roll was an important vector for the global diffusion, including to Pakistan, of the spirit of the Sixties.

Sixth, as in the United States and Europe, the student protests of 1968 in Pakistan were a revolt against the Cold War and the stultifying structures it imposed.[14] The focal point for Pakistani students, too, was opposition to the Vietnam War. The radical writer Habib Jalil's poem, calling on "Global defenders of human rights" to speak and reminding his audience that "Vietnam is on fire," caught the mood of the students.[15]

The students were also acutely alert to the fact that the authoritarian, military-bureaucratic regime was being propped up by the Cold War alliances in which Pakistan was entangled.

Finally, the language and forms of student protest in Pakistan were directly inspired by the upheavals in other places. In particular, the vocabulary and texts of the revolutionary left provided the terms on which much of the students' activity was conceptualized and debated. "Every student was reading Marx, Lenin, Mao," recalled a student of Punjab University who graduated in 1969. On the last night on campus, "we gave revolutionary speeches and were very emotional. At the end we sang the Internationale and tore apart our degrees and promised that from here on we will not go to our homes, rather we will go to the factories and the fields to work for revolution."[16] Similarly, the entire gamut of protest used elsewhere, from sit-in to street fighting, was adopted by the students of Pakistan.

All this was possible owing to technological advances that enabled almost instant transmission of news to different parts of the globe.

Throughout 1968, the English and vernacular newspapers in Pakistan extensively covered the protests in the United States, Western Europe, and elsewhere. Also, 1968 was the year that television came to Pakistan. In late 1967, three television stations had been set up in the West Pakistani cities of Karachi, Lahore, and Rawalpindi, and another station was inaugurated in early 1968 in Dhaka. Though television, like print and radio, was subject to censorship, Pakistanis congregating before their neighborhood television sets were exposed to news and images of the global uprisings.[17]

In addition to technology, the students in Pakistan had a direct link with the British student movement in the person of Tariq Ali. Born into a wealthy and well-connected family with socialist leanings, Ali was prominent in student politics in the early 1960s. His role in organizing protests against the Ayub regime made him a marked man. Fearing for his life, his parent bundled him off to Oxford. In 1965, he was elected president of the Oxford Union, and soon he was active in a Trotskyist splinter-group that was in the thick of the protests against the Vietnam War. By 1968, he had become the face of the protesting youth in Britain. For most Pakistani students, Tariq Ali was an iconic figure. But he was also a more direct source of inspiration and assistance. In early 1969, at the height of the student protests, Ali received a rousing welcome from the student groups in Pakistan.[18] In reviewing the situation, a British diplomat wrote that "the only agreeable aspect from the strictly British point of view is that Tariq Ali has left us to return to Pakistan, where I wish him no greater success than he has achieved here."[19]

All said, there were important differences between the student movements in the West and in Pakistan. For one thing, they differed in their objectives. Although the Western protests were couched in the language of the revolutionary left, the movements sought not to overthrow the regimes but to transform interpersonal relations and to open up decision-making processes in the state, the university, and the workplace. The essentially libertarian character of these movements was captured by the slogan "It is forbidden to forbid."[20] By contrast, the Pakistani students aimed at deposing the regime and effecting a fundamental transformation of the state. For another, unlike their counterparts in the West, the Pakistani students operated in an environment bereft of organized political forces or democratic structures. Their movement, in consequence, had a more direct impact on the political trajectory of the country.

II

The protest began on 7 November 1968 with a minor incident involving a group of students from Gordon College in Rawalpindi. The students were returning from an outing to Landi Kotal, a shopping center near the Afghan border, with a few thousand rupees worth of contraband. Though such "smuggling" happened routinely in a town filled with officials, the students' booty was impounded by the local authorities, and charges were leveled on them. Instead of tamely submitting to such treatment, the students of Gordon College organized a strike and marched in procession to the deputy commissioner's office. Soon they were joined by students from another college in Rawalpindi. When the crowd refused to disperse, the police charged with their truncheons and opened fire. One student was killed. Thereafter, the situation rapidly worsened. Over the next two days, students from various colleges in town picketed government offices and engaged in running battles with the police. Within days, campuses and towns across West Pakistan were aflame with protesting students.[21]

By 28 November, the protests had acquired substantial momentum. Ayub noted in his diary that "there have been widespread disturbances by students and hooligans in several towns. They indulged in looting and arson . . . The curious thing is that young school children of 10–12 years of age have also taken to violence."[22] The next day, the students issued a call for a general strike in Rawalpindi and asked workers, shopkeepers, and the unemployed to march with them. The workers responded to the call: "Many onlookers," a newspaper reported, "also joined the procession."[23] Unnerved by the scale of the turnout, the police attempted to break up the demonstration with force, resulting in a six-hour standoff with the students. The latter, joined by the workers, retaliated against government installations: two police stations were razed to the ground.

Soon, the students in East Pakistan joined the fray. On 6 December, they issued a call for a general strike in Dhaka, aimed to coincide with Ayub Khan's visit to the city. The authorities imposed a curfew but failed to deter students and workers from forming a massive procession. Hundreds of demonstrators were arrested and several wounded when the police opened fire.[24] This was followed by a string of strikes in Dhaka and other towns, in which workers and vendors, slum-dwellers and the unemployed, rag-pickers and white-collar employees joined the students.

More worrying for the authorities was the students' success in fanning out to the countryside and mobilizing peasants and rural workers. This was made possible by the students' organic links with the villages through their families and other networks of kinship as well as their skill in harnessing local grievances for larger causes.[25]

Initially, the students' objectives and demands were inchoate. On 6 December, the students in Rawalpindi held a convention and declared their intention to continue the struggle until an impartial commission was set up to inquire into the police excesses against them. When the government sought to fob them off, the students mobilized for their largest protest yet. On 25 December 1968, a demonstration of 10,000 students was joined by nearly 20,000 workers. That day, the students announced that they would no longer present their demands to the current regime: they would only place their program before a people's government. Thereafter, their sole demand was for Ayub Khan to quit.[26]

The student groups in East Pakistan came together in January 1969 to form a Student Action Committee (SAC). The main constituents of this alliance were the East Pakistan Students' League (EPSL) and the two factions (pro-Soviet and pro-China) of the East Pakistan Students' Union (EPSU). The EPSL owed allegiance to the Awami League led by Sheikh Mujibur Rahman, and the EPSU members to their respective factions of the East Pakistan Communist Party (EPCP). The student groups in East Pakistan were more politically attuned than their counterparts in West Pakistan partly because of a long-standing tradition of student activism in Bengal—Mujib himself had started out as a student leader—and partly because the education system in the province was a shambles, even by comparison with the other wing of the country.

At any rate, the SAC formally set forth an eleven-point program. The first point advanced a set of seventeen demands for educational reforms. The next three dealt with the political structure of the state: direct elections on the basis of universal adult franchise to establish a parliamentary democracy; full autonomy for East Pakistan within a federal constitution; and subfederation in West Pakistan, with full autonomy for all provinces. The next four points focused on economic issues: nationalization of big industries, the jute trade, and the financial sector; reduction of rents and taxes on peasants and remission of all arrears; a guarantee of fair wages and bonuses for workers, provision of other social facilities, and the granting of the right to form unions and to strike; and flood control measures for East Pakistan. On external relations, the program called for abrogation of the Cold War alliances in Asia and the military pacts with the United States as well as the formulation of a nonaligned foreign policy. Finally, the program sought the repeal of all emergency laws and the release of all activists jailed by the regime.[27]

The SAC also decided to join forces with other student groups across the country and to observe 17 January 1969 as "Demands Day." This led to the first coordinated general strike throughout Pakistan, with massive demonstrations in Dhaka and Rawalpindi, Lahore, and Karachi, among other cities in both the wings. The regime came down with unprecedented force. "Last two weeks," Ayub noted on 26 January, "have been tumultuous in the country. There have been demonstrations and protests against the government in the main cities. Rawalpindi has been particularly bad . . . Three days ago the situation in Dacca got out of control." The students in East Pakistan, he later observed, "are under nobody's control."[28]

The lack of leadership was true indeed. None of the political parties had gotten off the blocks quickly after the student protests had commenced. Besides, many political leaders were forced to cool their heels in prison, as was the case with the two most charismatic leaders from each wing: Sheikh Mujibur Rahman of the Awami League, and Zulfikar Ali Bhutto of the Pakistan People's Party (PPP).

Of humble origins, Mujib had entered politics in 1940 as a student volunteer for the Muslim League and a youthful campaigner for Pakistan. He came under the wing of Huseyn Shaheed Suhrawardy, who later became the last chief minister of undivided Bengal and prime minister of Pakistan in 1956. In 1949, Mujib joined the new Awami Muslim League formed by Suhrawardy and Maulana Bhashani. He shot to prominence during the language movement, and after Bhashani's exit from the party, Mujib became the acknowledged successor to Suhrawardy.[29] Despite his growing disenchantment with the reality of Pakistan, Mujib backed Suhrawardy in his quest for a role in national politics. Thus, when Prime Minister Suhrawardy assured the Bengalis that the constitution of 1956 provided 98 percent autonomy to their province, he quietly acquiesced in this outrageous claim. Only after the fall of Suhrawardy in the center did Mujib come into his own again as a champion of regional autonomy.[30] Nevertheless, like many Bengali Muslim politicians of his generation, Mujib hoped both to preserve the unity of Pakistan under a federal structure and to make a bid for national leadership by leveraging the Bengalis' potential electoral majority.

Through the Ayub years, the Awami League played an oppositional political role. In March 1966, Mujib advanced a six-point program of autonomy for East Pakistan. This called for parliamentary democracy and a genuinely federal constitution; for restricting the powers of the federal government to defense and foreign affairs; for establishing two separate currencies for each wing; for devolving fiscal policy to the federating units; for maintaining separate foreign exchange earnings for each wing; and for raising a separate militia for the defense of East Pakistan.[31] When the protests erupted in 1968, Mujib was on trial for allegedly conspiring with India to undermine the unity of Pakistan—the so-called Agartala conspiracy case, named after the eastern Indian town where Mujib was alleged to have met and schemed with Indian agents.[32]

Bhutto's career had followed rather a different trajectory. Born into a prominent and wealthy landed family in Sindh, Bhutto took degrees from Berkeley and Oxford before being called to the bar in 1953. On returning to Pakistan, he embarked on a meteoric political career. In 1958, Bhutto was handpicked by Ayub Khan to join his first cabinet. Five years on, after holding a succession of portfolios, he became the foreign minister. Bhutto played a pivotal role in maneuvering Ayub toward an entente with China. He also egged on the field marshal to attack India in 1965, with disastrous consequences. Bhutto fell out with his patron the following year over the Tashkent agreement, which he bitterly criticized. On resigning from the government, Bhutto traveled all over West Pakistan, excoriating his erstwhile master and tapping into local grievances. During this period, he also founded the Pakistan People's Party. Owing to Bhutto's fiery opposition to the regime, the West Pakistan student protesters of 1968 regarded him as a hero; for the same reason, he was taken into custody a few days into the uprising.

With Bhutto and Mujib in prison, the PPP and the Awami League were largely rudderless. In early January 1969, eight other parties formed a Democratic Action Committee (DAC), which failed to articulate a coherent set of demands. The DAC's dithering contrasted unfavorably with the eleven-point program of the Bengali students. As an East Pakistani newspaper noted, "The demand charter placed by them [students] exceeds the imagination of ordinary political parties. What the students are agitating for can very well form the basis of an anti-feudal, anti-capitalist, anti-imperialist democratic movement. Their programme and leadership have largely been accepted by the people of the country."[33] A British diplomat in Pakistan similarly concluded that "in East Pakistan, it is the students and their associates who have captured the imagination of the masses and who, by their 11-points (only one of which is strictly to do with education), have out-bid the D.A.C."[34]

The unremitting pressure from the protesters led Ayub to reassess his options. If he was to preserve the presidential system that he had inaugurated, Ayub concluded, he would have to relinquish power. That Ayub should be concerned in this hour of crisis about his legacy was not surprising. He was, after all, the man on horseback who had elicited deep admiration in the West and whose program of authoritarian modernization had inspired other dictators in the Third World. On 21 February 1969, Ayub Khan announced that he would not contest the next presidential election. By so doing, he hoped to calm temporarily the opposition and the army, and to use the interregnum to influence the election of an appropriate successor.[35]

The same day, Mujib was released from prison. Ayub's subsequent attempts to forge a political consensus through a roundtable conference came to naught. At their very first meeting, Mujib made it clear that he would settle for nothing less than his six points. "There was no give and take in his points," Ayub despondently noted. He shrewdly observed that Mujib "was greatly under the influence of extremists in his party and the students who were completely out of control."[36] Indeed, soon after his release, Mujib had been feted with a massive rally organized by the students at Dhaka's Race Course grounds; more symbolically, Mujib was conferred with the title "Bangabandhu" (Friend of Bengal). The students' eleven-point program, which was rather more radical than Mujib's six points, had been reiterated at that meeting. By acknowledging the students' demands and by opting to ride the wave of radicalism triggered by their protests over the past months, Mujib circumscribed his bargaining position vis-à-vis the West Pakistanis. Thenceforth, the six points became the minimum acceptable outcome for the Bengalis rather than being a maximum opening bid that could be diluted during the course of negotiations. The history of East Pakistan had reached a turning point—and began to turn.

III

As the Round Table Conference lumbered on, the military leadership grew eager to grasp the levers of state power. From their perspective, the nub of the problem was Ayub himself: the popular movement was evidently aimed at unseating him, and his own vacillations had aggravated the unrest. Besides, the military felt, it was time to clip the pretensions of the civilian bureaucracy, which had been so important a component of Ayub's regime and had proved so thoroughly incapable of governing the country. The military had yet again to demonstrate that it was the sole anchor against extremism and anarchy. By the third week of February 1969, the army leadership began to take the first steps toward deposing the field marshal.

Earlier that month, the governor of Punjab had met the president and requested the imposition of martial law in his province. Ayub had been "taken aback." He was understandably averse to this option, but decided to consult the commander in chief. General Agha Mohammad Yahya Khan was Ayub's prize protégé. A young brigadier when Ayub had taken over as commander in chief, Yahya had matured into a trusted associate. In 1966, Ayub appointed him commander in chief, superseding two senior claimants for the post. The promotion was all the more remarkable given that Yahya was a Shia in the predominantly Sunni officer corps. But Ayub now found that Yahya had grown comfortable in his shoes. The commander in chief told him that "partial martial law at this stage was not the answer."[37] The army was interested not in aiding the regime but in supplanting it.

Speaking to Ayub after a cabinet meeting on 23 February, Yahya was certain that "the time had come for imposition of countrywide martial law to save the country. Partial martial law won't do any good."[38] This stance reflected the collective wisdom of the senior army leadership. The chief of general staff held, for instance, that "partial martial law was no panacea for our problems," and that Ayub should hand over the reins to Yahya, who in turn should declare martial law.[39] The director of military operations claimed that "the army can't just sit on its haunches while the whole country burns" and believed that Ayub was "up to all sorts of tricks." The general headquarters had also summoned the corps commanders and apprised them of its thinking.[40] Indeed, by the time the cabinet met, the army had already begun drafting martial law regulations.

Within two weeks, Yahya was back with Ayub, saying that he was "very pessimistic" about the situation and insisting that "this rot could only be stopped by imposition of martial law."[41] Yahya's blandishments contained not a grain of subtlety. He wanted Ayub to secure an assurance from the opposition that they would support a compromise formula advanced by the regime. "If they do not give you such an assurance then you will be free to act." The government, he observed, had "lost all credibility . . . There is very little time left."[42] The best that Ayub could come up with was the setting up of a constitution commission, but Yahya shot the idea down, claiming the situation was "far worse than they imagined." Piecemeal changes could not work a miracle. Yahya declared that "he will carry out his duty to the country." Ayub knew that the game was up. "It was clear as to what Gen. Yahya Khan was heading for," he wrote in his diary.[43] Two days later, he made the formal decision to hand over power to Yahya.

On 26 March, Yahya Khan broadcast his first speech announcing the imposition of martial law. "We have had enough of administrative laxity and chaos," he declared. "I shall see to it that this is not repeated in any form or manner." Yahya averred that he had "no ambition" but to pave the way for a "constitutional government," but he was convinced that sound administration was "a prerequisite for sane and constructive political life."[44] The message was all too familiar to the people of Pakistan. East Pakistan crackled with protests, which were quickly suppressed, but the province continued to simmer with resentment.[45] The reception in West Pakistan was mostly placid.

Yahya anointed himself president as well as chief martial law administrator (CMLA). Yet the regime was actually run by a group of senior officers assisted by bureaucrats and handpicked civilian advisers. The key military leaders involved in decision making were Lieutenant General S. G. M. M. Peerzada, principal staff officer to the president; Lieutenant General Abdul Hamid, the army chief; Major General Ghulam Umar, secretary of the national security council (NSC); Lieutenant General Gul Hassan Khan, the chief of general staff; and Major General A. O. Mitha, the quartermaster general. All had known each other and Yahya throughout their professional lives, but their relationships with one another were hardly easy. Yahya considered these tensions to be not entirely problematic, as they at least ensured that his colleagues lacked the cohesion to conspire in overthrowing him. Yet the martial law administration was not a collection of marionettes stringed into action by Yahya; to the contrary, his room for maneuver on major policy matters was limited by the views of his senior military colleagues.

The problems in this system were compounded by the infirmities of Yahya Khan himself. Equipped with an uncluttered—some would say vacant—mind, though not slow on the uptake, Yahya exuded professional confidence. His military subordinates found him easy to work with, for he seldom stood on ceremony and focused quickly on the heart of a matter. But his brisk, unreflective style was unsuited to the demands of an office that fused the highest political and military power. A close civilian adviser would trenchantly recall that "his powers of understanding and of taking imaginative decisions were extremely limited."[46] Yahya's energies were also sapped by his hectic social routine. He was excessively fond of the bottle, and his pursuit of a string of liaisons was unblemished by concerns about public opprobrium or professional ethics. All this left the martial law authority ill-prepared to weather the storms that would be visited upon it.

IV

From the outset, Yahya publicly insisted that he was interested only in ensuring the establishment of a new constitution and a smooth transition to an elected civilian government. This did not mean—as the generals would subsequently maintain and as some historians have argued— that "the military leadership was committed to an early transfer of power." Nor did it imply that Yahya sought to "arrange for the withdrawal of the military from power."[47] The military governor of West Pakistan was pointedly told by Peerzada that "we are in no hurry to hand over."[48] To be sure, Yahya did initiate discussions with political leaders, but these only deepened his impression that the politicians were "a pack of jokers." Speaking at a regimental gathering in May 1969, Yahya claimed that the army "must be prepared to rule this unfortunate country for the next 14 years or so. I simply can't throw the country to the wolves."[49]

Yahya was clever enough to understand that direct military rule could not be ensured in perpetuity. The student protests had transformed the political climate in Pakistan and made it impossible to turn the clock back. So the martial law authority hazily envisaged a constitutional order that would entrench the military as the "guardian" of the elected government—quite possibly with Yahya Khan as the president. To some members of the administration, the "Turkish model" held out the beguiling prospect of such an arrangement.[50] A transition along these lines could only be ensured if the military could control the exercise of constitution making. Yahya was determined, therefore, to continue with martial law until an elected assembly had drawn up the constitution and received his approval.[51]

Between April and November 1969 Yahya met with leaders of parties across the political spectrum. The discussions centered on the principles that should govern the transition from the martial law administration to an elected government. On three overarching issues there was a convergence of views. All parties broadly agreed that Pakistan should adopt a Westminster-style parliamentary system, that it should remain an Islamic state, and that the federal system should be maintained. But there were major differences about the nature of the relationship between the center and the federating units. Almost all parties came out in favor of autonomy, but like the blind men sizing up the elephant they had widely differing views of what this principle might entail. Mujibur Rahman sought autonomy along the lines of the six points. The smaller Western-wing parties sought more regional autonomy than the larger ones were willing to concede. Bhutto sought to sound the tocsin by writing to Peerzada that the six points "spell the destruction of Pakistan."[52] More concretely, his party stood for central control on subjects ranging from irrigation to power and the location of heavy industries.[53] Confronted with this cacophony of views, the regime decided to sidestep the issue.

On 28 November 1969 Yahya Khan outlined his plans for the way forward. He had decided to evolve "a legal framework for general elections," which would be in place by March 1970. The general elections would be held on 5 October. Yahya conceded that the East Pakistanis were "fully justified in being dissatisfied" with the prevailing arrangements: "The requirement would appear to be maximum autonomy to the two Wings of Pakistan so long as it does not impair national integrity and solidarity of the country." The "National Assembly" so elected would have to draft and adopt the constitution within 120 days, else the assembly would be dissolved and fresh elections called.[54] This proviso was justified on the grounds that it was necessary to impart a sense of urgency to the elected leaders.[55] But given the crevasses between the positions of the major parties, this stipulation would enable the regime to control their trek toward the constitutional summit.

The published Legal Framework Order (LFO) carried an additional requirement: The constitution bill adopted by the assembly would be presented to the president for authentication. If the latter refused to accord his approval, the assembly would stand dissolved. Speaking to the press a few days later, Yahya observed that there was no reason why he should not authenticate a constitution that accorded with the framework laid down by the administration. More ominously, he reminded them that the president was "an integral part of the constitution and the constitution making body."[56] Even before the LFO came into force, the martial law administration removed the proscription on political activities. Pakistan was gearing up for its first general elections.

V

The political parties had already been operating in campaign mode for the past six months. Twenty-five parties—seventeen from the East and eight from the West—eventually entered the national elections; in all, 1,570 candidates vied for the 300 seats. The parties were permitted to use the state-owned radio and television for their political campaigns. This proved particularly useful for diluting the traditional filaments of patronage that many had assumed would determine the outcome of the elections. But it also cast into sharp relief the provincialism of Pakistani politics—a trend that had been visible since the mid-1950s and had now accentuated. Not a single party proved capable of mobilizing voters in both wings of the country. Even the larger parties were focused on tending their own parishes and were content with a tenuous toehold in the other wing. Efforts to create pan-Pakistan coalitions rapidly ran into the sands. As the campaign wore on, the political lines dividing the East and the West turned into barbed-wire fences.

The only parties that staked a serious claim on the allegiance of both the wings were the Jamaat-i-Islami and the three Muslim Leagues. The principal problem for these parties was that their appeals for a strong and Islamic government failed to strike a chord with the recently galvanized populace of West Pakistan, never mind those of the East. This self-professed "old guard" of Pakistan failed to feel the pulse of an electorate, over half of whom had been born after the heady days of 1947. In West Pakistan, the electoral nemesis of these parties proved to be the PPP led by Bhutto.

Bhutto chose to channel his electoral energies into the campaign in the West. Despite this restricted focus, the task ahead of him was stupendous. For one thing, his party suffered from an anemic organization—partly because of Bhutto's desire to play the prima donna. For another, he had to craft a campaign that would be attuned to the diverse interests of the various provinces and social groups of West Pakistan. Bhutto's solution was to reinvent himself as all things to everybody; in so doing, he ran the risk of ending up as nothing to anybody. It was the measure of his political genius that he managed to pull it off with great élan.

Bhutto's campaign focused on a set of core themes that were calculated to appeal to various constituencies. To court the poor, he concocted an amorphous populism that went by the slogan of "Islamic Socialism." Bhutto captured this rhetorical radicalism in a pithy phrase: "*Roti, Kapda aur Makan*," or "Food, Clothing, and Shelter." A related theme was an appeal to the religious sensibilities of the people. The first "long march," he once claimed, had been undertaken not by the Chinese communists but by Imam Hussein. On the campaign trail, the chairman of the PPP attired himself like Mao Zedong, but the fervor of his speeches and the swooning ecstasy of some of his followers lent to his meetings the feel of a revivalist congregation. His third theme was unceasing confrontation with India, which was aimed at warming the cockles of the Punjabis and the refugee communities in Sindh. A corollary to this was the call for Pakistan's withdrawal from military alliances with the West—a key demand of the student radicals. In private, however, Bhutto was quick to reassure the Americans of his goodwill and intentions.[57] Be that as it may, Bhutto's charismatic populism drew West Pakistani youth to him in droves. In consequence, the PPP was able to harness the radical currents of the student movement to considerable electoral advantage.

The political landscape of East Pakistan was also strewn with a number of parties. Here, too, one party—the Awami League—emerged as the dominant political force. The rout of the religious parties and the Muslim Leagues was predictable, as their notions of a centralized polity with paltry concessions to the East were wholly at odds with popular opinion. The Pakistan of the past was also represented by the People's Democratic Party (PDP), led by the oldest of the old guard Nurul Amin—chief minister of East Bengal from 1948 to 1954. The PDP was wiped out in the West, and in the East managed to scrape through with a single seat—won by Amin. But by a curious concatenation of circumstances Amin would end up as the last prime minister of united Pakistan in December 1971.

The only party in Bengal that could have challenged the Awami League was the National Awami Party (NAP), led by the left-leaning Maulana Bhashani. The Maulana had not read Marx, but his ideas about revolution had been forged by decades of activism among the peasantry.

Following a visit to China in 1963, he had grown enamored of the Chinese path to socialism—a move that also led him to moderate his criticism of the Ayub regime. With his simple *lungi* and shirt, his modest style of living, and his luxuriant white beard, Bhashani came across as a genial, grandfatherly figure—but his rhetoric could be incendiary. During the tumult of 1969, he addressed a meeting in Dhaka, "Oh, my children, why have you come here? Have you come here to see my beard? Go out to the countryside and spread fire."[58]

Bhashani's prowess as a demagogue far outstripped his skill as an organizer. With an anarchic streak to his temperament, Bhashani found it difficult to be corseted by party programs and discipline. In addition, the NAP had been beset by organizational problems almost since its inception. Principal among these was the presence in the NAP of members of the banned East Pakistan Communist Party, who brought with them their sectarian—pro-Moscow and pro-Beijing—schisms. In 1966, the NAP was also split in two, and Bhashani assumed leadership of the pro-Beijing faction, the NAP (B). But his relationship with the more radical rump of the EPCP soon entered troubled waters. The pro-Beijing communists were rent by rampant factionalism and eventually splintered into five groups. Many of the communist cadre, led by the party's general secretary Mohammad Toaha, walked out in May 1970. As the elections approached, Bhashani stood dangerously isolated. At the earliest opportune moment, he opted out of the electoral race.[59]

The pro-Soviet NAP (R) was led by Khan Abdul Wali Khan of the North-West Frontier Province and by Muzaffar Ahmad in East Pakistan. Wali Khan held that "if Pakistan is to be strong, it must inevitably have a weakened Center. Given the strength of regional sentiment in both the East and the West Wings, only the devolution of greater autonomy to the provinces can provide the basis of unity."[60] Given the affinity of their stances on autonomy, the NAP (R) was easily overtaken by the Awami League's juggernaut.

The failures of the left eased the way for the Awami League, but the latter's untrammeled dominance cannot be attributed, as some historians have asserted,[61] to the weaknesses of the left-wing parties. To be sure, the Awami League's main constituencies were East Pakistan's professional classes and students, businessmen, and industrialists. But in the run-up to the elections, Mujib was able to draw on the radical energies unleashed by the uprisings of 1968–69 and mobilize a wider set of constituencies, including the urban and rural destitute, labor, and the peasantry. Among Mujib's signal successes was to secure the support of the Hindus for his party's vision of Bengali nationalism, a relationship that was crystallized in the East Pakistan Minority Conference's decision to work closely with the Awami League.[62]

From the outset, Mujibur Rahman was confident that he would win 80 percent of the vote in East Pakistan. By October 1970, he believed that his party would carry 140 of the 163 seats in his province.[63] Even this proved to be a conservative estimate. The Awami League's electoral success was in no small measure due to its superb organizational machinery staffed by student volunteers. His campaign trail encompassed fifty-five cities, every district headquarters and subdivisional town, and nearly 400 *thanas*, or police administrative units. According to one estimate, "Sheikh Mujib addressed over 30,000,000 people . . . a figure representing almost half of the total population of East Bengal."[64] Underlying Mujib's campaign was a single, carefully constructed narrative that drew on Bengal's long catalog of grievances—economic and political, social and cultural. At the official launch of the Awami League's campaign, Mujib declared that the forthcoming elections should be treated as a "referendum" on his six-point program. The struggle for autonomy, he observed, was closely linked to the struggle for establishment of "workers' and peasants' rule in the country."[65]

Insofar as possible, Mujib wished to avoid a total breach with West Pakistan. The students and the younger Awami League cadre were more vocal about their willingness to consider outright independence. But the gap—between Mujib's propensity for constitutional methods and desire for autonomy, and the students' impatience with prim politics and inclination toward independence—was narrow, not least because of the constraining influence of the students' radicalism on Mujib. By this time, Mujib and his close associates were clear that if the West Pakistan leadership refused to concede the substance of the six points, the only alternative was an all-out struggle for independence: "Six points; if obstructed, one point" was the refrain of the Awami League leadership.[66] Asked by an American diplomat in January 1970 what would happen if the constitution could not be framed within 120 days, Mujib shrugged his shoulders: "We will try. We will try. If we cannot agree, then we cannot agree." Ten months later, he was more candid. The Awami League, he stated, was preparing a draft constitution based on the six points that he would present to the constituent assembly. He was willing to be flexible on "less important matters," but virtual economic independence for East Pakistan was non-negotiable. "This was the last chance, he [Mujib] said, and alternative to acceptance [of] East Pak [Pakistan] demands would be 'civil war' . . . While he and [the] Bengalis would prefer to remain peacefully in one Pakistan, their patience was now exhausted and there were other options."[67]

Mujib's public pronouncements echoed his private views. In a lengthy interview published in April 1970, the Sheikh artfully laid out the case for the six points. "I can assure you," he said, "Pakistan will remain strong and united . . . Our programme is not directed against the people of West Pakistan . . . [and] it has never been . . . [The] six point programme is as much theirs."[68] Responding to his critics, Mujib affirmed in June that "the six points will be realised and Pakistan shall also stay." In subsequent speeches, however, he was more explicit about his thinking. If the six-point program was not given "due consideration in the future constitution of the country," he would "launch a mass movement."[69] Mujib's hardening stance stemmed from the increasing polarization of politics in the country's two wings. His sole campaign visit to West Pakistan proved unsuccessful. And he was incensed by the martial law regime's attempts to dissuade industrialists from supporting his party and to engineer defections within the Awami League.[70]

The gathering steam of mistrust was given impetus by a succession of natural disasters that struck East Pakistan. In July 1970, the province was devastated by a flood that inundated large parts of eleven districts. This led to a postponement of the elections to 7 December, a measure that Mujib viewed with disquiet. Then, on the night of 12 November, a cyclone hit the coastal areas of Bengal, with winds billowing forward at 150 miles an hour. Close on the heels of the cyclone was a tidal bore twenty to thirty feet high. Hundreds of thousands perished in the worst natural disaster confronted by the province in the twentieth century. International assistance poured in, but the response from West Pakistan was languid and lackadaisical. Not a single political leader of any standing visited the eastern wing. Yahya had been on a trip to China and stopped in Dhaka on his way back. The president had been celebrating his freshly won commitment from Beijing for increased military assistance by a bout of drinking. He flew over the affected areas in an aircraft, downing several cans of beer to cope with a hangover and casting an alcoholic eye on the barely visible destruction beneath. Yahya concluded that the extent of the calamity had been blown out of all proportion. He instructed the governor, Admiral Ahsan, to take charge and swiftly left for Rawalpindi.[71]

In a tough but measured statement, Mujib ventilated the anguish and anger of the people of Bengal. Describing the devastation as a "holocaust," he condemned the government's response as "criminal negligence." The destruction wrought by the tidal bore had brought into sharp focus "the basic truth that every Bengali has felt in his bones, that we have been treated so long as a colony and a market." Mujib declared that "we must attain full regional autonomy on the basis of the 6-point/11-point formula." When queried by a foreign correspondent if his statement could be read as a call to independence, Mujib responded, "No, not yet."[72] Treading this thin line would become rather more difficult in the months ahead.

2

BREAKDOWN

"What in the devil's name is happening here?" hollered Yahya Khan. "Where on earth has your assessment gone?" It was 3 AM on the morning of 8 December 1970. Yahya had sat up all night watching the election coverage on television, and now he demanded an explanation from General Umar of the NSC.[1] In the final tally, the Awami League won 160 of the 162 seats in East Pakistan. Although it had failed to win a single seat in West Pakistan, it had a comfortable overall majority. In the West, the PPP took 81 of the 138 seats, winning 62 of 82 in Punjab, 18 of 27 in Sindh, and 1 of 25 in the North West Frontier Province.

The military leadership had expected that the electorate would return a splintered verdict. Such a fractured National Assembly, they believed, would render the task of constitution-making within 120 days nigh impossible, and so necessitate a fresh election. "This process, they hoped," recalled a member of the martial law administration, "would go on indefinitely, allowing martial law to remain in force."[2] Or, alternatively, compel the politicians to come to terms with the military with regard to future political dispensation. Indeed, the government had strained many a nerve to achieve this electoral outcome. In particular, it used the Intelligence Bureau and the NSC to sap the strength of the Awami League. In a trance of wishful thinking, the generals continued to believe that the polls would play out to their script. They persistently underestimated both the Awami League and the PPP. When the military governor of Punjab suggested just days before the poll that Bhutto might fare rather well, members of the administration derisorily sniggered.[3]

The regime was stunned by the Awami League's stupendous performance. The six-point program would now have to be taken seriously. Hitherto, Yahya and his colleagues had believed that after the elections the political landscape would be so fragmented that the Awami League would be in no position to plow ahead with its agenda. In consequence, Yahya had not paid much heed to intelligence inputs, which indicated that Mujib's objective might be independence. Nor had they undertaken any serious analysis of the Awami League's political options. Some memoranda on the constitutional and economic consequences of the six points had been prepared, but these had remained securely stapled in the musty files of the martial law administration.[4]

Of equal concern to the military was the preservation of its political position and corporate interests. According to one close observer, the cohort of senior generals with Yahya was planning for "a Turkish type of 'military-civilian (i.e. concealed) regime.' "[5] According to another, they were "obsessed with the attitude of the Awami League towards the Army."[6] Visiting Dhaka in late December 1970, a senior general reassured his fellow officers, "Don't worry . . . we will not allow those black bastards to rule over us."[7]

Three months later, the military leadership came down with massive force on the Awami League and its supporters. On the face of it, this decision seems easy to explain. The military was unwilling to concede the demands advanced by the Awami League, and Mujib was unable—even if he was willing—to dilute the six points. Hence, a breakdown was bound to occur. This explanation elides an important question: why did Yahya believe he could get away with repression when Ayub could not? After all, the tide of radical dissidence that had dissolved Ayub's regime had not yet receded. By clamping down on East Pakistan would he not run the risk of detonating another wave of uprisings in both the wings? If Yahya made so bold as to attempt to crush the Awami League and cow the Bengalis, it was because he was confident that West Pakistan would remain quiescent. For he had a willing West Pakistani partner who shared the military's outlook on key political issues as well as its desire to cut the Awami League to size.

I

"Let's back Bhutto," exclaimed Gul Hassan soon after the elections. Bhutto's power base, he explained, lay in Punjab, which was the traditional recruiting ground for the army. He would therefore keep well away from the army's affairs.[8] The chief of general staff's enthusiasm for the chairman of the PPP was not surprising. Bhutto's gift for connecting with the electorate was matched by his guile in maintaining close ties with the military. He had assiduously nurtured these relationships over several years. As Ayub Khan noted with a whiff of petulance, "Even when he was a minister he took great pains in cultivating people like Yahya, General Akhtar Malik, General Gul Hassan, General Peerzada etc. in the hope of making use of them when the occasion arose."[9] Yahya himself had a cautious admiration for Bhutto, referring to him in the same breath as a "young, bright demagogue" and as "power crazy and fascist at heart."[10]

Then again, Bhutto's stance on key political questions made him a potentially useful partner for the military. On the campaign trail, Bhutto repeatedly declared that his party stood for a fully fledged democracy, but privately he held that "the best model for Pakistan will be Turkey, for the military in Pakistan must continue to share in power, even if remaining in [the] background much of the time." Pakistan, he believed, was not yet ripe for parliamentary democracy: "The British model, how-ever modified, is not suited for Pakistan in its present stage of political development." His own desire was to govern the country "as a strong man within the Turkish model" with army in the wings.[11] These ideas, of course, were entirely consonant with the military leadership's views and its desires for the future political and constitutional dispensation in the country. And Bhutto was not shy of advancing fertile suggestions along these lines to them. According to Yahya, Bhutto advised him in the sum-mer of 1970 to not worry about the elections: "Yahya the soldier and Bhutto the politician will make a very good team and can together run the country."[12]

Further, Bhutto played a more insidious role by stoking the regime's concerns about Mujib and his six points. In public, Bhutto refrained from making any specific comments about the six points and their im-plications. But since late 1969, we may recall, he had been warning Yahya (through Lieutenant General Peerzada) that Mujib's six points "spell the destruction of Pakistan." When Peerzada sought, some months before the elections, his assessment of Mujib's intentions, Bhutto point-edly replied, "Separation."[13] These links and affinities enabled Bhutto to work with the military in derailing the constitutional process.

In the aftermath of the elections, Bhutto believed that his party's per-formance had entitled him to a great say both in the making of the con-stitution and in the formation of the government. Besides, he felt that he was destined to the leadership of Pakistan, and that he could wait no longer. At one point, he told Yahya that he had to accede to power "now."[14] Yet Bhutto knew that his maneuvers could only succeed if he enjoyed the military's patronage. "I will ensure Yahya remains on my side," he remarked to a close associate.[15] Bhutto fired his opening salvo at a victory procession in Lahore on 20 December. "Punjab and Sindh are the bastions of power in Pakistan," he declared. "Majority alone does not count in national politics."[16] In subsequent speeches, he asserted that his party was the "sole representative of the people of West Pakistan," that the PPP and the Awami League had to reach an agreement on the quantum of autonomy to be devolved to the provinces, and that he would not allow anyone to "chisel us out" of power and responsibility.[17]

Bhutto's stance deeply disconcerted the Awami League. Despite winning an overall majority at the polls, the Bengalis feared that the ruling elites of West Pakistan would prevent the convening of the National Assembly. A strong rejoinder was drafted by the party's constitutional expert, Kamal Hossain, and was issued by the general secretary and Mujib's principal lieutenant, Tajuddin Ahmad. The statement clarified that the Awami League was vested with a "clear electoral mandate" and was competent to frame the constitution and form the government "with or without any other party."[18] The Awami League also conveyed its views to an aide of Bhutto's: "Bengalis are no longer prepared to accept the dictates of the military-bureaucratic establishment for whom Bhutto is a spokesman." If the latter tried to impede the six-point program, the Bengalis would "stand up and resist to a man."[19]

The Awami League had already started preparing a draft constitution based on the six points. The political steering group for this exercise comprised the party's "high command," including Mujib, Tajuddin, Syed Nazrul Islam, A. H. M. Kamruzzaman, Khandakar Moshtaque Ahmad, and Mansoor Ali. Kamal Hossain led the drafting committee. As work on the draft constitution progressed, the Awami League leadership realized that they were proposing "a very loose form of political and economic relationship." As one member of the drafting team recalled, "We envisaged a confederation of economically independent and sovereign states with some common arrangements such as common defence and foreign affairs, financed by contributions from each state." Mujib realized that the proposed constitution was "barely a consolation prize to the West," and that the latter might well decide to part ways after a few years of the experiment. In any event, Mujib was keen to follow the constitutional route and to avoid the bloodshed that would necessarily ensue from an armed struggle for independence.[20]

On 12 January 1971, Yahya arrived in Dhaka. The purpose of the trip was to ascertain Mujib's stance on the six points, and, more subtly, to elicit his views on the form and composition of the future government. After a succinct reprise of the six points, Mujib asked the president to outline his objections to them. Yahya's response indicated the regime's approach to dealing with the Awami League: avoiding a direct showdown but constraining their options by using the PPP. Thus, Yahya claimed that he had no objections to the six points, but Mujib would have to carry the West Pakistan leaders with him. The Sheikh nodded his assent, asking Yahya to convene the National Assembly on 15 February. To assuage the military-bureaucratic establishment's concerns, Mujib stated that his party intended to elect Yahya as the next "elected President of Pakistan." He added that they had no intention either of trimming the armed forces, or of removing West Pakistani personnel from the military and civil services. Yahya coyly and disingenuously replied that he was a mere soldier and that he would prefer to return to the barracks or to his home. In closing, Mujib emphasized the need for the Assembly to meet no later than 15 February.[21]

Yahya was hardly drooling at the crumbs held out by Mujib. Prior to the meeting, his military colleagues had felt that Yahya should aim for an active presidency that would control the ministries of defense, foreign affairs, finance, interior, commerce, and communication as well as retaining control of the armed forces. Mujib seemed to suggest an altogether more ceremonial office for the president—a "Queen Elizabeth of Pakistan." Nor were they pleased with Mujib's perceived assertion of the Awami League's primacy. Indeed, they feared that once power was transferred without appropriate constitutional arrangements, they would be unable to prevent the erosion of the military's institutional interests.[22] In his public remarks, though, Yahya oozed reasonableness. He expressed satisfaction at the discussions with Mujib and referred to the latter as "the future Prime Minister of Pakistan." Asked if he would now meet Bhutto, Yahya jauntily retorted, "I am going for shooting of birds in Sind [sic] which is Bhutto's area. If he is there I will meet him also."[23]

The meeting had, in fact, been arranged in advance. On 17 January, Yahya, Hamid, Peerzada, and Umar among others were received by

Bhutto at his family estate. Bhutto played the consummate host but lost no time in expressing his displeasure at Yahya's statement declaring Mujib the next prime minister. Yahya replied that it was for Bhutto to work toward an arrangement with Mujib. Bhutto argued that the transfer of power involved three parties: the Awami League, the PPP, and the army. The Awami League's assurances were worth nothing; yet it was imperative to reach a consensus on the constitution prior to convening the National Assembly. In other words, the opening of the Assembly would have to be delayed. Bhutto craftily added that the postponement would also serve as a test of Mujib's fidelity to a united Pakistan: "if there is no reaction then Mujib is loyal but if he disobeys and starts an agitation, then he is disloyal." He further indicated that his party would support Yahya's efforts to preserve the unity of Pakistan. Prior to his departure, Yahya urged Bhutto to travel to Dhaka and meet Mujib. If he did not, the odium of a constitutional deadlock would befall his party as well. Bhutto reluctantly agreed.[24]

II

The PPP delegation arrived in Dhaka on 27 January. After two sessions of negotiations, it became clear that there was little progress. The Awami League team insisted on the six points as the basis for a new constitution; the PPP harped on socialist policies but had no concrete alternatives to present.[25] Faced with this impasse, Bhutto adopted a two-pronged approach. On the one hand, he tried to build a consensus among the West Pakistani parties against the six points and for the inclusion of his party in the future government. On the other, he sought to sow doubts about the Awami League's commitment to a united Pakistan, and so undermine its credibility in West Pakistan. Bhutto met Yahya on 11 February and tried to persuade the president to postpone the opening of the National Assembly for at least six weeks. He then proceeded to confer with leaders of the smaller West Pakistan parties, but his inability to forge a consensus was quickly apparent.[26] By this time, the situation in the East was almost on the boil. The delay in summoning the Assembly was generating immense impatience among the Bengalis. As one observer noted, "public meetings, processions, rallies, began taking place day and night in Dhaka and most major towns." Consequently, Yahya announced on 13 February that the National Assembly would convene in Dhaka on 3 March 1971.[27]

This did not, however, mean that the martial law administration was willing either to summon the Assembly without prior negotiations on future arrangements or to loosen their ties with Bhutto. Indeed, even before the announcement of 13 February, Major General Umar had been deputed to meet leaders of the smaller West Pakistan parties and dissuade them from attending the National Assembly. After the announcement, too, the regime sought to cajole these parties into staying away from the Assembly. On 20 February, for instance, Umar called on the leader of the Council Muslim League, Mumtaz Daultana, "to encourage a united front in West Pakistan against attendance at the National Assembly unless some sort of understanding could be worked out before."[28]

The government's moves were in concert with those of Bhutto. On 15 February, Bhutto declared that his party would not attend the National Assembly unless there was "some amount of reciprocity" from the Awami League. A constitution based on the six points, he claimed, could not provide a "viable future for the country." He had gone the distance to meet the Awami League's position and believed there was "hope for understanding." It was now for the Awami League to demonstrate flexibility.[29] Looking back years later, a close aide conceded that "there can be little doubt" about Bhutto's "collusion" with Yahya from January to March 1971.[30]

The Awami League leadership was concerned about the link between Bhutto and the regime. They were apprehensive that "Yahya, even while going ahead with [the] March 3 date, will move promptly thereafter to postpone further meetings for several months in view of non-attendance by West Pak[istan] MNAs [Members of National Assembly] and lack of consensus on constitution." Mujib was convinced that Bhutto "could not possibly have acted on his own" and that he was supported by the military.[31] For its part, the Awami League began consultations with leaders of other Western parties, seeking to alleviate their concerns about the six points. At the same time, Mujib carefully tended to his own constituencies. In a memorial service for the martyrs of the language movement, he declared that "no power on earth could subjugate the Bengalees [sic] any more." In subsequent speeches, he warned against any attempt to throttle the wishes of the people: "We will die but we will not surrender."[32]

In so doing, Mujib sought at once to signal the Awami League's resolve to the regime and to rein in the more militant sections of his supporters. The latter—mostly students—were convinced that Bhutto and Yahya would never allow the Bengalis to hold the reins of state. They believed, therefore, that the Awami League must issue a unilateral declaration of independence. However, Mujib felt that they should avoid taking any step that would allow the government to pin the blame on the Awami League and so justify a military crackdown. It would be better to allow the negotiations to play out, even if they were doomed to a dead end.[33]

At this point, Mujib was worried about vague reports suggesting that the army was building up its presence in East Pakistan. The Awami League's thinking was also colored by its concerns about the reaction of the international community to a unilateral declaration of independence. After all, obtaining recognition from the world community would be essential for an independent Bangladesh. In the first week of February, Mujib had sent a feeler to the American consulate in Dhaka exploring the possibility of the United States playing a mediatory role if the Awami League declared independence. The consul general, Archer Blood, politely indicated that the United States wished Pakistan to stay united and that it was loath to involve itself in Pakistan's internal affairs.[34] When meeting the American ambassador later that month, Mujib emphasized that "he did not want separation but rather he wanted a form of confederation in which the people of Bangla Desh would get their just and rightful share."[35]

In the meantime, the government was watching with chagrin the Awami League's increasing defiance. On 6 February, Yahya had sent a message to Mujib inviting him to Rawalpindi for further discussions on constitutional matters. Mujib declined and instead asked Yahya to visit Dhaka. The pent-up pique against Mujib led to an explosion of presidential temper on 20 February: "I am going to sort out that bastard [Mujib]," Yahya declared at a meeting. He was now considering postponing the National Assembly. When reminded that it could lead to military action, Yahya said, "So let it be."[36]

At another meeting on 22 February, Yahya spoke of Mujib's intransigence and observed that in the prevailing circumstances a meeting of the National Assembly could not be useful. Most participants—barring East Pakistan's governor Admiral Ahsan, and the martial law administrator for East Pakistan, Lieutenant General Sahibzada Yaqub Khan—concurred with this view. After the meeting, Yahya took the East Pakistan officials aside and disclosed his intention to postpone the National Assembly. As Yaqub recalled, Yahya was also keen "to impose open sword martial law to roll back the situation to what it was in 1969." Yaqub and Ahsan impressed upon Yahya the impossibility of doing so; for postponement of the Assembly would result in a major upheaval in East Pakistan. But Yahya was adamant. At a private meeting the next morning, when Ahsan and Yaqub yet again presented their case, Yahya continued to insist that enforcing order would not be a problem: "a whiff of the grapeshot" would suffice. He told them that he intended to announce the postponement on 1 March and directed them to inform Mujib 24 hours before then.[37]

On or around 20 February, the army began preparations for the military option. Contingency plans had been prepared as far back as 11 December 1970.[38] The first troop reinforcements began landing in Dhaka on 27 February.[39] Yahya started simultaneously to prepare the diplomatic ground for an eventual crackdown on East Pakistan. On 25 February, he met the American ambassador and conveyed his deep disappointment at the current impasse. Recounting all the "hard things" that he had done to restore democracy in Pakistan, he hinted at the postponement of the National Assembly. Yahya also agonized aloud about the possibility of Pakistan breaking up. Paraphrasing Ayub, he stated that he had no intention of presiding over the liquidation of the state. Ambassador Farland duly assured him of Washington's commitment to Pakistan's integrity—an assurance that naturally pleased Yahya.[40] At noon on 1 March 1971, the postponement sine die of the National Assembly was announced.

III

Minutes after the announcement, hundreds of thousands of people poured into the streets and public spaces of Dhaka. Government employees went on strike, banks and commercial concerns ceased functioning, and university campuses and law courts emptied out. A cricket match that was being played between Pakistan and the Commonwealth XI was abandoned, and thousands of spectators rushed out to join the crowds. A tumultuous throng of protesters brandishing bamboo sticks and iron rods, chanting slogans demanding independence and armed struggle, converged from all directions at the Purbani Hotel where the Awami League leadership was in a huddle.

At a press conference that afternoon, Mujib was characteristically forthright. The National Assembly had been indefinitely postponed "only for the sake of a minority party's disagreement . . . We are representatives of the majority people and we cannot allow it to go unchallenged." He announced a program for the next six days, including a complete strike in Dhaka the following day, a provincewide strike on 3 March (when the Assembly was to have met), and a public meeting at the Race Course on 7 March. When asked if he would proclaim unilateral independence, Mujib replied, "You wait."[41]

On the next morning, the streets of Dhaka were cluttered with numerous roadblocks erected by students and workers. The strike was a complete success, not least because the Awami League cadre proved capable of vigorously enforcing it. An observer recalled that the boisterous youth would "smash the windshields and cut the tires of any car moving in violation of the *hartal* [strike]."[42] By the evening, the authorities decided to curb the protests. A curfew was declared from dusk to dawn. In ensuing confrontations with the crowds, the army opened fire, leaving nine dead and fifty-one injured. These scenes would be repeated several times over the next days. On 8 March, the authorities issued a note stating that 172 people had been killed and 358 wounded. The Awami League's estimate of the casualties was much higher.

By the morning of 3 March, life in East Pakistan had ground to a halt. The events of the past 24 hours had further radicalized the Bengali students. Mujib was, of course, aware that the sentiment in the streets ran ahead of his own thinking. He was keen to maintain the momentum of the agitation, and yet ensure that it did not precipitate into a full-blown confrontation with the army. Besides, he was disturbed by the violent streak of the agitation, particularly the attacks on Urdu-speaking "Biharis," Muslim migrants from eastern India who had moved to East Pakistan after Partition and whose support for the ruling elites of West Pakistan drew the ire of the Awami League cadres. Speaking at a students' rally that afternoon, Mujib sought to strike a balance between activism and restraint. He called on the Yahya regime to withdraw martial law and transfer power to the elected representatives, but also underscored the importance of a "peaceful *satyagraha*." The Biharis and non-Muslims "are our sacred trust," he added.[43]

The radicals were disappointed at the tepid tone of Mujib's speech. Nevertheless, they continued to fix their sights on independence. A few days after the meeting, the major student bodies banded together to form the Central Students' Action Committee of Independent Bangladesh. They declared Rabindranath Tagore's *Amar Sonar Bangla* (My Golden Bengal) as the national anthem of Bangladesh and ensured that it was played regularly on the radio. Parties on the political left endorsed the call for independence. The National Awami Party, led by Muzaffar Ahmad, demanded the right to self-determination, including secession. The various communist parties called on the people to resist the authorities by taking up arms if necessary. The Maoists went so far as to call for the "liquidation" of landowners, moneylenders, and other oppressors.[44]

The government, for its part, was dismayed at this turn of events. On 6 March, Yahya broadcast a speech blaming Mujib for the prevailing impasse. Having read out the charge sheet, Yahya announced that the National Assembly would now meet on 25 March. In closing, he declared that it was "the duty of the Pakistan Armed Forces to ensure the integrity, solidarity and security of Pakistan, a duty in which they have never failed." That evening, Yahya sent a telex message for Mujib through the martial law headquarters in Dhaka: "Please do not take any hasty decision. I will soon come to Dacca and discuss the details with you. I assure you that your aspirations and commitments to the people can be fully honoured. I have a scheme in mind which will more than satisfy your Six Points. I urge you not to take a hasty decision."[45]

Yahya's immediate concern was to forestall a unilateral declaration of independence by Mujib, as rumors about it had flitted like bats in the press and political circles for several days. Such a declaration would be problematic both internally and externally. On the one hand, the military was not yet fully geared up to quash dissent in the East. The troop reinforcement begun in late February was progressing slowly. On the other hand, a declaration of independence would attract international attention and possibly some form of intervention. Yahya's moves were also aimed at setting the stage for the next round of negotiations with Mujib. His barely concealed threat of military action was issued at the insistence of Bhutto.[46] And his message to Mujib was aimed at anesthetizing the Awami League's concerns in the run-up to the negotiations.

Some historians have argued that in approaching these negotiations Yahya was committed to finding "a political solution but from a position of strength." This is too simplistic a reading of his motives and approach.[47] In the coming negotiations, Yahya sought, for the last time, to probe Mujib's intentions about political and constitutional arrangements. In so doing, he mainly looked for evidence to confirm his existing opinions about Mujib's obduracy and treacherousness as a precursor to a military solution. Indeed, by the time Yahya left for Dhaka the army's plans for regaining control of East Pakistan were well advanced.[48]

The option of declaring independence was discussed by the Awami League's working committee on 6 March. The party's leaders knew that the students and younger cadre "strongly favoured such a declaration." Indeed, there was "little doubt" that anything short of independence would "not be acceptable" to the bulk of their following. Yet the leadership wanted to move cautiously. For one thing, such a declaration would provide the military the "pretext" to use force. "Could an unarmed population absorb the shock of such an onslaught and emerge victorious?" For another, would the international community accord recognition to an independent Bangladesh? They concluded that the regime was looking for an opportunity to impose a military solution and that such an opportunity should be denied them. Yahya's message to Mujib was read as an attempt to create an "alibi." At the same time, they wanted to maintain the tempo of the popular movement and compel the government to realize that "use of military force could not result in their gaining any objective." Thus, a declaration of independence should be avoided, and instead specific demands should be advanced. At the same time, independence would be set as the "ultimate goal."[49]

The next afternoon, hundreds of thousands gathered at the Race Course grounds. Mujib was running late. As he was leaving home, a group of student leaders met him to petition for a declaration of independence from the rostrum. Mujib did no such thing, but his seventeen-minute address was a masterpiece of oratory. In a philippic against the military-Bhutto axis, he asserted that "it is a minority group of Western Wing which has obstructed and is continuing to obstruct the transfer of power." He announced that the Awami League would not attend the National Assembly unless its four core demands were met: revocation of martial law, return of troops to the barracks, inquiry into the recent incidents of firing, and immediate transfer of power to elected representatives. The Awami League, declared Mujib, had pledged "to lead this struggle and ultimately to attain for the people their cherished goal of emancipation." Punching his fist in the air, he concluded, "Our struggle this time is a struggle for independence." Mujib had thrown down the glove. As the US embassy in Pakistan grimly observed, "Question now is whether Yahya or Mujib will blink first—or whether neither will blink. Showdown cannot be put off much longer."[50]

The Awami League's "non-cooperation" movement gathered momentum. The party issued a slew of "directives" drafted by Tajuddin, Kamal Hossain, and another young barrister and party whip Amirul Islam. The directives covered a swath of issues, including timings of strikes; a "no-tax" campaign; functioning of offices, banks, and other economic agencies; and regulation of medical and other public services. Bureaucrats and police officials, judges and business leaders, all began to liaise with the Awami League to ensure a modicum of continuity in their functioning. Throughout this period, a ceaseless flow of processions snaked their way through the streets of Dhaka, usually ending at Sheikh Mujib's residence. To an American observer, all this seemed the "outpouring of the Bengali dream, a touching admixture of bravado, wishful thinking, idealism, animal cunning, anger and patriotic fervour."[51]

Mujib's speech and demands received wide approbation. Maulana Bhashani proclaimed his willingness to work with Mujib in the struggle for liberation. Interestingly, the smaller Western parties also came out in support of Mujib's stance. On 8 March, Maulana Mufti Mehmood of Jamiat Ulema-i-Islam called for a meeting of smaller West Pakistan parties to be held five days later. The meeting in Karachi was attended by leaders of the Muslim Leagues, Jamaat-i-Islami, and Jamiat Ulema-i-Pakistan. Wali Khan of the National Awami Party was unable to attend but extended his support for the initiative. The leaders present accepted Mujib's four demands and called for interim governments to be established in the center as well as the provinces. They criticized Bhutto's insistence on prior agreement on constitutional matters, and declared that Mujib had given the "clearest assurance" that the majority party would be responsive to suggestions. They called on Yahya to meet Mujib and remove "misunderstandings, apprehensions and suspicions."[52]

Sensing that he was being isolated, Bhutto met Yahya in Karachi on 14 March. By his own account, Bhutto told Yahya that Mujib's demands for a transfer of power and the lifting of martial law were acceptable to his party, but the modalities of these "had to be worked out on the basis of a common agreement."[53] In hindsight, it is clear that his discussions with Yahya ranged further than were suggested by his own anodyne account. Speaking at a large rally the same day, Bhutto called for a transfer of power to the Awami League in the East and the PPP in the West. The two parties would then frame a "comprehensive" constitution for Pakistan. The Urdu press quoted him as saying *Idhar hum, Udhar tum* (We here, You there).[54] Then again, Bhutto was actually opposed to the demand for repeal of martial law—as that move would weaken his main ally, the military leadership. His opposition was, however, couched in legalistic terms. As a senior colleague of Bhutto's put it, "the demand for lifting martial law . . . would deprive present government of legal basis to operate on until transfer of authority to civilian government can be accomplished."[55] This argument, we shall see, would be trotted out by the regime in the coming negotiations with the Awami League.

IV

On 15 March 1971, Yahya Khan and his military entourage landed in Dhaka. Negotiations opened the next morning with a preliminary meeting between the principals. Mujib formally advanced his four demands: withdrawal of martial law, transfer of power to elected representatives, withdrawal of troops to cantonment and cessation of reinforcements, and inquiry into the firings. He also suggested that the National Assembly initially meet separately in the two wings and then convene for drafting the national constitution. Yahya said that Mujib would have to carry the majority party of the West with him. He also insisted that there were legal difficulties in withdrawing martial law before framing the constitution. Mujib replied that his legal experts would discuss the matter further with Yahya's team. Mujib directed Kamal Hossain to discuss this matter with Peerzada the same evening. In their meeting, Lieutenant General Peerzada claimed that repealing martial law before preparing the constitution would lead to a "legal vacuum." Kamal Hossain countered that Yahya could promulgate an "Interim Arrangements Order"— effectively a provisional constitution—by the same order with which he revoked martial law. The meeting ended inconclusively.[56]

The next day, the negotiations remained mired in the same question. The military was evidently dissatisfied with the direction in which the talks were proceeding. That same evening Yahya told Tikka Khan, "The bastard is not behaving. You get ready." While the plan for military action was being finalized, the negotiations continued.[57] At their meeting on the morning of 19 March, Yahya and Mujib traversed the same ground. When the negotiating teams met later that day, Justice A. R. Cornelius, Yahya's constitutional adviser, forcefully argued that abrogating martial law without adopting a constitution would result in the abolition of the presidency and other basic laws governing the country. The Awami League team shot down this argument on the grounds that the issue at hand was not legal but political. There was no reason why Yahya could not divest himself of the powers of the chief martial law administrator while retaining the powers of the president.[58]

While the presidential team got working on a draft proclamation, the negotiations continued. In their meeting on 20 March, Yahya said that he was "a simple man": although he agreed with Mujib's demands, his advisers had told him about the difficulties of revoking martial law. After some discussion, it was agreed that they would seek the advice of an independent constitutional expert. Thereafter, the elements of a draft proclamation were discussed. Yahya now disclosed his hand. He said that it would be necessary for him to consult leaders of West Pakistan on these matters. In particular, he proposed to invite Bhutto for consultation. He would also want a signed letter from all the political leaders requesting a proclamation from him. Mujib icily replied that Yahya was free to meet anyone, but his party would not enter into any negotiations with Bhutto. In closing, it was agreed that a working draft would be prepared by the government team and sent to the Awami League.[59]

By this time, the Awami League leadership was coming around to the view that a political settlement might be in sight. Their lingering concerns about the military were by no means allayed, but the negotiations had held out a glimmer of hope—a sentiment that was reflected in the upbeat press coverage of the talks. The meeting of 20 March was unsettling because it brought Bhutto back into the scene. In fact, Yahya and Peerzada had been in touch with Bhutto over the past four days, and Bhutto had been "agitated at being excluded from the talks."[60] On the evening of 19 March, he had received a message from Yahya: "the talks are on. You can now come to Dhaka with your party men."[61] The next day, Bhutto announced to the press that he had received "clarifications" from the president and that he was proceeding to Dhaka.

Bhutto's remark and Yahya's stance led Mujib and Tajuddin to reconsider their position. They now thought it imprudent to press for the formation of an interim national government because Bhutto would surely try to wangle his way in. It was better, they felt, to seek an immediate transfer of power only in the provinces. There were other considerations as well. For one, the student leaders had importuned Mujib not to "compromise" on his program by taking power at the center. For another, they believed that such an arrangement would be congenial to Yahya, as he would be left fully in control of the central government in the interim period. Accordingly, Mujib and Tajuddin sought an urgent meeting with Yahya on 21 March and told him that power should only be transferred in the provinces.[62]

The next morning Yahya, Mujib, and Bhutto met at the presidential house. Mujib sought Yahya's response to his proposals for an interim constitution. Yahya replied that it was essential to secure Bhutto's agreement. Mujib maintained that it was up to Yahya to convince Bhutto and that he would join formal negotiations after Bhutto had accepted them in principle. After Mujib left, Bhutto conveyed to Yahya his strong reservations about the Awami League's proposals.[63] That evening, the Awami League leaders met to finalize their draft of the proclamation. The president's team had sent a draft the previous day, which the Awami League's experts felt was "a slipshod effort." Their own draft sought to be more complete and precise. Kamal Hossain and Amirul Islam worked through the night of 22 March to produce a fresh draft of the proclamation.

At the meeting with Yahya's team on 23 March, the Awami Leaguers presented their draft proclamation. They were informed that the president's chief economic adviser M. M. Ahmed and other experts had been flown in to examine the economic and financial provisions of the Awami League's demands. The ensuing discussions with Ahmed went surprisingly well: experts on both sides found that their differences, though real, were not unbridgeable.

However, differences on other matters persisted. The presidential team took particular exception to two provisions of the Awami League's draft. Where their draft had spoken of two "constituent committees" for writing the provincial constitutions, the Awami League's draft called them "constituent conventions." Furthermore, the latter mentioned that after the provincial constitutions were framed the National Assembly would meet to draft a constitution for the "Confederation of Pakistan." These changes were semantic rather than substantive. Mujib had wanted the term "confederation" mainly as a genuflection to popular sentiment in the province, especially the young militants. In fact, the draft envisaged federal as opposed to confederal interim arrangements. It explicitly granted powers to the central legislature to make laws for the "Islamabad Capital Territory and Dacca Capital Territory." In any event, when the presidential team contested these as "fundamental" changes, the Awami League team said that the issue was negotiable between Mujib and Yahya. Nevertheless, the president's team seized upon these as confirmatory evidence of the Awami League's perfidy.[64] The stage was now set for military action.

Later that night Yahya Khan summoned the leaders of smaller West Pakistan parties who had arrived in Dhaka a couple of days ago. The previous day, he had given them a slanted summary of the talks with Mujib. He had also asked them to meet Mujib and persuade him to be more reasonable. That night, the West Pakistani leaders found Yahya relaxing—in his cups. When informed that Mujib had refused to budge, Yahya threw up his hands with a dramatic flourish and asked, "Then what do you expect me to do? I am becoming the laughing stock of the world as well as of the Army and there is a limit to any man's patience."[65] Sensing that military action was afoot, the leaders implored Yahya not to resort to any hasty or irrevocable steps. At least one of them pointedly asked Yahya to extricate himself by transferring power to the elected representatives. By contrast, Bhutto and his party leaders concluded that "military action was necessary." The chairman conveyed the message to Yahya on the morning of 24 March.[66]

Yahya and his colleagues had already decided on the military course the previous evening. At the final meeting on the evening of 24 March 1971, the Awami League negotiators asked Peerzada when the draft would be finalized. They proposed that Kamal Hossain and Cornelius firm it up that night so that it could be discussed by Mujib and Yahya the next day. Cornelius was agreeable, but Peerzada said, "No, we have some discussions this evening, you may meet tomorrow morning." He said that the time of meeting would be intimated to Kamal Hossain by telephone. After the meeting, Peerzada informed Cornelius that all West Pakistan officials who were in Dhaka for the talks should leave the following day.[67]

The Awami League was, of course, unaware of these developments, but Mujib was already worried about the possibility that Yahya might have changed his mind. That afternoon he had sent an emissary, Alamgir Rehman, to meet with the US consul general Archer Blood, and inform the latter of the progress made in the negotiations. Only a final meeting of the principals was required before Yahya made an announcement, but Mujib feared that Yahya, under pressure of the "hawks" in the military, might renege on the agreement. Mujib hoped that the United States could "stiffen" Yahya by letting him know how much Washington favored a political solution. However, Blood was noncommittal. In a cable to the embassy in Islamabad, he opined that, at the brink of an agreement, Mujib was nervous that it might fall through.[68]

By this time, the preparations for military action were well under way. Following the meeting with the Awami League on 23 March, Yahya decided to set the plan in motion. General Mitha was summoned from Rawalpindi to assist in the implementation of the plans. The next day, 25 March, Yahya met the senior army officers in Dhaka and gave the final go-ahead. At 6 PM, the divisional commanders received orders that the operation would commence an hour after midnight. Yahya would leave Dhaka in an hour, and the operation was timed to coincide with his arrival in Karachi. Through the day, the Awami League leadership had nervously awaited for the call from Peerzada. As night approached, they were increasingly convinced that the regime had decided to embark on the path of war. Despite the army's best efforts at secrecy, Mujib learned of Yahya's departure. The Awami League cadre swung into action, felling large trees, putting up barricades, and erecting roadblocks to prevent the army from getting out of the cantonment. The army command responded by advancing the H hour.[69] At 11:30 PM on 25 March 1971, Operation Searchlight began.

V

The next evening, Yahya Khan addressed the people of Pakistan in a radio broadcast. After outlining his version of the talks with the Awami League, he claimed that Mujibur Rahman's "obstinacy, obduracy and absolute refusal to talk sense can lead to but one conclusion—the man and his party are enemies of Pakistan and they want East Pakistan to break away completely from the country. He has attacked the solidarity and integrity of this country—this crime will not go unpunished." Yahya went on to proscribe political activity in the country. The Awami League was "completely banned." Yahya claimed that he still aimed to "transfer power to the elected representatives of the people." As soon as the situation permitted, he would strive to move in this direction. Unsurprisingly, Bhutto echoed Yahya's argument. Landing at Karachi that afternoon, he told the press: "By the Grace of Almighty God, Pakistan has at last been saved."[70]

The military plan to "save" Pakistan rested on the premise that the Awami League's actions would be treated as "rebellion" and its supporters would be "dealt with as hostile elements." Furthermore, given the widespread support enjoyed by the Awami League, the operation would be "launched with great cunningness, surprise, deception and speed combined with shock action."[71] The army's crackdown began simultaneously across the province on the night of 25 March 1971. The sweep in Dhaka had several targets. The most important ones were the leadership of the Awami League and other radical political outfits, especially the student groups. The bulk of the top leadership of the various political organizations managed to elude the military dragnet, but the army did manage to hook its prize catch: Mujibur Rahman.

The student halls at Dacca University were the site of gruesome military action. In addition to the students, the troops also went after several faculty members of the university. This was in part a planned purge. The troops seemed to be working with a list of names, and they certainly asked for some individuals. Another locus of military action was Old Dacca—an area teeming with shops, markets, and the homes of artisans and workers—a stronghold of the Awami League. Hindus were particularly targeted during the operations in Dhaka and elsewhere. They were simultaneously seen as a key source of support for the Awami League and its secessionist plans, as a corrosive cultural influence that diluted the glue of Islam holding Pakistan together, and as a potential fifth column for India. The US consul in Dhaka would cable Washington on 25 May 1971 that "evidence of a systematic persecution of the Hindu population is too detailed and too massive to be ignored. While the Western mind boggles at the enormity of a possible planned eviction of 10 million people, the fact remains that the officers and men of the [Pakistan] Army are behaving as if they had been given carte blanche to rid East Pakistan of these 'subversives.' "[72]

By the end of March 1971, the army had established its ascendancy in Dhaka, but large swaths of the province remained out of its control. This was partly because the army's efforts to "disarm" the battalions of the East Bengal regiment and the East Pakistan Rifles (EPR) miscarried. The Bengali officers and troops of these battalions independently mutinied and prevented the army from securing control of large parts of East Pakistan.[73] Over two months would pass before the Pakistan army wrested control of all "liberated zones" from the Bengali forces. However, the "pacification" campaign, conducted with the assistance of local collaborators and militias, continued thereafter—the civilian population being the primary target of these military operations. Meanwhile, in the course of their engagements with the army and their attempts to defend "liberated zones," the Bengali officers began reaching out to Indian soldiers across the border. Political leaders, too, sought to evade the army and make their way to the borders with India.

On the evening of 31 March 1971, having traveled incognito for five days on horseback and foot, Tajuddin Ahmad and Amirul Islam sat anxiously at a culvert in the no-man's-land near an Indian border outpost. Their messenger had gone across to establish contact but had not yet returned. Tajuddin was pensive, but Islam felt strangely energized. "The sun is setting," he said to Tajuddin, "but there will be a new dawn." As night fell, they heard the thud of boots heading in their direction. A small group of soldiers stood before them, presented arms, and welcomed them to India.[74]

3

THE NEIGHBOR

K. C. Sen Gupta was a harried man. That morning—14 March 1971—
the deputy high commissioner of India in Dhaka had met Captain Sujat
Ali, an emissary of Sheikh Mujibur Rahman. Ali had been sent to him
with a "special appeal for help at this critical hour." Two and a half divisions of the Pakistan army were being flown into East Pakistan. Mujib
felt that this was possible "due to withdrawal of Indian troops from
West Pakistan border." He believed that if India intercepted "troops,
ships and aircrafts to East Pakistan on [the] pretext of violation of Indian borders [it] can only shake military morale." Mujib requested that
"India's decision in this connection be communicated immediately" so
that he could "decide his next move." "East Pakistan has gone to the
point of no return," he insisted. They were prepared to strike at the army
if "India could stop further reinforcement . . . Mujib has no alternative
but to fight for independence."[1]

This was not the first message from Mujib for the Indian leadership.
On 5 or 6 March, Sen Gupta had been approached by Tajuddin Ahmad.
The Awami League's general secretary inquired about the prospect of
Indian assistance in terms of offering political asylum to activists or
material assistance to a liberation movement in the event of a Pakistani
attack on East Bengal.[2] The absence of a response from the Indian government had peeved Mujib. Indeed, Sujat Ali emphasized Mujib's "dissatisfaction" and sought India's "decision immediately." Now, merely to
please Mujib, Sen Gupta had to make a quick trip to Calcutta for consultations with his government.[3]

Mujib's message, conveyed through intelligence conduits for secrecy,
reached the prime minister's office on the morning of 19 March. In the
meantime, Sen Gupta had returned to Dhaka and conveyed to Tajuddin

a vague and general assurance that India would offer "all possible assistance" to victims in the event of an attack.[4] New Delhi's unwillingness to accede to Mujib's request raises important questions. Why was India reluctant? Might it not have been more feasible and fruitful to intervene early and tilt the scales in the favor of the Bengalis? Should it not have been obvious to decision makers that an independent East Bengal would be highly desirable from India's standpoint? How did this stance impinge upon India's subsequent attempts to manage the crisis?

I

In the run-up to the East Pakistan crisis, India was busy with its own general elections. In late 1969, Prime Minister Indira Gandhi had split the Congress Party in order to secure her grip on power. The grand old party splintered into two curiously named outfits: the Congress (Organization) led by the old guard and the Congress (Requisionist) led by Indira Gandhi. On the heels of this move, she called for national elections in March 1971—a year ahead of schedule. This broke the link between the national and provincial elections, which had always been held simultaneously, and so fixed the electorate's attention on national as opposed to local issues. Pitted against Mrs. Gandhi's party, Congress (R), was a hastily cobbled coalition of the Congress (O), the right-wing Jana Sangh, the pro-business Swatantra, the socialists, and a smattering of regional parties. This self-styled Grand Alliance adopted the slogan *"Indira Hatao"* (Remove Indira), and her response was *"Garibi Hatao"* (Remove Poverty). Indira Gandhi's electoral strategy paid off handsomely: she returned to power with 352 out of 518 seats. The next largest party garnered a pitiable 25. So when the crisis erupted, Mrs. Gandhi was no longer the leader of a minority government. This strengthened her position in handling the crisis, though it did not insulate her from political pressures.

Even as the country was gearing up for elections, the government had kept a watch on Pakistan. New Delhi believed that Yahya Khan was interested in transferring power to an elected leadership both because he had "seen the end of Ayub in circumstances which were not very flattering" and because "personally he is not a hard-working man and is not prepared to put in the solid hard work to master . . . the intricacies of a modern administration." Moreover, India had "never thought that Sheikh Mujib would get this outstanding majority."[5] Be that as it may, the electoral outcome was welcomed in New Delhi. An Awami League government was seen as offering the best hope for normalization of India's relations with Pakistan. First, the Bengalis did not share the West Pakistanis' obsession with perceived threats from India or with wresting back Kashmir. Second, there was the prospect of reviving the trade links between India and East Pakistan that had been disrupted and suspended by the 1965 war. Third, the secular outlook of the Awami League was expected to ease communal tensions in East Pakistan and so reduce the migration of Hindus into India. Finally, the new political dispensation might cease supporting anti-Indian insurgent groups (the Nagas and Mizos, in particular) that were operating out of safe havens in East Pakistan.[6]

The possibility of secession by East Pakistan was recognized—only to be assessed as antithetical to India's interests. The Indian envoy in Islamabad observed in December 1970 that a secessionist East Bengal might seek to create a United Bengal in association with West Bengal. Besides, an independent East Pakistan was likely to fall under the control of pro-China communists. The foreign secretary, Triloki Nath Kaul, agreed that India should do nothing to encourage the secession of East Pakistan, although it was incapable of preventing such an outcome.[7] These assumptions were not as idiosyncratic as they seem in hindsight and were widely shared at the time. At a meeting of the parliamentary consultative committee on foreign affairs, Balraj Madhok of the Jana Sangh warned that "East Pakistan is going to get out of Pakistan and West Bengal is going to get out of India, perhaps Assam would also get out of India . . . the Russian and Chinese mind is working along with these lines."[8] Against the backdrop of the Maoist "Naxalite" movement that had been raging in West Bengal since 1967, such fears did not seem entirely fanciful. Indeed, the concern that the Maoists would hijack the Bangladesh movement would deeply inflect Indian thinking throughout the crisis.

Interestingly, India's major strategic concern at this point was rather different. The prime minister's principal secretary, Parmeshwar Narain Haksar, believed that the Awami League's massive victory had made the resolution of internal problems in Pakistan "infinitely more difficult." Consequently, "the temptation to seek solution of these problems by external adventures has become great."[9] In mid-January 1971, the external intelligence agency, the Research & Analysis Wing (R&AW), prepared a detailed assessment of the situation. The paper noted that although the Awami League had an absolute majority, it would "find it necessary to enlist the support of some parties and groups from the Western Wing in the National Assembly"—especially the PPP. "It is likely that because of political compulsions and the realities of the situation as it develops, Sheikh Mujibur Rahman and Bhutto would reach a working understanding." The quantum of autonomy for East Pakistan and the power of taxation would be subject to "hard bargaining." Yet, the paper argued, it would be "very difficult for Yahya Khan to withhold the authentication of any Constitution framed by the National Assembly"—the more so "if Bhutto's PPP joined the Awami League in passing the Constitution." The expectation, then, was that Mujib and Bhutto had a common interest in working together to keep the military out. The possibility of an attack on India to divert attention from internal issues was judged to be "somewhat remote." Yahya had "so far tried to appear responsive to public opinion and has shown a sense of realism in his actions." The possibility of such an attack would, however, increase "if the democratic process is aborted."[10]

By this time, the R&AW had begun to receive inputs suggesting that Mujib considered secession to be a real possibility and that he was preparing for such an eventuality. The agency's chief, Rameshwar Nath Kao, felt that Mujib would have no option but to stand firm on the six points.[11] A Kashmiri Brahmin from Uttar Pradesh, Kao had joined the Imperial Police Service in 1940 and had been seconded to the Intelligence Bureau (IB) on the eve of independence. His acumen, competence, and discretion drew the attention of B. N. Mullick—the second and long-serving director of the IB. The assignment that established Kao's professional standing was the investigation into the crash of the Indian aircraft *Kashmir Princess* that was carrying members of the Chinese delegation to the Bandung Conference in 1955. In 1968, the Indian government decided—following the perceived intelligence failures in the wars of 1962 and 1965—to split the IB and create a separate external intelligence agency. Prime Minister Gandhi tasked Kao with building the new organization and placed the R&AW directly under her control. So Kao not only had the prime minister's confidence but had unmediated access as well. The brewing crisis in East Pakistan, he well understood, would be the first serious test for his agency.

After the postponement of the National Assembly, members of the Awami League conveyed to the R&AW their requirements in the event of a showdown: machine guns and mortars, 3 million tons of food supplies, medicines, communication equipment, transportation for quick movement inside India, including a small passenger aircraft and a helicopter, and a radio transmitter with facilities for broadcasting. Kao believed that although the Pakistan army may gain "some temporary successes . . . it will be impossible for them, any more, to completely crush the liberation movement." If the fighting became prolonged, the movement would go underground and "develop on the lines of a widespread guerrilla movement." "The longer the liberation struggle takes to achieve success," he added, "the greater are the chances of its control moving into the hands of extremists and pro-China communists in Bangla Desh." This would be "greatly to the disadvantage of India." Kao argued that it was in India's interest "to give aid, adequate and quick enough, to ensure early success of the liberation movement under the control and guidance of the Awami League and its leaders."[12]

On 2 March, the prime minister ordered a committee comprising Cabinet Secretary K. Swaminathan, Haksar, Kaul, Kao, and Home Secretary Govind Narain to "examine the issue of giving help to Bangla Desh and give their assessment to the PM [Prime Minister]." Given the possibility of a unilateral declaration of independence by Mujib on 7 March, it is not surprising that the first issue she wanted to consider was the implications of according recognition to an independent Bangladesh. Second, regardless of whether recognition was given, what would be the political, economic, and military implications of assisting the movement? Curiously, the military dimension of their discussion did not envisage offensive moves by India; rather, they examined the likelihood of a Pakistani attack on Kashmir or military reaction by China "as a close ally of Pakistan."[13]

It was against this backdrop that Mujib's renewed requests for help were received in New Delhi. These appeals went unanswered for at least two reasons. The Indian government was nonplussed by the turn of events in the middle of March. Immediately after Mujib's request for assistance, Yahya had arrived in Dhaka, and his negotiations with the Awami League seemed to be progressing. Reports from the missions in Islamabad and Dhaka suggested that an agreement on some substantive issues was at hand. The military buildup in East Pakistan was seen as a tactic to cow the Bengalis into diluting their demands.[14] Further, over the past couple of years Mujib had kept a conspicuous distance from his Indian contacts. He would later admit that "it was true he had lost touch with India . . . he had to be extremely cautious after the Agartala

Conspiracy Case."[15] Unsure of his aims and intentions, Indira Gandhi and her top advisers—with the exception of Kao—thought it prudent to wait and watch. Mujib's own tactlessness could not have helped his cause. In the message that was conveyed through Sen Gupta, for instance, he claimed that the US ambassador to Pakistan had "agreed to ensure withdrawal of Pakistan Army from East Pakistan on [the] condition of leasing a bay island for seven years." Mujib added that he was reluctant to agree to this proposal but might have no other option if India did not come to his aid.[16] The use of such crude baits might have exacerbated the doubts in the minds of the Indian leadership about his plans. In any event, Mujib made no further contact with the Indians.

II

When the first reports of the military action trickled in, the prime minister and her key advisers thought that negotiations would be resumed after a short, sharp show of strength. The issue at stake was nothing less than the "territorial and ideological foundations of the state," and it was difficult to see why the Pakistan army would want to completely alienate the Bengalis. Besides, given the intensity of popular support for Mujib and the Awami League, they believed that the army would realize that it would not be able to hold down the Bengalis by the jackboot.[17] These assumptions were soon swept away by the flood of refugees and their tales of woe. Yet, for a variety of reasons, India's initial response to the crisis was stamped with circumspection.

Looking back through the distorting prism of the Indian military victory, most accounts tend to credit Indira Gandhi with exceptional foresight, impeccable timing, and an assured touch in handling the crisis. To be sure, Mrs. Gandhi had a keen sense for the role of power and interests in politics, and a remorseless and highly developed instinct for cutting her adversaries to size. Yet her response to the crisis was more tentative and improvisational than is usually assumed. After all, this was her first major international crisis. She was also mindful that her father's legacy had been undone by his disastrous handling of the China crisis in 1962.

The prime minister's caution was reinforced by her foremost adviser, P. N. Haksar. An erudite and experienced diplomat, Haksar habitually thought in terms of historical parallels and cast a weary eye on the workings of the international community. He had known Mrs. Gandhi from his own days as a student at the London School of Economics in the 1930s: his Primrose Hill apartment had been a favorite haunt of Indira and her then boyfriend, Feroze Gandhi. During those years, Haksar had been active in left-leaning student circles and had known Rajni Palme Dutt of the Communist Party of Great Britain. Unsurprisingly, these radical sympathies left their mark on his international outlook, for Leninism in international politics tends to shade into a form of realism. Haksar had been a lawyer in Allahabad when he was invited by none less than Jawaharlal Nehru to join the new foreign service of independent India. Haksar belonged to the generation of Indian diplomats who had a ringside view of the rise and fall of Nehru's nonalignment—an experience that undoubtedly shaped his views on the bubbling crisis in East Pakistan.

Although their sympathies lay with the Bengalis, Indira Gandhi and Haksar believed that "India, as a state, has to walk warily." Pakistan was a member of the United Nations, so "interference in events internal to Pakistan will not earn us either understanding or good-will from the majority of nation-states." The recent example of Nigeria, where the secessionist movement in Biafra had not been supported, was instructive. Further, where a state of civil war does prevail, "international law and morality only accords legitimacy to a successful rebellion." Until Mujib and his colleagues established their legitimacy, the international community was unlikely to accord recognition to an independent Bangladesh. Finally, India had to be careful not to fire a blunderbuss from an exposed piquet. For India had consistently maintained "in respect of Kashmir that we cannot allow its secession and that whatever happens there is a matter of domestic concern to India and that we shall not tolerate any outside interference." All things considered, India had to "tread our path as a State, with [a] great deal of circumspection and not allow our feelings to get the better of us." The prime minister was aware that there would be considerable parliamentary and public pressure on the government to do something. To avoid being painted into a corner, she met the leaders of the opposition parties on the evening of 26 March and explained her thinking. She also requested that the government's policy on this issue "should not become a subject matter of public debate."[18]

Proceedings in parliament over the next three days were impassioned all the same. The foreign minister, Swaran Singh, made a statement in both the houses that the government was "gravely concerned" at the developments in East Pakistan and that "our hearts go out in sympathy to the people who are undergoing great suffering."[19] The tepid tone of his remarks was sharply censured on the floor of the parliament, with the opposition demanding a clearer statement of intent. The prime minister had to intervene and assure parliament that "we are fully alive to the situation." "At the same time," she insisted, "we have to follow proper international norms." Underlining her cautious approach, she held that "a wrong step, a wrong word, can have an effect entirely different from the one that we all just [*sic*] intend." She reiterated that "it would not be wise if this becomes a matter for public debate."[20]

But the government was already struggling to control the public narrative. Several political parties, including the local unit of the ruling party, Congress (R), organized demonstrations outside the Pakistan embassy in New Delhi, demanding immediate withdrawal from "Bangla Desh." Similar protests were held in Calcutta outside the Pakistan mission. Public meetings involving academics, intellectuals, and students were held all over the country, condemning the military crackdown. A cohort of students even met the prime minister and demanded full support to the people of East Bengal. Indira Gandhi realized that this issue could rejuvenate the opposition that was licking its wounds after the mauling defeat in the elections. To contain parliamentary and public opinion, she moved a resolution in parliament on 31 March, strongly criticizing the military action, demanding an end to the violence "which amounts to genocide," and promising "whole hearted sympathy and support" for the people of "East Bengal."[21] Over the next two weeks, Indian policy on the crisis began to take shape within this cautious framework. Deliberations in New Delhi were lent urgency by the news that Tajuddin Ahmad had crossed over to India in the early hours of 30 March.

III

At the border post, Tajuddin and Amirul Islam were met by the senior Border Security Force (BSF) officer in West Bengal, Golok Majumdar. The BSF had received intelligence about senior Awami League leaders, perhaps Mujib himself, coming in from Khushtia. Tajuddin briefed his host on the situation in East Pakistan and handed over a list of Awami League leaders and members of the National Assembly. Later that evening, Majumdar drove them to the airport in Calcutta, where they met the Director-General of BSF, K. F. Rustamji, who had arrived posthaste from Delhi. Over the following three days, Tajuddin and Islam had extensive discussions with BSF officials. Emphasizing their determination to resist the Pakistan army and to secure independence from Pakistan, they requested that Rustamji provide arms and ammunition to the Bengali soldiers who were already establishing contact with BSF posts along the border. Rustamji observed that such a decision could only come from the highest levels of the government and that he could arrange for them to meet the prime minister. On 1 April, Tajuddin and Islam were flown to Delhi in an old military aircraft and were ensconced in a BSF safe house.[22]

Before his meeting with Mrs. Gandhi, Tajuddin was beset by several concerns. Foremost of these was the question of how best to present himself to the Indian prime minister. Tajuddin was worried that if he met her merely as a senior leader of the Awami League, he might elicit a great deal of sympathy but little material assistance to conduct a liberation war. Both Islam and Tajuddin felt that India—for that matter any foreign government—would not be open to offering such assistance until a formal Government of Bangladesh was constituted and until this government unequivocally declared its intention to wage a war of liberation. En route to India, they had heard a declaration of independence on behalf of Mujibur Rahman broadcasted by a Bengali officer, Major Ziaur Rahman. In Delhi, Tajuddin met other Awami League activists who had separately made their way to the Indian capital. Following consultations with M. R. Siddiqi, Sirajul Haque, Abdur Rauf, Rehman Sobhan, and Anisur Rahman, Tajuddin decided to present himself as the member of a duly elected government that had declared Bangladesh independent. By so doing, he hoped to convince the Indian leadership both of the legitimacy of his mission and of the need to recognize the government of Bangladesh. By this time, Tajuddin had also decided to establish the government in the Chuadanga subdivision in East Bengal opposite Krishnannagar in India. Following from this, Tajuddin was eager to secure sanctuary and matériel for Bengali soldiers and fighters as well as assistance for refugees. Lastly, he was anxious to ensure that the crisis did not turn into an India-Pakistan problem with all its attendant complications. Barring this last point, Tajuddin aired his views in preliminary meetings with intelligence officers in Delhi.[23]

The Indians, for their part, had decided on the contours of the assistance that they would offer. These included arms and ammunition, communication equipment and broadcasting facilities, civil supplies and medicines, safe passage and transit arrangements. The Indian leadership saw that the Awami League had "overwhelming enthusiasm and spontaneous support," but they were concerned that "our Friends do not yet have an organization to harness this meaningfully." So apart from providing material assistance, India had "to advise them about the organization they should set up and their channels of command and communication." In particular, the Bengalis decision to carve out "a liberated area near our border" ought to be encouraged. This would not only advance their aims, but would "also enable us to have some capability to influence the turn of events, and to ensure that the help given by us is utilized properly." Apart from establishing a headquarters in the liberated zone, a small liaison group with "the authority to take decisions" would be set up in Delhi as well as a "small servicing facility in Calcutta to help movement of personnel and material." The requirements of the liberation movement would be considered by the committee constituted earlier by the prime minister, now expanded to include the defense secretary, K. B. Lall. The relationship at the political level would be handled "only through the agency of the R&AW." The agency would guide the committee's deliberations and "provide adequate coordination." At this stage, the "main executive agency" would be the BSF, though for "specialised needs we may have to get the help of the Army too." A premium was placed on "as much secrecy as possible" to avoid generating "the wrong kind of pressures."[24]

On the evening of 3 April 1971, Indira Gandhi met Tajuddin Ahmad at the office in her residence. The prime minister began by asking for news of Mujib. Tajuddin said that he had had no contact with his leader since the night of 25 March, but added that Mujib had proclaimed the independence of Bangladesh and had formed a cabinet for his government comprising all five members of the Awami League's high command. It is not clear whether Tajuddin presented himself as the prime minister of the government, but he appears to have indicated that after Mujib's arrest and the dispersal of the rest of the cabinet, he was effectively in charge of the movement. At another meeting the next day, Tajuddin informed the prime minister that Mujib had been arrested by the Pakistan army. In these meetings, Mrs. Gandhi did not touch upon on the question of recognition but offered support along the lines that had already been decided, though the magnitude of the assistance remained to be worked out.[25]

While in Delhi, Tajuddin tasked Amirul Islam with preparing a formal proclamation of independence of Bangladesh. In light of the US stance on the crisis, it is ironic that Islam chose the American Declaration of Independence as one of his models (the other was the United Nations Covenant on Civil and Political Rights). Islam and Rahman Sobhan also worked on an accompanying speech by Tajuddin, which was recorded in Delhi for subsequent broadcasting.[26] Tajuddin, however, was reluctant to go any further before consulting other Awami Leaguers who were gathering in India. Over the next week or so, he managed to reestablish contact with the rest of the high command.

On 11 April, the Swadhin Bangla Betar Kendra (Independent Bengal Broadcasting Centre) broadcast Tajuddin's speech, announcing the formation of a "mighty army" around the nucleus of the East Bengal regiment and the East Pakistan rifles.[27] The announcement of a cabinet for the government of Bangladesh came two days later. On 17 April, at a ceremony—carefully orchestrated by the BSF—in a mango grove across the Indian border called Baidyanath Tala (renamed Mujibnagar), the government of Bangladesh was formally proclaimed in the presence of Indian and foreign journalists. Syed Nazrul Islam took guard of honor as acting president and made a passionate plea to the international community for assistance.[28]

IV

A week later, Nazrul Islam wrote to the president of India requesting immediate recognition of his government. Well before this missive, the question of recognizing the government of Bangladesh was being debated in Delhi. As early as 26 March, we may recall, Mrs. Gandhi and Haksar had felt that recognition could only be given if the liberation movement demonstrated its ability to take on the army and gain the upper hand in the civil war. Mandarins in the Ministry of External Affairs took a different view from the Prime Minister's Secretariat. By the end of March 1971, officials in the ministry felt that because the idea of united Pakistan was effectively dead, India's main interests lay in ensuring that the new state of Bangladesh started out with friendly feelings toward India and that the regime that took over was not oriented toward China. The foreign office felt that recognition should not be withheld for long: if the liberation war proved to be a prolonged affair, the leadership would pass to the extreme left. But India should grant recognition only after ensuring that at least two or more powers would simultaneously do so.[29] But the foreign minister as well as the prime minister preferred to move gingerly.

Pressure for recognition, however, began to mount outside the government. Several political parties passed resolutions demanding immediate recognition of Bangladesh. Legislative assemblies in Uttar Pradesh, Bihar, Assam, Nagaland, and Tripura adopted resolutions urging the central government to formally recognize Bangladesh. The opposition parties castigated the prime minister's stance as vacillating and complacent, and equated it with her father's stand on Tibet. More uncomfortable to the government was the demand for recognition from its principal ally, the Communist Party of India. These calls were echoed in the press and lent credence by the pundits.[30]

The prime minister was particularly worried about the demand for recognition voiced by the veteran Gandhian leader Jayaprakash Narayan. "JP," as he was popularly known, had for long been the conscience of the nation, championing successively the cause of the Tibetans, the Kashmiris, and the Nagas. But Narayan did not base his argument merely on morality. Rather, he sought expert opinion to contest the government's claims about international norms of recognition. The eminent jurist and erstwhile cabinet minister M. C. Chagla told him that the normal requirements for recognition—control of part of the territory and effective administration—did not apply in the case of Bangladesh. The Bengalis were the majority in Pakistan, so they could not be held to have seceded from the minority. If anything, it was Yahya Khan's regime that lacked legitimacy. Others suggested that recognition of a government was different from the recognition of a state and that the former had less stringent criteria than the latter.[31] Armed with this advice, Narayan assailed the government's stance. In a widely circulated press release, he emphatically claimed that "my sense of history and knowledge of international affairs tell me that it will not be any violation of international law to accord immediate recognition to Bangla Desh."[32]

This many-voiced chorus strengthened the position of the advocates of early recognition within the government. In early May, Foreign Secretary Kaul wrote to Haksar that "our refusal to recognise Bangla Desh Government cannot be maintained for very long in the face of mounting pressure in our press and at the next sitting of Parliament."[33] Haksar demurred, insisting to the prime minister that "so far there is no evidence that the Provisional Govt has any area in Bangla Desh under its effective control." The Bangladesh leadership was offered an anodyne assurance that the matter was "constantly under consideration."[34] Leaders of the opposition parties were told that "no Government recognises a revolt unless it acquires legitimacy. That legitimacy is acquired by control of territory and by its writ running. From this point of view the Government of Bangla Desh has not succeeded in satisfying the criteria. The public posture in most countries was that these developments were Pakistan's internal affairs."[35]

Questions of international law and diplomacy apart, New Delhi harbored two important concerns that deepened its circumspection. The first pertained to fractures within the Bangladesh leadership. These had begun to surface in the aftermath of Tajuddin's initial consultations with the Indian prime minister. At a meeting of Awami Leaguers held in the BSF's office in Calcutta, Tajuddin's proposal for constituting a government was contested by a small but influential faction of the party. Led by Sheikh Fazlul Haq Moni, a nephew of Mujibur Rahman, this group asserted that a liberation war needed a revolutionary council rather than a regular government. The group also demanded the cancellation of Tajuddin's impending radio broadcast. In the tempestuous debate that followed, Amirul Islam pointed out that a revolutionary council had not worked elsewhere in similar situations, most recently in Biafra. There was an ever present risk of the council splitting. In such a situation, he asked, who would India support? Although Moni backed down in the meeting, he sent an appeal—signed by forty-two Awami League functionaries—to Indira Gandhi requesting the cancellation of Tajuddin's broadcast.[36]

Sheikh Moni's clout did not derive from the number of his supporters; rather, it stemmed from his proximity to the R&AW and Kao, who in turn shaped the prime minister's position on the crisis. In any event, the news of these dissensions sowed doubts in the Indian official mind about the solidity of the Mujibnagar enterprise. A senior envoy would later confess to Mujib that "doubts lingered in our minds as to what his [Mujib's] actual wishes were regarding the whole situation. We had Mr. Tajuddin's word to go by, the authenticity of which was unfortunately disputed by some of his colleagues."[37] In consequence, New Delhi thought it "politic to adopt a policy of watch and wait for some until the situation in Bangladesh crystallizes further." Meanwhile, India would continue "to exhibit its full-fledged support to the people of Bangladesh in their saddest hour and to render them moral, financial, medical and other facilities" and to keep "propaganda constantly focused on the issue."[38]

The second major concern for New Delhi was that the very act of recognition would "raise false hopes that recognition would be followed by direct intervention of the Armed Forces of India to sustain and support such a Government."[39] This was not just a question of managing the expectations of the Bengalis. Indeed, the Indian government was eager to avoid direct military intervention in East Pakistan.

The received wisdom is that Prime Minister Gandhi actually wanted to undertake a military intervention in April 1971 and that she was dissuaded by the army chief, General S. H. F. J. "Sam" Manekshaw. This is perhaps the most tenacious of all myths about the 1971 crisis.[40] Manekshaw's own version was embellished with each telling, not least because he outlived Indira Gandhi and most of her senior advisers. At his most imaginative and expansive, Manekshaw recalled a "terribly angry and terribly upset" Indira Gandhi demanding, "Can't you do something? Why don't you do something . . . I want you to march in . . . I don't mind if it is war." After outlining his reasons for avoiding war at that point, Manekshaw claimed to have said at a cabinet meeting, "If you still want me to go ahead, Prime Minister, I guarantee you 100 per cent defeat. Now give me your orders." Manekshaw added that he had even offered to resign if the prime minister did not agree with his assessment. In the event, the prime minister reposed her confidence in his judgment. "So there is a very thin line," reminisced Manekshaw, "between becoming a Field Marshal and being dismissed!"[41] Not to be left behind, Lieutenant General J. F. R. Jacob, chief of staff of the eastern army command, claimed that Manekshaw was wobbling under political pressure and that he had stiffened his chief's spine.[42]

These claims hardly comport with reality. Contrary to the assertions of Manekshaw and his military colleagues, the prime minister did not contemplate such an intervention in the early stages of the crisis. Indira Gandhi's strategic outlook was shaped by an assessment prepared earlier in the year on the threat posed by Pakistan. This assessment had underscored the "impressive increase in Pakistan's armed might since her confrontation with India in 1965." Not only had Pakistan refitted and modernized its armor, artillery, and air force, but it had "accumulated sufficient stockpile to sustain a war with India of a duration of 90 to 150 days." The assessment had concluded that "Pakistan's military preparedness is such that she has the capability of launching a military attack against India on the Western front."[43] Mrs. Gandhi was aware that "there are many weak spots in our defence capabilities. These need to be remedied without loss of time."[44] By the time the crisis broke, these problems had not been rectified. Hence, India was vulnerable to a Pakistani attack along the western border in response to an Indian intervention in the east. This had, in fact, been Pakistan's traditional strategy for the defense of East Pakistan—one that it had adopted both in the refugee crisis of 1950 and in the war of 1965.

Furthermore, New Delhi was alert to the possibility of a Chinese intervention in a war with Pakistan. "It is unlikely," the assessment had noted, "that China will actively get involved, militarily, in an India-Pakistan conflict." Nonetheless, "it is to be expected that in the event of all out hostilities between India and Pakistan, China would adopt a threatening posture on the Sino-Indian border and even stage some border incidents and clashes, to prevent the diversion of Indian troops . . . to the theatres of war with Pakistan." Besides, China would ensure "a steady flow" of military supplies to Pakistan.[45] This judgment, too, reflected the experience of the 1965 war, when China had tried to create incidents along its borders with India but refrained from direct military involvement in support of Pakistan. Yet even limited moves by China would cause serious complications to India's military strategy vis-à-vis Pakistan. It is not surprising that the possibility of a Chinese intervention bulked large in New Delhi's mind in the early stages of the crisis.[46]

Finally, Mrs. Gandhi and Haksar thought that an armed intervention by India would "evoke hostile reactions all over the world and all the sympathy and support which the [sic] Bangla Desh has been able to evoke in the world will be drowned in Indo-Pak conflict."[47] From the outset, therefore, the prime minister went with Kao's advice to support a guerrilla movement led by the Awami League. By 1 April 1971, the prime minister and her top advisers were clear that the rebels would have to be given "some orientation training in guerrilla tactics, to prepare for a long struggle."[48] The advice given by her close associates serving abroad chimed with this view. D. P. Dhar, the prime minister's hand-picked ambassador to the Soviet Union and an old associate, argued that "our main and only aim should be to ensure that the marshes and quagmires of East Bengal swallow up the military potential which West Pakistan can muster. This may even open up perspectives of a long drawn struggle. I have no doubt that in the end and that too in the not very distant future the West Pakistani elements will find their Dien Bien

Phu in East Bengal." The resistance, he emphasized, "must not be allowed to collapse."[49]

The advice from the military chiefs fit snugly with the prime minister's views on appropriate strategy. This was conveyed to her by Manekshaw in his capacity as the chairman of the chiefs of staff committee. Manekshaw observed that the existing contingency plans for the east were limited to defending the "chicken's neck corridor" that linked north Bengal with the other northeastern states of India. A military intervention in East Pakistan would require a reorientation of operational plans, major redeployment of forces into the eastern theater, and considerable logistical and administrative preparation. Moreover, there was a shortage of stockpiled reserves of armored vehicles and bridging equipment, which would need time to redress. In any case, military operations in East Pakistan were best undertaken after the coming monsoon, and better still after November, when snowbound Himalayan passes would impede any military moves by China.[50]

The most sophisticated argument for an early military intervention was advanced by K. Subrahmanyam, a senior bureaucrat with acknowledged expertise on military matters and director of the Institute for Defense Studies and Analysis in Delhi. In a paper that was circulated to the prime minister, key cabinet members, and some senior officials, Subrahmanyam argued that "it will not be possible" for the Bangladesh fighters "to exert unacceptable military pressure" on the superior Pakistani forces. If these operations were prolonged, they would lead to severe attrition of the rebel force and would create incentives for Pakistan to escalate the fighting to a war against India. A policy of limited intervention carried other costs as well: parliamentary pressure on the government, possible emergence of a militant leadership among the Bengalis, "adverse impact" on the prime minister's image, and the dilution of India's "military credibility."[51]

Subrahmanyam observed that there was "a large body of opinion in the country which favours covert assistance." But he advocated a more decisive strategy. Beginning with the supply of arms, India should aim "for rapid escalation to subsequent overt limited intervention, quarantine of Bangla Desh, full-scale intervention and a full-scale war with Pakistan." The "initiative for escalation," he argued, "must always be held to extract maximum advantage out of this situation." At the highest rungs of the escalator, if India undertook a "short swift operation likely to be completed in 4 to 5 days," it could present the great powers with a fait accompli and minimize its own vulnerability to intervention by China. Subrahmanyam concluded that "intervention on a decisive scale sooner than later is to be preferred."[52]

Subrahmanyam's standing in the defense bureaucracy and his proximity to the defense minister Jagjivan Ram and the finance minister Y. B. Chavan ensured that his views were echoed in the system. But the prime minister's thinking continued to be molded by her own outlook and those of her trusty advisers. Dhar wrote from Moscow advising against the "policies and programmes of impetuosity" advocated by some analysts. What India had to plan for "is not an immediate defeat of the highly trained [army] of West Pakistan; we have to create the whole of East Bengal into a bottomless ditch which will suck the strength and resources of West Pakistan. Let us think in terms of a year or two, not in terms of a week or two."[53]

By the time the fabled cabinet meeting of 25 April was held, Mrs. Gandhi had ruled out the option of a military intervention. In fact, she summoned Manekshaw to the meeting so that her colleagues—some of whom had been rattled by the criticism heaped on the government's cautious policy—could hear the military's views for themselves.[54] In a closed-door meeting with leaders of the opposition on 7 May, the prime minister observed that she envisaged a guerrilla campaign "with the object of keeping the West Pakistan army continuously off their balance and to, gradually, bleed them." "If the struggle could be sustained over a period of 6 to 8 months," she added, "it is not unreasonable to expect that the sheer burden of Pakistan carrying on this struggle will become, sooner or later, unbearable." The prime minister was clear, however, that "we cannot, at the present stage, contemplate armed intervention at all. It would not be the right thing to do."[55]

V

The principal strategic problem confronting India was organizing and shaping the liberation campaign. Initially, the Bengali soldiers—the Mukti Fauj (Liberation Army), in Indian parlance—were supported by the BSF troops without any specific orders from on high. This was naturally restricted to providing shelter, food, and small quantities of ammunition. Even after New Delhi approved the limited provision of weapons, the BSF was unable to provide meaningful assistance. A BSF liaison officer observed that the fighters needed more than the rifles and rifle ammunition on offer. Indeed, "the bullets supplied for the rifles created a handicap for them as these bullets did not fit the Chinese made rifles used by the Mukti Fauj personnel."[56] In the first week of April, the BSF prepared an assessment that identified the Pakistan army's Achilles' heel in the eastern wing as its lines of supply and communication.[57] Targeting these would, of course, aggravate the problems of the local populace trapped in a civil war. The BSF's chief, Rustamji, sought and obtained Tajuddin's approval: "he [Tajuddin] was quite clear in his mind that those bridges which had to be destroyed for military reasons should be destroyed without hesitation and even if there is some local feeling against their destruction."[58] Over the next few weeks, the Mukti Fauj—assisted by the BSF—targeted several bridges, railroads, and other logistics installations in East Pakistan.[59]

By this time, the battalions of the East Bengal regiment and the East Pakistan Rifles were getting their act together. On 4 April 1971, the commanders met at the headquarters of 2 East Bengal in Teliapara and conferred about the course ahead. At length, they decided that the liberation war should be conducted under a centralized command structure and that the command should be vested in a senior military officer. The choice of the overall commander suggested itself: Colonel M. A. G. Osmany, the retired but senior-most Bengali officer who was present at the meeting and who was also a member of the Awami League. The officers further decided that this military command should be subordinated to a political leadership. This was deemed essential to securing material assistance from India and other countries.[60]

When it was learned that the Awami Leaguers in India were preparing to proclaim a government of Bangladesh, the military commanders offered their allegiance. In his broadcast of 11 April, Tajuddin announced the establishment of the military command and named the various sector commanders. But the relationship between the political leadership and the military officers was anything but easy. The politicians felt that "there was a tendency among some army leaders to take up the absolute leadership of the movement." Major Ziaur Rahman, who had not only proclaimed independence on behalf of Mujib but also declared himself leader of the provisional government, had to be pointedly "instructed not to make any such further announcements."[61] The soldiers, on the other hand, thought that the politicians were not doing enough to meet their requirements and assist their operations. Consequently, meetings between the two sets of leaderships tended to have an acrimonious edge.[62] This, in turn, bred a degree of mistrust among the Bangladesh leaders about India's intentions. Prior to a meeting with Tajuddin, Haksar reminded the prime minister to "ask them not to suspect our motives, if some times it appears that their demands are not immediately met."[63]

Of greater concern to New Delhi was the progress of military operations inside East Pakistan—or rather, the lack thereof. By mid-April it was becoming clear that the Bengali forces were unable to hold their own in the face of Pakistani offensives. Indian intelligence reports noted that the "Liberation Forces have had to yield ground in some areas and the Army is slowly gaining the upper hand."[64] In the coming weeks, the Mukti Fauj suffered a succession of setbacks. By the third week of May, most of the liberated areas under their control had fallen to the Pakistanis, though the latter's mopping-up operations continued to the end of June. This debacle was partly because of the Pakistan army's superior weaponry and partly because of the flawed organization and tactics adopted by the Bengalis.

An operational assessment by a percipient Bengali officer observed that the Pakistanis were making effective use of amphibious capabilities as well as parachute and helicopter landings to isolate the Mukti Fauj. Besides, they were also bringing to bear their heavy artillery and airpower. The Bangladesh forces had "practically no answer to the air menace." Nor did they have heavy mortars and mines to stymie the army's advance. The larger problem was that the Mukti Fauj offered pitched battles to the Pakistan army—a form of combat in which the latter's superiority was brought into play. The assessment called for a reorientation toward "a people's war" strategy that adopted "guerrilla methods": "no more op[erations] at day time," "no action unless a local superiority of at least 3 to 1 in fire power," and a focus on ambushes and raids to "jitter the en[emy]."[65]

All this was eminently sensible, even if the realization came a little too late. It was precisely in this direction that New Delhi sought to reorient the Bangladesh forces. Plans were drawn up for training the available forces and the civilian volunteers coming in from East Pakistan. On 22 April, the BSF was instructed—much to its chagrin—to act under the "broad directions" issued by the Indian army's eastern command.[66] Following a more detailed review of the operations, the army chief issued an operational instruction to the headquarters of the eastern command on 1 May. The overall aims were "to assist the government of Bangla

Desh in rallying the people in support of the liberation movement" and "to raise, equip and train East Bengal cadres for guerrilla operations in their own native land." The aim of these Indian operations initially was to tie down the Pakistani forces; subsequently, by gradual escalation of guerrilla attacks, to sap the Pakistanis' morale, impair the logistic capability for any offensive against Assam and West Bengal; and to use the Bengali fighters as ancillaries "in the event of Pakistan initiating hostilities against us." The plan was to organize and equip a guerrilla force of 20,000 men, which "could subsequently be enlarged to 1,00,000." The scope of guerrilla activities in East Pakistan would gradually be intensified in stages.[67]

These plans were explained to the Bangladesh leadership by the eastern army commander, Lieutenant General Jasjit Singh Aurora. At her meeting with Tajuddin on 6 May, Mrs. Gandhi reiterated the broad contours of the strategy and impressed upon him the need for complete agreement between the two sides. Then again, the prime minister and her advisers had their own doubts about Mujibnagar's ability to work this strategy. In particular, they were concerned about the Awami League's unwillingness to collaborate with other political parties or individuals without party cards. The Awami League's insistence that every recruit should be "politically certified" resulted in the rejection of hundreds of eager, able-bodied Bengali youth for guerrilla training.[68] Haksar urged the prime minister to tell Tajuddin that "every attempt should be made irrespective of political party affiliations to evolve a commonly accepted programme of action on a national level." This would allow the National Awami Party (led by Muzaffar Ahmad), Bhashani, and the East Pakistan Communist Party to join the liberation movement. The provisional government, Haksar insisted, "would have to raise themselves above the purely party loyalties."[69]

More generally, India's initial enthusiasm for the Awami League was beginning to curdle. Thus, when the Bangladesh government advanced ambitious schemes for training young volunteers for suicide missions, Haksar swatted them aside. The Bangladesh leadership, he noted with asperity, had not shown itself capable of inspiring the youth to such an extent. "This would require greater vision than they have displayed at present, greater flexibility than they have shown, greater organizational skill, capacity to bring together [a] wide variety of people who may not wear the label of the Awami League." Indeed, they "must, first of all, understand that the necessary pre-condition to carrying on the struggle is existence of Bangla Desh Government which would inspire confidence."[70] The smaller political outfits were, in fact, clamoring for the formation of a national coalition government, but the Awami League was unwilling to share power with parties that had been pulverized at the polls. All this ensured that the liberation forces did not receive the complete support of New Delhi until early August 1971—and only then after significant shifts in the wider strategic picture.[71]

VI

Even as India was fine-tuning its strategy, the situation was in rapid flux. The flow of refugees, which had begun as a trickle toward the end of March, had turned into a torrent by mid-April and broadened like the Brahmaputra River by the end of May 1971. In the month of May, the average daily influx of refugees was a staggering 102,000,[72] with around seventy-one refugees entering India every minute. Even these numbers understated the magnitude of the problem, for they counted only the registered refugees. Many others merely melted into the landscape of northeast India.

No sooner had New Delhi learned of the military crackdown, than it began to prepare for the possibility of more refugees trooping into India. There had already been a steady flow of refugees—mostly Hindus—

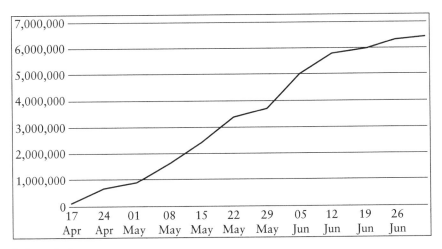

Influx of refugees.

Source: Visit of Henry Kissinger, WII/121(54)71, MEA, 1971, National Archives of India, New Delhi.

from East Pakistan since 1947, and India had also faced serious refugee crises in 1950 and 1964 when communal tensions had flared up in Pakistan. On 27 March 1971, the Indian government decided that the refugees should be afforded relief—shelter, food, and medical aid—on humanitarian grounds and that the costs would be borne by the central government. The governments of states abutting East Pakistan were enjoined to execute the relief program, and a branch of the secretariat of the Ministry of Rehabilitation was set up in Calcutta to direct these efforts.[73]

However, the relief preparations were overwhelmed by the speed and scale of the inflow from mid-April. The unprecedented influx of refugees posed a series of grim challenges to India. To begin with, it touched off outrage among the Indian people and enhanced the domestic pressures weighing on the government. Then there was its deleterious impact on the economy. After having had a torrid time managing economic problems in her first term, Indira Gandhi was looking forward to a period of self-sufficiency in food and to implementing a left-leaning economic program. Soon it became apparent that "there is a limit to our capacity and resources. Even the attempt to provide minimum facilities of shelter, food and medical care is imposing an enormous burden on us."[74] This burden was magnified by the serious health problems that broke out in the refugee camps, which intensified with the onset of the monsoon. In early June 1971, an estimated 9,500 cases of cholera were reported,

Influx of Non-Muslims from East Pakistan to India

Year	Number of Refugees
Partition to 31 December 1961	4,078,000
1962	13,894
1963	18,243
1964	693,142
1965	107,906
1966	7,565
1967	24,527
1968	11,649
1969	9,768
1970 (until Aug 1970)	159,390
Total	5,124,084

Source: Brief for the Parliamentary Consultative Committee, PI/125/82/70, MEA, 1970, National Archives of India, New Delhi.

with 1,250 fatalities. This shot up to 46,000 by the end of September, with nearly 6,000 dead.[75]

New Delhi was further alarmed at the composition of the refugee groups. Initially, the ratio of Muslims to Hindus among the refugees was 80 to 20. But by the end of April this had reversed: nearly 80 percent were Hindus, and only about 20 percent were Muslims.[76] The Indians concluded that "apparently, Pakistan is trying to solve its internal problems by cutting down the size of its population in East Bengal and changing its communal composition through an organized and selective programme of eviction."[77] The government kept these data under wraps. The prime minister was worried that parties on the Hindu right would make capital out of this and stoke retributory violence against Muslims in India, as had happened during earlier refugee crises. As Swaran Singh told Indian envoys, "In India we have tried to cover that up, lest it may inflame communal feelings but we have no hesitation in stating the figure to foreigners."[78] Mrs. Gandhi also reached out to the leader of Jana Sangh, Atal Behari Vajpayee, and asked him not to politicize the issue, for it would only help Pakistan to portray the refugee problem as a Hindu-Muslim and India-Pakistan problem.[79] The composition of the refugees was also problematic because of the possibility that the Hindus might seek to stay on in India rather than return to their homes.

The states bordering East Pakistan bore the brunt of the influx. By the end of May, for instance, 900,000 refugees had swept into the small state of Tripura, which had had a population only of 1.5 million. In West Bengal, places such as Bongaigaon, whose population had been only 5,000, were inundated by the 300,000 refugees who arrived in only two months. Parts of Assam, too, faced similar situations.[80] These were among the poorest parts of India, and the inflow of the refugees portended social tensions. For one thing, the unregistered refugees were bringing additional pressure to bear on volatile labor markets. For another, there was the danger that the local populace might consider the refugees to be better off than them. So, New Delhi sought to provide only minimum relief to the refugees.[81]

Equally worrisome were the security implications of the influx. Northeast India, a close adviser of Mrs. Gandhi would note later, "was demographically askew, economically retarded, politically unstable and socially volatile."[82] The region teemed with ethnic insurgent groups who operated out of safe havens in East Pakistan. Moreover, the recent Maoist, "Naxalite," uprising in West Bengal had hurled the state down a spiral of violence. The refugees, New Delhi feared, would come as touch paper to this tinderbox. As Haksar observed, "The regions which the refugees are entering are overcrowded and politically the most sensitive parts of India. The situation in these areas can very easily become explosive." Moreover, there was concern about the prospect of Maoists on both sides jointly exploiting the presence of such an immense number of refugees. "With our own difficulties in West Bengal," wrote Haksar, "the dangers of a link-up between the extremists in the two Bengals are real." The influx of refugees, he concluded, "constitutes a grave security risk which no responsible government can allow to develop."[83]

Writing to practically all heads of states and governments in mid-May, Indira Gandhi emphasized the range of problems posed by the refugees. She requested them to convey their concerns about the "personal safety" of Mujib and to "persuade the military rulers of Pakistan to recognize that the solution they have chosen for their problem in East Pakistan is unwise and untenable."[84] Over the next week, the prime minister's stance on the crisis became rather more robust. The point of inflection was her visit to Assam, Tripura, and West Bengal on 15–16 May. P. N. Dhar, who accompanied her on the trip, would recall that the prime minister "was so overwhelmed by the scale of human misery that she could hardly speak." At the end of their visits, she told Dhar, "The world must know what is happening here and do something about it. In any case, we cannot let Pakistan continue this holocaust." However, this did not mean that she was prepared to undertake an early military intervention to put an end to slaughter and ethnic cleansing in East Pakistan. Indeed, her principal concern was to ensure that refugees did not stay on in India. Thus, on returning to Delhi, Mrs. Gandhi made a firm decision that India would not absorb these refugees and that Pakistan must allow them to return to their homes in safety. In the meantime, it was essential to ensure that the refugees did not disperse and that they remained in their camps. Accordingly, the scale of the humanitarian effort was stepped up.[85]

Over the next week, Mrs. Gandhi and her advisers carefully crafted a speech that the prime minister delivered in parliament on 24 May 1971. It marked a departure from the stance hitherto adopted by the government. The speech was aimed at multiple audiences: to convince domestic opinion that the government was resolved to tackle the problem, to convey to Pakistan that India would not accept the refugees as a fait accompli, and to convince the great powers that Pakistan's actions were pregnant with dangerous possibilities. The prime minister stated that "what was claimed to be an internal problem of Pakistan has also become an internal problem for India." She was, therefore, "entitled to ask Pakistan to desist immediately from all actions which it is taking in the name of domestic jurisdiction." Pakistan, she declared, "cannot be allowed to seek a solution of its political or other problems at the expense of India and on Indian soil." India neither could nor wished to provide perpetual relief to the refugees. The operative part of the speech read: "Conditions must be created to stop any further influx of refugees and to ensure their early return under credible guarantees for their safety and well-being . . . If the world does not take heed, we shall be constrained to take all measures as may be necessary to ensure our own security." The prime minister reminded the great powers that they had "a special responsibility." If they exercised their influence over Pakistan quickly, peace would be preserved on the subcontinent. "But if they fail—and I sincerely hope that they will not—then this suppression of human rights . . . will threaten peace."[86]

Mrs. Gandhi was indeed sincere in her hope that external powers would succeed in pressuring Pakistan. As her foreign minister told senior diplomats a few days later, "we do not want war." What India did want was "changes in the governmental set-up there [in East Pakistan]. It is quite clear that refugees will never go back if the present regime continues. Therefore, this regime must be replaced by a regime which is responsible to the people . . . Our ultimate objective is that this military regime there must give way to a regime which is truly representative of the Awami League."[87] To be sure, the dominant opinion within the government was that independence for Bangladesh was inevitable. For instance, Kaul wrote to D. P. Dhar that "Bangladesh will be an independent nation sooner or later."[88] Yet New Delhi was open to the idea that there might be other, intermediate stations en route to that eventual destination. At one point, the foreign office even toyed with the possibility that "if they [Pakistanis] are not prepared to restore conditions under which these refugees could return to East Bengal, then the least they should do is to set apart a portion of their territory on which the refugees could be rehabilitated." Kaul hinted to the Soviet ambassador on 21 June that India might help the refugees "to create a belt of land on Bangladesh territory to which they could go back."[89]

Although this particular trial balloon was abandoned as being impractical, New Delhi did not insist on an independent Bangladesh as the only solution to the crisis. This was not merely an expedient stance. As Swaran Singh told Indian envoys, New Delhi was "not stating that we stand for independent Bangla Desh because this is a stage at which you cannot think of that." India's position was that the military regime in Pakistan should negotiate with Mujib and his colleagues and reach an agreed solution: "If they want to have autonomy according to six-point programme it is for them to agree. If they want independence it is for them to settle between the Central rulers and the Awami League." This stance also reflected New Delhi's awareness of the discord within the exile government and the fact that no one knew what Mujib really wanted. "Although they continue to say that they want a separate Bangla Desh," it was possible that "the Awami League tomorrow abandons this idea and they are content with the six-point programme or autonomy or even lesser autonomy."[90] India's stance, therefore, was at once diplomatic and prudent.

In the weeks ahead, New Delhi launched a frenetic diplomatic effort to persuade the international community to bring Pakistan to heel. Ministers and special emissaries were dispatched to capitals in Europe, North Africa, and East and West Asia. The foreign minister himself undertook a whistle-stop tour of Moscow, Bonn, Paris, Ottawa, Washington, and London. The government also roped in Jayaprakash Narayan into touring the major capitals and presenting the moral case of the Bengalis. Indian diplomats were exhorted not to be content with receiving assurances of "a few tons of medicine or some money" but to make energetic efforts in presenting India's arguments to their host governments. "Plug this once, twice, thrice, four times. Start from the lower rung and go up to the highest levels. Come to the lower level and try and all levels."[91] The outcome of these efforts would determine the subsequent course charted by India in navigating the crisis.

4

THE GRAND STRATEGISTS

On 28 April 1971, Henry Kissinger got down to composing a memorandum on the Pakistan crisis for President Richard Nixon. Kissinger's ire had been roused by an interdepartmental paper prepared on the crisis. The malice and ignorance of his colleagues were threatening to capsize his carefully laid plans. As national security adviser, he had to contend with many adversaries, but in his own estimation the real enemies resided in the Washington bureaucracy. After a brilliant and somewhat unconventional career at Harvard, Kissinger had joined the government barely two years before.[1] But his zest and skill in bureaucratic battles put many a professional to shame. These qualities, as well as his analytic powers and strategic acumen, made Kissinger an indispensable adviser on foreign and strategic affairs to President Nixon.

In his memorandum, Kissinger highlighted three judgments that applied to the unfolding situation. The Pakistan army seemed poised to overpower the resistance. This did not, however, guarantee the restoration of normality. Even if the resistance was presently snuffed out, there would be "widespread discontent and hatred in East Pakistan" that could threaten the unity of Pakistan. There was also the danger, if the crisis dragged on, of a conflict between Pakistan and India. Kissinger believed that the Pakistanis would try to reestablish their administration, but that they might see the need "to move towards greater East Pakistani autonomy in order to draw the necessary Bengali cooperation." This period of transition could lead to "perhaps, eventual independence."[2]

Kissinger presented three options to the president. The first would entail "unqualified backing for West Pakistan." This would ensure the preservation of the relationship with West Pakistan but would encourage the Pakistanis to prolong the present situation, with all its attendant risks. The second option would be to adopt "a posture of genuine neutrality." This might be "publicly defensible," but it would entail cutting back military and economic assistance—moves that would effectively favor East Pakistan. The third option would be to "make a serious effort to help Yahya end the war and establish an arrangement that could be transitional to East Pakistani autonomy." Kissinger's preference for the last option was unstated but evident. To ensure that the president did not muddy the waters, Kissinger's office wrote separately to Nixon requesting that he add a note stating that he did not want any moves that would end up squeezing West Pakistan. On 2 May, Nixon approved the third option and scribbled a note: "*To all hands. Don't* squeeze Yahya at this time." The "Don't" was underlined three times.[3]

Nixon's refusal to "squeeze" Yahya at this point in the crisis had important ramifications. Yet if there is an image that is almost universally associated with Nixon and Kissinger's response to the crisis, it is that of a "tilt." That term was used by Kissinger in interdepartmental meetings during the latter half of the crisis to convey the president's (and his) desire for a more pro-Pakistan stance. Even before the war ended, the nationally syndicated columnist Jack Anderson published excerpts from the record of these meetings about the White House's tilt toward Pakistan.[4] Kissinger himself titled the chapter on the crisis in his memoir as "The Tilt." He was, of course, being ironic, for his account is a labored attempt to argue that the tilt within the government (especially the State Department) was actually toward India and that the White House was merely seeking to rectify this imbalanced posture.[5] Subsequent scholarship, too, has focused on the origins of the tilt. Much of this work explains it with reference to Nixon and Kissinger's obsession with great power or triangular diplomacy and their propensity to view regional developments in a geopolitical framework.[6]

However, an excessive—not to say exclusive—focus on the tilt tends to obscure other aspects of US policy during the crisis. For one thing, it blurs the line between the different stages in which this policy evolved. For another, it lavishes too much attention on the latter part of the crisis—when American actions were spectacular but futile—and gives short shrift to the earlier part—when American policy could have been more effective in managing the crisis. The White House's unwillingness to squeeze Pakistan was rather more consequential than its willingness to tilt.

I

When Nixon took office in January 1969, Kissinger recalled, "our policy objective on the subcontinent was, quite simply, to avoid adding another complication to our agenda." The administration's foreign policy reports to Congress in 1970 and 1971 devoted no more than a few paragraphs to South Asia—the latter clearly stating that US strategic interests were confined to ensuring that neither China nor the Soviet Union attained a commanding influence in the region.[7]

Few American presidents have entered the White House with greater experience in foreign policy than Richard Nixon; none with greater exposure to South Asia. As often, this proved not an asset but a liability. Nixon wheeled with him to office a trolley of biases against India and in favor of Pakistan. These prejudices were sown during the Eisenhower administration's dalliance with Pakistan, which Vice President Nixon had enthusiastically endorsed, and they were nurtured during his subsequent travels to South Asia. Nixon's biases were further fattened by the politics of US foreign policy. The pro-India leanings of the Democrats struck him as "a prime example of liberal soft-headedness."[8] Kissinger shared many of these prejudices, though on occasion he merely echoed his master's voice.

To what extent did Nixon's ingrained prejudices influence his policy toward South Asia? It is frequently argued that they played a major and distorting role in his handling of the crisis.[9] To be sure, declassified documents and tapes are replete with Nixon's sneering references to Indians in general—"a slippery, treacherous people," who are "devious" and ruthlessly self-interested—and to Indira Gandhi in particular—"bitch" and "witch." By contrast, Yahya Khan is certified as an "honorable" man faced with an impossible situation.[10] Moreover, Nixon had an undeniable propensity for imagining slights and nursing grievances. Even so, it is difficult to disentangle the relative importance of such prejudices and too easy to exaggerate them, especially when dealing with such uncongenial historical figures as Nixon and Kissinger. In analyzing their response to the crisis, we need to ask counterfactual questions about what decisions might have been taken had these biases been the key driver, and whether certain decisions could have been taken in the absence of more concrete interests.

Interestingly, India saw Nixon's ascent to the White House as an opportunity for a fresh start in its relationship with the United States. "The most important single factor about the American administration in so far as India is concerned," the foreign office noted, "is that the USA is now in the process of a major reappraisal of its global policies." The key drivers here were the worsening war in Vietnam and the India-Pakistan war of 1965 "in which the American ally, Pakistan, did so unexpectedly badly vis-a-vis India." In consequence, the United States evinced little appetite for embroiling itself in regional disputes. Indeed, the Indians discerned a "new American posture of neutrality between India and Pakistan." "Under these circumstances," the foreign office concluded, "it is possible that we could arrive at a reasonable understanding with them."[11] Before Indira Gandhi's first summit with Nixon in 1969, P. N. Haksar, the prime minister's principal secretary, observed that "the obvious focus of our efforts must be to convince President Nixon that apprehension felt in the United States regarding growth of Communist influence in Asia, whether of Soviet or Chinese variety, can be dealt with effectively only by strengthening or stabilising forces in Asia, which, they must see, inevitably depends on the stabilising influence of India."[12]

Visiting India in the summer of 1969, Nixon reiterated to Indira Gandhi his commitment to India's economic development. "We will go to Mars together," he assured her.[13] From the Indian standpoint, the principal—if only potential—sticking point was the possibility of a revivified military relationship between Pakistan and the United States.[14] This was not an unfounded concern. Weeks after assuming office, Nixon had ordered "a thorough review of our military supply policy in South Asia." Nixon and Kissinger believed that the Johnson administration's arms embargo was iniquitous: "the practical consequence was to injure Pakistan, since India received most of its arms either from Communist nations or from its own armories."[15] When the secretary of state, William Rogers, visited Pakistan in May 1969 Yahya Khan made an emphatic pitch for resumption of military supplies, arguing that Pakistan's security was imperiled. Rogers questioned this claim but assured his host that the policy was under review. In his subsequent interactions with the press, Rogers had said that the administration's proposals would "go a long way to meeting Pakistan's requirements."[16]

Mrs. Gandhi had looked askance at Rogers's comment, and the issue was brought up in the officials' meeting during Nixon's trip. The Indians pointed out that Pakistan's military strength had nearly doubled since 1965. "Each side has military needs," said Foreign Secretary Kaul, "but India [is] facing China. What is the threat to Pakistan!!" "Don't repeat the mistake of 1954," he tactlessly added.[17] The president's next stop was Pakistan, where the question of military supply predictably cropped up. The Pakistanis insisted that they sought nothing more than a "minimum deterrent" against India. Kissinger replied, "We want to avoid [an] arms race. We are looking at military supply policy and will attempt to be sympathetic."[18]

Notwithstanding the president's biases, then, the Nixon administration was not rushing headlong to meet Pakistan's military demands. As late as July 1970, the Indian embassy in Washington believed that "the danger was not an imminent one and possibly had passed at least for the present." Indeed, until the summer of 1970, policy toward South Asia seemed to be drifting listlessly. Ambassador L. K. Jha believed that "the real problem [in US-India relations] is not of differences but of indifference."[19] By the end of September, however, the United States conveyed to India its decision to grant Pakistan a "one time exception." On 8 October 1970, Washington formally announced the decision to allow Pakistan to procure nearly US $50 million worth of replacement aircraft and some 300 armed personnel carriers.

The official Indian reaction was measured, though the American ambassador was told that the decision was "extremely explosive."[20] Prime Minister Gandhi was more scathing on this matter when she met with Rogers later that month. "I do not say that you should not take decisions in your own national interests," she said, "but I want to make you aware of our feelings." Above all, India was concerned about the "great collusion between China and Pakistan." When Rogers interjected, "You have no concern regarding China," the meeting turned acrimonious. Mrs. Gandhi alleged foreign interference in India: "It has been in my father's time and it is so now." Asked for details, she loftily replied, "I cannot pin down anything. We have no proof. I am not personally concerned."[21] Subsequent conversations between American and Indian officials helped lower the temperature.[22] By early 1971, Kissinger rightly observed, US-India relations "had achieved a state of exasperatedly strained cordiality, like a couple that can neither separate nor get along."[23]

II

Why did the Nixon administration lift the arms embargo, even if temporarily? New Delhi regarded it as merely a continuation of US policy toward Pakistan since 1953—that Washington had apparently learned nothing and forgotten nothing.[24] On the contrary, the decision cannot be understood as being primarily driven by Nixon's personal affinity for Pakistan; rather, it was the outcome of a profound departure from the old US strategy of harnessing Pakistan for anticommunist alliances in Asia. The administration, as we have seen, proceeded more cautiously on this issue than might have been the case if the president's predilections were the principal driver of policy. Then, too, the "one time exception" fell short of Pakistan's desire for a return to business as usual. More importantly, this exception was carved out owing to a major American interest at stake: the opening to China.

The establishment of relations with the People's Republic of China was undoubtedly the most significant accomplishment of the Nixon presidency. The initiative was spurred by a series of considerations: the relative decline in American power since the early 1960s and the seeming shift in the superpower strategic balance toward the Soviet Union; the rise in the Soviet Union's assertiveness in Eastern Europe and its activism in the Third World; the irrevocable split between the Soviet Union and China; and the domestic upheaval of the Sixties that threatened to thwart America's ability to play a global role. By crafting a new relationship with China, Nixon and Kissinger hoped to transform the bilateral relationship between the United States and the Soviet Union into a triangular one, and to leverage this new equilibrium into arranging an honorable exit from Vietnam and preserving America's wider global interests.[25]

From the outset, Nixon was candid about his desire for a new relationship with China, even in his talks with India. In his first meeting with the Indian foreign minister, Nixon said that "India had its own difficult experience with China, and so has the USA. However, he saw danger in trying to isolate China ... the world must go forward without isolating what will one day be one billion people."[26] Nevertheless, the actual opening to China was thickly veiled in secrecy. Paranoid about domestic opponents and Washington's propensity to leak like a sieve, Nixon and Kissinger kept everyone in the dark, including senior colleagues in the administration (especially the loathed State Department), the Congress, and America's closest allies. To explore China's willingness to recast its relationship with the United States, Nixon almost simultaneously opened two parallel, secret channels of communication through Romania and Pakistan.

Of these, the line through Pakistan was the better bet. For one thing, the Romanian channel could easily be tapped by Moscow. For another, Pakistan enjoyed a closer relationship with China than any fraternal socialist state. The hitch was that Pakistan had felt seriously let down by the United States after the 1965 war, and hence needed a strong incentive to serve as a conduit. Meeting Yahya alone on 1 August 1969, Nixon expressed interest in seeking an accommodation with China, and asked him to pass that message to Beijing and use his influence to promote it. Yahya agreed that such a move would be desirable, but "stressed that Pakistan's influence and relationship with Peiping tended to be overrated in the West."[27] Yahya's coy response was a subtle indication to Nixon that messengers needed to be tipped. Nixon, for his part, was deeply impressed by Yahya "as a real leader, very intelligent, and with great insight into Russia-China relations."[28]

A few weeks later, Kissinger told the Pakistanis that Yahya should communicate on this subject only through Pakistan's ambassador to the United States, Agha Hilaly, who in turn should speak only to Kissinger. Almost three months passed before Yahya replied to Nixon's overture, suggesting an approach to the highest level of the Chinese government and asking for "specific points of discussion."[29] Hilaly was worried by the dilatory style of his government. In mid-October 1969, he wrote to Yahya asking if any message had yet been sent to Beijing, reminding him that "anything we can do to help Nixon is likely to prove beneficial to us."[30] The reference was obviously to resumption of military supplies.

Over two months later, Hilaly informed Kissinger that Yahya had met the Chinese envoy in Islamabad in early November and asked him to convey Nixon's message to Premier Zhou Enlai. The ambassador's immediate response was that "the U.S. always 'double-talked.'" When Hilaly asked Kissinger if there was anything more substantive that Yahya could discuss with the Chinese leadership, Kissinger replied that Yahya could convey to Beijing that "the U.S. appreciates this communication and we are serious in our desire to have conversations with them." Hilaly then brought up the question of military supplies, which he said were personally important to Yahya. The president was likely to travel to Beijing in the spring and hoped to "have a decision on U.S. arms supply policy before then."[31] Writing to Nixon in January 1970, Yahya wished him success in his endeavor to reach out to China, and reminded him "to press ahead urgently" with the review of arms supply policy:

"The ban imposed more than four years ago has operated greatly to Pakistan's disadvantage."[32]

Two more months passed before Yahya sent a handwritten message to Hilaly for transmission to Kissinger. The initiatives taken by the United States had encouraged the Chinese leadership, but they were loath to give an impression that their willingness to talk reflected either their own weakness or concerns about the Soviet Union. Yahya observed that "negotiations will be hard and difficult," but with patience and trust progress could be made. On 23 February 1970, Kissinger asked Hilaly to inform Yahya that Nixon was "prepared to open a direct White House channel to Peking, if Peking would agree. The existence of such a channel would not be known outside the White House and we can guarantee total discretion."[33]

Meanwhile, the discussion on military supplies was reaching the decision point. The State Department formally wrote to the president opposing any change in the military supply policy. The United States had no "overriding political or security interests in South Asia," India was "relatively more important to our interests than Pakistan," and Pakistan's "unhappiness would be containable." If the president felt "some obligation" to Yahya, then the department would prefer making a one-time exception and offering the six F-104 supersonic interceptor aircraft that Pakistan had sought. Kissinger ran with the idea of a one-time exception, though by the time the presidential decision was taken the inventory of sales had considerably expanded.[34] In his memoirs, Kissinger claimed that for their role in the opening to China, "Pakistan's leaders, to their lasting honor, never sought any reciprocity or special consideration."[35] The record, however, shows that the Pakistanis were as adept practitioners of "linkage" as Kissinger fancied himself.

The China express now chugged along. Nixon asked Yahya to convey two points to the Chinese leadership. First, "we will make no condominium [with the Soviet Union] against China and we want them to know it." Second, Nixon was willing to send an envoy to Beijing "to establish links secretly."[36] During his visit to China in November 1970, Yahya conveyed Nixon's message to Zhou Enlai. After three days of deliberation, Zhou reverted to Yahya with a message for Nixon from Chairman Mao Zedong: "In order to discuss the subject of vacation of China's territory called Taiwan, a special envoy from President Nixon would be most welcome in Peking."[37] In response, the White House proposed that American and Chinese representatives meet at "an early convenient moment" to discuss the modalities of a higher-level meeting in Beijing. The latter meeting "would not be limited only to the Taiwan question but would encompass other steps designed to improve relations and reduce tensions."[38] This message was passed to the Chinese on 5 January 1971. For the next three months, though, there was no word from Beijing. During this diplomatic lull, the East Pakistan crisis erupted.

III

In mid-February 1971, Kissinger ordered the National Security Council (NSC) to examine options in case the move toward independence gathered momentum. "The highly uncertain situation in East Pakistan," Kissinger wrote to Nixon, "has forced us to walk a very narrow tightrope." A realistic assessment might conclude that "there is very little material left in the fabric of the unity of Pakistan." But set against this was "the fact that the division of Pakistan would not serve U.S. interests."[39]

The contingency study argued that so long as the separation of East Pakistan remained uncertain, the United States should stick to its current position of supporting the unity of Pakistan and refusing to intervene in that country's internal affairs. An East Pakistani declaration of independence was judged to be "very unlikely." Equally unlikely was an intervention by the army, owing to the possibility of Bengali resistance and the logistical difficulties of carrying out military operations in East Pakistan. If such an intervention became imminent or actually occurred, then the United States had an interest both in avoiding violence and in checking its escalation. "We should be willing to risk irritating the West Pakistanis in the face of such a rash act on their part," the study held; "the threat of stopping aid should give us considerable leverage."[40]

The Senior Review Group (SRG) of the NSC met on 6 March to consider the contingency choices. The State Department's Christopher Van Hollen pointed out that "despite all the problems, our mission in Islamabad estimates that Yahya is prepared to use force." Kissinger insisted that any attempt to dissuade Yahya would "almost certainly be self-defeating." The president, he added, "will be very reluctant to do anything that Yahya could interpret as a personal affront." This cautionary remark puzzled the other participants. They were, of course, unaware of the secret opening to China or Yahya's importance in this enterprise. Nevertheless, Alexis Johnson of the State Department and Richard Helms of the Central Intelligence Agency (CIA) agreed that there was "a case to be made for massive inaction." A week later, when the military buildup in East Pakistan became clear, Kissinger informed Nixon that "it is undesirable for us to intervene now since we could realistically have little influence on the situation and anything we might do could be resented by the West Pakistanis as unwarranted interference and jeopardize our future relations."[41]

On the afternoon of 26 March, Kissinger chaired the Washington Special Actions Group (WSAG) to consider the situation in East Pakistan. Expressing surprise at the breakdown of talks, Kissinger asked for a prognosis. Van Hollen observed that the military would make an effort to prevent secession, but its ability "to maintain law and order in East Pakistan over the long run approaches zero." Kissinger said that he had spoken briefly to the president earlier that day: "He doesn't want to do anything. He doesn't want to be in the position where he can be accused of having encouraged the split-up of Pakistan. He does not favor a very active policy. This probably means that we would not undertake to warn Yahya against a civil war." The State Department officials agreed, and the WSAG concluded that the United States should "continue its policy of non-involvement."[42]

Meanwhile the US consul-general in Dhaka, Archer Blood, sent a series of cables, detailing the terror being unleashed on the populace by the Pakistani army. Labeling the military action a "selective genocide," he questioned the "continued advisability of present USG [US government] posture." "We should be expressing our shock at least privately to GOP [government of Pakistan]," urged Blood. Ambassador Joseph Farland in Islamabad stoutly resisted this suggestion. "Righteous indignation is not of itself an adequate basis for our reaction," he argued. "Deplorable as current events in East Pakistan may be," wrote Farland, "it is undesirable that they should be raised to the level of [a] contentious international political issue."[43] Blood responded a week later with a collective message from American foreign service personnel in Dhaka. Titled "Dissent from U.S. Policy Toward East Pakistan," this cable argued that the current policy "serves neither our moral interests broadly defined nor our national interests narrowly defined." The administration, it claimed, "has evidenced what many will consider moral bankruptcy" in dealing with a conflict "in which unfortunately the overworked term genocide is applicable."[44]

Why did the White House turn a deaf ear? The foremost consideration was the need to conserve the China channel and avoid a break with Yahya Khan. At this point, Nixon and Kissinger were on tenterhooks awaiting a response from Beijing. Furthermore, human rights simply did not rank among the priorities of Nixon's foreign policy. Kissinger and Nixon evinced not an iota of outrage at the atrocities. What drew their wrath was the wide distribution that Blood had given his cables, and the possibility of their being leaked.[45] Indeed, the atrocities in East Pakistan only mattered to Nixon and Kissinger because of their concern that it would give further ammunition to the administration's critics over Vietnam. As Nixon exclaimed, "The people who bitch about Vietnam bitch about it because we intervened in what they say is a civil war . . . Now some of those same bastards want us to intervene here—both civil wars."[46] But Nixon and Kissinger also believed that the outrage would die down on its own, just as it did over the Biafran crisis.[47]

A third, and important, reason underpinning this stance was their belief that the use of force had worked: the Pakistanis had rooted out the resistance. On 29 March, Kissinger called Nixon to say that Yahya had apparently got control of East Pakistan: "The use of power against seeming odds pays off. Cause all the experts were saying that 30,000 people can't get control of 75 million." Nixon claimed that history was replete with examples that "30,000 well-disciplined people can take 75 million any time . . . Look at what the British did when they came to India . . . anyway I wish him [Yahya] well."[48] Developments in East Pakistan over the next couple of weeks confirmed this impression. Kissinger told the Indian ambassador: "I am afraid, we were very badly advised. All our experts in the Pentagon and elsewhere were dead sure that West Pakistani military forces could not overpower the people of East Bengal, but it seems they have done so. What options do we now have? We must be Machiavellian and accept what looks like a *fait accompli*—don't you think?"[49]

Not everyone in the administration shared this optimistic assessment. In particular, the regional experts in the State Department had rather a different view. At an SRG meeting chaired by Kissinger on 9 April, Joseph Sisco said that it was likely "that East Pakistan will end in some form of separatism. Our job is to maintain reasonable relations with both wings." To Kissinger's annoyance, he went on to assert that "our interest in India is probably greater than our interest in Pakistan." Secretary Rogers, too, sent a memorandum to Nixon stating that the time had come to "re-examine our basic stance towards Pakistan."[50]

An exhaustive paper prepared by the interdepartmental group of the NSC reflected the views of the regional specialists. It advocated the "Use of Selective Influence" by continuing support for certain development activities but holding off on programs "which would contribute directly to the prolongation of the civil war." The paper proposed a series of steps: defer implementation of the one-time exception; postpone all deliveries of ammunition and spare parts; and indicate to Pakistan that food aid for the East could only be dispatched on assurance of safe delivery and equitable distribution. The State Department had already taken "interim decisions which will require formal reaffirmation" on the question of military supplies. These had been taken owing to evidence that American arms had been "used extensively by the army in East Pakistan."[51]

The State Department's effrontery sent Kissinger flying into a rage. He regarded it as nothing less than a "preemption of Presidential prerogatives"—a move that was "heavily influenced by its [State Department's] traditional Indian bias."[52] Matters came to a head in an SRG meeting on 19 April. Kissinger challenged the interdepartmental group's analysis of options: "These choices all seem to assume a prolonged war. How realistic is this since West Pakistani superiority seems evident." Undersecretary of State John Irwin demurred. "We have no evidence," he said, "that there will be cooperation by any East Pakistani elements with any influence." Kissinger testily argued that the recommended steps "would be interpreted by Yahya as a cut-off of military assistance." He insisted that "we must go to the President before we hold up any shipments. This would be the exact opposite of his policy . . . The President thinks he has a special relationship with Yahya; he would be most reluctant to take him on."[53]

By the time Kissinger wrote to the president, he had read a memorandum from Harold Saunders, his NSC aide on South Asia. Saunders underlined the point that *the situation is settling down to one of prolonged conflict*. In such a situation, the United States should aim to "encourage movement towards the greatest possible degree of East Pakistani autonomy." Saunders was not thinking of any substantive measures. "By creating the impression of movement in that direction," he wrote, "Yahya might just succeed in spinning out this process and averting for the time being the worst of a continued war of independence."[54]

IV

Against the backdrop of conflict with the US government's area specialists, Kissinger got Nixon to state unambiguously that Yahya must not be
squeezed and that the administration's policy was to help him create an
arrangement conducive to transitioning to East Pakistani autonomy.
Such a posture would put a leash on his opponents within the administration, and would buy time for both Yahya and the China initiative.

In fact, the day before Kissinger sent his memorandum, Ambassador
Hilaly had given him a handwritten note containing a message from
China. Zhou Enlai had expressed his government's willingness to "receive publicly in Peking a special envoy of the President of the U.S. (for
instance, Mr. Kissinger) or the U.S. Secretary of State or even the President of the U.S. himself for direct meeting and discussions." The modalities
and other details of the meeting were of "no substantive significance,"
and it was "entirely possible for proper arrangements to be made through
the good offices of President Yahya Khan."[55]

After toying with a few names—much to Kissinger's discomfort—
Nixon decided that Kissinger would undertake a secret trip to Beijing
and lay the ground for a presidential visit. The Pakistanis were delighted
at being accorded a key role in this process. As Hilaly wrote to Yahya,
"So far as we are concerned we will be placing Nixon under an obligation to us at this particularly delicate moment in our national life." Sure
enough, Kissinger assured Hilaly that "President Nixon would continue
to see to it that the United States Government does nothing to embarrass President Yahya's Government."[56] By early June 1971, the stage was
set for Kissinger's momentous visit to China.

In this context, Nixon and Kissinger's desire to refrain from squeezing
Yahya and to place the problem on the ice pail was understandable.
They believed that the United States needed just enough time to ensure
the success of their opening to China. When Ambassador Farland observed that, in the long run, West Pakistan could not hold on to the eastern wing, Kissinger exclaimed, "All we need is six months."[57]

At this point, the Yahya regime was toying with the various options
open to it after the imminent collapse of armed resistance in East Pakistan. The army was riding a wave of confidence about its role in keeping
the country together. Even a politician like Bhutto, who had connived
with them, was now being kept at arm's length. As the head of military
intelligence put it, "We have no particular love for him . . . if he misbe-

haves he will get the same treatment [as Mujib]."[58] So, realistic options for a political settlement never got off the ground. This is clear from the four broad alternatives that were mooted in Rawalpindi in April–May 1971. The first, which called for a restoration of the status quo ante, was summarily rejected. The second entailed convening the National Assembly, granting selective amnesty to the rebels, and appointing a national government with Mujib as prime minister. The military release of Mujib—never mind installing him as the head of government. The third option, to start afresh with new elections and the appointment of a committee to draft a constitution, was also turned down by the military. They deemed fresh elections to be potentially dangerous, for these could end up empowering Bhutto. The fourth, least risky option was to grant selective amnesty and charge a committee with drafting a new constitution.[59]

Yahya supported the fourth option. In April, he put together a committee comprising M. M. Ahmed, Justice Cornelius, Lieutenant General Peerzada, and G. W. Choudhury to frame a constitution. At the time, Yahya was unsure whether to proclaim an interim constitution or a permanent one. At a meeting with the committee on 26 May, he announced that the constitution prepared by them would be permanent. In a sharp departure from the Legal Framework Order, Yahya issued a set of directives to the committee: provincial autonomy would be restricted, the senior-most military officer would be responsible for "preserving and defending the constitution," no more than three political parties would be allowed in the country, and no general amnesty would be granted— the president would decide who would be granted amnesty.[60] In a speech on 28 June, Yahya invited the refugees to return to their homes. Yet he clearly stated that there would be neither new elections nor a return to the status quo. The Awami League would remain banned, and Mujib would be debarred from public life.

The US State Department was by now convinced that "genuine political accommodation remains the crux of Pakistan's internal crisis." Analyzing Yahya's speech of 28 June, Sisco of the State Department wrote to Secretary Rogers that it "offers little basis for optimism over his chances of early success under the terms and conditions he has prescribed." The White House continued to pretend otherwise; writing to Yahya a few days later, Nixon commended his announcement as "an important step."[61]

Could the United States have adopted a different stance—one that might have pushed Yahya toward a realistic political settlement without jeopardizing the China channel? The time when this might have been feasible lasted until the end of May 1971. Up to that point, the decision-making process in Pakistan was still fluid, and equally important, the refugee exodus had yet to reach the proportions that it would over the coming weeks. Did the Nixon administration have any alternatives at hand?

V

On 6 April 1971, a ten-member special team arrived in Dhaka to examine the eastern wing's economic situation. The team's report painted a bleak picture of a devastated economy in East Pakistan. Ports, railways, inland roads, and waterways were damaged and dysfunctional. Industrial activity had completely ceased after 26 March. The export of jute and jute products, which contributed 43 percent to the total export earnings of Pakistan, had juddered to a halt. Central government revenues from East Pakistan—custom duties, sales tax, and excise tax—had shriveled to the point of vanishing. The report recommended that the central government's outlay for East Pakistan be considerably expanded. This, of course, implied a diversion of resources from West Pakistan.[62]

At this time, Pakistan was also facing a major liquidity crisis—the most serious one its history.[63] Owing to a combination of mismanagement and Micawberism, Pakistan's foreign exchange reserves had plummeted from US $353 million in March 1970 to US $164 million in March 1971. The situation was, in fact, worse than these numbers suggested. At this point, short-term liabilities against letters of credit amounted to US $263 million. But the reserve figure of US $164 million included capital assets like gold and foreign securities that are not normally liquidated to meet current requirements. The "own reserves" position of ready-at-hand foreign exchange to cover the current account was already in the red. The negative "own reserves" indicated that current expenditure was being financed either by liquidating capital assets or by foreign commercial loans at high interest rates—or both. Further, political turmoil and the military crackdown had ensured that exports from East Pakistan were suspended from March and that no shipments had taken place until the end of April. This was particularly problematic because most of the jute shipments usually occurred between January and May. By implication, in May and June 1971, Pakistan would not receive the foreign exchange earnings to the tune of US $25–30 million a month that normally would have accrued. The suspension of economic activity in East Pakistan thus greatly exacerbated the problem and catalyzed the country's liquidity crisis.

At the end of April 1971, Pakistan's foreign exchange holding stood at US $137.6 million. The Ministry of Finance prepared a forecast of the balance of payments covering the five months from May through September 1971, taking into account exports during March–July (payments for which were likely to be realized within two months), payments for imports, invisible earnings and payments, and debt service payments. The prognosis was grim, not to say alarming. It suggested that, during this period, Pakistan would lose US $162 million in exchange assets. Suspension of conversion rights on certain debt obligation—on which more anon—would reduce the reserve loss by US $54 million to US $108 million. By the end of September Pakistan would be left with just US $20 million in exchange assets.

Even this was too optimistic. It assumed that exports would average US $22 million a month for the three-month period from May to July. The figure based on actuals for the same period in 1970 was US $27 million a month. In any case, exports from East Pakistan had failed to get off the ground by April. Further, the projection of invisible earnings, especially home remittances, was also questionable. From July through December 1970, these had fallen by 35 percent compared to the same period in the previous year. In February and March 1971 they dropped to a third of the average monthly inflow for the first six months of the financial year. Further, most of Pakistani expatriates hailed from the Sylhet district of East Pakistan and lived in Britain. The communication links for remitting funds from the UK to Sylhet had broken down. Besides, an active Bangladesh lobby in Britain was dissuading Bengali expatriates from sending money back home. Finally, the forecast excluded payments for military imports from the US to the tune of US $39 million—a figure that would have pushed the balance of reserves into the red. Thanks to the restrictions imposed on arms sales by the administration, Pakistan was eventually able to procure only US $5 million worth of equipment in all. But in April 1971, when these assessments were being made, Pakistan was hopeful that much of these sales would come through.

The state of the foreign exchange reserves had not come as a bolt out of the blue to Islamabad. Even before these forecasts, Pakistan had approached the International Monetary Fund (IMF) for standby assistance in the form of an emergency drawing and the World Bank for

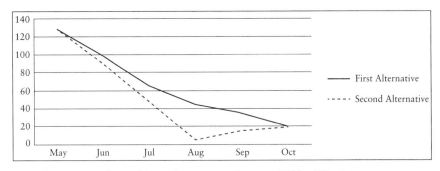

Two alternatives of monthly exchange asset forecast (US$ million).

Source: Attachment to "A Note by Mr. Cargill on Recent Discussions with the Government and a Possible Course of Action for the Consortium," World Bank, Center for the Advanced Study of India, University of Pennsylvania, Philadelphia.

debt rescheduling. The IMF had turned down this request owing to Pakistan's unwillingness to revise its Byzantine exchange rate policy and liberalize its imports regime. The World Bank, which led the Aid to Pakistan consortium,[64] declined to take any initiative in rescheduling Pakistan's debt and asked it to open bilateral negotiations with donor countries.

At a meeting presided by Yahya on 24 April 1971, it was decided that Pakistan would announce a moratorium on debt. Donor countries were informed that Pakistan "feels compelled to apply a moratorium on conversions for a period of six months in respect to maturities of principal and interest falling due from 1 May 1971 on all credits obtained under Consortium auspices." Islamabad also requested a special session of the Consortium to discuss its plans, pending long-term rescheduling. Similar steps were taken vis-à-vis non-Consortium donors. Of its total debt service obligation (to Consortium and non-Consortium countries and international agencies) of US $90.5 million for the period of 1 May to 30 September 1971, Pakistan announced a moratorium to the Consortium and non-Consortium countries of US $55 million.[65]

The announcement of a moratorium was a grave step for Pakistan to take. External assistance was critical to the Pakistani economy for bridging both its savings–investment gap and its export–import gap. Much of this aid flowed from the Consortium, and within the Consortium the United States loomed large. By comparison, the largest non-Consortium donors, the People's Republic of China and the Soviet Union, accounted for a measly 2 percent and 3 percent of the total aid received by Pakistan over the past decade.[66]

In response to Pakistan's request for convening an urgent meeting of the Consortium, the World Bank's president, Robert McNamara, sent the head of the bank's South Asia department, Peter Cargill, to Islamabad to take stock of the situation.[67] A former Indian Civil Service officer, Cargill had served for a few years in Pakistan after independence. After his discussions with Pakistani officials in the first week of May, Cargill was left with "no room for doubt that the situation is extremely serious"—even after taking into account the government's intention to defer US $55 million of debt service payments. To avoid complete evaporation of exchange assets and to prevent imports from falling to a crippling level, Cargill estimated that aid to the tune of US $500 million—US $300 million in cash and commodity aid, and US $200 in food aid—would be required. "If Pakistan's economic collapse is to be prevented," Cargill observed, "action will have to be taken quickly and the amounts of external assistance required will be large."

Yahya was willing to accept any reform program prescribed by the IMF and Wold Bank in order to secure assistance from abroad. However, Cargill rightly believed that economic stability to Pakistan could not be restored until there was a political settlement in the east. Nor could external assistance be taken for granted under the prevailing circumstances. Cargill's discussions with Yahya and others on the political aspects of the crisis were "highly disconcerting." They seemed entirely oblivious of the international obloquy drawn by the military campaign. In any case, the "realism of Yahya Khan's plans for a political settlement is open to serious questions." Unless economic conditions in East Pakistan were quickly restored, a program of economic assistance and reform would be difficult to draw up and implement.[68]

In the wake of Cargill's visit to Islamabad, most members of the Consortium decided to delay or suspend new economic assistance to Pakistan. Britain felt, for instance, that providing even a limited amount of foreign exchange would require "a degree of faith which it is difficult to justify on performance so far," and that it would be unacceptable to "British public opinion."[69] Soon, Yahya's economic adviser, M. M. Ahmed, landed in Washington to present Pakistan's case. After hearing Ahmed, Nixon instructed his aides to ensure "that the Bank understood that we feel strongly that it and other aid donors should do what they could to be helpful."[70]

Buoyed by Nixon's supportive stance, Ahmed met the World Bank's president. Robert McNamara told him that the bank and the IMF would jointly prepare and present to the Consortium an economic program for Pakistan, but he cautioned that "political constraints were the dominant obstacle to any donor coming forward with assistance." McNamara emphasized that "only the Government of Pakistan could remove these constraints, by demonstrating through its actions over the next several weeks that it was seeking a political, rather than a military solution to the problems of East Pakistan."[71]

Prior to Ahmed's departure, it was agreed that a joint World Bank–IMF mission would prepare an appraisal of Pakistan's economic situation. The team led by Cargill reached Dhaka on 1 June 1971 and spent ten days in each wing. The team's report presented a graphic picture of the devastation wrought on East Pakistan by the military crackdown. "The overall assessment of the situation," the report concluded, "is not encouraging." The obstacles in the path to normalization were "overwhelming." Infrastructure was "severely damaged," the authorities had "little understanding" of the problems of economic revival, and there was "all-pervasive fear as a major inhibiting factor," which together "amount to a formidable problem that would defy early resolution."[72]

Discussions with Pakistani officials on devising an economic program foundered on the rocks of widely divergent assessments. The Pakistanis proceeded on the assumptions that economic activity in East Pakistan, including foreign trade, would function normally from the second quarter of the next fiscal year beginning 1 July 1971; that the West Pakistan economy would operate at "a very high level of activity"; and that sufficient aid, including standby credit from the IMF, would be available to meet normal needs. The World Bank–IMF team, by contrast, held that the government might lose as much as 1,000 million rupees (US $212 million) in revenues and that more thorough-going economic reform was necessary. The Pakistanis, however, stuck to their guns and handed the team a letter of intent for the Consortium outlining their plans.[73]

The Consortium met in Paris on 21 June and agreed to continue disbursing aid against existing commitments. However, barring food aid to East Pakistan for humanitarian purposes, it was not prepared to consider providing new aid to Pakistan. This was because "public and parliamentary opinion were strongly opposed to aiding Pakistan in present circumstances" and because even limited resumption of aid was "likely to be misinterpreted by the powers that be in Pakistan and therefore further delay necessary reforms." Although some members, notably Japan and the Netherlands, took exception to Pakistan's unilateral suspension of debt payments, it was decided that this issue would be taken up subsequently. Cargill closed the session by noting that a full meeting of the Consortium scheduled for July would serve no purpose.[74]

Yahya wrote to Nixon protesting the outcome of the Consortium meeting. He had been "greatly encouraged" by Nixon's assurance to Ahmed, but now had no option other than publicly denouncing "external assistance with political strings" as unacceptable. Yahya entreated Nixon to maintain "your personal interest and support in this regard." Nixon promptly replied that the misunderstanding over the Consortium meeting was "regrettable." He assured Yahya that the meeting had been an informal one. There was no unanimous agreement that "all members of the Consortium would jointly suspend future aid." The Consortium members were awaiting the final reports of the World Bank–IMF mission and the "completion by your government of a revised national development plan." As soon as these were ready, the Consortium would meet formally "to review new aid requirements." The administration wished "to proceed with new agreements, subject to US legislative criteria."[75]

The reference to legislative constraints was significant. The administration was aware that the mood on Capitol Hill was censorious of the military repression unleashed by the Pakistan government. A few days before, Representative Cornelius Gallagher had introduced a bill in the House that sought to amend the Foreign Assistance Act to suspend all aid to Pakistan until there was "reasonable stability" in East Pakistan and the refugees in India had returned to their homes. When excerpts from the World Bank–IMF mission report on East Pakistan were published in the *New York Times* and *Washington Post,* Gallagher wrote to McNamara requesting a copy of the report: "the opinion of the prestigious World Bank would lend much credence to the arguments of those of us who want sanity brought back to our relations with Government of Pakistan." Eventually Senator Walter Mondale managed to procure a copy, which was circulated to his fellow senators with a plea to "consider this remarkable report most carefully and lend your support to Senate action to bring to an end any further complicity of the United States in this tragedy." On 15 July, the House's Foreign Affairs Committee passed the Gallagher amendment by seventeen votes to six.[76]

Yet the White House publicly announced that fresh US economic and technical aid would be withheld only until a revised plan was submitted by Pakistan. Further, the administration's previously declared request for an appropriation of $188 million in 1972 would be submitted to

Congress. Kissinger told Nixon that owing to "mounting press and Congressional pressures" they had to hold up $75 million "against the time when a revised Pakistani development plan is available." In the meantime, a pipeline of US $82 million was continuing to flow from earlier commitments. Pakistan's unilateral moratorium would reach an end in October, and at that point it would require further assistance. Kissinger observed that Pakistan's proposals "may well not satisfy either the World bank/IMF or the other aid donors." Unless the situation in East Pakistan improved, "the US may well be alone in proposing support."[77]

Nixon and Kissinger's unwillingness to use their economic leverage over Pakistan effectively reinforced Yahya's intransigence. Had they made it clear that come October they would be unable to bail out Pakistan, the military regime might well have been stopped in its tracks. It was the expectation of American economic support that gave them the confidence that they could pull back from the brink of bankruptcy and serious economic retrenchment, with all the attendant political consequences. The nub of the problem, as Cargill observed, was that "the difficulties of the situation are very largely obscured by the assumption that Pakistan will receive very considerably more aid in 1971/72 than it did in recent years."[78] Even after the Gallagher amendment was passed, the White House did little to disabuse Pakistan of this illusion and held out the hope of renewed aid.

Then again, would antagonizing Pakistan have wrecked the opening to China? Not necessarily, especially if the US position was conveyed quietly through the back channels that Nixon and Kissinger so favored. The central fact that applied to this situation was Pakistan's overwhelming dependence on the United States for foreign aid—a situation that was considerably magnified by the onset of the liquidity crisis. It is no coincidence that at the very outset Kissinger's staff had picked out economic leverage as a key tool in shaping Pakistan's behavior during the crisis. Kissinger himself had observed that "US economic support—multiplied by US leadership in the World Bank consortium of aid donors—remains crucial to West Pakistan. Neither Moscow nor Peking can duplicate this assistance."[79] By declining to use this leverage, Nixon and Kissinger deepened the East Pakistan crisis and aided the demise of united Pakistan.

VI

Eager to preserve the China initiative and reluctant to squeeze Yahya, Nixon and Kissinger turned their attention to the country that could scuttle their plans: India. From April 1971, the United States had been receiving intelligence on India's activities in support of the Bengali rebels. Early in the crisis, the CIA was even sounded out by an Indian contact about helping arm the rebels.[80] Meeting Kissinger on 21 May, Jha observed that the situation was "very explosive." "But what can we do?" retorted Kissinger. Emphasizing the need to handle the situation with "great delicacy," he asked Jha to tell Indira Gandhi that "we are concerned and are doing here what we can with a low visibility."[81]

Meanwhile, a report on Indian troop concentration along the eastern border with Pakistan alarmed Kissinger. He told Nixon that the ambassador in New Delhi had been asked to tell the government that "we were strongly opposed to military action." Nixon replied, "If they go in there with military action, by God we will cut off economic aid . . . they have got to know that if [sic] what is in jeopardy here is economic aid. That is what is in jeopardy."[82] Three days later, Kissinger urged Nixon to reply to an earlier letter from Mrs. Gandhi and "use it to bring pressure on her not to take military action." The Indians were "such bastards," "the most aggressive goddamn people around there." Nixon agreed: what India deserved was a "mass famine."[83]

In fact, an NSC memorandum summarizing the intelligence noted that Prime Minister Gandhi had decided only to "maintain constant military readiness" and that she had deflected demands from the opposition for military action.[84] Furthermore, at a WSAG meeting on 26 May, the State Department and the CIA took a more measured view of India's military intentions. When Kissinger asked, "What can we do to avoid military action?" Alexis Johnson promptly told him, "The refugees are the imminent incitement to military action. The only cure for the flow of refugees is some political accommodation in East Pakistan."[85] Nevertheless, Nixon wrote to Mrs. Gandhi expressing concern about the possibility of war, emphasizing that "India has a special responsibility for maintaining peace and stability of the region."[86]

On 16 June 1971, the Indian foreign minister reached Washington. Prior to his meeting with Nixon, Kissinger told the president that they ought to give him a combination of sympathy and "great firmness": "I am just trying to keep them [the Indians] from attacking for 3 months." He asked Nixon to say that the United States would provide $60 million in refugee aid and that they were working with Yahya in their own way. "It's a little duplicitous," he conceded, "but these bastards understand that." Swaran Singh told Nixon that refugees were pouring into India "every second" and that the tally had touched the 6 million mark. India wanted conditions to be created in East Pakistan for the return of these refugees. Nixon asked if it was in India's interest to have an independent country to its east. Swaran Singh cautiously replied, "we have no fixed position on that . . . we leave it up to the Pakistanis and the leaders of the Awami League to decide about their future in any manner they like." Nixon assured him that he understood the need to tackle the "deeper causes" of the refugee problem. "One way the public pressure, another way the private, shall we say persuasion," he observed. "I have always believed in the latter myself as the most effective way, particularly when I know the individuals fairly well." The meeting ended in this crescendo of disingenuousness.[87]

Within a week of Swaran Singh's visit, the *New York Times* reported that two Pakistani freighters were ready to sail from New York carrying military equipment for Pakistan, followed by reports indicating that a third ship was loading. Although the amount of equipment being shipped to Pakistan was small, the response from India was swift and sharp. Jha warned Undersecretary of State John Irwin that this development would deeply dent US-India relations. The Indian government lodged a formal protest, urging the State Department to stop the shipments from reaching Pakistan.[88] As the US-India relationship spun into a downward spiral, Kissinger set off for the subcontinent.

On the evening of 6 July Kissinger met Haksar. The two brilliant and powerful advisers spent over an hour trying to gauge each other's policy and intentions. Kissinger asked about the refugee situation: did India think they would go back? Haksar pointed out that "now nearly 90% of those coming out of East Pakistan are Hindus" and that this created a communal time bomb in India. "As to whether they will go back or not," Haksar said, "quite clearly, they would not go back, nor can we push them back, if the political situation and the regime in East Pakistan is such that they feel that they would be subject to the same sort of butchery which they have only recently experienced." But if East Pakistan had "a democratic government of the kind which the Awami League envisaged, not only the Muslims would go back but also the Hindus."[89]

Was India preventing the return of refugees by its support to the guerrillas, asked Kissinger? Haksar blandly replied that "we have given no arms . . . they are probably living either on the arms they had or the arms they might have snatched. Of course, our frontier is such that . . . we could not possibly seal it at every point." Kissinger observed that a war with Pakistan would not be in India's interests: "China would certainly react and this would lead you to rely upon Soviet assistance. Such a development will cause complications for us in America." Haksar insisted, "We in India are not seeking the conflict. In fact, we wish to avoid the conflict. We want a peaceful solution." In the event of Chinese involvement, he added, "It is not unreasonable for us to expect and to hope that the United States would take a sympathetic attitude towards our country." He was "a bit puzzled by your saying that if we got involved in a conflict which is not of our choosing and the Chinese intervene in one way or another, [the] United States, instead of assisting us, would feel some sort of discomfiture." Asked for his views on China, Kissinger gave a peek into recent developments: "We are desirous of improving our relations. We think that we can now quickly move forward in this direction."[90]

In his meeting with the prime minister the next day, Kissinger asked how long it would be before the problem turned unmanageable. Indira Gandhi replied that it was unmanageable right now: "We are just holding it together by sheer will power." Referring to the domestic pressures on her, she said there were "hardly two people in Parliament who approve our policy." She insisted that this was not an India-Pakistan problem: the settlement must be reached between East and West Pakistan, and India was not wedded to any particular solution. Haksar noted that it was "important to make clear [to Yahya] that future aid is dependent on well-timed political developments." Kissinger replied that it was important to avoid "extreme measures" for another few months. Mrs. Gandhi observed that India did not want to take extreme measures. "What India will do will be a question of how the situation develops and what it can do." The arms shipment to Pakistan may not make a practical difference, "but psychologically the US has made the situation more worse."[91]

Kissinger's meeting with Swaran Singh was mostly devoted to clarifying US policy on arms sales to Pakistan. On the possibility of a political settlement, the foreign minister was "very doubtful if people of East Pakistan will accept any solution unless Yahya Khan changes his policy basically." Yahya's speech of 28 June was unhelpful. "His statement has dispelled any possibility of even regional autonomy. Whether Mujib is there or not is not so important. Yahya Khan's statement means he wants to continue military rule." In a brief, one-on-one chat, Kissinger asked why India insisted that there could be no political solution without Mujib and the Awami League. "When we say Mujib or Awami League," Singh observed, "we are not keen on any particular individual or set up. What we mean is that a military regime or a communal regime will not inspire confidence among the refugees."[92]

Kissinger's last meeting was with the defense minister. Jagjivan Ram asked if "China will start something without some justification." "We think it highly unlikely," replied Kissinger; "I might also tell you that we would take a grave view of any Chinese move against India." Turning to the crisis, Ram told him, "The pressure on us here and particularly on me as Defence Minister to take some action has been mounting but we have been resisting this." Kissinger said, "We are strongly opposed to a military conflict here." "So are we," retorted Ram, "but there is a limit to what we could take."[93]

After these meetings, Kissinger felt that the Indians were "playing power politics with cold calculations" and that they were "bent on a showdown with Pakistan." In a memorandum prepared for Rogers, he was more measured: "There seems to be a growing sense of inevitability of war . . . not necessarily because anyone wants it but because in the end they fear they will not know how to avoid it."[94] The summer of 1971 in South Asia seemed to have shades of the summer of 1914 in Europe.

Kissinger's next stop was Rawalpindi. In his meeting with officials, he stressed the need for Pakistan to "defuse the refugee issue so that it could be separated from the issue of the political structure of East Pakistan." Pakistan should "internationalize" its response to the refugee problem by inviting international observers. "Linking the two," he said, "will only prolong the current situation which could lead to war. War would be catastrophe." "The lady is unpredictable," said Ambassador Hilaly. "She is maneuvering for a fight." Kissinger insisted that "time must be gained. The world must see that Pakistan is trying to solve the [refugee] problem." Refugees could be presented by India as a cause of war, but "what kind of political arrangement Pakistan makes in East Pakistan cannot be presented as a justifiable cause of war." Kissinger made the same points to Yahya and urged him to consider appointing a new civilian authority in East Pakistan to coordinate a program for the return of refugees. Yahya agreed to consider these suggestions.[95] At this point, Kissinger must have been concerned about a lot more than the subcontinental crisis; the next day, feigning an upset stomach, Kissinger took his furtive flight to Beijing.

VII

After Kissinger's trip to China, US policy began shifting from a disinclination to squeeze Yahya to an active tilt in favor of Pakistan. The opening to China and Nixon's forthcoming trip to Beijing were formally announced by the president on 15 July. The next day, the NSC convened to consider the South Asia crisis. Nixon said that it was imperative that the Pakistanis were not embarrassed. The Indians were "a slippery, treacherous people," who would like nothing better than to use this opportunity to destroy Pakistan. Admitting that he had "a bias" on this issue, the president insisted that India would not get "a dime of aid, if they mess around in East Pakistan." The United States could not allow—over the next three to four months, until "we take this journey" to Beijing—a war in South Asia. The CIA director noted that pressures were building in India for war. Kissinger agreed: "The Indians seemed bent on war. Everything they have done is an excuse for war." When Nixon asked how the Chinese would respond, Kissinger said that "he thought the Chinese would come in." He concluded that "if there is an international war and China does get involved, everything we have done [with China] will go down the drain."[96]

However, Kissinger's preferred approach to managing the crisis—by sequestering its humanitarian and political dimensions—was challenged by other agencies. In particular, the State Department felt that war could only be averted if Yahya was serious about political accommodation. Tensions between the State Department and the White House came to a boil at an SRG meeting on 30 July.[97] "Why is it our business to tell the Pakistanis how to run their government?" demanded Kissinger. When told that the United States could tell them what it thought, Kissinger let fly: "What would an enemy do to Pakistan? We are already cutting off military and economic aid to them. The President has repeatedly said that we should lean towards Pakistan, but every proposal that is made goes directly counter to these instructions." According to another set of notes taken of this meeting, Kissinger used the word "tilt" toward Pakistan, adding that "sometimes I think I am in a nut house."[98]

"You mention the question of tilting our policy," said John Irwin, but "it will be very hard to solve these problems unless there is some start in the political field." The State Department's Van Hollen also insisted that "the two things [the refugee problem and the political settlement] are directly related." What was the right direction for Yahya to move? Kissinger asked. "For Yahya to begin to deal with elected representatives in East Pakistan," replied Irwin. This occasioned another outburst: "We're holding up military shipments to Pakistan and not giving them economic assistance. What would we do if we were not opposed to Yahya? How does our policy differ from a hostile policy?" Eventually, Kissinger ordered the preparation of a comprehensive relief program for East Pakistan and contingency planning for an India-Pakistan war.[99]

Why did Nixon and Kissinger decide to overtly tilt in favor of Pakistan? After all, following Kissinger's trip to Beijing, Pakistan was no longer important as a diplomatic conduit to China. If Pakistan came to acquire heightened importance in their calculus, it was because of their reading of China's stance on the crisis.

The subcontinental crisis had been discussed in detail by Kissinger and Zhou Enlai. The Chinese premier told Kissinger that "Pakistan would never provoke a disturbance against India because in all military fields Pakistan is in a weaker position than India." But, he added, "If they [the Indians] are bent on provoking such a situation, then we cannot sit idly by." In their final conversation, just before Kissinger's departure, Zhou asked Kissinger to "please tell President Yahya Khan that if India commits aggression, we will support Pakistan." "We will oppose that," said Kissinger, "but we cannot take military measures."[100]

Kissinger interpreted Zhou's statement as "a gesture intended for Washington, since Peking had an Ambassador in Islamabad quite capable of delivering messages."[101] By indicating its determination to stand by Pakistan, Kissinger and Nixon believed that China was testing America's commitment to a close ally. In such a situation, if they stood aside and allowed Pakistan to be humiliated by India, their credibility in the eyes of Beijing would suffer—resulting in deep, possibly irreparable harm to the budding relationship with the People's Republic. Hence, they believed that a war between India and Pakistan would destroy all their efforts vis-à-vis China.

India had, therefore, to be served a stern warning against attacking Pakistan. As Kissinger observed, "The Indians should be under no illusion that if they go to war there will be unshirted hell to pay."[102] Meeting Ambassador Jha on 17 July, Kissinger warned that if war broke out between India and Pakistan and if China became involved on Pakistan's side, "we would be unable to help you against China." It is not clear whether he said explicitly that this applied only to a war that was begun by India.[103] The Indian government believed that Kissinger had stated that the United States "would not intervene in any conflict between India and Pakistan even if China did so."[104] New Delhi had already concluded that "this rapprochement with Peking would be at the expense of India and some of the other countries of the region . . . A strong India is certainly not in their scheme of things. The improvement of relations with Peking will only make this more evident."[105] Against this backdrop, Kissinger's statement came as a thunderclap and forced India to look elsewhere for a deterrent against Chinese intervention.

5

THE RELUCTANT RUSSIANS

On 9 August 1971, the foreign ministers of India and the Union of Soviet Socialist Republics (USSR) signed a treaty of "Peace, Friendship and Cooperation." The treaty, valid for twenty years, was aimed at "expanding and consolidating the existing relationship of sincere friendship" between the two countries. Both the context in which the treaty was concluded and the provisions of the document occasioned considerable commentary and speculation. After all, the treaty was signed at the height of the crisis in South Asia. The fact that Bengali rebels were operating against the Pakistan army from sanctuaries in eastern India was an open secret. And the treaty itself seemed to be designed to backstop India's approach to the crisis. Article IX of the treaty stated, "In the event of either Party being subjected to an attack or a threat thereof, the High Contracting Parties shall immediately enter into mutual consultations in order to remove threat and to take appropriate effective measures to ensure peace and the security of their countries."

Unsurprisingly, many contemporary observers saw the treaty as setting the stage for an armed intervention by India. Kissinger held, for instance, that the Soviet Union had "seized a strategic opportunity" by not only assuring India of its continued support but also providing a hedge against Chinese intervention in support of Pakistan. "With the treaty," Kissinger wrote later, "Moscow threw a lighted match into a powder keg."[1] Interestingly, most Indian accounts tend to see the treaty in a similar, if more positive, vein. Writing on the fortieth anniversary of the treaty, an adviser to Indira Gandhi claimed that it was "difficult to exaggerate the importance" of the treaty. "Armed with the treaty," Mrs. Gandhi moved decisively to tackle the crisis in a manner of her own choosing.[2]

Such interpretations err in inferring causes from consequences. The treaty was not the product of a strategic consensus between India and the Soviet Union on the crisis in South Asia. For New Delhi and Moscow sought rather different objectives in concluding the treaty. These divergent interests were being pursued well before the Bangladesh crisis erupted in March 1971. Although the crisis enabled the two countries to muffle their differences and find common ground, those differences persisted even after the treaty was inked.

I

In the aftermath of the Tashkent agreement of 1966, the Russians basked in the warmth of their newfound influence in South Asia. Indeed, they began to take their role as a peace broker between India and Pakistan rather seriously. In July 1968, Premier Alexei Kosygin wrote to Indira Gandhi expressing hope that the two neighbors would be able to make significant progress in normalizing their relations. He suggested that the Indus Water Treaty of 1960 could provide a framework for the solution of the problem posed by the Farakka Barrage in sharing the waters of the Ganges between West Bengal and East Pakistan. Mrs. Gandhi wrote back that Pakistan showed "no sign of departure from the normal pattern." The Pakistanis had evidently given him a "wrong picture" of the state of the relationship. Gently but firmly, she suggested that there was no scope for third-party mediation on the core problems between India and Pakistan. She asked Kosygin to "exercise your growing influence with Pakistan and persuade them to start direct discussions with us with the object of normalising our relations."[3]

Around the same time, Moscow dropped a bombshell by announcing military sales to Pakistan. The amount of arms sold to Islamabad was small in comparison with what New Delhi had received, but the reaction in India was decisively negative. Opposition parties had a field day castigating the government's foreign policy, especially its relations with the Soviet Union. The right wing Jana Sangh organized a huge demonstration outside the Soviet embassy—a gathering that had to be dispersed by the police, using tear gas and batons. Moscow's decision to arm Pakistan drove home to the Indian leadership both the importance of shoring up ties with the Russians and the domestic political implications of the Indo-Soviet relationship. P. N. Haksar told the prime minister that the Soviet decision was undoubtedly "erroneous and misguided," and that India should convey to them "both our feelings and reasons for our assessment." But he also emphasized the importance of not overreacting to this development, as Indo-Soviet relations were "many-sided and complex. We have, therefore, to carefully strike a balance sheet of debits and credits." The recent Soviet move was "heavily on the debit side," yet, on balance, India still had a favorable economic and military relationship with Moscow.[4]

The silver lining to the clouds that gathered on the Indo-Soviet relationship was Moscow's proposal of a treaty of friendship and cooperation in early 1969. From the outset, however, the two sides sought to pursue different objectives in working toward such a treaty. From Moscow's standpoint, the main aim of the treaty was to secure a special relationship with India and ensure that India stood with the Soviet Union in the latter's escalating rivalry with China. A Soviet military delegation led by Defense Minister Marshal Andrei A. Grechko arrived in New Delhi on 2 March 1969. That same day, Russian and Chinese forces clashed at the Ussuri River. In their meetings with the Indian defense minister and the chiefs of the armed forces, Grechko and his colleagues discussed various aspects of Soviet military assistance to India's defense efforts "against the backdrop of [the] growing Chinese threat to world peace." The Russians were also eager to probe whether India was hopeful of normalizing relations with China. Their concerns were kindled by Prime Minister Gandhi's recent speech, wherein she expressed a desire for better relations with China.

On returning to Moscow, Grechko and the Soviet ambassador to India, Nikolai Pegov, met with officials from the Indian embassy. The marshal assured the Indian envoy, D. P. Dhar, that "the Soviet Union would come to India's assistance in case of aggression from China or Pakistan" and suggested "some kind of a Treaty of Friendship and Cooperation between India and USSR." Pegov also conveyed to Dhar's deputy, Romesh Bhandari, that they were "extremely keen" to conclude such an agreement. "It would not be a military agreement, but one which would cover cooperation in all fields—technical, scientific, cultural, economic." But it would be "a very good insurance against any possible aggression by China or Pakistan." It was evident to Dhar that the Soviet Union's suggestion was driven by "the increasing tension in their relations with China which posed a threat to them as well as us." Back in India in early April 1969, Dhar told Foreign Minister Dinesh Singh and Foreign Secretary T. N. Kaul that India should explore "the possibility of cashing in on this offer and if the Soviet Union was forthcoming and made certain commitments, then we might agree to enter into a Treaty of Friendship and Cooperation with them."[5]

The Indian government shared the Soviet assessment about the potential threat from China. The Soviet assurance of support in the event of an attack by China was welcomed in New Delhi, particularly by Kaul who had been the ambassador in Moscow during the Sino-Indian war of 1962. He had seen up close the unwillingness of Nikita Khrushchev and his colleagues to take sides between the Chinese "brother" and the Indian "friend." Haksar, too, was enthusiastic about the idea of a treaty. "My own reaction," he informed the prime minister, "is entirely favourable as such a treaty will reflect coincidence of our interests at present."[6] But by "cashing in" on the Soviet offer, the Indians' objective was rather different—their main concern was Moscow's attitude to India-Pakistan relations and its relationship with Islamabad.

India's central aim was to restore the exclusivity in its political and strategic relationship with Moscow and to ensure that the flow of arms to Pakistan was stanched. Dhar's immediate reaction was that if India agreed to consider this proposal, "the Soviet Union would perhaps be inclined to supply us the more sophisticated weapons, bombers, etc. which we badly needed." Besides, the Russians should be told about the "need to curb the rising military trends" in Pakistan "which were anti-Indian."[7]

The prime minister agreed with Dhar, Kaul, and Haksar that the treaty would help strengthen ties with Moscow, but she was more concerned about the potential implications of such a treaty and wanted to move deliberately. To begin with, she was worried about the domestic political fallout of such a treaty. Some sections on the Left—especially the pro-Soviet Communist Party of India—might welcome it, but the rest of the political spectrum was likely to react negatively. The main opposition parties on the Right—the Jana Sangh and Swatantra—would mount a political offensive accusing her of locking India into an embrace with Moscow and alienating it further from the West. More important, Mrs. Gandhi was engaged in a tussle with an influential section of senior members of her own party and government. Many of her opponents in the Congress Party were politically conservative, and they distrusted, not to say disliked, the Soviet Union. A treaty with Moscow would give them a solid handle to take on the prime minister.

Indira Gandhi was also concerned about international reaction to a treaty. Relations with the United States were already on a low ebb, owing to India's vocal criticism of the American war in Vietnam. Washington had not eased the arms embargo imposed during the 1965 India-Pakistan war, but the United States was providing much-needed food aid and was closely involved in launching the Green Revolution to spur India's food production. The prime minister also weighed the possible response from China. She realized that the treaty would ensure Soviet assistance in the event of another conflict with China; but she had been looking out for signs of change, however slight, in Beijing's attitude and posture toward India. Hence she was sensitive to the possibility that Beijing might react negatively to an Indo-Soviet treaty.

Underlying both sets of concerns, domestic and international, was Mrs. Gandhi's unwillingness to abandon the central tenet of nonalignment: the need to avoid being ensnared in military alliances. She was clear, therefore, that the treaty should be carefully drafted to avoid the impression that India had become a Soviet ally. Her key advisers insisted that this was easily done. Haksar, for instance, claimed that "if we enter into arrangements with the USSR, we can offer the same to the rest of the world, including the USA."[8] The prime minister was not entirely convinced.

Mrs. Gandhi wrote to Kosygin in April 1969 welcoming the assurances and overtures from Moscow. "The time has come when these ideas should be examined in detail." Underlining India's main concern, she questioned the Soviet assertion that its military aid to Pakistan— unlike that of the United States—would be conducive to the promotion of better India-Pakistan relations. "This matter is not quite clear to us. Perhaps, it could be clarified."[9]

When Kosygin met her in New Delhi the next month, he referred to the uproar in India over the Soviet-Pakistan arms deal. "I think the noise that has been raised over this question far exceeds [the] importance of the small quantities of armaments we have been supplying." Mrs. Gandhi tartly summarized India's objections. "Nothing should be done," she said, "from which it could be inferred that the Soviet Union treated India at par with Pakistan . . . an equidistance between India and Pakistan tended to cause irritation in India." Further, she was "specially worried with regard to Soviet [military] help [to Pakistan], as such help might neutralise what we have obtained from the Soviet Union." Kosygin heard her out and suggested that she should arrange a summit meeting with Yahya Khan. Grechko had met him in Pakistan and "was of the view that Yahya Khan seemed to be earnestly anxious to come to terms with India and reach some kind of accommodation." The prime minister made it clear that she did not share this assessment.[10]

Kosygin also sought her views on the idea of a treaty. Mrs. Gandhi's response underscored her cautious approach to this issue: "she would not say that it was a wrong step to take, but she did think that the matter had to be considered very carefully and specially the reaction both within the country or in China. One had also to carefully consider in what way such a Treaty should be formulated." Referring to a draft prepared by the Russians, she observed that "it would not be appropriate to have any phraseology in the Treaty which might be misunderstood and construed as a shift from our stand of non-alignment." Further, "the Treaty should not contain anything which might be construed—even though we may not mean it that way—by others as directed against a third party. Such a thing would not be appropriate." Kosygin agreed with those points. Even so, it was obvious to both the leaders that China was a common cause for concern. When Mrs. Gandhi raised the possibility of a Chinese attack on India, Kosygin said that the "Soviet Union was ready to incorporate in the Treaty something on 'mutual assistance.'" Mrs. Gandhi noted that "such a clause would then become a military agreement." "It would be so provided India wants to solve her military affairs," replied Kosygin. He added that "India would probably resort to such consultations" regardless of whether the clause existed. The Soviet Union would not insist on it either way.[11]

The first draft of the treaty prepared by the Indians had had no reference to "mutual assistance" or to military and security matters. Besides, the treaty was valid initially for five years and was extendable for another five. Following Mrs. Gandhi's meeting with Kosygin, the draft was further revised. Clause 6 of this draft spoke of mutual consultations in the event of a threat to either party.[12]

The draft was initially discussed at the level of officials—by Dhar in Moscow and Kaul in New Delhi. These discussions were soon overtaken by political developments in India. From June 1969 onward, it was increasingly clear that Indira Gandhi was headed for a showdown with the old guard of the Congress Party. The point of no return was reached in August, when she opposed the party's nominee for election as president of India and ensured that her own candidate prevailed. Although a formal split in the Congress Party did not occur until November 1969, it was evident that Mrs. Gandhi would soon be heading a minority government. Her concerns about the domestic fallout of the treaty were accentuated.

The Indian foreign minister, Dinesh Singh, visited Moscow in September 1969. He handed over to his Russian counterpart, Gromyko, a more or less finalized draft from the Indian side. He also hinted that India could not sign the treaty at this point. Gromyko assured him that they understood Mrs. Gandhi's difficulties. Dhar was unhappy that "the document seems to have been put into cold-storage for the time being." He felt that India could have played for time by keeping the discussions going at the officials' level.[13] The Soviet politburo approved the treaty, including the clause on mutual consultations.[14] And there the matter rested.

During official exchanges and ministerial visits to the Soviet Union, the Indians continued to emphasize their concerns vis-à-vis Pakistan. These efforts paid off, when Moscow decided to stop military sales to Pakistan in early 1970. Foreign Secretary Kaul thanked Kosygin during a subsequent visit. "We deeply appreciate this gesture on the part of the Soviet Union and we have no doubt that it will contribute greatly to the preservation and maintenance of peace in the sub-continent."

However, the Soviet decision was prompted not by their concurrence with India's assessment regarding arms for Pakistan, but by their desire to buttress the domestic standing of Indira Gandhi, who was heading a minority government and was swerving to the left in matters of domestic policy. There is some evidence to suggest that Dhar had sold this line to the Soviet leadership. Furthermore, the shutting down of the arms pipeline to Pakistan did not mean that the Russians had abandoned their efforts to ensure stability in South Asia. Kosygin was particularly keen to promote "a trade and transit agreement" between India, Pakistan, and Afghanistan, which would be "beneficial for the whole region." He also kept insisting on "the relevance of [the] Tashkent [declaration]." The Indians, in the meantime, persisted with their request for advanced military equipment and technology—often in the context of Soviet attempts to drag their feet, if not demur.[15]

The Russians, for their part, patiently awaited the resumption of discussions on the treaty. A. A. Fomin, head of the South Asia Department in the Soviet foreign ministry, told Dhar on the eve of the elections in India that the Soviet leadership "fully appreciated the difficulties of the Indian government regarding this matter and, as such, allowed this whole question to hibernate in dormancy." Fomin felt that "after the elections if the Indian Government was of the view that the time was opportune and propitious for resuming a discussion on the 'Document,' we would not find the Soviet Government wanting in their desire to reciprocate fully."[16] A few days later, Indira Gandhi won, voted into power with a decisive majority. Soon after, the crisis in East Pakistan flared up.

II

On 2 April 1971 the Soviet president, Nikolai Podgorny, wrote to Yahya Khan expressing "great alarm" at the turn of events in East Pakistan. He urged Yahya to take "the most urgent measures to stop the bloodshed and repression against the population in East Pakistan and for turning to methods of a peaceful political settlement." This would be in the interest of Pakistan and in "the interest of preserving peace in the area." Anxious to avoid being seen as interfering in the internal affairs of Pakistan, Podgorny added that he was guided by "the generally recognised humanitarian principles recorded in the universal Declaration of Human Rights." In closing, he hoped that Yahya would "correctly interpret the motives by which we are guided in making this appeal."[17] The text of the letter was released to the press the same evening.

Podgorny's letter was, in fact, a follow-up message to an earlier one to Yahya from Premier Kosygin. In his oral message of 28 March, which had been conveyed through the Soviet consul-general in Karachi, Kosygin had stated that "extreme measures taken by the military administration and continuation of bloodshed in East Pakistan will not solve the existing complicated problems." He asked Yahya to "take immediate measures for the cessation of bloodshed in East Pakistan and for the resumption of negotiations." In a thinly veiled reference to the United States and China, Kosygin warned that "imperialist circles" and "forces in Asia" could use the situation in detriment to the "integrity of Pakistan." This was entirely in keeping with earlier assurances from the Soviet foreign ministry that Moscow stood for a peaceful resolution of the East Pakistan problem on the basis of a united Pakistan.[18]

From the outset, then, the Soviet Union emphasized the need for peace and stability in Pakistan and in the subcontinent. In contrast to Nixon and Kissinger, who were fixated on Cold War geopolitics and grand strategy throughout the crisis, the Soviet leadership regarded the crisis as a challenge for regional stability and balance of power in South Asia. To the extent that the Cold War entered their calculus, it was their erstwhile ally China rather than the United States that bulked large. Then, too, their concerns about China were located in the regional context rather than that of the Cold War itself. Throughout 1971, only one superpower regarded the crisis as central to Cold War geopolitics—and it was not the Soviet Union.

The Russians were averse to the fracturing of Pakistan on both strategic and ideological grounds. They believed that a breakaway East Pakistan would be vulnerable to the influence and domination of China. They also thought that if the crisis turned into an India-Pakistan conflict, the resulting instability would redound to the advantage of China. From an ideological standpoint, the Soviets regarded the leader of the Awami League, Sheikh Mujibur Rahman, as a "bankrupt bourgeois."[19] The Communist Party of the Soviet Union (CPSU) made it clear to the Communist Party of India (CPI) that it stood for a speedy settlement on the basis of regional autonomy for East Pakistan. As a senior member of the CPI would later note, the Soviet Union "was against the redrawing of boundaries and would, if it came to that, have condemned but condoned Pakistan's repression of the people of East Pakistan to keep its state identity intact."[20]

Moscow adopted a two-pronged approach to the crisis. On the one hand, it sought to dissuade India from a military intervention in East Pakistan. The Soviet leadership was particularly concerned that the public clamor in India to support the Bengalis might force the hand of the Indian prime minister. On the other hand, Moscow tried to nudge the military regime in Pakistan to move toward a peaceful, political resolution of the problem.

Pakistan did not take kindly to the efforts by the Soviet Union. Replying to the Soviet president on 5 April, Yahya claimed that he had had no alternative left to safeguard "Pakistan's integrity, sovereignty and unity" and that the situation in East Pakistan was "well under control and normal life is being gradually restored." He went on to state that India's stance was "causing us grave concern." Recent public statements by Indian leaders "constitute a clear interference in our internal affairs." India, he claimed, had also concentrated six divisions of its army on the borders with East Pakistan—a move that "constitutes a direct threat to our security." Yahya asked the Soviet leadership to use its "undeniable influence with India to prevent her from meddling in Pakistan's internal affairs."[21]

India was naturally pleased with Podgorny's public message. In fact, Kosygin had consulted Ambassador Dhar about the message. Both in Moscow and in New Delhi, the Indians had been urging their Soviet interlocutors to take a tough stand on the developments in East Pakistan. On the publication of Podgorny's message, Dhar wrote to Haksar that "we have got every reason to feel satisfied about this unique diplomatic achievement; there is no doubt that a great and in diplomatic matters essentially a conservative power like the Soviet Union would not have made up its mind to make a public pronouncement criticising the Yahya regime unless it was independently convinced about the rightness of their stand." Dhar claimed that the Soviet leadership had "overcome their inhibitions about so-called principles of national integrity etc., which controlled their policy regarding [the] similar situation in Biafra." He believed that India "should fully take advantage of this unusual development" to bring to bear international pressure on the Pakistan government.[22]

The Indian ambassador overestimated both the extent to which the Soviet Union would turn the screws on Pakistan and the willingness of the Soviet leadership to support a secessionist movement. The first indication of the former came even as Dhar was penning his optimistic missives to Haksar. The Soviet chargé d'affaires in New Delhi called on Foreign Minister Swaran Singh and handed him a message from Moscow for Indira Gandhi. The note observed that Pakistan's foreign secretary had told the Soviet envoy in Islamabad that India had massed six divisions of its army on the East Pakistan border and that "small armed groups" from Indian territory were "infiltrating into East Pakistan to help the freedom fighters." Sultan Khan had said that "Indian actions cannot but provoke reaction . . . leading to an international conflict." The Soviet government "thought that it was their duty to bring this to the notice of their Indian friends and particularly of the Prime Minister. It would be highly appreciated in Moscow if P. M. [Prime Minister Gandhi] could share her views." Moscow evidently wanted to ensure that New Delhi was not stirring the pot in East Pakistan.[23]

Swaran Singh patiently but firmly responded that "India had no intention of intervening militarily in the matter and it was obvious that the Pakistani authorities were trying to build up a hate-India campaign and making unwarranted allegations to divert the attention of people, particularly in West Pakistan." He said that the allegation of Indian infiltration into East Pakistan was "entirely incorrect." If anything, India was worried about the people pouring in from East Pakistan. Similarly, the charge that India's navy was interfering was "without foundation." If India had any such intention, "we would have done so when they [Pakistan] were moving large numbers of troops and equipment to East Pakistan." When the chargé d'affaires requested again that the message should be conveyed to the Indian prime minister and her reply obtained, Swaran Singh tersely replied that his reply should be conveyed to Moscow and that if the prime minister "had anything to add to what he had said, this would be communicated." Mrs. Gandhi read the record of the conversation the next day, and she directed that a reply to the Soviet leadership be drafted stating India's position.[24]

Meanwhile, Moscow also was conveying its thinking through party channels, particularly during the 24th Congress of the CPSU held from 31 March to 10 April. The leader of the CPI delegation, Rajeshwar Rao, met with Ambassador Dhar on 2 April. Dhar asked Rao to circulate material on the developments in East Pakistan to the other party delegations and to seek permission for the East Pakistan delegation to make a statement at the Congress. To this end, Rao spoke with Boris Ponomarev, the head of the International Department of the CPSU Central Committee. Ponomarev made it clear that although he had some sympathy for the Bengalis' struggle, he was certainly not in favor of rushing to their aid. On the contrary, he advised Rao "to use his influence with Indira Gandhi to work for a negotiated settlement." The Soviets were reluctant even to help Rao prepare copies of the résumé on the East Pakistan situation. The representative in charge of the India desk pleaded that his cyclostyling machine was out of order. Rao had to get the material cyclostyled through a journalist friend in Moscow and then had to push the CPSU apparatchik to distribute it. The party leadership was willing to go no further, and it again urged Rao and other CPI delegates "to persuade Indira Gandhi not to precipitate matters."[25]

In the following weeks, Moscow adopted a careful equipoise between India and Pakistan, urging restraint on the former while prodding the latter toward a political settlement in East Pakistan. It ended up displeasing both. The Soviet leadership's response to the letter from Indira Gandhi was tepid. Not only did it fail to offer any positive promise of action, it also asked India to exercise restraint and keep the Soviet Union fully informed of its thinking. The Soviet leadership also conveyed its concern over the pitch of the public response in India to the happenings in East Pakistan. The only crumb of comfort held out by Moscow was the promise of another appeal to Pakistan.

Even the ebullient D. P. Dhar found the message quite "bleak" and "unhappy." Then he characteristically put the most positive gloss on the Soviet Union's stance. "What more really can we expect of a major power in such circumstances?" he wrote to Haksar. "They really cannot commit themselves to any concrete offer of aid and endorsement of an aggressive policy of intervention at this stage. These are matters which they would like to be understood than recorded and perhaps this could explain their reticence to be explicit." It was important, he urged, "to read between the lines" and not to read too much into their request that India should "carry on the present policy of restraint and caution."[26]

If the situation in East Pakistan failed to improve soon, claimed Dhar, the Soviets "would be the one people most likely to understand our reaction even if that reaction is a departure from the present policy of restraint." He also observed that a contact in the Central Committee of the CPSU had taken a slightly different line. Dhar was sharp enough to realize that all this amounted to clutching at straws: "I hope I do not sound too optimistic," he wrote in conclusion.[27] But it was clear that the ambassador and his government had their work cut out for them.

The Soviet leadership was simultaneously in touch with the Pakistanis. In a long meeting on 12 April with Pakistan's ambassador in Moscow, Jamsheed Marker, Kosygin "categorically and frequently stressed that the Soviets had no desire to interfere in the internal affairs of Pakistan." He was emphatic that Podgorny's message was not intended to do so. Kosygin made no reference at all to Mujibur Rahman or to the arrest of other political leaders. On the contrary, he stated at least five times that "it was for the Pakistani leaders to themselves decide what kind of a political system they wanted." After receiving the letter from Prime Minister Gandhi and the subsequent exchange of views, the Soviet leadership decided to lean a bit more on Pakistan. In another message to Yahya on 17 April, Kosygin adopted a formal tone and stressed the need for a peaceful settlement. The Pakistanis noted with concern the reference in the message to "the lawful wishes of the parties" and to "the interest of the population of both West and East Pakistan."[28]

Instead of replying to this message, Yahya sent to Moscow a special envoy, M. Arshad Hussain, an erstwhile foreign minister and ambassador to the Soviet Union. Hussain had to wait a week before he could meet the chairman, and by all accounts, the meeting was testy. On his return to Pakistan, Hussain would tell his former boss, President Ayub Khan, "Kosygin was very cross and unhappy. His fear was that Bhutto was being helped to get into power and should that happen war between India and Pakistan might well be precipitated. He accused us of genocide and [had] an unduly harsh reaction to the situation in East Pakistan."[29] When Hussain elaborated on Yahya's political plans, Kosygin heard him out and reiterated the need for a peaceful settlement with East Pakistan and peaceful coexistence with India.

The Pakistan ambassador's assessment of Moscow's stance was perceptive. The Soviet position, Marker informed the foreign ministry, was ambivalent and not clearly committed to supporting Pakistan. "They would, in the overall interests of peace and stability, prefer a united Pakistan, but they had doubts about our ability to bring the situation in East Pakistan under control, and feared that a continuation of instability would help Chinese interests to prosper in the region." Islamabad's reading of the situation was less sanguine. The foreign ministry and the military leadership believed that "the Soviet Union was not interested in sustaining the unity of Pakistan, assurances to the contrary notwithstanding."[30]

Soviet officials apprised the Indians of the meeting between Kosygin and Hussain. Fomin met with D. P. Dhar and gave him a summary of the discussion with the Pakistanis. Dhar made it clear that India could not remain content with such palliatives from the Soviet leadership. New Delhi's principal concern was the billowing inflow of refugees from East Pakistan. Judging by the tempo of military operations in East Pakistan, this was expected to swell further. "This was too high a price to pay for one's restraint," Dhar observed. He noted that the Pakistan army and its affiliates had now embarked on "a discriminatory and preplanned policy of selecting Hindus for butchery." The Indian government was trying its best to prevent this aspect of the crisis from being publicized. But the continued targeting of Hindus in East Pakistan could result in "a massive retaliation in India" against the Muslims. Indeed, the communal situation in the subcontinent was "highly explosive."[31]

Emphasizing the mounting magnitude of the refugee problem, Dhar told Fomin that "a few tins of milk powder or a few blankets would not be enough." The financial burden would run into hundreds of millions of rupees, and "we cannot bear it alone." Fomin replied that his government was actively considering such assistance. Dhar further argued that "while we should do our best to alleviate the sufferings of the refugees through organised relief work, we could not afford to ignore or forget the cause which leads to these unfortunate events. An international scrutiny to discover the main cause of which this human exodus was only an effect [was] absolutely essential." Dhar's remarks underlined New Delhi's stand on the developing refugee crisis. Although India was canvassing for international aid and assistance for the refugees, it was also insisting that the refugee influx could only be stemmed and reversed if the fundamental political problem in East Pakistan was addressed to the satisfaction of the Bengalis. Fomin nodded his sympathy and said that "he was personally aware of the strong and bitter feelings entertained by East Bengalis."

In two long letters to Haksar, Dhar laid out his assessment of the situation and the way forward. As usual, he began by minimizing the differences with the Soviet Union. Moscow, he claimed, had "by now reached a stage where their hope of bringing Pakistan round to a sensible position is receding very fast." The Russians apparently believed the rupture between the two wings of Pakistan was "complete, emotionally and otherwise." The Soviet leadership would "slowly, in spite of their native and sometimes irritating conservatism, bring their policies on the same grid as ours. India could "trust the Russians to be helpful," if it took care in "cultivating them and keeping them fully informed."[32]

But Dhar knew better: persisting with the current approach to the Soviet Union might not result in a concordance of views about the crisis, at least not within a time frame acceptable to India. So, he drew attention to the wider dimensions of the crisis. The "blatant and aggressive statements emanating from China" against India were a matter of concern. The possibility of a Chinese military intervention in support of Pakistan brought into focus the "poignant fact that in case such an eventuality materialises, we shall have to go it alone." Dhar reminded Haksar that it was "in the context of such situations and with a view to dealing with them specifically and with greater self-confidence that we had mooted the desirability of drawing up the 'Document' between us and the Soviet Union. How about signing this 'Document' now?"[33]

III

In reviving the idea of the treaty, Dhar revisited the factors that had previously given pause to the prime minister. He argued that the context had dramatically changed owing to the East Pakistan crisis. If the treaty was signed now, "we shall give a counter blow to the Pakistani morale and they may succumb to the continuing pressures of the East Bengal situation." From a domestic standpoint, "it will immediately lift the morale of the average Indian sky-high." To be sure, the treaty would be attacked by the opposition, but this was "the psychological moment to have this Document as a new weapon in our armoury." The reaction of China and the United States had to be considered as well. The treaty could "jeopardise our chances of initiating a dialogue with China." Then again, the prospects of opening such a dialogue did "not seem to be very bright at the present moment." Yet Dhar suggested that New Delhi should "explore all possibilities of coming to some terms with China, reaching some preliminary accord with her before the Document is signed." As for the United States, India could offer the same document "without any change . . . for being signed and concluded between them and us as a Treaty." The real question, as Dhar was all too aware, was whether the Russians would be amenable to signing the treaty at this juncture. "I am not sure about their willingness or otherwise . . . But their mind can be probed."[34]

The prime minister, however, remained ambivalent about the merits of concluding the treaty. Dhar grew anxious at New Delhi's refusal to make a positive move. Unless India took the lead on the treaty, it would not be able to ensure a convergence of interests with Soviet Union regarding the ongoing crisis. Dhar was also troubled by the fact that his time in Moscow was running out. Mrs. Gandhi wanted him back in New Delhi to help manage the crisis. In the time that was given to him, Dhar made valiant efforts to highlight the crucial point of convergence of Indian and Soviet interests in negotiating the treaty: the threat from China. He also strained every nerve to secure a substantial Soviet contribution for the Bengali refugees and increased military supplies and spares for the Indian forces.

Thus, while delivering a letter from Indira Gandhi to Kosygin, Dhar told Fomin that he wondered "whether these new tensions and strains were not perhaps being created by China using Pakistan as its usual pawn in order to impede the normal course of development in our country." A few weeks later, he called on Marshal Grechko to bid him farewell. Dhar observed that India was "passing through a very difficult phase." It already had 4 million Bengali refugees on its hands and 50,000 to 60,000 refugees were coming into India every day. The gravity of the situation was exacerbated by "regular provocations by Pakistan on our borders." While the Indian side of the border was manned by the Border Security Force, Pakistan had deployed its regular army, including artillery units. To add to India's woes, "our friend from the North" had also assumed a threatening posture.[35]

Grechko took the bait. He said that India should "not be worried by Pakistan," but it should "take into account the unpredictable enemy from the North." He assured Dhar that if China started "to use aggression, the USSR would not hesitate to use its strength and force in repelling it."

Grechko added that it would be of "vital importance" to India and the USSR if their relationship was "fixed" in a "treaty of mutual help" of the kind recently concluded between the Soviet Union and Egypt. "Such a document would deter any one from embarking on an adventure against India." Dhar replied that "an agreement had been reached in principle" on the text and contents of the treaty: the "meal was ready on the plate." Grechko said that the time was "opportune and appropriate," and that the treaty should "contain some reference to military cooperation also." The massive presence of Soviet troops on China's borders, he added, does "help India directly in her defence against China." "If the Chinese had not to contend against our forces, they would release their hordes for use against you. We have to understand these problems in the military sense—in the operational sense." Dhar undertook, with some satisfaction, to convey the marshal's views to his government.

Reporting on his meeting with Grechko to Kaul and Haksar, Dhar made a strong pitch for signing the treaty. He wondered if India was "being wise in reacting in a lukewarm manner to the Soviet offer of unequivocal help to us." The treaty would work to India's benefit "in the event of our country being involved in a conflict with Pakistan singly or with her allies." He emphatically stated that he was "not talking merely in terms of the political requirements of the situation as it will develop as a consequence of a conflict of this type. I am more interested in the military aspects of the aid and assistance which we will need and which we are bound to seek."[36] Dhar was, of course, exaggerating the Soviet willingness to support India in the unfolding crisis. Grechko, in fact, had twice said that he saw the treaty as a deterrent against aggression from Pakistan and China. The Russians regarded the treaty as a step toward stabilizing the situation in the subcontinent by reassuring India—and forestalling it from precipitating a war.

IV

The day after Dhar's meeting with Grechko, Foreign Minister Swaran Singh reached Moscow for consultations with the Soviet leadership. His discussions with the Soviet leaders made it clear that there was a convergence of views regarding China. But on the crisis itself, the two countries continued to hold different positions.

In a long meeting with Kosygin, Swaran Singh observed that the tally of refugees had just touched the 5 million mark. Prime Minister Gandhi had "made it clear that these refugees will remain with us only for a short while." Two steps had to be taken without delay. First, "the military regime must stop all its activities so that an end is put to the daily influx of refugees." Second, "conditions must be created in East Bengal, conditions of normalcy, so that these refugees can return with some sense of safety." This was possible only if negotiations were commenced with the leadership of the Awami League, "so that the party which was chosen by the people is installed in power." India, he observed, had "shown a great deal of restraint but there is a limit to this restraint. Unless there is a rapport and a solution which is brought about quickly, we fear that a situation, though we wish to avoid it at all costs, may develop which may endanger peace."[37]

India saw the two parts of the problem—refugees on Indian soil and a political solution in East Pakistan—as inextricably intertwined, but the Soviet Union preferred to treat these issues separately. From Moscow's standpoint, addressing the refugee problem would remove the potential casus belli for India and so ensure stability in the subcontinent. So, Kosygin insisted that "these events could be divided into two separate parts." "Refugees must go back, all of them, every one of them," he stated. He suggested that "we should concentrate, in the first instance, on this issue of refugees." The second question "deserves intense political consideration." He claimed to agree that this was a "legitimate question," but hastened to add that "technically speaking . . . it can be resisted on the grounds of being a matter which relates to a domestic jurisdiction." If India linked the second question to the first, Pakistan would claim that India was only interested in meddling in its internal affairs. In dealing with the second issue, India should act to ensure the Bengalis' struggle "continues, so that it succeeds after the return of the refugees." Kosygin suggested, "in strict confidence," that India could continue to support the Bengali guerrillas as well as the mass struggle. "Therefore, let us not bundle the two [issues] together, but give all possible help to the democratic forces . . . You are a politician, you know what I am implying."[38]

In his meeting with Gromyko, Swaran Singh tried to elicit some firm commitment that the Soviet Union would bring pressure to bear on the Pakistani regime. Gromyko was evasive about Moscow's plans. "Unfortunately," he observed, "we have not yet reached the stage of planning this action." Swaran Singh also raised the threat from China, "A situation may arise which may demand the entry of the Soviet Union into it in order to encounter the difficulties which may be created by the

Chinese support to Pakistan." He urged Gromyko "even now . . . to consider some appropriate steps." Gromyko recalled the earlier discussions on the treaty. "What do you think about the feasibility or otherwise of resuming this exchange of views and ideas regarding their Draft Document?" he asked. It was Swaran Singh's turn to be cautious: "we may be too late, events may over-take us. Can we think of something quickly? When Gromyko stressed the idea of a treaty, Singh tentatively said, "We could resume the threads of discussion." That evening, the Indian foreign minister was asked by New Delhi to convey India's willingness to resume negotiations on the treaty. He told Gromyko the next day that India was ready and that "such an agreement will . . . act as a deterrent to China and Pakistan against embarking on any military adventure."[39] The ball was set rolling again.

V

Back in New Delhi, Foreign Secretary Kaul began revisiting the draft treaty drawn up two years before. He compared this draft with the recent treaty between the Soviet Union and Egypt. The latter broadly accorded with the Indian draft, but it went further, explicitly referring to cooperation "in the military sphere." Grechko had told Dhar that the Indo-Soviet treaty should include some reference to military cooperation. Kaul demurred: "I do not think a specific reference to military cooperation is necessary in our draft as it might give the impression of entering into a military alliance." Instead, Article IX of the Indian draft, which called for "mutual consultations" in the event of an attack or threat, would be strengthened by adding words "with a view to removing the threat." Another modification to Article IX was the inclusion of a provision that each side would undertake "to abstain from providing any assistance to any third party that engages in armed conflict with the other Party."[40] In so doing, India sought to foreclose on the possibility of Soviet political assistance or military sales to Pakistan in the event of active hostilities.

In the meantime, Mrs. Gandhi wrote to Kosygin about the worsening crisis in the subcontinent. The situation "is extremely serious, even grave." The number of refugees was rising rapidly and was imposing serious strains on India. Hinting at Kosygin's advice to Swaran Singh, she added, "we can hardly expect the refugees to return unless political conditions in East Bengal are such as to give them a feeling of assurance that they will be able to live in peace and safety." India, she said, had been exercising great restraint. In closing, she sought Kosygin's "assessment of the course that events are taking."[41]

In the wake of Swaran Singh's visit and of the letter from Mrs. Gandhi, the Soviets began to step up their diplomatic efforts. Kosygin had a long meeting with the Pakistani ambassador in Moscow on 22 June. Ambassador Marker conveyed a message from Yahya Khan that contained two main points. First, Yahya was committed to finding a political solution in East Pakistan and to restoring democracy. Second, both of these would be accomplished within a framework that safeguarded the territorial integrity of Pakistan. Marker added that the Pakistani president was expected to make a formal pronouncement on these matters on 28 June. In response, Kosygin emphasized the importance of the forthcoming announcement by Yahya. "The President will be speaking at an acute moment upon issues which are almost about war and peace. If the President's statement does not take into consideration the Indian attitude there will be a sharp response from the other side. If both sides make sharp public pronouncements then it would be difficult to control the situation."[42]

The Soviet premier then turned to the question of atrocities in East Pakistan and the flow of refugees into India. This was "a matter of grave concern to us." "If people flee," he said, "it is because unbearable conditions have been created for them that they are forced to leave everything behind." When Marker tried to controvert this claim, Kosygin replied, "I do not want to turn this conversation into a debate . . . We say with all sincerity that Pakistan and India should resolve their differences without resorting to a conflict. We say it to you and we say it to India." However, Moscow would continue its economic collaboration with Islamabad. More importantly, he said, "We do not want to interfere in your internal affairs. This is for you alone to decide. We think a democratic government should find its legitimate rights. It will find it, sooner or later."[43]

Clearly, the Soviet Union was adopting a similar line, albeit with different emphases, in its dealings with India and Pakistan. Moscow's ability to maintain this posture would come under increasing strain owing to the Yahya regime's unwillingness to take positive steps toward creating conditions for the refugees to return.

Meanwhile, the Russians tried to encourage India to conclude the treaty. Ambassador Pegov met Haksar and sought to allay India's misgivings about the implications of the treaty. "The loudest and most vociferous opponents would be the Chinese," but the treaty would put an end to their "tactics of blackmail," and Pakistan would be "down cast and dismayed." He insisted that aid and assistance from the West would not stop flowing to India because of the treaty. In case it did, the Soviet Union would step into the breach with "special assistance in the field of defence and also essential raw materials." At the same time, Moscow wanted to ensure that India would not bring matters to a head vis-à-vis Pakistan. As Haksar noted, Pegov "was very keen to know whether we were making any offensive preparations against Pakistan."[44]

VI

In the end, the impetus to sign the treaty came not from the Russians but from developments with the United States. On 17 July, we may recall, Kissinger met the Indian ambassador, L. K. Jha, and told him that if China intervened in an India-Pakistan war, the United States would be unable to help India. It was at this point that Mrs. Gandhi overcame her lingering doubts about the treaty and moved ahead to conclude it. Moscow was informed that D. P. Dhar would return for final negotiations to seal the accord.

Before Dhar's departure, Kaul sent a note to the prime minister outlining the case for signing the treaty. The foreign secretary observed that Kissinger's message to Jha "changed the whole perspective in which the Soviet proposal has to be considered." Kaul focused on the strategic advantages flowing from the treaty, the implications for India's policy of nonalignment, and the likely international and domestic reaction to the treaty.[45]

From a strategic standpoint, the two main concerns were continued Russian support for Pakistan and the need to restrain China. Article IX, he wrote, was "perhaps the most important from our point of view." It would "safeguard us against the supply of any Soviet military support to Pakistan if she engages in a conflict with us." Further, it would "in the case of a conflict with Pakistan and/or China . . . act as deterrent on both." If war seemed likely, India "could ask the USSR to tie up [the] bulk of the Chinese troops along Sinkiang, Mongolia, and their far-eastern borders with China." This would "greatly reduce the Chinese pressure on us" along the Sino-Indian borders.

What about India's long-standing policy of nonalignment? Kaul emphasized the point that the treaty "does not conflict with our conception of non-alignment." Nonalignment did "not mean if our security and territorial integrity are threatened we cannot enter into any arrangements we may consider necessary to meet and avert such a threat." The treaty "did not put us in the Soviet camp," he insisted. On the contrary, India could sign similar treaties with a host of other countries.

Regardless of what India believed, the response of other major players would matter more. The Indian assessment of these factors was realistic, but it also was laced with a dose of wishful thinking, especially with regard to the United States. "It is possible," Kaul conceded, "that the US government will not like the treaty at first," but once other countries were ready to enter into such an arrangement with India, the United States "might approach us for signing similar treaties and US opposition will diminish." Britain and other Western European countries were "unlikely to react sharply." They had détente with the Soviet Union themselves and could not "logically oppose" the treaty. The only countries that would be "openly hostile" to the treaty were Pakistan and China, but the treaty "would have a deterrent effect on both."

Kaul observed that any further delay in concluding the treaty "would be to our detriment," and he recommended that India should enter into it "at the soonest date possible . . . time is of essence because of the outbursts of Yahya Khan and the possibility of his staging some kind of misadventure." The Indians, however, continued to overestimate the Soviet Union's willingness to support their stance on the crisis. Thus, Kaul believed that "with the signing of this treaty we can be assured of Soviet support . . . regarding our stand on Bangla Desh." It would soon transpire that matters were not resolved quite as easily.

VII

On 3 August, D. P. Dhar reached Moscow for final negotiations on the treaty. Over two long meetings with Gromyko, Dhar ironed out the text of the treaty. The amendments suggested by the Soviet side were minor and acceptable to the Indians. But, when it came to discussing the crisis, the Soviets stuck to their earlier stance. In the second meeting, Dhar conveyed a message from Indira Gandhi to the Soviet leadership, highlighting the problems posed by the influx of nearly 8 million refugees, and emphasizing that the movement for Bangladesh was "bound to succeed." India was sitting "on the top of a volcano which might explode any minute," but it "did not want a war." The prime minister wished to impress upon the Soviet leaders that "it was absolutely necessary to put our heads together to prevent a war, to take steps so that adventurers did not unleash it." However, if "a war was forced on India," the two countries would have to "determine the means and methods of cooperating with each other in the economic, political and defence fields so as to meet the situation effectively." Gromyko's response was noncommittal. Soviet policy on the crisis "was well-known to the Indian leaders." He assured Dhar that they "felt very strongly" about the situation and were "doing everything possible to prevent aggravation." He promised to convey Indira Gandhi's message to Kosygin, Podgorny, and Brezhnev.[46]

Meeting Kosygin the next day, Dhar went over the same ground. Mrs. Gandhi, he told Kosygin, "has asked me to convey to you her assurances that we will do everything to preserve peace." But India had "to take into account the possibility of a conflict also." How should India and the Soviet Union "confer with each other to act to meet such a contingency?" he asked.

Kosygin conceded that "the situation is complicated and becoming more complicated everyday." Yahya Khan had sent two messages requesting him to receive a special envoy from Pakistan. Kosygin would make it "absolutely clear" to the envoy that Moscow would not provide any military equipment or spares to Pakistan. They would also "apply economic pressure to moderate the bellicose policy of the Pakistan Government." Yet Kosygin was emphatic that "war is not in the interests of India." He observed that Pakistan and the United States were fully aware of the support being given by India to the Bengali rebels. "It is my advice that you should be more careful . . . otherwise you will face many difficulties and many dangers." The Russians were evidently pulling back from their earlier stance of a wink-and-nod toward India's assistance for the insurgency. India, said Kosygin, should ensure that "Pakistan and her friends . . . know that you have the strength to counter-act all their nefarious designs." That fact "alone will enable you to avert war."[47] In short, the Russians continued to have a very different view on tackling the crisis and saw the treaty as increasing India's deterrent capability and so preserving peace in the subcontinent.

Moscow's reluctance to get drawn deeper into the crisis was also obvious from its response to Dhar's persistent requests that the two sides begin consultations on contingencies. Dhar, in fact, asked Gromyko to bring with him to New Delhi an expert each from the army and the intelligence services. The Soviet politburo considered the request and decided against it. Gromyko told Dhar that "it was extremely difficult to select the proper persons and collect the required material at such short notice." When Dhar responded that Gromyko could himself engage in some discussions in India, he politely suggested that "matters of this nature will have to be discussed at a fairly high and restricted level."[48]

Gromyko and Swaran Singh signed the treaty on 9 August. In his meeting with Mrs. Gandhi the next day, the Soviet foreign minister reiterated his government's view on dealing with the crisis. Moscow believed that "the Pak [sic] military will not succeed in keeping down the people of East Pakistan for long and the rule is doomed." But, he added, "it is not for us to prejudge whether East Pakistan should be separate from West Pakistan or one with it." "You may rest assured," said Gromyko choosing his words carefully, "that in regard to the refugees we shall always support your position." Mrs. Gandhi raised the possibility of Mujib being executed by the military regime, and pointedly said that "we will not remain indifferent and will take certain steps." Gromyko responded, "We believe it would be very good if your Government continues the restraint and regards the situation in a cold blooded way . . . The heart should be warm but the mind should be cool as we say."[49]

Mrs. Gandhi said that the "situation is not static"—refugees were continuing to pour in. "I do not know what we can do unless some solution is found. I am posing the question to you what can we do?" Gromyko said, "it is not an easy problem and there is no easy solution." He assured her that they would apply "considerable pressure" on the visiting Pakistan special envoy. The "Pakistan government must give guarantees of security to those people who left because of unbearable conditions."[50] As earlier, the Russians refused to commit themselves to addressing the political problem in East Pakistan. The gulf between the two sides had not been spanned by the treaty of friendship.

6

POSTER CHILD AND PARIAH

Harold Evans had not met his visitor earlier. The well-dressed, thickset man in his early forties who walked into his office on 18 May 1971, was Anthony Mascarenhas, a Pakistani journalist of Goan Christian descent. Evans, editor of the *Sunday Times,* knew that Mascarenhas worked for the *Morning News* in Karachi and was a stringer for his paper. He had also been following the developments in East Pakistan. Not only had the *Sunday Times* covered some of the events, but Evans's youngest brother was a British diplomat serving in Islamabad. Yet Evans was utterly unprepared for the story he heard that afternoon.[1]

Mascarenhas was one of eight Pakistani journalists taken on an officially sponsored trip to East Pakistan in the last week of April. The Yahya regime had been concerned about the campaign launched by the Bangladesh exile government and its network of supporters across the globe.[2] The idea, Mascarenhas told Evans, "was to show in a patriotic way the great job the Army was doing." "But what I saw," he added, "was genocide." Mascarenhas had covered and been shocked at the violence against the non-Bengalis in March, but he maintained that the army's current campaign was incomparably worse and orchestrated on a grand scale. "The top officers," he said, "told me they were seeking a final solution."[3]

Evans was a bit unsure. Why had the story not been run in the *Morning News*? Mascarenhas replied that given the levels of censorship prevailing in Pakistan, it was impossible for him to publish the story at home, so he had come all the way to London. "Either I had to write the full story of what I'd seen or I would have to stop writing. I would never be able to write again with integrity." Impressed by Mascarenhas's "decent Christian passion," Evans decided to risk publishing this explosive story. Before filing it, however, Mascarenhas wanted his wife and five children to leave Pakistan. On returning to Karachi, he managed to arrange their passage to Italy and from there to England. But Mascarenhas himself was forbidden from accompanying them: only one foreign trip a year was permitted. Staying on in Karachi was not an option, so he took a flight to Peshawar and crossed on foot into Afghanistan. Before wending his way back to Europe, he sent an agreed-upon message to a staffer's residence: "Export formalities completed. Shipment begins Monday."[4]

The centerfold of the *Sunday Times* on 13 June 1971 carried a single story with the headline "Genocide." The article cracked the casing of censorship imposed by the Pakistani regime and laid bare the brutalities being perpetrated on the Bengalis. Mascarenhas's 5,000-word story was a carefully crafted report of the ten days he had spent in East Pakistan. It stood out for its vividness and precision—he named names—as much as its grit and humanity. Mascarenhas emphasized the systematic character of the murderous campaign waged by the military. He quoted military officers stating that they were "determined to cleanse East Pakistan once and for all of the threat of secession, even if it means [the] killing of two million people and ruling the province as a colony for thirty years." Hindus were the special target of what the authorities called the "cleansing process." The Pakistan government, wrote Mascarenhas, was "pushing through its own 'final solution' of the East Bengal problem."[5] The accompanying editorial—"Stop the Killing"—added that "there is no escaping the terrible charge of premeditated extermination leveled by the facts against the present Pakistani Government."

Mascarenhas was not the first journalist to write about the atrocities in East Pakistan. Some foreign journalists had filed stories about the military crackdown before being evicted at the end of March 1971. The international press had continued to report and editorialize on the subject. But unlike Mascarenhas's eyewitness account, these were drawn from stories related by the refugees and put out by Mujibnagar. Further, most of these stories referred to the events as "massacre," "slaughter," or "tragedy."[6] With the exception of *The New Nation* (Singapore) and the *Saturday Review* (New York),[7] none had invoked the term "holocaust" or "genocide." And neither of these publications commanded the prestige and readership of the *Sunday Times*. By authoritatively levying the charge of genocide, Anthony Mascarenhas transfixed global attention with a single shaft of investigative journalism.

I

In the wake of Mascarenhas's story, the Bangladesh crisis garnered increasing amounts of column inches and airtime in the media across the world. In Britain alone, from March to December 1971, the *Times* carried twenty-nine editorials on the crisis, the *Daily Telegraph* thirty-nine, the *Guardian* thirty-seven, the *Observer* fifteen, and the *Financial Times* thirteen. No fewer than eight episodes of BBC television's most-watched program *Panorama* were devoted to developments in the subcontinent.[8]

The role of the international press in highlighting the murderous military campaign should not, however, be exaggerated. Of the front-page reportage in the *New York Times* and the *Times* (London), only 16.8 percent focused on human interest stories relating to the Bengali people, victims, and refugees. By contrast, 34 percent dealt with the military-conflict dimension of the crisis and 30.5 percent with its potential consequences. Nor was the coverage in these newspapers particularly favorable to the Bangladesh movement. Nearly half of it was neutral in tone, with only 35.1 percent being positive and 14.4 percent negative. Interestingly, almost three-fourths of these reports drew on official sources, which helps explain their focus and tone.[9]

Moreover, global reactions to the crisis were not mediated only through the press. Rather they were conditioned by larger and disparate historical currents that coursed and crisscrossed throughout the period. On the one hand, the late 1960s saw the beginnings of globalization, particularly the emergence of a new form of humanitarianism that was self-consciously transnational insofar as it refused to accept national governments as the sole source of authority and aimed to address a global audience. On the other hand, there were trends within the international system, especially the acceleration of decolonization, that built a breakwater against the erosion of state sovereignty by such considerations.

The rise of transnational humanitarianism—the "globalization of conscience,"[10] to use Daniel Sargent's resonant phrase—reflected the confluence of four trends. The first was an exponential growth in nongovernmental organizations (NGOs) dedicated to humanitarian causes: principally, provision of relief to victims of natural and man-made catastrophes. Although such NGOs had existed in the West since the late eighteenth century, they came into their own only during World War II, a conflict in which the civilian casualties far outstripped military ones. The onset of decolonization at once increased their numbers and broadened their orientation. In the postwar years, humanitarian NGOs went global as development and aid became the watchwords for the West's interaction with the newly independent states. Traditionally, these NGOs had focused on succoring victims rather than shaming their persecutors or shaping their political circumstances. The archetypal humanitarian NGO, the International Committee of the Red Cross, had notoriously remained silent during the Holocaust. By clinging to the principles of impartiality, neutrality, and independence, they hoped to create a "humanitarian space" that would provide sanctuary to aid workers and victims alike.[11]

Strict adherence to these principles, however, became difficult and contentious owing to the second trend: technological advances that underpinned globalization. The explosion of radio and television broadcasting in the 1960s spread the news and images of suffering in distant lands with unprecedented speed and immediacy. This enabled NGOs to appeal to an ever-widening set of audiences across the world. Advances in satellite telephony and the proliferation of commercial air travel made it easier and cheaper for NGOs and activists to establish global connections and to step up their activities.[12] But these developments also forced them both to conceive of their own roles in different ways and to justify their stances before global audiences.

Third, there was the impact of the global protests of the 1960s. The movement against the Vietnam War generated widespread antipathy to militarism and an expanding circle of global solidarity. The protests of 1968 in Western Europe and America also had an impact, if at one remove. These movements, as we may recall, were fundamentally libertarian. After 1968, when many young radicals began weaning off the Marxist catechism, the libertarian dimension of their revolt found other avenues of expression. In particular, their demand for freedom and rights at home sensitized them to the question of freedom and rights abroad.[13] Interestingly, a prominent vehicle for the "globalization of conscience" was the counterculture of the Sixties.

Of greater importance were the protests of 1968 in Eastern Europe. Dissidence in the Soviet bloc had begun in the era of de-Stalinization under Khrushchev.[14] But the dissident movement embraced human rights only after Soviet tanks crushed the Prague Spring in the summer of 1968. Among the enthusiastic supporters of the Prague Spring was the Soviet physicist Andrei Sakharov. Only weeks before the invasion, he had published in the *New York Times* his famous essay "Progress, Coexistence, and Intellectual Freedom," arguing for international cooperation to exorcise the specter of nuclear war and for removal of restrictions on individual rights.[15] In the years ahead, Sakharov would become the most prominent figure in the Soviet human rights movement. Another well-known dissident, the writer Alexander Solzhenitsyn, also championed human rights after 1968. In his acceptance speech for the Nobel Prize in 1970, delivered in absentia, Solzhenitsyn would famously proclaim that "no such thing as INTERNAL AFFAIRS remains on our crowded Earth!"[16]

The language of human rights emanating from Eastern Europe was picked up by activists in the West. Few NGOs at this time were exclusively focused on human rights as opposed to humanitarian causes: the former aimed to secure individual rights, and the latter sought to alleviate suffering. Among the exceptions was Amnesty International. Founded in 1962 and devoted to the cause of securing the release of "prisoners of conscience," Amnesty International cut its activist teeth in the campaign against the Greek junta's use of torture in the late 1960s.[17] Not until the mid-1970s would Amnesty International become the best-known human rights NGO owing to its championing of the cause of Soviet and Latin American dissidents. Yet the incipient human rights movement was beginning to percolate the emerging circuit of transnational humanitarianism.

The fourth trend that contributed to this phenomenon were the changes in historical imagination and popular memory in Western Europe and the United States. For over a decade after World War II, there had been little reference to the Holocaust in public discourse. The unwillingness to squarely confront its enormity stemmed from a combination of psychological trauma and the demands of the Cold War. Too many Western European countries had been witnesses to if not accomplices in Germany's crimes against the Jews. At the same time, it was essential to foster the reconstruction of Western Europe (including West Germany) and its integration in the Atlantic alliance against the Soviet Union.[18]

Paradoxically, the country that first began coming to terms with the Holocaust was West Germany. This was triggered by belated investigations into the crimes against the Jews, starting with the revelations that came of the 1958 trials of former Nazis in Ulm. Consciousness of the Holocaust was also dramatically catalyzed by the arrest and trial of Adolf Eichmann by Israel in 1961, and was further amplified by the Frankfurt trials between 1963 and 1965 of Auschwitz guards. The shift in German consciousness was symbolized by Chancellor Willy Brandt dropping to his knees at the Warsaw Ghetto Memorial during his visit to Poland in 1970. These developments led American Jews and liberals to shed their Cold War–induced reticence over the Holocaust. Other European countries were slower in coming to terms with this legacy, but the curtain of silence was no longer drawn.[19]

Together, these four trends nourished the budding transnational humanitarianism and delimited its features. But it was pitted against other developments in world politics. The international order that emerged after World War II affirmed the importance of human rights—at least on paper. The preamble to the United Nations (UN) Charter affirmed a faith in "fundamental human rights," and Article 1 stated that a prime purpose of the United Nations was "promoting and encouraging respect for human rights." However, Article 2 then muddied the waters: "Nothing contained in the present Charter shall authorize the United Nations to intervene in matters which are essentially within the domestic jurisdiction of any state." This tension in the Charter reflected the fact that the UN founders essentially saw it as an organization geared to coordinating and advancing the global interests of the Big Three: the United States, the Soviet Union, and Great Britain.[20]

The Cold War belied these hopes and vitiated further efforts to enshrine human rights in the state system. On 9 December 1948, the General Assembly adopted the Genocide Convention, which called for both the prevention and punishment of genocide. Although it came into effect in 1951 after ratification by a sufficient number of signatory states, the Convention remained toothless. For one thing, the United States did not ratify it until 1988, owing to the concern of Southern senators that it might be invoked against racial segregation.[21] So no moves were made toward establishing a standing international court to deal with prosecutions under the Convention. The Universal Declaration on Human Rights (UDHR) adopted by the General Assembly fared worse still. Even as the declaration was being drafted, the Big Three maneuvered behind the scenes to ensure that it was not binding. The British and the Americans were concerned about embarrassment over colonies and segregation, and Stalin was opposed to any effort to "turn the United Nations into a kind of world government placed above national sovereignty."[22]

This emphasis on sovereignty was echoed by the new states emerging out of colonial control with fresh memories of the humanitarian benevolence of the imperial powers. With the onset of decolonization, their burgeoning number led to the adoption in 1960 of a General Assembly declaration equating colonialism with the denial of human rights and insisting on self-determination as a component of human rights. The decolonized states also supported the Soviet Union's demand for incorporating economic and social rights into any definition of human rights. Redressing the physical, moral, and intellectual degradation of colonialism, they argued, was essential to enjoying other rights. However, representatives of the "Free World" led by the United States held that human rights should be restricted to civil and political rights. The ensuing divide led the United States to step back from the process of drafting a human rights covenant. Further, the draft covenant itself was split into two: one each on civil and political rights, and economic and social rights. These were adopted by the General Assembly in 1966, though they did not come into effect until a decade later. Importantly, both these covenants upheld the right to self-determination as the very first right. Sovereignty reigned supreme in the postcolonial age.[23]

The Third World's campaign had positive as well as negative outcomes. The foregrounding of racial and gender equality certainly advanced the cause of human rights. But their tireless advocacy of sovereignty and their insistence on the primacy of socioeconomic rights over individual rights did not bode well. For it coincided with a wave of authoritarianism that washed over the decolonized world. Between 1960 and 1969, there were twenty-six coups in Africa, and the situation in postcolonial Asia was only marginally better: Pakistan, Burma, and Indonesia slipped into authoritarian control. The new dictators invariably argued for the model of authoritarian modernization—a model that was pioneered by Ayub Khan of Pakistan under the approving and admiring eye of American social scientists.

The problematic dimensions of this turn taken by the postcolonial states were apparent at the first UN human rights conference, held in Tehran on the twentieth anniversary of the UDHR. Inaugurating the conference in April 1968, Shah Reza Pahlavi—another autocrat coddled by the United States—brazenly claimed, "While we still revere the principles laid down in the Universal Declaration, it is nevertheless necessary to adjust them to the requirements of our time."[24] The Proclamation issued by the conference stated that respect for human rights was "dependent upon sound and effective . . . economic and social development." Interestingly, the United States did not demur from this position. The

American delegation to the conference was in a defensive mode following the recent assassination of Martin Luther King Jr. Subsequently, under Richard Nixon the United States willingly worked with dictators in the Third World. Even as vice president in the Eisenhower administration, Nixon had been skeptical of the possibility of democracy in these countries. "The peoples of Africa," he once argued, "have been out of the trees only for about fifty years."[25]

Thus, by the early 1970s, there were two opposing sets of trends at work: the beginnings of a transnational humanitarianism, reflecting the incipient process of globalization; and the reification of sovereignty and derogation of human rights in international politics, flowing from the authoritarian turn in the postcolonial world. The tension between these was evident during the Biafran crisis of 1967–70, when humanitarian NGOs championed the Biafran cause but the United Nations and its member states refused to intervene in an internal affair of Nigeria's.[26] Biafra proved to be a curtain-raiser for Bangladesh. These contending global forces pulled the 1971 crisis in different directions, and the resulting torsions told on its development and denouement.

II

Within weeks of the military crackdown, Britain emerged as the focal point for efforts to rally international public opinion on behalf of Bangladesh. For one thing, the British media and humanitarian organizations had a greater interest in and closer ties to the Indian subcontinent than their counterparts elsewhere. More importantly, the United Kingdom hosted the largest community of Pakistani migrants, the overwhelming majority of whom were Bengalis from the Sylhet district of East Pakistan. Here again, the larger historical process of globalization intersected with the Bangladesh crisis: the presence of Bengali diasporas in the West being a prime example of another dimension of globalization, the circulation of labor. Indeed, the Bengali diasporas played a critical role in publicizing the cause of Bangladesh and in mobilizing political opinion against the Pakistan government.

The Bengali community in Britain quickly organized itself to work for the liberation movement and established contact with the Mujibnagar authorities. Links were forged with other humanitarian organizations, and the latter were continuously supplied with information about the plight of the Bengalis. The Bengali diaspora in Britain also raised substantial contributions from within the community and beyond. The bulk of these finances were used for assisting the victims, but some was diverted to procuring matériel for the freedom fighters.[27] Equally significant was the diaspora's decision to stop remitting money back home. By March 1971, overseas remittances had plunged to a third of the average monthly inflow for the first six months of the financial year. This, we may recall, contributed in no small measure to accentuating the liquidity crisis faced by Pakistan. The Bengali diaspora in other Western countries undertook similar activities, such as producing new reports and publicity documents, selling souvenirs and raising funds, organizing lectures and teach-ins. The diaspora in the United States was particularly active in lobbying Congress and supplying information to sympathetic senators and representatives.[28]

The efforts to mobilize international concern received a jump-start with the formation of Action Bangladesh by a group of young, internationalist, activist Britons. This umbrella organization brought together several assorted outfits, including Peace News, Peace Pledge Union, and the Young Liberals. Action Bangladesh was headed by thirty-year-old Paul Connett, a veteran of the pro-Biafra campaign, and by Marietta Procopi, a student of philosophy with a Bengali boyfriend. Their aims for the campaign were succinct: "Getting the Pakistani army out of East Bengali and relief in." Toward these ends, they launched a campaign aimed at bringing public pressure to bear on the parliament and government. Action Bangladesh sponsored a number of innovative advertisements, mostly full page, in leading newspapers. These blurred the line between purely humanitarian action and a human rights–oriented political campaign. An advertisement issued in the *Times* on 13 May 1971 carried the caption "This Is the Moment to Show That Man Is More Than 'An Internal Problem.'" The advertisement's text ran: "Tomorrow May 14th 1971 the House of Commons will debate the events taking place in Pakistan. Please cut this ad out, sign it and send it to your M.P. today . . . Call upon the British Government to suspend all aid to West Pakistan until its rulers remove their troops from East Bengal."[29]

A similar campaign was undertaken later in the year by Oxfam, one of Britain's most respected humanitarian organizations. Established in 1942, Oxfam had many firsts to its credit. It was the first European NGO that went global to aid humanitarian causes. It was the first humanitarian NGO that dispensed with the tradition of volunteerism and went professional. And it was the first to use the growing international media for promoting both its causes and itself. Like most humanitarian NGOs, Oxfam in its early years sought to steer clear of the human rights agenda, but adhering to that distinction became increasingly difficult. During the Biafra crisis, Oxfam not only developed a relief program but publicly supported the rebels, even at the risk of incurring the wrath of the Nigerian and British governments.

When the crisis broke in East Pakistan, Oxfam had already been involved in the relief efforts following the cyclone of December 1970. These efforts were coordinated by the office in the Indian state of Bihar, where Oxfam had been working for famine relief since the mid-1960s. Oxfam's assistant field director in Bihar, Alan Leather, had gotten to know well the veteran Gandhian activist Jayaprakash Narayan. Tipped off by Narayan about the torrential inflow of Bengali refugees, Leather set out for Calcutta in late April 1971 armed with a paltry sum of $10,000. The enormity of the problem floated into view only after he left the camps in Calcutta and traveled out toward the border. Leather reported to Oxford: "The first place we stopped was a small town between Krishnanagar and the border. All the talk about numbers and the state of some camps had not prepared me for suddenly finding 6,000 people clustered along verandas, under trees, around handpumps, queuing for food, ration cards, registration, spilling out of makeshift offices." At another halt, "we found that 13,000 had gathered at a site for a new camp. Here again there was no shelter, just a great mass of people waiting to be fed."[30]

Overcoming its initial incredulity at the scale of the problem, Oxfam headquarters swung into action. It took the lead in reviving the Disaster Emergency Committee (DEC), a consortium of humanitarian NGOs—originally formed in 1963 for cyclone relief in Ceylon—that was composed of Oxfam, War on Want, Save the Children Fund, Christian Aid, and the Red Cross Society. In July 1971, DEC mounted an appeal that raised over £1 million in Britain alone. Initially Oxfam concentrated on filling critical gaps in the provision of relief, such as acquiring Land Rovers for workers to reach far-flung camps and administering cholera vaccine. From July onward, Oxfam focused its efforts on five areas where over 500,000 refugees were located, supplementing the rations provided by the Indian government with additional medical care, sanitation, clean water, child feeding, clothing, and shelter.[31]

Between July and October 1971, Oxfam spent £350,000 to supply the program and maintain its teams. By the end of August, Oxfam headquarters realized that it would need an additional £120,000 a month to continue its work with the refugees. The communications director, Philip Jackson, felt that an attempt must be made to rouse the world's conscience, but Oxfam's director, Leslie Kirkley, was concerned that they might be accused—as in the case of Biafra—of taking an overtly political line. After a round of consultations with editors of newspapers and television news programs, Kirkley decided to launch a high-profile media campaign. Advertisements were placed in the press, carrying coupons that could be sent to members of the British parliament: "I add my plea that the United Nations use the power invested in it to press for an urgent political solution to the Pakistan problem and immediately organize the relief programme desperately needed to avert further suffering."[32] The public response exceeded Oxfam's expectations. The Oxfam headquarters noted that "HLK [Kirkley] was phoned by an MP [member of parliament] last week that they are being besieged by signed copies of the Oxfam advertisement. They are having to work until all hours of the night to acknowledge them and their Secretaries are threatening to go on strike!"[33]

Oxfam's campaign climaxed with the publication of an unusual document titled *Testimony of Sixty,* which contained short statements and articles by fifty prominent public figures, including Mother Teresa and US senator Edward Kennedy. These punchy pieces were accompanied by poignant photographs of the refugees. In the opening statement, Kirkley sought to strike a balance, highlighting both the humanitarian and human rights dimensions of the problem. Thus, he asked the world community to contribute to the relief operations, but he also wrote that the crisis was "a story of millions, hounded, homeless and dying. It is, too, a story of the world community engaged in a communal ostrich act." Kirkley called on Pakistan to "create conditions genuinely compatible with the return of refugees to their homes."[34]

Oxfam headquarters also rallied to its banner Oxfam franchises and NGO partners, especially church organizations, across the globe. In late September 1971, the chairman of Oxfam Council, Michael Rowntree, went to New York to lobby at the UN General Assembly. He drew a blank. In fact, a group of twenty-two international NGOs—including the International Commission of Jurists, the International Federation for the Rights of Man, and the Women's International League for Peace and Freedom—that had consultative status with the UN Economic and Social Council (ECOSOC) had already attempted to petition the United Nations. In July, they had requested that ECOSOC's Subcommission on

Prevention of Discrimination and Protection of Minorities act on "the reports of gross violations of human rights and fundamental freedoms occurring in East Pakistan." They had also demanded the appointment of a working group to "review communications on human rights regarding the situation in East Pakistan"; to recommend measures "to protect the human rights and fundamental freedoms" of the Bengalis; and to consider the extent to which the developments in East Pakistan might be relevant to the subcommission's studies on "minorities, indigenous populations and genocide."[35] The UN system, as we shall see, remained impervious to such pleas.

Similar appeals had been made by international organizations across the world. The Commission of the Churches on International Affairs issued a statement in July expressing concern over the plight of the Bengalis and urging their member churches to influence their own governments to press Pakistan toward a just political settlement. The Pugwash Conference held in August asked Pakistan to create conditions for a peaceful political settlement and for the return of refugees to their homes. The Latin American Parliament at Caracas adopted a resolution on 27 August calling on Pakistan to desist from further violations of human rights and to enter into immediate negotiations with the elected representatives of East Pakistan. The resolution itself was prompted by a humanitarian appeal issued by twenty-nine leading Latin American intellectuals and artists, including Victoria Ocampo and Jorge Luis Borges.[36]

III

Above all, the crisis in East Pakistan was inscribed on the global imagination by the Concert for Bangladesh. The concert was conceived by the famous Indian musician Pandit Ravi Shankar, a Bengali from West Bengal who lived in Hollywood, California. When Ravi Shankar learned of the massive flow of refugees into India, some of his own distant relatives included, his sympathies were immediately with Bangladesh, and he was anxious to help the refugees, especially the children. Ravi Shankar wrote several songs in Bengali, including "Joi Bangla," and he cut a record with Apple Records. However, given the scale of the humanitarian crisis, the meagre profits from the sales of his record could hardly help. Realizing that something larger was needed, in late May 1971 Ravi Shankar suggested to his friend George Harrison the idea of a charity concert.[37]

Harrison readily agreed. Though it had been over a year since the Beatles had broken up, he knew that he could leverage "the fame of the Beatles." John Lennon, he recalled, had "made me more aware of . . . that aspect of using the Beatle power."[38] Harrison spent the next six weeks drawing up a list of musicians for the concert, calling the potential performers, and cashing in favors. The concert was scheduled for 1 August 1971 at Madison Square Garden in New York, the only date when the venue was available. It left them very little time for rehearsals.

A more pressing concern was whether the ensemble would actually come together for the concert. Harrison had sought to bring together the brightest stars in the rock music firmament of the period, including John Lennon, Ringo Starr, Eric Clapton, Bob Dylan, Billy Preston, and Leon Russell. A week before the event, Lennon told Harrison that he would not be able to make it after all. Clapton, too, proved elusive. Though he was booked on almost every flight from London to New York for the week preceding the concert, he did not show up until the day before—then he failed to show up for the last rehearsal, arriving only in time for the concert's sound check. Clapton at the time was going through an intense phase of drug addiction: Harrison observed hours before the concert, "He's pretty messed up. Somebody is finding some heroin to give him as soon as he arrives."[39] Throughout the concert, Clapton could barely open his eyes, but he played every number like the genius that he was.

The other major star was Bob Dylan. Harrison was understandably eager to have him on stage. The Beatles and Dylan had had a musical relationship dating back to the mid-1960s. Indeed, the Beatles had revived Dylan's interest in rhythm and blues, a genre with which he had grown up but later abandoned for folk music. In turn, Dylan's songs, which memorably captured the antiwar zeitgeist of the Sixties, had taught the Beatles to combine their music with poetic lyrics, and to regard rock 'n' roll as an art form that gave utterance to the deepest feelings of their generation.[40] Although Dylan had agreed to appear at the concert, Harrison could not take it for granted; after all, the famously reclusive Dylan had given a pass to the iconic Woodstock festival. Dylan turned up the day before the concert, but he was apprehensive about performing before such a large crowd and a phalanx of video cameras. Harrison could heave a sigh of relief only when he saw the diminutive Dylan shuffle onstage with his trademark acoustic guitar and harmonica rack.

The announcement of the concert triggered a tidal wave of enthusiasm from fans across the globe. For this star-sprinkled event came at a time when rock 'n' roll had hit a trough. The leading voices of rock seemed to have gone silent: the Beatles had split up and were not performing even individually, and Dylan had not put out an original record since *Nashville Skyline* in April 1969. More worryingly, the seamy side of the Sixties counterculture had crept to the fore: the deaths of Jimi Hendrix and Janis Joplin underlined the pervasiveness of drugs in the music industry; and the violence, vandalism, and mayhem of the infamous Altamont Speedway Free Festival organized by the Rolling Stones in December 1969 in California had ripped open the ugly underbelly of rock 'n' roll. So the Concert for Bangladesh was not only assembling an unrivaled array of talent, but it was also supporting a cause that evoked the best spirit of the Sixties.

There was no mistaking the message of the concert. By invoking the name of "Bangladesh" and by refusing the more cautious alternative of "East Pakistan" or "East Bengal," Ravi Shankar and George Harrison laid bare their political sympathies. In a press conference, Harrison observed that "awareness is even more important the money." He would later write that "you can feed somebody today and tomorrow they will still be hungry, but if they are getting massacred you've got to try and stop that first of all."[41] The media coverage in the run-up to the conference reflected their concerns. A television reporter covering the crowds lining up for tickets noted that the concert was for "relief of refugee children of the holocaust in East Pakistan," and some fans confirmed they were "really into this East Pakistan thing."[42]

The scale of public enthusiasm led Harrison to organize two back-to-back concerts on the afternoon and evening of 1 August. The concert program was framed by two special compositions. Ravi Shankar and Ali Akbar Khan opened with a sitar-and-sarod duet called the "Bangla Dhun." Ravi Shankar began by observing that the concert was "not just a programme but . . . has a message. We are not trying to make any politics. We are artistes. But through our music we would like you to feel the agony, and also the pain, and a lot of sad happenings in Bangladesh, and also [of] the refugees who have come to India." Harrison's closing composition, "Bangla Desh," spoke for itself. Although the refrain of the song was "relieve Bangladesh," Harrison began by referring to his friend's country "where so many people are dying fast." The audiences were left in little doubt that the Bangladesh crisis was a political as well as humanitarian tragedy.

The concert was successful beyond the imagination of Ravi Shankar and Harrison. They had initially hoped to raise about $20,000, but they ended up with close to $250,000, which was funneled for relief efforts through the United Nations International Children's Emergency Fund (UNICEF). The impact of the event reverberated well beyond the venue. Not only did it attract wide coverage in newsprint, but images from the concert also were broadcast by television channels across the world. A boxed three-record set released soon after the concert climbed to the top of the charts across the world. The original cover of the album, which featured the photograph of an emaciated child sitting in front of an empty plate, became an iconic image of Bangladesh.[43] The notes accompanying the album held the Pakistan army responsible for "a deliberate reign of terror" and for perpetrating "undoubtedly the greatest atrocity since Hitler's extermination of the Jews."[44]

The medium and the message were perfectly matched. David Puttnam, filmmaker and later head of UNICEF in Britain, was in Madison Square Garden that evening. Decades later, he would observe that the Concert of Bangladesh showed that "the dreams of the Sixties could be realised."[45] Whether or not this was true, it certainly captured the contemporary feelings of his generation. The public impact of the concert can be gauged from the fact that the Pakistan government warned all its embassies and missions that the concert album "contains hostile propaganda against Pakistan" and that they should work their contacts "to have this excluded from broadcasts." For good measure, the record was officially banned in Pakistan.[46]

The concert was not, however, the only way in which the countercultural currents percolated into the Bangladesh crisis. Other iconic figures took up the cause of their own volition. Prominent among these was Joan Baez, whose songs had spoken to the concerns of her times even before her friend Bob Dylan had come on the scene. A committed Gandhian who had marched with Martin Luther King Jr., Baez was the most politically aware and morally sensitive artiste of her times.[47] Her music expressed solidarity at various points with causes and victims in North Vietnam, Argentina, Cambodia, Soviet Union, Czechoslovakia, Poland, and South Africa. In the last week of July 1971, Baez performed at Stanford University before an audience of 12,000.[48] At another huge concert at the University of Michigan, she sang the "Song for Bangladesh." Baez's song was an inspired attempt at portraying the Bangladesh crisis both as the latest instance of the international community's continued apathy to massive abuses of human rights and as a dastardly deed by Pakistan's military regime. Thus, she sang of the world standing aside and watching "families crucified" for the old principle on which nations were founded: "to sacrifice a people for a land." The song also referred graphically to the army's attack on the Dhaka University campus on the night of 26 March 1971: soldiers shooting students in cold blood and "pillows drenched in red." Baez's concerts may not have commanded the audience that Harrison and Ravi Shankar did, but her politically charged lyrics left a deep imprint on legions of fans and admirers across the world.

During the same period, Allen Ginsberg, the Beat poet and friend of Bob Dylan, also took a trip to India—a country that he had introduced to a generation of Westerners who came of age in the Sixties. During his previous passage to India, Ginsberg had befriended a group of radical intellectuals and writers in West Bengal led by the poet Sunil Gangopadhyay. On 9 September 1971, Ginsberg and Gangopadhyay traveled out on the Jessore Road from Calcutta to see the refugee camps near the East Pakistan border. At the border town of Bongaon, Ginsberg was shocked to hear from a local voluntary organization that "food is generally given to the destitute just on Thursday . . . The ration is being distributed once in a week." As they went along, Ginsberg recited his immediate impressions into a tape recorder: "Straw shops by the roadside waiting for food all day. Smells of shit and food and bidis. Heavy rain, cholera epidemic. A man standing on the road with a many-pronged spear. Tensions between poor residents and refugees. 'You are behaving like a lord,' the refugees complain to the poor villagers. 'The refugees are shitting on our lawns,' the residents complain."[49]

On returning home, Ginsberg wrote a poem "September on Jessore Road," which was published in the *New York Times* on 14 November 1971.[50] In his brilliant, idiosyncratic style, Ginsberg vividly described his journey on Jessore Road: the procession of refugees walking toward Calcutta, the squalor of the refugee camps, the children with distended bellies queuing up for food, and the infants dying of dysentery. America's apathy toward the humanitarian crisis was juxtaposed with its involvement elsewhere in Asia. Why were the US Air Force and Navy not delivering aid and relief? Busy "Bombing North Laos" and "Napalming North Vietnam." The poem ended with a call for "tongues of the world" and "voices for love" to ring in "the conscious American brain."

Ginsberg's poem, like the songs of Harrison and Baez, strummed the conscience of global opinion, particularly in the Western world, by braiding Bangladesh with the causes espoused by young protesters around the world. For a few months in 1971, Bangladesh seemed to distill all the hopes and fears of the Swinging Sixties.

IV

Although Bangladesh became the poster child of a globalizing world, it remained a pariah in the international system of states. The United Nations had been bound up with the crisis almost from the outset. On 29 March 1971, the Indian permanent representative at the United Nations, Samar Sen, handed a demarche to Secretary-General U Thant stating that India was "greatly shocked by the brutality with which the Pakistan army is suppressing the struggle for legitimate rights and aspirations of the majority of the people of Pakistan." The emphasis on the Bengalis as the majority in Pakistan was important, for India wished to differentiate this crisis from the Biafran precedent. Expressing India's "very strong feelings in the matter," the demarche made three formal requests: "Initiative of the Secretary-General to stop the mass butchery," arrangements to send an International Red Cross team to East Pakistan, and organization of relief "for expected large scale refugees" in the eastern states of India.[51]

U Thant had recently announced that he did not want a third term as the secretary-general. During his decade in office, he had dealt with several international conflicts—including those in Cyprus and the Middle East—and humanitarian disasters. But the crisis that was unfolding in the subcontinent was of an altogether more complex nature than anything he had previously handled. U Thant told Sen the following day that "I am never neutral on humanitarian issues . . . But I have often encountered two insuperable obstacles." The first was the claim of governments that "the Secretary-General has no right to interfere in their internal affairs or in matters pertaining to their national sovereignty." The second was the "lack of authoritative information without which the Secretary-General cannot speak without incurring the risk of being accused of prejudice," which was "one of the major challenges" for the secretary-general. The latter issue had, in the past, dented his "prestige in one segment or another of world public opinion." In consequence, his ability to act was "dependent on the facts of the situation" and was circumscribed by "what is granted to me by the consent of Member Governments." He asked India to approach the Red Cross directly, and he agreed to convey the Red Cross's request to the UN High Commissioner for Refugees.[52]

The secretary-general's unwillingness to climb the bully pulpit led Sen to circulate the Indian demarche as a press release on 31 March. Pakistan's response confirmed U Thant's observation. Indeed, it appears to have been drafted keeping in mind the secretary-general's confidential reply to India. It was "deplorable that India, while professing allegiance to the United Nations Charter, is attempting to demolish one of its cornerstones by flouting the principle of non-interference in the internal affairs of Member States." Pakistan claimed that India was already interfering in its internal affairs by a "virulent propaganda campaign," by adopting a parliamentary resolution on East Pakistan, by dispatching arms and fighters, and by deploying six divisions of her army on the borders with East Pakistan. The military action had been undertaken "to prevent the disintegration of the country" and the government was working to bring the democratic process back on track.[53]

However, the other "major challenge" invoked by U Thant was by no means insurmountable. On 19 April, he received a secret report from K. Wolff, the deputy resident representative of the UN Development Program (UNDP) for East Pakistan. The report contained a balanced and perceptive résumé of the crisis up to 4 April, when Wolff and his colleagues had left Dhaka. After detailing the course of events leading to the crackdown, Wolff observed, "In retrospect, it would seem that there was never any intention by the Army or by the Central Government to agree to autonomy for East Pakistan. It can be assumed that the negotiations were carried on and protracted chiefly in order to enable the Army to build up its strength in East Pakistan." The report then described the brutal "warlike" campaign launched by the army against the populace. "At midnight the Army moved into Dacca full strength and 30 hours of heavy shooting, shelling and burning followed . . . There were innumerable fires and almost all the quarters . . . of the poorest people were intentionally burned down by the Army. No living thing could be found in these burned quarters afterwards . . . Army trucks loaded with the dead bodies of civilians have been seen by UN personnel." Estimating the number of deaths after two days of shooting in Dhaka was "difficult, if not impossible." The Nepalese consul-general, who was also the doyen of the diplomatic corps in Dhaka, had toured the city on 28 March and told Wolff that "his conservative estimate would be between 5,000 and 7,000 civilians killed." A professor at the University of Dhaka had suggested a death toll of about 25,000.[54]

Wolff believed that while the army might be able to bring the major towns under control, "it is unlikely that it will be able to control the whole country." "All in all," he wrote, "a military solution to East Pakistan problem would seem impossible." Only a political solution involving negotiations with Mujib and the grant of "a large measure of autonomy" could preserve the bonds between the two wings of Pakistan. Wolff further argued that Pakistan "will not be in a position, militarily or economically, to carry on the present situation for any length of time." Hence, all foreign assistance—military or economic—should be "stopped immediately." "The UN," he urged, "could set an example in this respect." Nevertheless, planning and preparation to deal with famine and epidemic should be undertaken. The UNDP, he concluded, could do this with the major donor countries "without being physically present in East Pakistan."[55]

On receiving this paper, U Thant ordered a legal study on the kinds of action that could be taken when confronted with an internal conflict. The legal counsel's advice cast into sharp relief the conservatism of the UN machinery. The counsel acknowledged that "in view of the seriousness of the situation in East Pakistan . . . it is difficult for the Secretary-General . . . to remain entirely silent." Nevertheless, his reading of what the secretary-general could do was rather narrow. Article 2 of the UN Charter precluded intervention in domestic matters, but "there has undoubtedly been a development in recent years where it has been accepted that offers of *humanitarian assistance* in cases of internal armed conflict does not come within the prohibition of Article 2." The question of whether the secretary-general could speak out against gross violations of human rights enshrined in the Charter and the Declaration was not even raised—let alone answered. The Counsel advised U Thant to send "a personal and confidential letter to the President of Pakistan offering humanitarian assistance."[56]

U Thant wrote to Yahya the next day, affirming that the events in East Pakistan fell strictly within the domestic jurisdiction of Pakistan under Article 2. Nonetheless, "prompted purely by humanitarian considerations," U Thant believed that "the United Nations and its specialized agencies have a most useful role to play, with the consent of your government, in providing emergency assistance." Yahya replied a week later dismissing U Thant's suggestion, and saying that the gravity of the situation in East Pakistan had been greatly exaggerated. The Pakistan government had completed its own assessment of the requirements: "international assistance, if and when required, will be administered by Pakistani relief agencies."[57]

Yahya's brusque rebuff discomfited Washington. Nixon and Kissinger believed that Pakistan could do with international relief assistance and that by declining the offer Yahya risked inviting the opprobrium of other states. Secretary of State William Rogers encouraged U Thant to persevere with his efforts in securing Pakistan's acceptance, and simultaneously the US ambassador to Pakistan, Joseph Farland, urged Yahya to "take the constructive step of personally issuing a statement to the effect that GOP [Government of Pakistan] was seized with the matter of international humanitarian relief assistance."[58] On 22 May, Yahya sent a message to U Thant requesting "at least 250,000 tons" of food aid and 100,000 tons of edible oil as a grant from the UN's World Food Programme. Pakistan was prepared to accept the help of UN personnel with the planning and organization of relief. Yahya also expressed his willingness to receive a representative of the secretary-general to serve as a "focal point," but only "on the understanding that his role and activities would be within the framework of humanitarian assistance."[59]

U Thant was glad to comply with this stipulation. His special representative, Ismat Kittani, met the Pakistani president in Rawalpindi on 4 June. Kittani assured him of the "purely humanitarian character" of the secretary-general's offer and sought Islamabad's cooperation. Yahya was a font of reasonableness. "I found the President most receptive and personally warm," Kittani wrote to U Thant. "He readily agreed to every single thought and proposal from me." After this fawning encounter, Kittani prepared a press release on his meetings with Pakistani officials, taking care to ensure that the text was cleared by his hosts. "The [Pakistan] Government considers this very desirable," he observed without a trace of irony.[60]

In the meantime, Yahya had become amenable to the appeal from the UN High Commissioner for Refugees (UNHCR), Prince Sadruddin Aga Khan. An urbane and cosmopolitan Iranian aristocrat—his nephew Karim Aga Khan was the leader of the Ismaili sect of Shia Muslims—Sadruddin had been in his post since 1966. As an admiring subordinate would later recall, "He was willing to take risks and make big bets in the cause of a long-term vision. He rarely deviated from the strategic direction he set himself."[61] These qualities, alas, were not evident in his approach to the Bangladesh crisis. Like many senior UN functionaries, Sadruddin was wary of making any move that might smack of violating Pakistan's sovereignty. What was more, he was averse to turning the spotlight on the causes of the refugee flow and was content to merely tend to the needs of the victims.

In mid-June 1971, Sadruddin visited Pakistan as well as India to offer the UNHCR's services. He was apparently encouraged by Yahya's announcement that all bona fide Pakistani refugees in India could return to Pakistan. Speaking to the press after his trip, Sadruddin observed that he had discussed "purely on a humanitarian basis with Pakistan the modalities of the return of refugees" and had received their "full co-operation." He said that the East Pakistan authorities had kindly organized a trip for him by helicopter, and that the aerial tour had been admittedly limited but "in these parts he could see that life was slowly returning to normal." Sadruddin acknowledged in passing that the refugee flow was "closely correlated to the need for a political solution," but stressed that his mission was "purely humanitarian with nothing to do with the political aspects." His Indian interlocutors held rather a different view. They insisted that "the refugees could not stay in India . . . There was no question of . . . their rehabilitation in India."[62]

In fact, India had categorically refused to accept the UNHCR's presence beyond New Delhi. This, New Delhi felt, would impart an aura of permanence to the refugee camps. Furthermore, it would deflect the international community's focus from the task of tackling the root cause of the problem within Pakistan. After considering various options, India made the camps accessible to foreign journalists and observers so that they could highlight the plight of the refugees.[63]

Sadruddin, however, took a jaundiced view of India's stance. When speaking with Secretary Rogers the day after his press conference, Sadruddin said that India's refusal to station UNHCR personnel in the camps reflected its "desire [to] protect cross border infiltration from international view." According to him, not only was India seeking to shield its support for the Bengali rebels, but India's stand on the refugees was inconsistent. "On the one hand, India complains about [the] presence of six million refugees and insists they must return and on the other hand it imposes conditions (negotiations with Mujib, etc.) for their return." Sadruddin emphasized that India "seems uninterested in repatriation [of refugees]. It is important that India not insist upon political solution as prior conditions for return of refugees." Indira Gandhi had been very "hawkish" in their meeting, and she had sought to impress upon him the seriousness of the situation, saying "we may have to resort to other means." As for Yahya Khan, Sadruddin had found him as congenial as had the White House. The pressures on Yahya, he said, were "very great"; "he is not happy about army actions in East Pakistan and agreed that actions against Hindus were unfortunate."[64]

Faced with the solicitude of high UN officials for the domestic jurisdiction of Pakistan and pressure to maintain an ostensibly neutral stance on the crisis, U Thant sought to assuage his conscience by initiating a private attempt to bring about a political settlement in Pakistan. After reading Wolff's report, U Thant wrote secretly to Tunku Abdul Rahman, the former prime minister of Malaysia who was now secretary-general of the Islamic Conference of Foreign Ministers, asking him to facilitate a political solution in Pakistan. U Thant was anxious, however, that he should not be associated with this initiative in any manner. Tunku felt that "tempers were still too hot for any chance of success,"[65] but he made the attempt. It took him three months to approach Yahya and another month to meet with Indira Gandhi. In early September 1971, he gave up. That abortive venture's sole outcome was that it allowed U Thant to claim the moral high ground in his memoirs.[66]

It is hardly surprising therefore that India's attempts to highlight the brutalities perpetrated by the Pakistan army failed to stir the United Nations. India sought to persuade other countries to raise the issue in a meeting of the Economic and Social Council, which was charged with advancing the cause of human rights. The response of Britain was typical: while Britain did "recognize the competence of the Economic and Social Council (ECOSOC) of the United Nations to discuss the matter," it had decided that "we should not seek to raise it ourselves."[67] So India decided to raise the matter: invoking the Universal Declaration and the Geneva Conventions, Samar Sen requested that the ECOSOC's opinion be "expressed in no uncertain manner," insisting that "international conscience must be roused and international effort must be made to restore some semblance of civilised existence in this part of the world." Five days later, Sen reiterated that the Pakistan government should be asked "to restore human rights to the people of Pakistan . . . in accordance with the international obligations and declarations that Government have subscribed to or supported."[68]

These appeals fell on stony ground. Pakistan predictably responded that "a sovereign state has the right to suppress secession," referring for good measure to the American Civil War as an honorable precedent. The only country that came out in support of India's stance was New Zealand, Pakistan's ally in the Southeast Asia Treaty Organization (SEATO), whose delegate insisted that "violations of human rights wherever they occur on a scale that could call into question the obligations of Member States under the Charter may be discussed in the relevant United Nations bodies."[69]

This situation persisted in the next session of the ECOSOC held in July 1971. The member states confined themselves to praising India's relief efforts and calling for the return of the refugees and maintenance of restraint. A report on the refugee crisis submitted by the UNHCR was dispatched to the General Assembly without any debate. Other UN bodies were no more responsive to the gross abuses by the Pakistan army. The Committee on Elimination of Racial Discrimination, which had been in place since 1969, met in April and September 1971 without paying much attention to the events in East Pakistan. The Subcommission on Prevention of Discrimination of Minorities—a part of the ECOSOC's Human Rights Commission—met between 2 and 20 August 1971 but chose not to take up the case of East Pakistan. The Pakistani delegate invoked domestic jurisdiction, and the other member states, particularly the United States, China, and the Arab and African states, agreed that they should not discuss "political" issues.[70]

U Thant might have been chary of infringing on Pakistan's sovereignty, but he could not shut his eyes to the worsening crisis, which seemed pregnant with the possibility of war. After all, upkeep of international peace and security was the primary mission of the secretary-general. After consultations with Sadruddin, he wrote formally to India and Pakistan underlining the importance of repatriating the refugees and requesting them to permit "a limited representation of the High Commissioner for Refugees on both sides of the border."[71] U Thant also took the unusual step of presenting a memorandum on this issue to the Security Council. In the ongoing crisis, he wrote, "humanitarian, economic and political problems are mingled in such a way as almost to defy any distinction between them." This did not mean that U Thant was moved by the violation of human rights—indeed, he claimed that it was "all too easy to make moral judgments." Mainly, he was concerned about the possible consequences of the crisis "not only in the humanitarian sense, but also as a potential threat to peace and security." This was the aspect underscored in his submission: "Border clashes, clandestine raids, and acts of sabotage appear to be becoming more frequent." He urged the Security Council to attempt not only "to mitigate the human tragedy which has already taken place" but also "to avert the further deterioration of the situation."[72]

The secretary-general's assumption that the human tragedy had run its course was startling, but it was entirely in keeping with his approach to the crisis. The Security Council ignored his message. The Indian government, however, took a dim view of the steps initiated by U Thant. New Delhi responded to his suggestion for posting UN observers on the borders with a blistering missive. "The chaos and the systematic military repression and the decimation of the Bengali-speaking people continue unabated." India was receiving forty to fifty thousand refugees every day, and under these circumstances was "unable to understand what purpose the posting of a few men on the Indian side of the border will fulfil . . . they can in no way help or encourage the refugees to return home . . . it would only provide a façade of action to divert world attention from the root cause of the problem which is the continuation of military atrocities." Further, India "resent[ed] any insinuation that they are preventing the refugees from returning to East Bengal" and was "most anxious" that they should go back, but "as a first step, conditions must be created in East Bengal to prevent the further arrival of refugees into India." This could only be done "through a political settlement acceptable to the people of East Bengal and their already elected leaders."[73] India's refusal to accept observers led Pakistan to reject them as well.[74] So there the matter rested until war clouds unmistakably gathered over the subcontinent.

7

POWER AND PRINCIPLE

"I am fully convinced about the total ineffectiveness of the UN organization," said Swaran Singh, "whether they are [*sic*] political, social or human rights. They talk and talk and do nothing." The foreign minister was addressing heads of Indian missions in Europe in mid-June 1971. The response of the United Nations came as no surprise to India. New Delhi was certain that the United Nations would switch to the default mode of viewing this crisis as yet another manifestation of India-Pakistan hostility. Indeed, from India's standpoint the principal reason for engaging with the United Nations was to avoid being outflanked by Pakistan in that forum.[1]

The minister was preaching to the converted. The Indian ambassador to France, Dwarka Nath Chatterjee, held, for instance, that if India sought a solution to the crisis, then "the United Nation is to be avoided." The UN General Assembly was dominated by the Third World, where "a great number of these countries are suspicious of democracy, human rights etc. They have had long practice at suppressing them at home . . . The United Nations as a body will tend to preserve the *status quo*." Besides, the great powers that dominated the UN Security Council "have committed, at one time or the other, massacres of adequate dimensions. The records of Russia and America are sufficiently impressive . . . They all have skeletons in their cupboards and they continue to add to the collection."[2]

India, therefore, channeled its diplomatic energies toward bilaterally engaging important countries. From the end of May to July 1971, practically every member of the Indian cabinet was sent as a special envoy to canvass the support of key countries. These missions covered all the major West European, Scandinavian, East European, and Southeast

Asian countries as well as Japan and the major Muslim states of West Asia and North Africa. In addition, the government encouraged Jay-aprakash ("JP") Narayan to undertake an independent international tour and rouse the conscience of the major powers, acting as "a sort of informal John the Baptist."[3] In six weeks starting from mid-May 1971, Narayan traveled to no fewer than sixteen countries in Europe, Asia, and North America. The results were not encouraging.[4] The only consolation for this erstwhile socialist was the opportunity to visit Lenin's mausoleum in Moscow, where he paid tearful homage.[5]

The stances adopted by the major powers were intricate tessellations of interests and expedience, power and principle—or the lack thereof. Yet their reactions did not fall into any predictable pattern. For the major powers' responses to the evolving crisis were shaped and constrained by globalizing trends in the emerging transnational public sphere and by other developments that were diminishing the salience of the bipolar Cold War dynamic of an earlier period. The lineup of the major powers in the Bangladesh crisis was hardly predetermined.

I

Among the Asian countries that India contacted, Japan was the power that counted most and was the most understanding of the plight of the Bengalis. Yet Tokyo's response underscored the limitations of India's efforts to channel international pressure on Pakistan. The Japanese told the visiting Indian minister of education (and a confidant of Indira Gandhi), Siddhartha Shankar Ray, that the crisis was no longer an internal matter of Pakistan but an international problem. "It was necessary to find a political solution through discussion with Mujibur Rahman though it would be difficult." Although Japan realized that ultimately an independent Bangladesh "was bound to emerge," it had "very little influence with Pakistan." Japanese officials assured Ray that they would give no further aid to Pakistan, but were unwilling to state their views publicly and hoped that "the U.N. could be brought in to find a solution."[6] Even so, the Japanese were vocal in the discussions of the Pakistan Consortium, and they were increasingly willing to defy the wishes of the United States. After the shock administered to Tokyo by Kissinger's secret visit to Beijing, the Japanese were growing wary of China's enlarging clout in Asia. On the one hand, Tokyo wished to avert any conflict on the subcontinent that carried the possibility of Chinese intervention. On the other, Japan had little desire to palliate Pakistan, one of China's key allies. The smaller Asia powers echoed Japan's ambivalence.[7]

The Eastern European countries took their cue from the Soviet Union. Thus, Poland and Czechoslovakia expressed their sympathies for the refugee problem facing India, but they refused to acknowledge either the strength of the resistance movement or the necessity for a political solution involving the creation of an independent state.[8] Interestingly, the only Soviet bloc country that took a different tack was East Germany, the German Democratic Republic (GDR).

At the time, East Germany had no formal diplomatic ties with New Delhi, although it had had trade missions in India since 1954.[9] The East German stance on the crisis was driven by its long-standing desire to secure full diplomatic recognition from India. In the second week of April 1971, the East German representative in Calcutta anticipated the proclamation of independence by the provisional government of Bangladesh.[10] East Germany moved swiftly to establish contact with the Mujibnagar authorities.

The following month, East Germany not only invited the foreign minister of the Bangladesh exile government to visit East Berlin, but received him with all the protocol due the representative of a sovereign state. By dangling the prospect of diplomatic recognition for Bangladesh, East Germany sought to coax India into formally recognizing East Germany as a quid pro quo. As the East German foreign minister, Otto Wintzer, would later tell the Soviet foreign minister, Andrei Gromyko, East Berlin sought "to make progress in establishing diplomatic relations with India, through the process of recognizing Bangla Desh."[11] Toward the end of July 1971, Rehman Sobhan, the special emissary of Mujibnagar, met with the East German consul-general in New Delhi and offered full diplomatic recognition for East Germany in exchange for military and economic aid. Sobhan also mentioned that this move had been cleared by India, which did not want to be the first country to recognize Bangladesh.[12] New Delhi, for its part, welcomed East German offers of political as well as humanitarian aid, but sought to leverage East Germany's willingness to ingratiate itself with India by reaching out to the Bengalis. The Indian minister of tourism and civil aviation, Karan Singh, visited East Berlin in June 1971, but he politely brushed aside his hosts' requests for diplomatic recognition, stating that his visit was merely a small step on the long road to recognition.[13]

II

India's stance on the question of recognizing East Germany stemmed from the desire to not antagonize West Germany. The Federal Republic of Germany (FRG) had for two decades insisted that India, like the other countries, should refrain from formally recognizing another German state.[14] India had gone along with this owing to both the importance of economic ties with West Germany and the desire to avoid compromising its nonaligned stance. Nevertheless, Prime Minister Jawaharlal Nehru's unwillingness to criticize the construction of the Berlin Wall had led Bonn to nurture ties with Islamabad. During the 1965 Indo-Pakistan war, West Germany had made few efforts to conceal its sympathies with Pakistan. In the aftermath of that war, Bonn had gone on to sign two major defense deals with Islamabad to supply fighter aircraft and tanks. When the fighters began arriving in Pakistan, Indira Gandhi put the West German leadership on notice.

Relations between New Delhi and Bonn began to improve only after the election of a coalition government led by Christian Democrat Chancellor Kurt Georg Kiesinger and Social Democrat Foreign Minister Willy Brandt. Both men were known friends of India. Brandt had made a strong impression on Nehru and Indira Gandhi, owing to his personal credentials as an anti-Nazi resistance fighter and his eagerness to normalize West Germany's relations with its eastern neighbors. Brandt's election as chancellor in 1969 was warmly welcomed in India. His subsequent efforts to achieve a détente with the East European countries—the Ostpolitik—fit well with Mrs. Gandhi's policy toward these countries and the Soviet Union. In consequence, India avoided making any moves toward East Germany that might embarrass Brandt. As Mrs. Gandhi would tell Brandt during their meeting in November 1971, "For the first time since the Weimar Republic there was a government in Germany led by the Social Democrats, and therefore India would avoid everything that might create problems for this government."[15]

New Delhi sought, in turn, to stem the flow of military aid from West Germany to Pakistan. After the outbreak of the Bangladesh crisis, India added the cessation of West German economic aid to Pakistan to its wish list. Briefing Secretary of State Frank Paul on the crisis the Indian ambassador to Bonn, Kewal Singh, requested that West Germany "exert pressure on the government of Pakistan and persuade them to cease the use of military measures, by withholding the development aid grants." Paul conveyed his government's admiration for India's restraint and its willingness to contribute to humanitarian relief, but he emphasized that "the Federal government will at the very least adopt a discrete stance on the India-Pakistan conflict, if not a neutral one." India, he advised the ambassador, "must be anxious not to intensify the existing problems between the two countries and also not to disregard the difficulties posed by the stance taken by China and the Soviet Union."[16]

By early June, Bonn feared that "the refugee problem may force India to seize the bull by the horns and take the initiative in the form of a military intervention." The only hope was that India would bear in mind the larger consequences of a military intervention in East Pakistan: "Logic and reason speak against it." Nevertheless, the West Germans concluded with more than a touch of Orientalism that "in Asia sober deliberations are often clouded by emotions."[17] When Swaran Singh visited Bonn a few days later, he found that West Germany's position was gradually evolving. In meetings with Foreign Minister Walter Scheel and Chancellor Brandt, he sought "international pressure on the Pakistan government so that the refugee influx stops, and a political environment is established in East Pakistan that makes a repatriation of the refugees favourable. India is in a position to accommodate the refugees only temporarily. What is urgently required is an unequivocal statement from the international community." Scheel admitted that "the actual crux of the problem is the necessity to normalize the political situation in East Pakistan. A politically sound solution should be arrived at by all the participants in Pakistan." But, he added, "This is an internal matter of the Pakistanis." Although West Germany was ready to work with the Aid to Pakistan Consortium in bringing pressure to bear on Pakistan, "external political pressure on Pakistan could . . . be counter-productive." Brandt lent a more sympathetic ear to the Indian foreign minister and assured him of "the willingness of the Federal government, within the scope of our possibilities, to contribute to a solution."[18]

Swaran Singh recounted that Brandt was "very familiar with this problem of refugees and he was greatly moved . . . I must confess it came to me as a pleasant surprise." True to his word, "Willy Brandt did a great deal of canvassing" in Western Europe and even the United States.[19] Brandt's empathetic stance on the crisis was shaped by his own experiences during the Nazi regime, his attentiveness to the growing humanitarian interests of the West German people,[20] and his concerns about the possibility of a war in the subcontinent. West Germany not only voted in favor of terminating fresh aid to Pakistan from the Consortium, but also imposed, in September 1971, an arms embargo on both Pakistan and India.

III

In contrast to Brandt's quiet activism, France took a more conservative position. Toward the end of April 1971, President Georges Pompidou told Yahya Khan's special envoy that France wanted everything to end "for the best on the human, moral and political levels under President Yahya's leadership."[21] When Swaran Singh visited Paris on 12 June, the foreign minister, Maurice Schumann, took the line that while the refugee problem needed international attention, the political situation was an internal matter for Pakistan to resolve. Fortunately, Swaran Singh was able to meet with Pompidou at an official lunch and impress upon him India's concerns. Owing to the president's intercession, the French Ministry of Foreign Affairs issued a statement that the Indian foreign minister had been told that "no effort [should] be neglected to provide a political solution to this crisis which stops the flood of refugees and enables their return to their homes."[22] Swaran Singh wryly observed that this statement was "definitely much better than the talk Schumann had with me."[23]

Soon the French government was finding itself under increasing pressure from the tide of public opinion, which had turned sharply against Pakistan. *Combat,* the newspaper that had begun life as the organ of French Resistance during World War II, noted that "journalists made a heart-rending appeal on the waves of the French National Radio and TV . . . The pictures shown on the programme '24 hours,' and the accounts of those who brought them back, shook the French."[24] Prominent French figures were weighing in against the government's posture. The seventy-year-old André Malraux—famous novelist, veteran of the Spanish Civil War and the French Resistance, and culture minister under de Gaulle—denounced the Yahya Khan regime and declared himself willing to bear arms on behalf of Bangladesh. The physicist and Nobel laureate Alfred Kastler compared the tragedy of East Pakistan to Hiroshima, Dresden, and Auschwitz. "Will no shock occur to rouse consciences, to assert human solidarity on our planet?" he wrote. "If humanity witnesses this tragedy unmoved, is it not ripe to destroy itself?"[25]

The French Committee of Solidarity with Bangladesh, a civil society group, systematically highlighted the atrocities perpetrated by the Pakistan army. In October 1971, the Committee published a manifesto accusing the Pakistan government of violating the Universal Declaration of Human Rights, the UN Charter, the International Covenants, and the Genocide Convention. The manifesto lambasted the French government for providing only "a trifling part of international aid," which itself amounted to a mere fraction of the overall needs. In addition to humanitarian concerns, it underlined the need for a "political solution" to the crisis involving negotiations with Mujib. Finally, the Committee called for the complete suspension of economic and military aid to Pakistan.[26]

By the time this manifesto was published, the French government had already placed economic and military aid to Pakistan on hold, but had been reluctant to rock the boat with Pakistan any further. However, by the summer of 1971, it became clear that government's position on the crisis would need to be modified in keeping with public pressure. Senior French leaders "privately hinted" to the Indian envoy that "India should take 'suitable action' in her own self-interest and she would find that no one would attack. At worst, there would be some proforma criticism and then there would, probably, be 'some admiration and even support for India' when some other country rushed to the Security Council crying 'foul.' "[27] The "other country" in question was, of course, the United States.

On 2 October 1971, the French ambassador in Islamabad warned Foreign Secretary Sultan Khan that "he expected worsening of the French public attitude against Pakistan in the coming weeks." This, as Sultan Khan well understood, was a discreet signal of a shift in France's stance. The ambassador said that this trend was "the accumulated result of the publicity which had been going on and which tarnished Pakistan's image . . . Moreover, people like Mr. Malraux, although not representing any one, had a certain hold on sections of public opinion, and their antipathy towards Pakistan would influence others."[28]

Sure enough, France's position began to move in October 1971. In his speech of 25 October, President Pompidou proclaimed the need to "unite our efforts with others to push aside the spectre of armed conflict, to encourage a political solution which will allow East Pakistan to find a new calm and to welcome back those who have taken refuge in India."[29] Interestingly, Pompidou's meeting with Soviet leader Leonid Brezhnev spurred the French further down this path. The joint declaration issued at the end of Brezhnev's visit "declared their wish to continue their efforts towards preserving peace in the region . . . expressed their understanding of the difficulties facing the Indian government . . . [and] expressed their hope for a rapid political settlement of the problems which have arisen in East Pakistan."[30] The French, D. P. Dhar would observe a few months later, "moved slowly but ultimately decisively in favour of the Indian stand on Bangla Desh . . . even Brezhnev had made his contribution during the course of his visit to France in moulding Pompidou's opinion."[31]

The governments of Austria, Belgium, and the Netherlands also bowed to public opinion that had grown censorious of Pakistan, and they suspended further economic aid. The only countries that bucked this trend were Italy and Spain. Notwithstanding the critical coverage by the media, Italy refused to follow the Pakistan Consortium in declining further economic aid to Pakistan. Franco's Spain was the only European country that "completely understood Pakistan['s] stand. Spain not only fulfilled with promptitude all the arms order[s] placed with them but had offered additional supplies at favourable terms."[32]

IV

The great power with the closest historical connection to South Asia was, of course, Britain. In the aftermath of partition and decolonization in 1947, Britain had hoped to buttress its position as a world power by enlisting India and Pakistan in a refashioned Commonwealth. Although Washington had initially deferred to London in its dealings with South Asia, the erstwhile colonial master soon found itself dislodged from its position of primacy in the region. The United States and Britain frequently found themselves at odds in South Asia: the former acted according to the imperatives of the Cold War, while the latter sought to preserve its regional interests.[33]

The crisis of 1971 was continuous with this pattern of divergent perceptions and preferences. In addition, three related, overarching considerations shaped Britain's approach to the crisis. First, the events in the subcontinent occurred in parallel with Britain's renewed bid to join the European Economic Community (EEC). Burnishing its European credentials may not have been the impetus for Edward Heath's government distancing itself from the United States, but it certainly prompted Britain to find a stance consonant with that of the other major Western European countries.[34] Second, Britain's move toward the EEC entailed turning away from the Commonwealth. The Conservative government's white paper of 1971 explicitly stated that the Commonwealth did not "offer us, or indeed wish to offer us alternative and comparable opportunities to membership of the European Community. The member countries of the Commonwealth are widely scattered in different regions of the world and differ widely in their political ideas and economic development. With the attainment of independence, their political and economic relations with the United Kingdom in particular have greatly changed and are still changing."[35] This did not mean that Britain would forsake the leadership of the Commonwealth or did not have substantial interests in those countries. Rather, it merely meant that Britain did not see the former as helping secure the latter—or indeed that it bolstered Britain's status as the "Third Power" on the global stage.

Third, 1971 was the year when Britain's military presence east of Suez was being wound down. By the mid-1960s, it was becoming clear to British leaders and officials that their military deployment in the region stretching from Aden to Malacca was financially unsustainable. The sterling crisis and ensuing currency devaluation of November 1967 had made it impossible to avoid recognizing this bitter reality. To pull back from the fiscal abyss, Britain had not only to push for entry into the EEC but also to accelerate and complete its withdrawal from east of Suez by the end of 1971.[36] This implied that Britain's wider strategic interests in the Indian Ocean region had to be secured by working with the major regional players. In this context, India loomed large. If Britain needed any reminder about India's strategic importance, it was provided by Singapore's prime minister Lee Kuan Yew, who had urged Indira Gandhi to proclaim a "Monroe Doctrine" for Southeast Asia and act as a balancing force against Communist China.[37] Taken together, these considerations led Britain to adopt a narrower, hard-nosed view of its interests during the Bangladesh crisis—the first global crisis that Britain confronted as a postimperial power.

British diplomats had been closely following the developments in Pakistan well before the crisis erupted in March 1971. Indeed, their dispatches from the region both before and after the military crackdown were the most detailed, careful accounts of the events on the ground. A week into the military crackdown, the high commissioner in Pakistan, Cyril Pickard, advised London that the "eventual end result is likely to be an independent East Pakistan. In terms of investment and raw material sources, our long-term interests may prove to be with a future regime in the East, rather than with the Western rump. We must not prejudice our long-term interests, and offend the Indians, in seeking unwisely to defend short-term interests in West Pakistan."[38]

Pickard's cable set the tone for Britain's approach to the crisis, but it left open the question of how best to preserve these interests. London initially sought to do this by adopting a strictly neutral stance. The foreign secretary, Alec Douglas-Home, told the House of Commons that while the government was "deeply concerned" at the loss of life, they had "no intention of interfering in Pakistan's internal affairs . . . It is the people of Pakistan themselves who must decide their own destinies."[39] Douglas-Home thought that Britain might be able to prod Yahya Khan to reach a political accord that preserved the unity of Pakistan. This, he believed, might be possible "if Mujib could be got publicly to renounce secession in favour of co-operation in the central legislature." Alternatively, Yahya could "find other East Pakistanis to take over from Mujib."[40] These hopes were rapidly punctured. In a meeting with the foreign secretary, the Pakistan high commissioner in London, Salman Ali, bluntly stated that "it would be impossible for him [Mujib] to re-emerge as a political leader after what has recently happened."[41]

This prompted a minor course correction. Writing to Yahya two days later, Prime Minister Edward Heath took a tougher line. "There must be an end to bloodshed and the use of force as soon as possible and a resumption of discussions," he wrote. "Political leaders, who received such massive support, must at some stage participate in these discussions."[42] Yahya took umbrage at the tone of the missive: "it was sometimes necessary to take firm action to prevent more appalling bloodshed later on." Blaming the crisis on Indian machinations, he demanded that Britain should pressurize New Delhi to desist from destabilizing Pakistan. He also made it clear that he had "no intention of negotiating with Mujib."[43] Meanwhile, the deputy high commissioner in Dhaka informed the foreign office that "the Army is acting in unrestrained fashion, wantonly killing and destroying, and generally comporting itself like an Army of conquest." Under these circumstances, "any talk of political settlement [by Yahya] must be discarded as wilful nonsense."[44]

Toward the end of April, Yahya's special envoy, Arshad Husain, met the British prime minister. Husain assured Heath that the secessionist movement had run out of steam and that the government was moving toward a political settlement of its choice. Heath conceded that this was an internal affair of Pakistan. "It was, however, difficult to isolate the impact which it made outside, particularly in this country." Expressing concern over the "conduct of the Army in East Pakistan and the economic position [of Pakistan]," he made it clear that "the extent to which [economic] help could be given was bound to depend to some extent on public feeling and how far the Pakistan Government showed that it was tackling the situation in East Pakistan."[45] Douglas-Home reiterated to Husain that Pakistan "should not underestimate the political difficulties building up for Her Majesty's Government because of public anxiety in Britain about the way in which the Pakistan Army had operated in East Pakistan."[46]

The British government was indeed under unprecedented pressure from public and parliamentary opinion. Britain was the center of the campaign launched by the international NGOs and the media. Anthony Mascarenhas's article in a British newspaper had set off a huge wave of public indignation, and after its publication, the South Asia Department of the foreign office received "76 letters from MPs . . . 184 letters and telegrams from the public . . . 14 petitions and 220 copies of a letter that had appeared in *The Guardian* . . . headed 'East Bengal Atrocities.'" There were also requests to the prime minister: "Please do not allow Britain to become an accomplice in genocide." The letters demanded the suspension of aid to Pakistan, condemnation of Pakistan's actions, recognition for Bangladesh, and the raising of the issue in the UN Security Council. "None of the letters," the foreign office noted, "have offered unqualified support for the British Government; they have all asked for a stronger line . . . demand[ing] that more should be done."[47]

In response to these pressures, London stiffened its stance toward Pakistan. Writing to Yahya in June, Heath noted that "there can be no future for a united Pakistan unless you can resume the process which you started."[48] Britain decided to suspend further economic aid to Pakistan, although, like other members of the Pakistan Consortium, it continued to support existing programs.[49] Public opinion also impinged on Whitehall's arms supply policy. In early April, the foreign office initiated administrative action to place on hold all supplies of ammunition from government depots.[50] Subsequently, Douglas-Home decided that "military equipment and supplies which are not by themselves lethal"—such as mortar cartridges, fuses for artillery shells, and chemical compounds— "may be delivered against existing orders." Because most British military supplies to Pakistan came under this category, it was not tantamount to "an obvious change of policy."[51] Under sustained public pressure, Whitehall was compelled to halt the supply to Pakistan of "lethal weapons or their components." At the same time, Britain continued to supply arms to India on "normal commercial terms," including self-propelled artillery and fire units with missiles. This was a significant departure from the earlier British policy of imposing embargoes on both Pakistan and India in the event of a major crisis or war.[52]

Indeed, the Indian and British prime ministers had been in touch since the outbreak of the crisis. British officials had no love lost for India: the high commissioner in Delhi referred to the Indian government as a "bunch of psychotics."[53] Yet when Indira Gandhi wrote to Heath apprising him of the gravity of the refugee influx, the foreign office advised Downing Street that "in present circumstances our interest lies in retaining with Mrs. Gandhi as close and satisfactory a working relationship as we can."[54] Heath accordingly replied to her that he had impressed upon Yahya "the importance of . . . halting the movement of population" and "the need for early political advance." Heath also proffered aid to help the refugees in India, though he muddied the waters by referring to "arranging, *if possible,* for their ultimate return home."[55]

This touched off the tocsin in New Delhi. When Swaran Singh met Heath later that month, he was emphatic that "India was determined not to keep the refugees. There was no space for them and the areas in which they had moved adjoining East Pakistan were highly sensitive politically." He also underscored the need for "a political settlement involving the Awami League." There were "some good leaders" in the Bangladesh government-in-exile, "but the need was for Mujib and it was essential that there should be talks with him." Hinting at India's importance in light of the impending British withdrawal from east of Suez, Swaran Singh said that the two countries had an interest in ensuring that the crisis was not prolonged, with the attendant risk of the liberation movement being taken over by radical groups. "We both were concerned to see stability in the area and indeed in the whole of the Indian Ocean region." He referred to "the maintenance of trade and the safety of sea lanes and suggested that Britain and India had common objectives . . . India considered it against her interest that the balance in the area should be upset." Heath replied that he "fully understood India's concern" and asked Swaran Singh "to assure Mrs. Gandhi that we would continue to do all we could to persuade President Yahya Khan to bring about a political solution as quickly as possible."[56]

Meeting the Pakistani envoy the next day, Heath said that "Mrs. Gandhi was standing up firmly against the pressures to which she was being subjected." When Salman Ali claimed that India was insisting on a political solution of her own choosing, the prime minister responded that "he did not think they were doing this." He went on to note that Pakistan "should understand the real fear felt in India about the instability that could be caused by the refugee problem."[57] Heath's letters and statements coupled with his government's aid and arms policies sent Islamabad into a lather. Pakistan lashed out against the "persistent anti-Pakistan activities being conducted in Great Britain," accusing Britain of taking the lead in attacking Pakistan and threatening to sever the Commonwealth link.[58] In the past, this threat had sufficed to bend British policy toward Pakistan, but given London's disenchantment with the Commonwealth, it now proved to be a damp squib. If anything, Britain's discontent with Pakistan deepened, and its willingness to tilt toward India grew stronger.

Britain was not amenable to American advice or arm-twisting either. After his visit to the subcontinent, Kissinger told the British ambassador to the United States, the Earl of Cromer, that the Indians were in an "unrationally [sic] emotional state of mind" and were working themselves up toward war. By contrast, Yahya had seemed to him "a wholly honourable man but completely lacking in imagination." Kissinger candidly told Cromer that Britain's stance, especially on financial aid, "was having a harmful rather than helpful effect." The ambassador was aware of the differences between the White House and the State Department, and patiently sketched out the main lines of British policy.[59] Heath knew that the Nixon administration looked askance at Britain's approach to the crisis. London also realized that it might be unwise to "ignore the successive hints from Washington that we might bestir ourselves a little more vigorously on President Yahya's behalf; and that, if we did so, we should have the sympathy and (practical support) of the United States Government." "In terms of political action," the officials in Whitehall wondered, "is there any scope for a joint Anglo-American demarche to President Yahya"? To ask the question was to answer it—the British thought that "the point may come, quite soon, when it will be beyond our power to save him."[60] In these circumstances, Downing Street had no desire to be the doormat of the White House.

In early August 1971, the British foreign office noted that "there is virtually no evidence so far of any progress towards the settlement of the political crisis in East Pakistan." As for the plans announced by Yahya in his speech of 28 June 1971, "there is no evidence that they are likely to be acceptable to the people of East Pakistan."[61] Against this backdrop, officials in Whitehall began airing the view that "the logical course for British interests would seems [*sic*] to be to concentrate on cautiously backing the winners, namely India and Bangladesh, while hoping to gain some influence with them to mitigate the coming shambles."[62] Unsurprisingly, London maintained a careful distance from the plan advanced by U Thant to station observers in India and Pakistan. As the British envoy in Delhi wrote, "I believe we should recognise as a fact that India is going to be increasingly more important to us than Pakistan, in whatever shape she emerges. That therefore we should not sponsor ideas or actions which have no chance of running with the Indians, and which (apart from the effect on Indo-British relations) will make them more stubborn than ever."[63]

The new high commissioner in Islamabad painted a bleak picture. "My first impressions," wrote J. L. Pumphrey, "are of more intemperance, arrogance and ineptitude among decision-makers ... than anywhere else I have served, not excluding Zambia." He believed that Yahya had reached an impasse. "The road forward to civilian government lies through a bog which is at present impassable and may turn out to be studded with mines as well: to the right the ruinous course of indefinite maintenance of colonial rule in the East Wing; to the left, the precipice of its abandonment. This fourth way, though officially unthinkable, is certainly not unthought-about; nor of course is the fifth—to blow up the whole caravan sur place by launching or provoking an all-out war with India: the consequences would be fateful." Britain had to reconcile itself to the fact that "when the time comes to pick up the bits of our shattered relationship we shall find that some of them have been lost." That, he added, "need not necessarily be a wholly bad thing." In the meantime, they had to get used to Pakistani displeasure: "our shoulders are fairly broad; and lightning conductors, safety valves and Aunt Sallys also have their uses."[64]

Douglas-Home met Swaran Singh during the UN session in New York at the end of September. When he mildly broached the possibility of talks between Yahya and Bengali leaders other than Mujib, Singh dismissed it outright. When he expressed concern about guerrilla operations, Singh frankly said that "one had to accept the existence of the freedom fighters; one could not simply wish them away."[65] The foreign office wrote to Downing Street that Britain should "recognize that our ability to influence either the Indian or the Pakistani Governments is limited; and in any such action as we may take we should avoid taking sides with either party while recognizing the relative importance and strength of India."[66] Britain's core interests in South Asia—expanding trade, investment, and influence, while limiting Chinese and Soviet influence "particularly in the Indian Ocean, naval, context"—lay with India rather than Pakistan: "whatever happens India is now and will remain the dominant power in the sub-continent."[67] While conceding that the breakup of Pakistan was almost inevitable, Whitehall mandarins believed that Britain's interests would be better served if this came about without a major war. "The only policy compatible with our long term interests . . . is still one of restraint and conciliation. This is the cardinal point which we should try to get across to Mrs. Gandhi."[68] Edward Heath hoped to do this when Indira Gandhi visited London in late October 1971.

V

Britain's stance on the crisis influenced that of the other middle powers in the Commonwealth, if only by prompting them to cast aside considerations of Commonwealth unity and chart their own course. The Commonwealth power most directly affected by the wider trajectory of British policy was Australia. For over a decade, Canberra had harbored concerns about the viability of the British presence in Southeast Asia. Australia regarded this region as holding the key to its own security. Japan's wartime offensive through Southeast Asia had underscored its potential as a vestibule for power projection from Asia to Australia. Following the advent of the People's Republic of China and assorted communist insurrections in Southeast Asia, Canberra adopted a strategy of "forward defence" aimed at containing the threat of communist expansionism as far north of Australia as possible. Australian forces had been stationed in Malaya as part of the Commonwealth Strategic Reserve and had been factored into the Southeast Asia Treaty Organization's strategic plans.[69]

In so doing, Australia was playing the junior partner to Britain. But London's ability and willingness to shoulder the main burden of defending Southeast Asia seemed increasingly dubious, owing to its financial weakness, its loosening hold on colonial possessions, and its desire to embrace the EEC. Concerns about Britain's staying power had led Australia to cultivate a close strategic relationship with the United States.[70] Yet London's decision in 1968 to draw down its presence from east of Suez caused more than a flutter in the dovecotes of Canberra. Australia initially sought to persuade Britain, directly and through the United States, to reconsider or postpone the decision—not least because of its own heavy involvement in Vietnam alongside the Americans. By early 1971, Canberra was forced to reexamine its "forward strategy" in Southeast Asia and come into its own as a regional power.[71]

Australia had been keeping a weather eye on East Pakistan even before the crisis commenced in late March. In the wake of Yahya's decision to postpone the National Assembly, the Australian foreign office prepared an assessment titled "Implications for Australia of the Disintegration of Pakistan." The paper argued that the division of Pakistan into two states was nigh inevitable, but also held that the prospects of an independent Bangladesh were not bright, as the Awami League leadership might well be swept aside by a current of radicalism. At any rate, the emergence of a new nation of 70 million with a greater orientation toward Southeast Asia was bound to pose a variety of challenges for Australia, especially because Australia would (apart from Japan) be the most developed nation in its neighborhood.[72]

Two weeks into the military crackdown, the Australian high commissioner in Islamabad wrote to Canberra that "the evidence of the past month has confirmed your view that the present state of Pakistan will split into two." Given the brutality of the military operations and the levels of disaffection, "the Army will almost certainly be forced to abandon the East Wing in a 'Dunkirk' operation." He also agreed that an independent Bangladesh might not be an edifying development for Australia: "we shall be faced with the task of preventing an unstable 'Bangla Desh' sandwiched between India and South East Asia, from becoming a magnet for all dissident forces in the region and a dangerous catalyst for extremist forces in South East Asia."[73]

Australia thus perceived direct interests at stake in the subcontinental crisis. And it believed that these interests would best be served by the emergence of an independent Bangladesh without further bloodshed or an India-Pakistan war. The high commissioner in New Delhi pointed out that "the only way in which East Bengal could be restored to anything like normal would be for Pakistan to reverse its present policy of military oppression and re-open discussions with the Awami League. So far from acknowledging any past error, however, the Pakistan Government seems to be compounding it."[74]

Australian prime minister William McMahon accordingly wrote to Yahya urging him to consider releasing the Awami League leaders as a step toward finding a political solution. McMahon also assured Indira

Gandhi that he was seized with the gravity of the refugee influx. "We believe," he wrote, "that a return to civilian rule in East Pakistan, based on the transfer of power to elected representatives of the people, offers the best hope of progress towards a solution." McMahon also requested that both sides "show restraint and prudence" in the deployment of their armed forces.[75] The Australian position, British officials noted, "went rather further than anything we had said to the Pakistanis."[76]

When Siddhartha Shankar Ray visited Canberra in late June, he found the Australians quite sympathetic. "You are in a hell of a jam," said Leslie Bury, the foreign minister. Bury also said that "he hoped the Awami League could set up a government. This was something we must work on. We are well seized of the seriousness of the situation, but if fighting broke out the situation would be even more serious." Ray's assessment was that the Australians "do not seriously expect that a political solution is feasible. While realising that if conditions were not created for the safe return of refugees India would be forced to take steps on her own they tend to counsel restraint against drastic action."[77]

Canberra was initially hopeful that India would be wary of direct military intervention in East Pakistan. By the time Ray had returned to India, the envoy in New Delhi, Patrick Shaw, had grown pessimistic about the possibility of avoiding war. Remarking on the lack of progress in Pakistan toward a settlement, Shaw wrote, "it is hard to foresee the establishment of conditions in East Pakistan under which India would feel that the threat to itself had been removed. Seen in these terms, the outlook looks gloomy."[78]

Three weeks later, Shaw went to Pakistan and conferred with his counterpart in Islamabad, Francis Stuart. The two high commissioners produced a joint assessment of the situation for Canberra. Shaw and Stuart wrote that Pakistan was "unlikely to maintain its control over East Pakistan for very long." Further Australian advice to Islamabad would be futile: "the Yahya regime is an obstinate military one without the political flair of military regimes elsewhere, such as Sadat's or Suharto's." Nor would it be productive to continue pressing India to exercise restraint. The diplomatic duo concluded that "there seems little hope of Australia's reconciling the opposing view points which are leading to the likelihood of armed clashes in East Pakistan."[79] With a resigned realism, then, Australia looked ahead to the possibility of war. The fact that London seemed reconciled to an Indian military intervention undoubtedly made it easier for Canberra.[80]

VI

Unlike Australia, the other middle power in the Commonwealth, Canada, had more leverage in Pakistan. Over the past two decades, Canada had emerged as an important—at one point, the principal—supplier of weapons to Pakistan. During the 1965 war, Canada had imposed an arms embargo on both India and Pakistan, though it was relaxed within a few months to encompass sales of nonoffensive matériel. Canada was also the supplier of nuclear power reactors to Pakistan and India, and was a key provider of economic aid to both countries. Indeed, Canada ranked only behind the United States as the second-largest contributor of aid to Pakistan. By so doing, Canada sought both to sustain its standing as an important power and to bind Pakistan to the Western alliance in the Cold War.[81]

Unsurprisingly, Prime Minister Pierre Trudeau of Canada was among the first world leaders to whom Yahya Khan wrote after the military action to justify his decision. The Canadian high commissioner in Islamabad, George Small, informed Ottawa that "the Pak[istan] of . . . Jinnah is dead," and the emergence of an independent East Bengal was, in time, inevitable. Yet he also advised that Canada should stand aloof from the subcontinental quarrels and adopt a neutral, noncommittal posture. His counterpart in New Delhi, James George, argued against this advice: "Are we to gloss over [the] fact that the majority (75 million) is being suppressed by the minority (55 million)? Are issues only legal and constitutional or also political and moral?" Small shot back that Canada should "distinguish between rumours and emotions . . . on the one hand and facts and genuine [Canadian] interests on the other." He insisted on the continuation of Canadian development aid to West Pakistan while holding in abeyance any aid to the eastern wing: this, he thought, would ensure the preservation of Canada's investments and influence in Pakistan. Foreign Minister Mitchell Sharp concurred with this assessment and advised Trudeau that "humanitarian objectives in Pakistan will best be served by declining to adopt a public posture against the military government . . . Canada can best exert an influence by maintaining contact with the military government and, without threatening to cut off aid or assigning blame, nevertheless use our position to help them [Islamabad] realize the futility of trying to apply a military rather than a political solution."[82]

In principle, Ottawa adopted a four-pronged approach to the crisis: maintaining a neutral public posture, urging restraint on both Pakistan and India, providing humanitarian relief to East Pakistani victims, and encouraging Islamabad, softly and privately, to move toward a political solution. In practice, the last strand of Ottawa's policy was so soft as to be useless. It only served to salve the conscience of the Liberal government led by Trudeau.

Part of the reason for Canada's reluctance to use her leverage more effectively was the uncomfortable parallel between East Pakistan and her own secessionist province of Quebec. In October 1970, Trudeau had sent the Canadian army into Quebec to tackle an incipient insurrection led by the Front de Libération du Quebec. Although the insurrectionary sparks were blanketed down, the political project of secession remained alive. Ottawa was anxious not to throw stones from a glass house. This was entirely consonant with its stand on the Biafra crisis.[83]

In the run-up to Swaran Singh's visit to Ottawa on 13 June 1971, the Canadian foreign ministry held that "the continuance of this [economic] aid provides far better opportunities to bring constructive influence to bear [on Islamabad] than any abrupt decision to terminate it." Ottawa's thoughts on the modalities of a political solution were curious: "Our judgement is that the precipitate withdrawal of the Pakistan Army would probably turn East Pakistan over to chaos . . . What is needed from the Pakistan Government is a resumption of the search for an agreed political solution and we have been encouraged by recent indications that they are moving in this direction."[84] In his meeting with Swaran Singh, Sharp made it clear that they regarded the crisis as an internal affair of Pakistan. As far as the humanitarian problem was concerned, they would do their best to help. "This was to me quite unexpected," reported Swaran Singh, "because we have our traditional friendship and close relations with Canada." When he raised the issue of creating conditions for a political settlement, Sharp asked how India expected Canada "to do anything to bring about a political thing" and insisted that "aid [to Pakistan] should be without strings."[85]

The high commissioner in India sought to provide a touch of reality to the roseate view held by Ottawa. Writing the day after Swaran Singh's visit, George argued that "by political window dressing he [Yahya] might pacify to some extent world opinion," but this was unlikely to change the situation on the ground. "If Yahya does not move in this direction [of political negotiations with the Awami League] then there will be guerrillas to help him make up his mind and behind the guerrillas the Indian Army."[86] As a concession to reality, the government set up an India-Pakistan Task Force to examine various contingencies in the event the crisis escalated into war. Yet Canada retained a remarkable capacity for self-delusion. As the chairman of the Task Force observed in its inaugural meeting, Canada's aim in the crisis was "the establishment of a form of government in East Pakistan having the confidence of the people with *a less obvious role* for the military and a greater civilian participation, repatriation of the refugees and their rehabilitation, and resumption of efforts aimed towards economic development of East Pakistan."[87]

In pursuit of this Panglossian objective, Trudeau wrote to Indira Gandhi urging her to accept U Thant's proposal for stationing UN personnel on both sides of the India-East Pakistan border. "I think," he added, "the Government of Pakistan is increasingly coming to recognise the need to adjust its policies but while this evolution is in progress I hope India will continue to avoid taking any positions which might serve to increase tensions."[88] Informing Yahya of his missive to Mrs. Gandhi, Trudeau wrote, "From a Canadian vantage point the crucial issue in this whole situation is the future of displaced persons from East Pakistan who are now in India." The best way to create "a more normal situation in East Pakistan," he observed, "is a question to be decided among Pakistanis themselves." He hoped ways would be found "to achieve a realistic political settlement and to establish a climate of confidence in East Pakistan if the Bengali refugees are to be persuaded to return from India."[89] The conditional "if" was significant, for the Canadians would soon come around to the view that the refugees did not need to return to East Pakistan after all.

In the meantime, the Canadian government found itself under increasing pressure from domestic opinion to adopt a more robust stance on the crisis. Leading Canadian newspapers had covered the East Pakistan crisis almost from the outset. The major English newspaper, the *Globe and Mail*, had devoted several front-page articles to developments in the subcontinent. It also broke the news of Anthony Mascarenhas's *Sunday Times* story. In early July, the *Globe and Mail* editorialized on the government's "tawdry way of approaching the crisis," demanding that Ottawa call for "the duly elected to govern East Pakistan," turn off aid to West Pakistan, and increase assistance for the refugees.[90] Armed with information from the Bangladesh Association of Canada, several parliamentarians criticized the happenings in East Pakistan and the government's stance. A group of three parliamentarians visited the refugee camps in India and urged their government to take the issue to the United Nations, "stressing the right of humanitarian intervention on behalf of the world community."[91]

In deference to these pressures, Ottawa decided to suspend any further aid to Pakistan under the auspices of the Consortium. The government also invited flak for its arms supply policy toward Pakistan. As early as 6 April 1971, the Canadian foreign office had decided against granting any further licenses of military sales to Pakistan. But the government then released $2.5 million worth of military communications equipment to Pakistan. When news broke of a shipment of maritime aircraft equipment ready to sail from Montreal, there was a furor in parliament. Sharp was forced to review the entire military supply pipeline and assure the House that it had completely dried up.[92]

The Pakistanis were greatly nettled by Canada's decision to withhold military sales. In explaining the decision to them, Small dwelt on the "strength of CDN [Canadian] public opinion on the sub[ject]," but to no avail.[93] Against this backdrop, Small personally delivered his prime minister's letter to the president of Pakistan. Yahya read the letter carefully, "snorted . . . and commented 'He puts the blame on Pak[istan].'" Passing the letter to an official from the foreign ministry, Yahya sighed, "I have heard it all before." He had been writing to heads of governments regularly, "but all he received in return was advice." Yahya added for good measure that "because of my long friendship with President Nixon," the sole country that had "shown real understanding" was the United States.[94]

Yahya's opacity to the mildest advice had an interesting impact on the Canadian government. Instead of toughening its stance toward Islamabad, Ottawa decided to come down heavily on New Delhi. India had politely turned down Trudeau's espousal of U Thant's idea of stationing observers. P. N. Haksar informed George that the road to a political settlement began in the prison cell of Mujibur Rahman: "If Mujib is released he would still have sufficient authority to accept a settlement falling short of independence. No other [Bengali] leader could make such a deal for fear of losing whatever support he might have in the party and in the resistance."[95] But Canada quailed at the thought of persuading Yahya to do any such thing. Rather, it decided to strike a more public stance on the refugee problem and on the danger of war in the subcontinent. In preparation for a UN General Assembly session, Ottawa decided to try to "restrict the debate to the humanitarian side of the problem." If this proved difficult and the debate acquired political overtones, Canada "would take the position that the internal problem of East Pakistan will be settled sooner or later, but it is inevitable that an important proportion of the ten million refugees in India (perhaps as much as 80 per cent) will not wish to return to East Bengal . . . We would suggest therefore that the world community (developed nations) should be prepared to assist India [to] integrate those refugees as productive members of the economy." This, of course, cut against the core of the Indian position on the crisis. The Canadians conceded that India might not agree to this proposal, but they felt that merely advancing it "could help take the edge off the present impression of a hopeless situation." As far as the civil war in East Pakistan was concerned, "we should be careful to continue to observe the maxim of 'a domestic solution to a domestic problem.' "[96] It is just as well that the General Assembly debate did not take this turn, for had these ideas been aired, they might have done lasting damage to Indo-Canadian relations.

VII

While the bigger players in the Commonwealth went their own ways, the smaller countries sought to take the lead. On 27 June 1971, the secretary-general of the Commonwealth, Arnold Smith, received a message from Prime Minister Sirima Bandaranaike of Ceylon asking him urgently to consult all Commonwealth countries with a view toward finding a solution to the crisis. Smith had earlier attempted, without success, to offer the services of the Commonwealth secretariat. At the end of March, he had called on the Pakistani envoy in London, Salman Ali, and proffered the Commonwealth's assistance in arriving at a political solution. The high commissioner undertook to transmit this to Islamabad, but unsurprisingly there was no response. Smith repeated his offer to Yahya's own envoy, Arshad Husain, when he visited London in May, and again drew a blank. Smith would not give up, however. On 16 June, he wrote directly to Yahya, extending the Commonwealth's good offices. During this period, Smith also met with Jayaprakash Narayan and Swaran Singh during their visits to England. The Indian foreign minister "made no commitments and blandly said that it was up to Islamabad to decide how it proceeded."[97]

On receiving Prime Minister Bandaranaike's message, Smith suggested that she invite to Colombo a small group of "carefully selected governments" to confer on the crisis. He specifically recommended that Pakistan and India should not be invited to this meeting. Smith thought it would be better for the Commonwealth group to travel separately to both countries as well as meet the Awami League leadership in India. Smith believed that the "root of the problem was the need to persuade the Pakistan government to take steps which would bring about a political solution tolerable to the Bengalis." Sirima Bandaranaike liked the idea of chairing a small Commonwealth contact group, but she overreached by inviting India and Pakistan to the meeting.[98]

The idea of Commonwealth mediation found no favor with either Britain or Australia. Already weary of dealing with the Commonwealth, Heath took the position that "there is a long standing Commonwealth convention that we do not interfere in each other's internal affairs."[99] Canberra held that "it would not be in Australia's interests to get caught up in mediation efforts between India and Pakistan. Mediation efforts would inevitably fail, and our relations with both countries would suffer."[100]

Indeed, both Pakistan and India took exception to the idea. Disappointed with the statements emanating from London and Canberra as well as Ottawa's decision to withhold military supplies, Islamabad was already threatening to leave the Commonwealth. The "time had come to cut [the] link," said Pakistan's additional foreign secretary Mumtaz Alvie to the Ceylon high commissioner. Sultan Khan curtly added that Pakistan was not interested in Ceylon's initiative under the Commonwealth umbrella—if Prime Minister Bandaranaike wished to proceed, she should do so on her own.[101] India's response was starkly negative. As Haksar told the Canadian envoy, "What is in it for Mrs. Gandhi? What is she to say to him in present circumstances after his Jun[e] 28 statement makes it perfectly plain his mind is closed? . . . To talk to him would be a waste of Mrs. Gandhi's time and an admission that [the] problem was essentially [a] bilateral one between India and Pak[istan]. He would say everything is normal in East Pak[istan] except for what is still being stirred up by Indians."[102]

The Indians not only rebuffed the Ceylonese initiative but told them to stop meddling in the crisis.[103] New Delhi was already upset over Ceylon's willingness to provide transit facilities for military flights from West Pakistan to East Pakistan. Ceylon's stance on this matter struck India as particularly ungrateful because New Delhi had recently assisted

Sirima Bandaranaike in putting down a communist insurrection against her government. In late August 1971, Swaran Singh traveled to Colombo and made it clear that unless the transit facility for Pakistani military planes was stopped, India might be compelled to intercept the planes en route to Ceylon. Prime Minister Bandaranaike acquiesced.[104]

VIII

The prime minister of Ceylon was not the only one to take the initiative in mediating between Pakistan and India. The first such offer had been made by the Shah of Iran, the United States' stalwart ally in the Middle East and a close friend of Pakistan. Throughout the crisis, Mohammed Reza Pahlavi was concerned about the consequences of a breakup of Pakistan—especially because the restive province of Balochistan bordered Iran—as well as the possibility of the Soviet Union stepping into the crisis. In mid-May 1971, the Shah met with the Indian foreign secretary T. N. Kaul, who had flown in to brief him on the crisis. New Delhi had received intelligence suggesting that Iran had recently dispatched arms to Pakistan. Kaul asked the Iranian leadership to desist from arming Pakistan and to knock sense into Yahya's head before the crisis escalated into a larger conflict. A prolonged crisis, he observed, would inevitably lead to increased Chinese influence in East Pakistan.[105] In fact, the Shah had already been trying to persuade Yahya to change tack. As the Shah later confided to Bhutto: "I urged the need for political action suggesting that he [Yahya] should clear the elected representatives of the Awami League, disqualify only a few, and hold only a few by-elections."[106]

Yahya's imperviousness to such advice led the Shah to consider direct mediation. On 23 June 1971, the Iranian ambassador called on Prime Minister Gandhi and delivered a verbal message from the Shah proposing a meeting between her and Yahya. Mrs. Gandhi felt that "this was quite an extraordinary suggestion divorced from any sense of reality." She promptly dispatched a cabinet minister to Tehran, instructing him to tell Pahlavi that "so far as any settlement is concerned, it must be between the Govt. of W. Pakistan and the leaders of East Bengal." India would not agree to turn the crisis into a bilateral dispute with Pakistan.[107] Writing to the Shah, Mrs. Gandhi "confess[ed] to a feeling of bewilderment." She could "only conclude that we have failed to convey to Your Majesty the full magnitude of the problem which Pakistan has created by its action and the extremely grave reaction it has created in our entire country."[108]

Scotching the efforts of an ally of Pakistan was easy, but it was trickier for India to deal with its own friends. Yugoslavia took the position that Pakistan should find its own solution to the crisis and that the international community should focus on providing relief for the refugees. Rather like the Soviet leadership, Marshal Josip Broz Tito was not in favor of a carving out of an independent Bangladesh. Tito, who was concerned about ethnic secessionism in Yugoslavia, was not keen to support external intervention in such matters. The tragic history of Yugoslavia two decades later would bear out Tito's anxiety, but at the time the marshal felt confident enough to lecture the Pakistanis about the futility of using force in such situations. "Over here in Yugoslavia," he boasted to the Pakistan ambassador, "we have solved these problems once and for all. There will be no Balkan question ever again in the world!"[109]

Tito's stance was doubly uncongenial to the Indian prime minister. Not only was Yugoslavia one of the founders of the nonaligned movement with India, but Tito and Indira Gandhi had been good friends for years. With an eye to the forthcoming session of the UN General Assembly, Mrs. Gandhi wrote to Tito in early September 1971 about the 8 million refugees who had already streamed into India and the forty to fifty thousand who continued to pour in every day. The situation in East Bengal had "assumed serious proportions and deserved the immediate attention of the world community both on humanitarian, economic, political and other grounds." India did not wish to provoke a war, but "we cannot be indifferent to this struggle for freedom against colonial and ethnic domination that is going on in our neighbourhood."[110]

Belgrade informed the Pakistani envoy that the Yugoslav president had "the most serious forebodings about the prospect for peace in the subcontinent." Tito was prepared to mediate, if so desired by Pakistan. The offer was relayed to Islamabad, and a meeting of Tito and Yahya was arranged for the following month at Persepolis, on the sidelines of the celebrations organized by the Shah to mark the 2500th anniversary of the Iranian monarchy. The meeting, the Pakistani envoy to Yugoslavia recalled, was "a dialogue of the deaf. Tito could not get much of a word in and Yahya spent the whole time hectoring him about India's expansionism, duplicity, mischief-making and so forth." Tito came away with the impression that Yahya was not serious about a political settlement in East Pakistan.[111]

Tito's initiative troubled the Indians. At Indira Gandhi's invitation, Tito came to New Delhi from Iran. The crisis figured prominently in their discussions as well as those between officials. The joint communiqué issued at the end of Tito's four-day trip noted that "both sides had agreed that the problem could only be solved by a political solution acceptable to the representatives who had been elected by the people . . . any attempt to by-pass the so clearly expressed wishes of the people would further aggravate the problem."[112] The formulation, however, concealed the fact that even this late in the crisis Tito did not believe that an independent Bangladesh was the only feasible solution. Furthermore, he still urged Indira Gandhi to desist from recourse to war. Speaking to an American television channel a week after their meeting, Tito observed that "a solution granting autonomy to the Eastern part within Pakistan itself would be a very good one" and that he was "seriously concerned" about the possibility of an armed conflict in the subcontinent.[113] Once war broke out, as we shall see, Yugoslavia would go on to support a UN General Assembly resolution calling on India to immediately withdraw its troops from East Pakistan.

No less troubling to India was the stance adopted by another founding member of the nonaligned movement, Egypt. President Anwar Sadat admitted to the Indian ambassador that Mujib was the key to a solution in East Pakistan. He was, nonetheless, unwilling to adopt even a mildly critical stance on the military operations launched by the Pakistan army. Nor did he evince any appreciation of the problem posed by the millions of refugees in India. "Ignoring realities," wrote the Indian ambassador in Cairo, "[Sadat] was excessively concerned about preventing the break up of Pakistan." More damaging to the Indian position was his persistent "hope that the matter could be settled bilaterally between India and Pakistan or through the help of a third party."[114]

Egypt's stance was not entirely surprising. Gamal Abdel Nasser, too, had been equivocal during India's wars with China and Pakistan in the previous decade. In 1971, Sadat was still finding his feet and was desirous of staying in step with the Arab and Islamic countries. A twenty-two-nation conclave of Islamic countries in Jeddah, held at the end of June 1971, had proclaimed its support for "Pakistan's national unity and territorial integrity"—a formulation advanced by Islamabad.[115] Cairo's stance was deeply disappointing to New Delhi, for India had been "one of the most forthright, consistent and vocal supporters of Egypt and the Arab countries" during and after the Arab-Israeli war of June 1967.[116]

India had also called for Israel's withdrawal from the territories occupied during the war. Much to Mrs. Gandhi's consternation, Egypt would not only go on to vote in favor of an Indian withdrawal at the UN General Assembly, but would justify its stance on the grounds that it could not vote against this resolution while calling for an Israeli withdrawal from West Bank and Gaza.

IX

India's inability to muster support from its traditional friends turned it toward a strange bedfellow. Given Sadat's unyielding solicitude for the Pakistani regime, it was fittingly ironic that India reached out to Israel. The relationship between India and Israel was threaded with ambivalence. This was nicely captured by Sarvepalli Gopal, the former director of the Ministry of External Affairs's historical division, during a visit to Israel in 1973: "The Israelis are modern, socialist, democratic; on the other hand they are squatting on land which is not their own, [and] are arrogant and racist with relations with South Africa—'an outpost of Europe.' Where does the truth lie and will one's feelings always be ambivalent about Israel? Can India's relations with Israel be improved without modifying the broad realpolitik policy of supporting the Arabs?"[117]

In 1947, India had opposed the partition of Palestine and proposed a federal plan for an Arab-Jewish state that was rejected by both parties. New Delhi did not formally recognize Israel until September 1950, and even then India refused to institute normal diplomatic relations with Israel. The principal driver behind India's policy of "recognition without relations" was its desire not to antagonize the Arab states, particularly owing to its own dispute with Pakistan over Kashmir. Israel's attack on Egypt during the Suez Crisis of 1956 drew strident criticism from New Delhi, and pushed Egypt and India into a closer embrace. The 1967 war further frayed the relationship of New Delhi and Tel Aviv. The Israeli attack on Gaza resulted in the death of five Indian soldiers stationed there as part of the UN Emergency Force led by an Indian general. In consequence, India was staunchly critical of Israel's preemptive resort to war and its occupation of West Bank and Gaza.[118]

At the same time, India had sought and obtained small quantities of weapons and ammunition from Israel during the wars of 1962 and 1965. Notwithstanding New Delhi's desire to maintain an arm's-length relationship, Tel Aviv was anxious to establish full-fledged diplomatic ties with India. Given Israel's willingness to accede to Indian requests at critical moments, it was perhaps not surprising that Indian officials and leaders cast a furtive glance toward Tel Aviv at the height of the Bangladesh crisis.

Ambassador Chatterjee in Paris wrote to the Ministry of External Affairs that "India is truly at the cross roads and she is half-turned the wrong way." He suggested that New Delhi should "discreetly improve" its relations with Tel Aviv. "The state of Israel is small (though energetic)," he argued, "but the Israeli 'nation' spreads all over the world and is powerful out of all proportion to its numbers." In terms of assistance with "propaganda, finance, and even procurement of armament and oil," Israel's support would be "invaluable." Chatterjee suggested that India should quietly send a consul to Israel. "If the Muslim World sets up a howl, we can point to Iran and Turkey [which had ties with Israel] apart from inventing bland excuses."[119]

Indira Gandhi was unwilling to go so far as to establish full diplomatic ties with Israel—a move that would have further isolated India from the Arab world. Nevertheless, she did reach out to Israel with a request for vital weapons and ammunition—especially heavy mortars to support the Mukti Bahini's operations—that India had been unable to obtain from other countries. The conduit was the armaments firm Establissements Salgad, which was based in Liechtenstein and manufactured weapons for Israel, among other countries. During the 1962 and 1965 wars, Establissements Salgad had helped India secretly procure weapons from Israel. New Delhi's request in the summer of 1971 was a tricky one. The only stocks available with the firm were destined for Iran, and in any case their holdings were inadequate to comply with India's demand.

The managing director of the firm, Shlomo Zabludowicz, was known to Haksar from the latter's stint in London during the 1965 war. At Haksar's request, Zabludowicz cut short his summer vacation and flew to London to meet the Indian deputy high commissioner Prakash Kaul on 3 August 1971. When asked to expedite the deliveries, Zabludowicz "promised that as before he will do what is possible and not disappoint you [Haksar]. [The] situation [is] not easy this time because he has to seek your releases from the Israeli Army." Zabludowicz had already spoken to the Israeli government and was "hopeful of airlifting ammunitions and mortars in September." He also agreed to send Israeli instructors with the first lot.[120]

Zabludowicz did more than he had promised. He not only diverted the weapons produced for Iran to India,[121] but also prevailed upon Tel Aviv to release additional quantities from the Israeli Defense Force's stocks. In fact, Israeli prime minister Golda Meir was eager to accede to Indira Gandhi's request. After the consignment was airlifted to India, she asked Zabludowicz "to inform the Prime Minister, Mrs. Indira Gandhi, that we believe she will know how to appreciate our help at a time when they were in difficulties in the past and our complying with their approach now."[122] A copy of Golda Meir's letter, duly translated into English by the Israeli counselor in Helsinki, reached Indira Gandhi's desk in the last week of September. But Prime Minister Meir's hint about establishing diplomatic relations as a quid pro quo was politely ignored. Indeed, Israel would have to wait a little over two decades to receive an Indian ambassador. It is not inconceivable that Mrs. Gandhi may have returned the favor when Golda Meir faced *her* gravest crisis two years later during the Yom Kippur War, but the submerged channels of India-Israel cooperation will only surface when archives in both countries are thrown open.

Help from Israel, however critical and welcome, could hardly compensate for India's failure to persuade the major countries to pressure Pakistan into a political settlement to the crisis. At best, India had found sympathetic ears among some of its interlocutors; at worst, India found itself being portrayed as part of the problem. India's disappointment over the international community's response and foreboding of increased international isolation over the crisis were captured in a personal note written to Haksar by Ambassador Chatterjee:

> Where does India stand? India is regarded warily in the West because she is against the concept of Imperialism and because she "invented" the "Third World."
>
> India is looked on with suspicion in the "Third World" because of her (subversive) sentiments for democracy, human rights etc.; the Muslim World is wrathful because of our secularism.
>
> The Communist countries regard India as insolent—and potentially dangerous—because we have rejected Communism as the prime condition for Progress.
>
> We are, of course, on the side of God. But, is God on our side?[123]

8

THE CHINESE PUZZLE

As the aircraft crossed the Karakoram mountain range, it commenced its descent. When it landed at Urumqi, a team of Chinese navigators came on board and joined the pilots for the next leg. On the evening of 5 November 1971, the special flight finally touched down in Beijing. Premier Zhou Enlai was waiting at the runway to receive the Pakistanis. The visiting delegation comprised Yahya Khan's special envoy, Zulfikar Ali Bhutto, along with Foreign Secretary Sultan Khan, Air Chief Marshal Rahim Khan, and Chief of General Staff Gul Hassan Khan.

The next afternoon, Bhutto and Sultan Khan had a substantial meeting with Zhou. The Pakistanis were surprised to find that "the Chinese assessment of the situation differed considerably from how we looked at it."[1] Zhou told them that the Soviet Union and the United States would not permit India to start a war. If war did break out, the United States would come to Pakistan's assistance. In the event of war, Zhou advised them, Pakistan should aim at limiting and prolonging the conflict, which would ensure that India was seen as the aggressor and that world opinion would turn against it. Pakistan, he opined, should prepare to absorb the initial blows, if necessary by ceding some ground; to mount only limited offensives to dislodge the enemy; and to go all out in mobilizing political support across the world and so deter India.[2]

The Pakistanis tactfully refrained from raising the question of China's military involvement in the event of war. The Chinese, for their part, remained silent on the subject. Zhou only assured them of military supplies to the extent possible.[3] More discomfiting to the Pakistanis was Beijing's stance on the political aspects of the crisis. At a formal dinner for the guests, the foreign minister, Ji Pengfei, made a speech outlining China's position. The crisis in East Pakistan was an internal problem of Pakistan, and India's interference was unacceptable. But Ji went on to say that a "reasonable settlement" should be made by "the Pakistani people themselves." Beijing was clearly dissatisfied with Yahya Khan's approach to the problem and was publicly urging political negotiations with the Bengalis. Ji assured Pakistan of China's support "in their just struggle to defend their state's sovereignty and national independence." This carefully worded assurance made no mention of defending Pakistan's territorial integrity.[4] At the return banquet hosted by Bhutto, Zhou spoke about Sino-Pakistan relations but made no mention of any external threats to Pakistan.

An irate Bhutto remarked to an accompanying journalist that "Pakistan can hope for little help from China."[5] Immediately after the war, he would tell the Shah of Iran that his trip to Beijing had been prompted by the fact that "China stopped the supply of planes" that had earlier been promised to Pakistan. The Chinese "gave hints, polite and subtle, to warn us of the gravity of the situation. I returned empty handed."[6]

Given its strategic propinquity to Pakistan, why did China adopt so cautious a stance? The standard explanation, particularly offered in Indian accounts, is that the onset of winter and snow in the Himalayan passes prevented direct Chinese involvement in an India-Pakistan war. These accounts also argue that China was deterred from taking action by the conclusion of the Indo-Soviet treaty in August 1971. In fact, China had no desire, from the outset, to become embroiled in the East Pakistan crisis. The Pakistanis were not the only ones who failed to read accurately the intentions of the People's Republic of China.

I

Since the fall of Ayub Khan, China had been keeping a watchful eye on the internal situation in Pakistan. When Yahya visited Beijing in November 1970, Zhou Enlai advised him to seek a fair solution to the problems of Pakistan.[7] By the end of the visit, the Chinese premier's reading of the situation was heavily tinted by Yahya's own assessment of the forthcoming elections. At a dinner hosted by the Pakistanis, Yahya invited Zhou to visit Pakistan. Zhou replied that he would, but only after the elections—when Yahya had become president of Pakistan. He teasingly said that this was bound to happen: "Chou En-lai does not eat his words."[8] The actual electoral results came as something of a surprise to the Chinese. Zhou wrote soon after to both Mujib and Bhutto, urging them to work toward a settlement between East and West Pakistan.[9]

Like other external observers, China was caught out by the breakdown of negotiations between Yahya and Mujib, and the ensuing military action. Going by the public statements of both sides, the Chinese had believed that an agreement was in the offing. Immediately after Operational Searchlight was launched, Yahya sent messages to the Chinese leadership justifying his actions. For almost two weeks, there was no response. Beijing's reticence reflected its reluctance to plunge headlong into the domestic whirlpool of Pakistan. A united Pakistan was undoubtedly in Beijing's best interests. A breakaway East Pakistan could easily slip into the orbit of India and, at one remove, that of the Soviet Union. From an ideological standpoint, China—very like the Soviet Union—saw the Awami League as a bourgeois party and Mujibur Rahman as a bourgeois leader backed by Bengali businessmen and industrialists.

Yet there were other, competing considerations. For one thing, China had to couch its response in a manner that did not conflict with its much avowed support for "national liberation movements." After all, compared with other struggles that had received Beijing's patronage, the Bangladesh movement seemed to have massive popular support. For another, Beijing did not want to lose its standing among the Bengalis. Bengali intellectuals and politicians had been the most vocal and enthusiastic supporters of the idea of a Sino-Pakistan entente. It was a Bengali prime minister, Huseyn Shaheed Suhrawardy, who had undertaken a visit to China in October 1956—the first official visit by a ranking Pakistani politician—and accompanying him on that trip was his young protégé Mujibur Rahman. When Zhou had visited Dhaka later that year, he had received a rousing welcome. In addition to the Awami League, East Pakistan was the home of two of the most pro-China political parties in Pakistan, the National Awami Party led by Maulana Bhashani and the Maoist faction of the East Pakistan Communist Party. Beijing was concerned that the military action unleashed by Yahya not only targeted the Awami League but the pro-China parties as well as the Bengali populace.[10]

So, in the immediate aftermath of the military crackdown, China was apprehensive that the longer the military campaign continued, the stronger would be the popular sentiment for secession and the greater the chances of intervention by the Soviet Union or India. Beijing's position was calibrated to reduce the possibility of either of these outcomes and to ensure residual Chinese influence among the Bengalis as well as the West Pakistanis in the event of a parting of ways.

While China was fine-tuning its approach to the crisis, Yahya grew anxious at Beijing's unresponsiveness. Following the open letter he had received from Podgorny, Yahya looked eagerly to China for an encouraging, off-setting reply. When this was not forthcoming, he was worried that the Chinese might have placed their ties with Pakistan in cold storage. Yahya's concerns were understandable, as this was also the period when the Chinese response to Nixon's message via Yahya was overdue and eagerly awaited. At Yahya's request, the Chinese agreed to receive a delegation led by Sultan Khan and Gul Hassan Khan. The delegation arrived in Beijing on the night of 9 April 1971, and held detailed discussions with Zhou over the next two days.

In their first substantial meeting, Sultan Khan conveyed Yahya's concerns to Zhou Enlai and said that they had expected that "China would categorically express its solidarity and support for Pakistan." He urged Zhou to issue a formal statement clarifying China's stance. After quizzing Sultan about various aspects of the crisis, Zhou observed that Pakistan was experiencing "a time of turmoil." China stood for noninterference in the internal affairs of any country. The prospects of external intervention, however, depended on the strength of the rebellion. If "the rebellion did not grow into bigger proportions, then the U.S.S.R. and India might not intervene, but if the 'pacification' dragged on then Pakistan should brace itself for outside interference." Yahya, he said, had informed the Chinese ambassador in Pakistan that the campaign would last up to three months. Zhou emphasized the need to take political action alongside military operations and to work through the Bengali leaders who were not sold on the idea of secession.[11]

Zhou reported the details of this meeting to Mao Zedong. After consultations with the chairman, he sent a letter to Yahya Khan and suggested that the Pakistanis might release it to the press. The letter stated that "the unification of Pakistan and unity of people of East and West Pakistan are basic guarantees for Pakistan to attain prosperity and strength." It deplored India's "gross interference in the internal affairs of Pakistan," adding for good measure that "the Soviet Union and the United States are doing the same one after the other." Yet his letter was strewn with veiled qualifications: Zhou expressed his confidence that "through wise consultations and efforts of Your Excellency and *leaders of various quarters* in Pakistan, the situation will certainly be restored to normal." And just in case this adjuration to initiate political steps went unnoticed, Zhou wrote that "it is most important to differentiate the broad masses of people from a handful of persons who want to sabotage the unification of Pakistan."[12] The most important bit of the Chinese letter, which was promptly excised by the Pakistanis before releasing the rest, unambiguously stated that "the question of East Pakistan should be settled according to the wishes of the people of East Pakistan."[13]

China's strategic reassurance to Pakistan was similarly hedged. Zhou assured Yahya that "should Indian expansionists dare to launch aggression against Pakistan, Chinese Government and people will, as always, firmly support Pakistan Government and people in their just struggle to safeguard state sovereignty and national independence."[14] Nowhere was there a specific commitment to help protect the territorial integrity of Pakistan, nor was any hope held out of Chinese assistance in case Pakistan decided to pull the trigger on India.

In their last meeting on the night of 11 April, Zhou emphatically told Sultan Khan, "Please tell the President to hold the army tightly, improve relations with the masses, take impressive economic measures and commence political work." The premier presented two specific considerations for Yahya. First, he should induct more East Pakistanis into the two new divisions that were being raised with Chinese equipment. Second, he should announce a political measure that would still the demands of the separatists and forestall external intervention. "Participation by the army is only the first step," noted Zhou. "The major problem of winning the hearts of the people through economic and political measures should be tackled quickly." Zhou emphasized the fact that this was not his thinking alone—it was being conveyed after much deliberation and consultation with Mao.[15]

Thus, from the time the crisis broke, China adopted a cautious stance. The Chinese leadership expressed support for a unified Pakistan but urged Yahya to reach a political accord with the East Pakistanis. They also looked askance at the military crackdown and took a dim view of the army's rampage. Beijing was vociferous in the attempt to dissuade military action by India, but gave no concrete assurances of military support to Pakistan. China's circumspection arose not merely from the exigencies of the current crisis in East Pakistan, but also reflected wider strategic, ideological, and domestic political considerations.

II

During Pakistan's war with India in 1965, China had provided rhetorical support by issuing two ultimatums to India. In aftermath of that war, China's relations with Pakistan had remained on an even keel. Even while China convulsed under the Cultural Revolution, Mao took care to ensure that Pakistan enjoyed reasonably normal relations with the self-proclaimed center of world revolution.[16] Not only did China emerge as the major supplier of arms to Pakistan, Beijing did not object to Pakistan's efforts to mend ties with the United States (such as by maintaining a sympathetic stance on Vietnam) and with the Soviet Union (by Ayub Khan's successive visits to Moscow).[17]

Nevertheless, the Soviet decision to supply arms to Pakistan in 1968 had unexpected consequences for China's policy toward South Asia. Ever since the humiliating defeat in the war of 1962, India had regarded China as the major strategic threat. The Sino-Pakistan entente was seen by India as aimed at containing its standing within the subcontinent. China's role during the war of 1965 raised the specter of a two-front war for which India was hardly prepared. These considerations led New Delhi to undertake a major program of military modernization and to shoulder an onerous fiscal burden.[18] The expanded defense outlay was not much more than 3 percent of the country's gross domestic product, but its impact was magnified by its coinciding with an economic crisis triggered by the failures of monsoon in 1965–66. The Indian leadership was well aware that the standoff with China "distorts the country's economy by obliging us to maintain a high level of defence spending. This led to shrinkage both of the external and internal resources."[19] It was evident that a rapprochement with China would enable India to lighten its load of military spending; but domestic opinion in India—which had barely recovered from the psychological shock of 1962—as well as Beijing's hostility made this idea a nonstarter.

However, Moscow's decision to arm Pakistan forced the Indian government to reconsider its stance toward China. India regarded the Soviet move with considerable anxiety, and the loss of exclusivity in its military relationship with Moscow rankled deeply in New Delhi. Even as India sought to stanch the flow of Russian arms to Pakistan, Indian officials were forced to reconsider their options vis-à-vis China. Among those nudging the government in this direction was R. K. Nehru, a former ambassador to China and a cousin of the prime minister.

In two long notes prepared in late 1968, Nehru argued that in light of the Soviet move it was time to revisit the policy of maintaining a mission in Beijing without appointing an ambassador. He identified three key trends that India should keep in mind while undertaking this reassessment. First, "the Soviet Union has now emerged as the principal adversary of China." Second, Moscow was attempting "to fill some of the vacuums created by the USA's declining interest in Asia." By supplying arms to Pakistan, the Soviet Union was "seeking to strengthen its influence and keeping Pakistan apart from China." And, third, "from the Chinese point of view, the Soviet move in regard to Pakistan is an attempt to create a new link in the anti-China alliance." In this changing situation, Nehru argued, "there is need for greater flexibility in our policy." The Chinese, too, were "not unlikely to reappraise the situation in the light of the new developments." While it was possible that Beijing might redouble its efforts to keep Pakistan in its embrace, "they may find that more normal relations with India and a peaceful border are more in their interests than reliance on Pakistan and attempts at subversion."[20] As a first step, he urged the appointment of an ambassador to China, "who alone can establish worth-while contacts with the top leadership." The ambassador should then be tasked with assessing the mood in China and whether negotiations should be offered. "A more important consideration," he added, "is that the appointment of an Ambassador is an indication to our friends [i.e., the Russians] also that if our interests are jeopardised, we may move in some other direction."[21]

It is not difficult to guess who Nehru had in mind for this important assignment, but as an old China hand his counsel seems to have carried weight. The prime minister's principal advisers in this matter—P. N. Haksar, T. N. Kaul, and D. P. Dhar—were loath to make any move that might undermine India's relations with the Soviet Union. At their urging, Indira Gandhi moved more cautiously in reaching out to China. In early January 1969, she publicly stated that India was willing to begin a dialogue with China without preconditions in hopes that it would lead to settlement of the boundary dispute. The next month, she reiterated that India was prepared to talk to China.[22] Two weeks later, Chinese and Soviet forces clashed along the Ussuri River.

III

For the past few years after the Sino-Soviet split, these erstwhile socialist allies had had minor standoffs along their disputed border.[23] The Soviet intervention in Czechoslovakia in 1968 and the proclamation of the "Brezhnev doctrine"—which asserted Moscow's prerogative to intervene in any fraternal country deviating from the socialist track—jangled Chinese nerves. To deter the Russians from entertaining any such ideas vis-à-vis China, Beijing authorized an attack on Soviet troops. On 2 March 1969, a battalion-sized Chinese force ambushed a troop of sixty-one Soviet soldiers on the Zhenbao/Damansky Island on the Ussuri.[24] The Russians were taken aback by both the suddenness and the ferocity of the attack. As they told their East German comrades, "the Chinese military committed incredibly brutal and cruel acts against the wounded Soviet border guards."[25] On 15 March, the Russians returned to the island with a battalion, and they fought the Chinese to a standstill. Two days later, they launched their biggest assault yet with tanks, armored personnel carriers, and heavy artillery. This last battle was never publicized by the Chinese because they took a severe beating at the hands of the Russian forces.[26] American satellite photographs showed that the Chinese side of the Ussuri "was so pockmarked by Soviet artillery that it looked like a 'moonscape.' "[27] As Zhou Enlai reported to Mao Zedong five days later, "it is possible for the enemy to occupy Zhenbao Island by force today."[28] Having demonstrated their ability and willingness to escalate an armed standoff, the Russians did not return to the island again.

Mao Zedong was unnerved. Over the previous months, he had already been worried about the adverse international circumstances that were confronting China. In response to the escalation of the war in Vietnam, Beijing had deepened its own involvement by providing both personnel and military supplies. The possibility of China being drawn into a direct military engagement with the United States could not be discounted. This, coupled with the mounting tensions with the Soviet Union, led the chairman to fret about the possibility of a war with the superpowers.[29]

In the wake of the Ussuri clashes, Mao repeatedly warned of the need to prepare for war in the event of an attack by the Soviet Union. This theme was also featured in the Chinese Communist Party's Ninth Congress held in April 1969. In August, Soviet and Chinese forces clashed again, this time along the border in Xinjiang. An entire Chinese brigade was wiped out, though the Russians suffered heavy losses as well.[30] Later that month, fearing another surprise attack, Mao ordered a general mobilization in the border provinces "to defend the motherland, to defend our borders . . . to prepare to smash the armed provocation by the US imperialists and Soviet revisionists at any time, and to prevent them from launching sudden attacks."[31] Three weeks later, he told a hastily convened strategic conclave of the People's Liberation Army (PLA), "The international situation is tense. We must be prepared to fight a war."[32] In October 1969, anticipating a Soviet attack, the top Chinese leadership was evacuated from Beijing, and the armed forces were placed on emergency alert.[33]

It is tempting to conclude that strategic forecasting was not among the chairman's strengths. Not least because in September 1969 the Soviet premier Alexei Kosygin had met Zhou Enlai and offered talks on the boundary dispute. But the fact remained that the Soviet military buildup along the borders with China was unprecedented. As Marshal Grechko later told the Indian envoy, the Soviet Union had increased its concentration of forces by "five to seven times more than before." This included land and air, naval, and missile forces. In Mongolia, for instance, the Russians had stationed "1000 tanks and several thousand aircraft." By contrast, Chinese defenses along this border were weak. "The terrain permitted them [the Soviets] to move straight to Peking," said Grechko with a dash of hyperbole, "even if half of these forces were destroyed, the other half would comfortably reach its destination." The Chinese were well aware of this awesome mobilization of the Soviet military power. Grechko claimed that "Chou En-lai had been repeatedly grumbling about it."[34]

Against this backdrop, Mao roped in four veteran marshals of the PLA to ponder China's strategic response. The group led by Chen Yi met several times between February and September 1969. Their final report underscored the fact that the principal threat to China now emanated from the Soviet Union, but concluded that an attack was not imminent. Chen also suggested that China should look to exploit the rivalry between the superpowers and take the initiative in proposing high-level talks with the United States.[35]

It was in this context that the idea of an opening to the United States took hold among the Chinese leadership. In the same context, the possibility of a thaw in relations with India began to be considered as well.

India was not seen as posing a significant military threat to China on its own, but it was certainly capable of pinning down China's strategic resources and attention on the borders along Xinjiang and Tibet.[36] More problematic from Beijing's perspective was the tightening strategic nexus between Moscow and New Delhi. This concern was heightened by the Soviet announcement in June 1969 of the so-called Brezhnev Plan for an Asian collective security system.[37] The plan was seen by Beijing as a lightly decked-up attempt to create an anti-China alliance in Asia.[38] The deterioration in China's overall strategic environment led Beijing to respond to New Delhi's overtures for a rapprochement.

The decision to probe India's offer also reflected the cooling of the doctrinaire fires lit by the Cultural Revolution.[39] During the ideological firestorm of the Cultural Revolution, Beijing had supported several insurgent groups active in northeast India who were fighting for separate ethnic homelands. The outbreak of the "peasant revolution" in the village of Naxalbari in north Bengal with its avowed allegiance to Maoist thought and praxis was regarded favorably by Beijing. A group of "Naxalite," Maoist revolutionaries was granted an audience by the chairman in December 1967. Mao was fulsome in his praise for their activities and asserted that only workers and peasants could solve India's myriad problems. He assured them that when they took power, China would sign an agreement giving up its claims to the territory south of the McMahon Line. China also trained "Naxalite" cadres in guerrilla warfare at Changping Military School on the outskirts of Beijing. When the embassy in Beijing protested China's provision of arms to insurgent groups active in India, it was baldly told that China's policy was to support weak and small nationalities.[40]

As the Cultural Revolution began to wane, the political climate for an attempt to mend fences with India became more favorable. The combination of altered strategic and ideological contexts set the stage for China's attempts to probe India's sincerity. Given Beijing's internal and external preoccupations, the outreach to Delhi was tentative and certainly not high on its list of priorities. Yet by mid-1969, the signs of change were visible.

IV

The first prominent indication of change in China's stance toward India was the appearance of the Chinese chargé d'affaires at the funeral of the

Indian president in May 1969. Prime Minister Gandhi not only noticed this, but mentioned it to Kosygin during their talks. "This was a change," she observed, "from the position which obtained after 1962." She also noted that the Chinese had handed a demarche on 23 April demanding the removal within 24 hours of the Indian post at the Nathu La Pass in Sikkim. Indian and Chinese forces had clashed there in 1967, resulting in several hundred dead on both sides. Accordingly, Indian troops were stationed on alert, but "nothing happened at all." Kosygin warned her that "there were many strange elements in the policies pursued by the Chinese . . . One could expect almost anything from them. Mao was a completely unbalanced person and one must be ready to expect him to behave in an unpredictable manner."[41]

This piece of advice slotted smoothly with India's own reading of—or rather its inability to read—China. Although New Delhi could "discern some slight changes in Chinese postures . . . we do not know if that means anything."[42] Moreover, certain moves by China were kindling India's concerns. In August 1969, the newly constructed road connecting China and Pakistan via Gilgit had become active, and India had picked up signs of "considerable movement of Chinese troops in Sinkiang and Tibet." The Indians were willing to concede that those moves might have been directed against the Soviet Union; "however, we have to carefully weigh the possibility that having failed to make any impression on the Soviet Union, the Chinese might turn their thoughts towards our country and may find in Pakistan a ready response [sic]."[43]

Beijing also kept up its barrage of bitter propaganda against New Delhi. In fact, the Indian Chargé d'Affaires Brajesh Mishra's only substantive meeting in 1969 with the Chinese foreign ministry was to protest a vituperative attack on Indira Gandhi in the official press.[44] The Annual Report for 1969–70 published by the Chinese foreign ministry in late April 1970 accused New Delhi of "obdurately following an expansionist policy towards India's neighbours," of "serving as a lackey of U.S. imperialism and Soviet revisionism in international affairs," of "frantically vilif[ying] socialist China," of "wantonly sabotag[ing] the five principles of peaceful coexistence," of "still fostering a handful of traitor bandits headed by the Dalai [Lama]," and of "forcibly occupying Kashmir and refusing to settle the Kashmir question with Pakistan."[45] The Indians could be forgiven for assuming that rapprochement with China was a forlorn hope.

A couple of days later, the Indian mission was asked by the Chinese foreign ministry to collect invitation cards for the May Day celebrations on the evening of 1 May 1970. Indian officials were surprised to receive a separate invitation for Mishra to go up to the rostrum where Mao and other Chinese leaders would be watching the proceedings. The last time that the Indian chargé had been given this privilege was in 1967, when Mao had walked past the line of ambassadors and shaken hands. The Indians assumed that another handshake was in the offing.[46] Mao arrived an hour late for the celebrations. A little later he went around, accompanied by Lin Biao, Zhou Enlai, and three other members of the Chinese Communist Party Politburo, greeting the heads of missions and their spouses. After shaking hands with Mishra, Mao paused and said, "We cannot keep on quarrelling like this. We should try and be friends again. India is a great country. Indian people are good people. We will be friends again some day." Mishra promptly replied, "We are ready to do it today." To which Mao said, "Please convey my message of best wishes and greetings to your President and your Prime Minister."

No sooner had the ceremony ended than Mishra dashed to his office and sent a personal cable to the prime minister and foreign minister reporting his conversation with Mao. Underlining the significance of such an expression of friendship from Mao himself, Mishra urged them to give it "the most weighty consideration." He also requested that they instruct officials in New Delhi "not to say or do anything which might give the Chinese the impression that we have disregarded or slighted the offer of friendship by the great Chairman himself."[47]

Mishra's concern was not unfounded. A garbled and trivialized account of this meeting was soon leaked to the press, stating that Mao had smiled at Mishra during the May Day celebration, which led to the opposition asking in parliament whether the government would succumb to a mere smile. The government's unwillingness to correct this popular misapprehension did not go over well with the Chinese.[48] This was in line with the approach advocated to the prime minister by Haksar: "My own feeling is that whereas the words used by Chairman Mao are certainly of some significance, we must not rush to any conclusions . . . We must neither over-estimate their significance nor under-estimate them." Accordingly, Mishra was instructed to reciprocate the Chinese desire for friendship, request a meeting with the vice foreign minister, and inform the Chinese that he would be returning to India for more instructions. "Our assessment," the instructions added, "is that whereas China would not be indifferent to normalising relations between India and China to the extent of exchange of Ambassadors, there will be no let up in their propaganda against us. We would like to test the validity of this assessment."[49]

Mishra called on the foreign ministry the same day and was received by a senior official from the Asia Department, Yang Kungsu. Yang had until recently been the ambassador to Nepal. More importantly, he had been closely involved in the Sino-Indian boundary negotiations in 1960 and had been responsible for the preparation of the officials' report published in 1961.[50] By designating Yang to hold exploratory talks, Beijing was signaling its willingness to move toward a resumption of negotiations on the disputed boundary. Yang referred to Mao's conversation with Mishra and said that for them Mao's word was the guiding principle in the relationship with India. When Mishra suggested some concrete steps, Yang made it clear that it was up to New Delhi to take them. "Our great leader, Chairman Mao, has talked to you personally," Yang loftily told him. "That, I think, is the greatest concrete action on our side and it is the principle guiding the relations between China and India. Mr. Mishra has heard personally what Chairman Mao said and we want to know what reaction the Government of India has after listening to Chairman Mao and what concrete action the Indian side will take." After dancing around the question of concrete action, Mishra said that he had taken "note of what you have said. And I hope you will also take note and consider what I have said, that concrete action must be taken on both sides." Yang replied, "Then, let both sides consider."[51]

New Delhi's response continued to be circumspect. When Mishra went to New Delhi for instructions, he was asked to pursue the discussion further and to let the Chinese know that India was open to any concrete proposals that Beijing may wish to place on the table.[52] The Indian government was hoping for no more than to "ascertain from the Chinese their reaction to the possibility of an exchange of Ambassadors."[53] In a meeting with Yang on 11 June 1970, Mishra apparently hinted at this.[54] But Pakistan remained a complicating factor in India's relations with China. Returning to Beijing on 1 June, Mishra learned that the Pakistani air force chief was on an official visit to China. "It would be advisable to watch the public posture the Chinese adopt," he wrote to Indira Gandhi. "In view of the cautious and step by step approach we have adopted it would be better not to disclose our hand."[55]

By the time the Pakistani air chief left China, Mishra could detect subtle changes in Beijing's public posture. He noted, for instance, that Chinese references to India were confined to Kashmir (there was no mention of the Sino-Indian war) and that they ignored Pakistani references to the 1965 war in the banquet hosted by the Pakistan embassy.[56] More significantly, at a banquet hosted for Norodom Sihanouk of Cambodia, Zhou Enlai asked Mishra, in the presence of the Pakistani ambassador, to send "his best regards to our Prime Minister."[57]

Mishra also reported that Beijing had agreed to send a new ambassador to Moscow and that it was doing the same with Hungary, East Germany, and Yugoslavia.[58] The following month, the Chinese vice foreign minister, Qiao Guanhua, told the Yugoslav ambassador that China was in the process of improving relations with many countries and was interested in doing so with India as well. "Even border problems could be easily solved. If India made concrete proposals she could be sure that they will favourably consider [them]."[59] The Yugoslav foreign ministry passed on the message to the Indian embassy in Belgrade.[60] There also was a discernible softening of Chinese propaganda against India. As Mishra reported toward the end of August 1970, "Clearly there is a quantitative as well as qualitative change in China's propaganda relating to India. It is now more in line with China's expressed desire to improve relations with India."[61]

The exploratory talks between Yang and Mishra continued through the end of 1970. The reluctance of both sides to take the first step ensured that these remained a diplomatic minuet. When the East Pakistan crisis erupted, China was still exploring an opening with India.

V

China's initial response to the South Asian crisis was shaped not just by its concerns about the consequences of the military crackdown and the possibility of intervention by the Soviet Union and India, but also by its desire to avoid reversing the thaw in its relationship with India and pushing New Delhi closer to Moscow. However, Beijing did raise the pitch of its propaganda against India. Under the circumstances, this was the least that it could do to keep Pakistan satisfied. As the crisis wore on, however, China believed that India was fishing in troubled waters. "The turmoil in East Pakistan in a very great way is due to India," said Zhou to Henry Kissinger during the latter's secret visit in July. "The so-called

Government of Bangla Desh set up its headquarters in India. Isn't that subversion of the Pakistani Government?"[62]

The Chinese believed that the United States had considerable leverage over India owing to the provision of economic aid. To nudge the Americans to come down heavily on India, Zhou put forth a rather stark statement of China's stance on the crisis. "If they [the Indians] are bent on provoking such a situation, then we cannot sit idly by . . . India, I believe, is one of the countries most heavily in [financial] debt . . . if such a disturbance is created, they will be the victims."[63] Zhou reiterated this point at the very end of his lengthy meetings with Kissinger: "Please tell President Yahya Khan that if India commits aggression, we will support Pakistan." When Kissinger replied that the United States too would oppose it but "cannot take military measures," Zhou replied, "You are too far away. But you have [the] strength to persuade India."[64]

For all his admiration of the diplomatic subtlety of the Chinese, Kissinger failed to recognize that Zhou was embellishing China's stance, and he took the premier's expressions of support for Pakistan at face value. When Nixon asked what China would do if India launched a war, Kissinger promptly replied that "he thought the Chinese would come in." This misapprehension, we shall see, would lead Kissinger and Nixon to grossly misjudge the situation when war broke out some months later. Worse still, based on Zhou's statements, Kissinger began weaving a fantastical web of strategic linkages between the South Asian crisis and America's wider interests. Kissinger believed that the Chinese would draw their own conclusions about America's credibility based on the US policy toward Pakistan during the crisis. If the Chinese thought that the Nixon administration was not supporting a country with which the United States had a formal alliance, the emerging Sino-American entente would be vitiated.[65] This excessive concern with reputation would lead Kissinger and Nixon to considerably overestimate the interests at stake in the crisis and to run needless risks to preserve those vaporous interests.

The Indians, for their part, were aware of the ambivalence in China's stance on the crisis, so they sought to persuade Beijing to consider their point of view. Even if China took a relatively neutral stance on the crisis, it would work to India's advantage. Further, Brajesh Mishra felt that India should attempt to mend fences with China before the Bangladesh crisis drove a deeper wedge in their relationship. He was particularly apprehensive that the escalating situation would deepen New Delhi's dependence on Moscow and so undermine the prospects for an improved relationship with Beijing.[66]

As the refugee influx touched the 7 million mark in July 1971, Indira Gandhi decided to write directly to Zhou Enlai. There were misgivings among her closest advisers, many of whom leaned toward the Soviet Union and were wary of handing a propaganda tool to the Chinese. Thus, even preparing an initial draft of the letter took unusually long. Mrs. Gandhi began by stating that India and China could "find a true basis for durable understanding." Her government's response to Mao's message had been "warm and positive." "It is in the context of these exchanges," she wrote, "that I am encouraged in the belief that the time may be propitious to seek an exchange of views with you on a matter of current importance." The tremendous burdens and dangers posed by the presence of such a large number of refugees on Indian soil meant that the crisis was no longer a purely internal affair of Pakistan. India now had "a legitimate interest in the problem and in the effort to find a solution." She made clear that any solution should create conditions that enabled the return of all the refugees, and her letter closed by seeking Zhou's "views on this problem" and by offering to resume consultation on this and "other matters of mutual concern."[67]

China did not respond to this overture.[68] For one thing, the Chinese were apparently wary of treading on the toes of their Pakistani allies. For another, they had to reckon with the Indo-Soviet treaty that had been signed within weeks of Mrs. Gandhi's missive. The Chinese realized that the treaty drew New Delhi and Moscow much closer together. However, unlike Nixon and Kissinger, they did not draw hasty and unbalanced conclusions from their observations. Zhou Enlai told Kissinger that the treaty did open up a new front against China, "but Madame Gandhi says this is not spearheaded against any country, and India is still non-aligned. Although the situation is such, we still recognize the times have changed and we should look at the future."[69] Kissinger informed him that Nixon would speak to Indira Gandhi "in the strongest possible terms" when she visited the United States in early November. Yet when Kissinger sought Zhou's assessment, the Chinese premier was guarded in his response: "We will like to make a further study of this matter before telling you."[70] In a brief private aside, Zhou told Kissinger that "he was thinking over possible coordinated action."[71] Nothing seems to have come of that, except for fueling Kissinger's concerns about the geopolitics of the crisis.

Indeed, when the Chinese took stock of the overall situation toward the end of October 1971, they were quite balanced in their assessment. The Chinese foreign ministry informed an East European ambassador that the war was not imminent. Beijing believed that the "U.S. will not encourage [the] two countries to embark on a war; [the] Soviet Union is also not interested in a war on [the] sub-continent."[72]

Although the Indo-Soviet treaty was concluded partly as insurance against the possibility of Chinese intervention, Mrs. Gandhi was anxious not to alienate China. Despite Beijing's refusal to acknowledge her letter, Mrs. Gandhi was keen to clarify that the treaty was not aimed at China. "Should we not indicate to Mishra," she asked Haksar just two days after the treaty was signed, "that the Indo-Soviet treaty does not preclude a similar treaty with China?"[73] This was, of course, the stock response given to any country that doubted India's nonaligned credentials following the treaty. But the fact that Indira Gandhi was prepared to suggest this to China as well underscored her eagerness to avoid becoming a frontline player in the Sino-Soviet clash. Haksar vehemently argued against the prime minister's inclination. "This attitude dilutes the impact of the treaty we have signed," he insisted, "and makes us look a little cheap." As for signing a treaty with China, "even a talk about it would not bring about a Treaty with China and it would certainly attenuate greatly the effect of the Treaty which we have signed with the Soviet Union."

A few days later, Indian intelligence agencies obtained a record of a discussion between Pakistani ambassadors at a conference held in Geneva on 24–25 August 1971. K. M. Kaiser, Pakistan's ambassador to China, summarized Beijing's stance on the crisis: China "had advised for a political settlement maintaining the integrity of Pakistan." China was also ready to provide economic aid for the rehabilitation of East Pakistan. Although the Chinese believed that the Indo-Soviet treaty was "directed against China," the "Chinese press did not publicize the Indo-Soviet Treaty." The most important part of Kaiser's presentation—which was highlighted for the Indian prime minister and was marked "Read" by Haksar—pertained to Chinese military support for Pakistan. "Amb. Kaiser was not sure about the nature of Chinese help in case of a war between India & Pakistan ... arms shipment to Pakistan since March 25 was almost nil. Most of the Chinese weapons Pakistan [was] now using were received during the years after 1965."[74]

VI

Why was China so reluctant in supporting Pakistan? Beijing's stance stemmed, as we have seen, from a combination of its concerns about the consequences of the Pakistani crackdown and its desire not to push India closer to the Soviet Union. These do not, however, explain why China refused to commit to protecting Pakistan's integrity or even to supplying weapons. The argument that China was deterred by the Indo-Soviet treaty does not really hold water: China's stance had crystallized long before the treaty was concluded. To make sense of China's puzzling behavior, we need to look at yet another, arguably the most critical, dimension of Chinese policy during this period.

From the summer of 1969, Mao was concerned about his hold over the PLA. After the clashes with Soviet forces, he had panicked at the prospect of a surprise attack and had ordered military preparations. During the evacuation of the top leadership from Beijing in October 1969, these preparations were overseen by Marshal Lin Biao, the defense minister and Mao's heir apparent. On 17 October, Lin Biao issued a six-point directive—subsequently billed as Vice-Chairman Lin's First Verbal Order—that placed the PLA on red alert. Three more orders followed in quick succession, resulting in the mobilization of nearly 1 million troops, 4,000 aircraft, and 600 naval vessels as well as considerable civilian resources. Though he had been informed of these measures in advance, Mao was incensed that such a massive military mobilization could be ordered by anyone other than himself. By unleashing the Red Guards against the party and the government during the Cultural Revolution, Mao had already, unwittingly, ensured that the PLA would become the key institutional actor in the People's Republic. During the 9th Party Congress earlier that year, Lin had formally been designated as Mao's successor, and the PLA's representation on the Central Committee and Politburo increased substantially. Of the twenty-nine first secretaries of the provincial party committees formed subsequently, all but seven came from the PLA. Against this backdrop, Mao regarded Lin Biao's moves as a challenge to his own authority.[75]

Mao's suspicions were sharpened by his differences with Lin over the rebuilding of state institutions following the devastation wrought by the Cultural Revolution. In March 1970, Mao informed the Politburo that he was not in favor of retaining, in a revised constitution, the office of the head of state—a position that had been held by Mao before being passed on to Liu Shaoqi, his original successor-designate whom the chairman had destroyed during the Cultural Revolution. Lin Biao, however, suggested that the post should be retained and occupied by Mao himself. The Politburo endorsed this idea. But Mao made it clear that he would not be persuaded to become head of state and instead suggested that Lin be appointed to the post. Lin declined the offer, and he persisted with the idea that Mao be the head of state. It is not clear whether Mao was serious about his proposal for abolishing the position, or whether he was merely trying to induce Lin to claim the office and so set himself up for denunciation by the chairman. In any event, the episode stoked Mao's paranoia. Matters came to a head at the Central Committee's plenum held in Lushan in late August 1970. Mao believed that Lin and his PLA associates were orchestrating a subtle campaign against him. Although he refrained from directly attacking Lin, he demanded self-criticism from Lin's supporters.[76]

The self-criticisms circulated by Lin's associates over the following months were deemed inadequate by the chairman. By early 1971, Mao sought self-criticism from Lin himself. The marshal evaded the demand and stayed away from Beijing. Lin was also absent at the Central Committee plenum of May 1971. In a meeting with Zhou in July, Mao was deeply critical of Lin and his followers. He said that the self-criticisms of the PLA generals were "nothing but fake. What happened at Lushan is not over, for the basic problem has not been solved. They have someone behind them."[77] By this time Mao seems to have resolved to rid himself of his recalcitrant heir. From 15 August to 11 September 1971, he toured southern China, addressing local party cadres, denouncing Lin and the generals, and corralling opinion among the rank and file.[78]

By early September, a showdown between Mao and Lin was imminent. At this point, Lin Biao's son, an air force officer, conjured an amateurish plot to murder Chairman Mao. When the plot failed to get off the ground, Lin's son flew to his father at the seaside resort of Beidaihe and urged him to set up a rival party headquarters in Canton. Lin, however, decided to flee to the Soviet Union. The leadership in Beijing was closely tracking these moves. When Lin's aircraft approached Mongolian airspace, Zhou asked Mao if it should be shot down. The chairman shrugged off the suggestion: "Rain has to fall, girls have to marry, these things are immutable; let them go."[79] As it happened, Lin's plane crashed in Mongolia, owing perhaps to lack of fuel.

Historians continue to differ over the motives of the central protagonists in the Lin Biao affair. The consequences of the episode were clear, however: it was one of the most serious political crises in the history of the People's Republic. Mao had to reestablish the party's and his own ascendancy against all comers. Immediately after Lin's flight, Mao had four senior generals of the PLA arrested on charges of conspiring with Lin. Having purged the Politburo of military influence, Mao began a spring cleaning of the entire PLA.[80]

VII

By the time Bhutto and Sultan Khan visited Beijing, China had little inclination to embark on a military venture of any kind. As the Chinese told a fraternal ambassador, "China certainly does not want a war between India and Pakistan; China hoped India will not embark on a war."[81] Even before Bhutto landed in Beijing, the Chinese ambassador in Nigeria told his Indian counterpart that "good and friendly relations between our two countries would be of immense significance for peace and stability in Asia and the world." He added that differences over the boundary could be resolved by negotiations. The Indian diplomat reported that "not even by implication did he [the Chinese envoy] say a word in defence of Pakistan."[82] New Delhi also learned that China had been urging Pakistan to maintain restraint, that Yahya had been advised to release Mujib and deal with him, that China wanted to keep lines of communication open with the Bengalis, and that the Chinese were in touch with Maulana Bhashani.[83]

Nevertheless, statements from Pakistan sowed doubt in Indian minds. On 1 November, Radio Pakistan quoted Yahya as having told an interviewer that China would intervene if India launched a war. On returning from Beijing, Bhutto publicly claimed that China had assured Pakistan of its support in the event of a war with India. This was evidently an attempt to heighten India's insecurity and uncertainty about China's intent, and so deter an attack on Pakistan. The Chinese were not pleased with these claims, but they let them pass.[84]

Soon after, Brajesh Mishra sent New Delhi an authoritative assessment of China's stance. Mishra concluded that "China has adopted an attitude of restraint and is advising Pakistan to do the same." It was also urging Pakistan to seek a political solution in East Pakistan. "At the same time," he added, "China wants to keep its options open in relation to India." China had already been stalling on supplying arms and equipment to Pakistan. "China has *not*," he emphasized, "played up Bhutto's visit." Indeed, the "military aspect of the delegation has not been emphasized at all."[85] After further consultations with an authoritative source, Mishra added a coda to his earlier assessment. China had assured Pakistan about the supply of all arms, ammunition, and matériel, and also said it would support Pakistan at the United Nations. "But China will not intervene in the event of war between India and Pakistan."[86]

The prime minister was in Bonn when Mishra sent these messages. Two days later, Mrs. Gandhi told the West German foreign minister that "she was not apprehensive of Chinese pressure on the borders of India, as China was occupied with its own internal problems."[87] India finally had the measure of China.

9

ESCALATION

Defense Secretary K. B. Lall rushed into the operations room at the Indian army headquarters at 5:00 PM on 3 December 1971. The army chief, General Manekshaw, was wrapping up for the day. Lall told him that the western army commander had just called to say that three Indian airfields in Punjab were under attack by Pakistani aircraft. Both the prime minister and the defense minister were out of Delhi and could not immediately be contacted. Manekshaw ordered the commanders on the western front to put into effect their operational plans.[1] The third India-Pakistan war was under way.

Yahya Khan's decision to launch preemptive strikes on Indian airbases—inspired by the Israeli strikes on Egypt in the 1967 war—allowed India to claim plausibly that the war had been started by Pakistan. The claim has echoed down the years. Indian historians continue to insist—and they are not alone—that the war of 1971 was triggered by the Pakistani attack of 3 December. This comforting fiction is true only to the extent that all wars are begun by defenders. The attacker, as Clausewitz observed, would like to enter his adversary's territory entirely unopposed. The war of 1971 was begun by India.

Why did Indira Gandhi escalate the crisis toward all-out war? Pakistani scholars argue that the war was the culmination of a deep Indian plot to emasculate Pakistan and establish India's preeminence in the subcontinent. Similarly, referring to India's "hegemonic ambitions" Kissinger claimed that Mrs. Gandhi moved toward war because she was aware that Pakistan was moving toward a political settlement with the Bengalis—a move that would deprive her of the coveted casus belli. "It was precisely the *near certainty* of a favorable outcome [to Yahya's efforts] that gave urgency to her actions."[2] This explanation is self-serving insofar as Kissinger claimed credit for having nudged Yahya toward this enlightened path of political reconciliation. It is also wrong insofar as it asserts that in resorting to war India sought a positive payoff. On the contrary, the decision to escalate flowed from New Delhi's assessment that without a war the crisis would get much worse. Indeed, by mid-November 1971, India's ability to steer events toward the desired denouement without force majeure looked increasingly uncertain. This was true along several dimensions: the international context, the situation in Pakistan, and India's relationship with the Bangladesh liberation movement.

I

The central concern for Indian decision makers was the continuing influx of refugees. Up to the end of July 1971, 7.23 million had taken shelter in India. By 15 December, an additional 2.67 million had poured in, taking the total to almost 10 million. From New Delhi's standpoint, the continuing flow of refugees gave the lie to the claims about impending normality in Pakistan. It also cast into sharp relief the problem of repatriating the refugees. So long as Bengalis continued to flee East Pakistan, there was no hope of persuading them to return. In this context, the religious composition of the refugees took an alarming color. As of 31 October 1971, the Indian government recorded that 82.3 percent of the refugees were Hindus. New Delhi was worried not just about the difficulty of persuading the Hindus to return to East Pakistan, but also about the prospect of their melting into the population of eastern India and providing cannon fodder for the Maoists in the region.[3]

Then there was the growing economic burden of maintaining the refugees. The budget presented in May 1971 had provided 600 million rupees for the relief of refugees, but this sum was submerged by the scale of the deluge. In August, the government was forced to present a supplementary demand of 2,000 million rupees. By the third week of September, it was assessed that maintaining 8 million refugees in camps for six months at the rate of just 3 rupees per person per day would amount to 4,320 million rupees—about US $576 million. At that point, the relief pledged by foreign countries and agencies amounted to US $153.67 million, of which only US $20.47 million had actually reached the coffers of the government. By October, the projected cost of maintaining 9 million refugees was assessed at 5,250 million rupees, while the external aid amounted only to 1,125 million rupees. The galloping costs of sheltering the Bengalis made a mockery of the government's original estimate for the fiscal deficit. In consequence, programs for economic development and social welfare had to be trimmed and additional resources mobilized by fresh taxation and commercial borrowing.[4]

A prolonged crisis would push the problem to unmanageable proportions. Although a war would entail significant costs, they would be more bearable than the burden posed by the refugees. In July 1971, an assessment prepared by P. N. Dhar, economist and secretary to the prime minister, underlined the potential consequences of embarking on war. The most significant of these would be the position of foreign exchange reserves, which had already worsened in the previous fiscal year. The level of the reserves depended, in the first place, on foreign trade. There was the possibility that India's trade partners would create difficulties in accepting its exports, so depriving it of foreign exchange earnings. This would "amount to a complete economic blockade." Dhar argued that this was "only an extreme [sic] imaginable situation, which I do not believe can be taken seriously." The second component of the reserves came from foreign aid. Dhar envisaged two scenarios in which the donor countries might seek to coerce India. They might, as with Pakistan, continue committed aid but suspend fresh commitments. Or they might cut all aid, both committed and prospective. In the first situation, India was "not vulnerable on account of foreign exchange" until March 1972. In the second, the amount of aid withheld would almost equal the amount owed by India to its donors in the current fiscal year by way of debt repayment and repatriation of profits. In this situation, India could reasonably threaten to impose a moratorium on debt. "Thus while as an aid-recipient country we are vulnerable to the adverse reactions of the aid-givers," wrote Dhar, "the size of our debts makes our creditors vulnerable to our reactions. Keynes once said that if I owe you 100 pounds, I should worry but if I owe you a million pounds, you should worry. We owe many millions to our creditors!"[5]

The economic considerations, however pressing, did not determine the decision to escalate the crisis. The initial move to mount the escalator was taken in late August 1971 in response to a series of developments. By this time, New Delhi had taken stock of its diplomatic efforts to persuade the international community to put pressure on Pakistan. It was now evident that most countries did not agree with India's view that the crisis needed a political resolution in Pakistan; rather, they preferred to regard the refugee problem in India and the situation in

East Pakistan as separate issues. The few countries that did appreciate India's position felt that it was unwise to put public pressure on the Pakistan government. The rare country that did impress upon Yahya the need to negotiate with the elected leadership of the Awami League did not seem to have any leverage in Pakistan. And the country that possessed the most leverage—the United States—was also the most energetic supporter of Yahya Khan.

Far from buckling under international pressure, the regime appeared to be becoming even more brazen. On 5 August, the Pakistan government published a white paper that pinned the blame for the outbreak of the crisis solely on the Awami League.[6] Four days later, Yahya announced that Mujibur Rahman would be tried for treason from 11 August. The trial was held in camera, with the government issuing only an occasional statement about its progress. At the same time, the Martial Law Administration announced that it had sifted through the list of elected representatives in East Pakistan and had disqualified 79 of the 160 Awami League members of the National Assembly and 195 of the 228 Awami League members of the Provincial Assembly. The rest were permitted to remain in their respective assemblies, but not as members of the Awami League.[7] The idea of disqualifying the Awami League had originally been put forward by Zulfikar Ali Bhutto in May 1971. In the aftermath of the crackdown, Bhutto was straining at the leash to be appointed the leader of a new civilian government. The military leadership had acted on his suggestion, but—much to his chagrin—refused to transfer power to a government led by Bhutto.[8]

This transparent attempt to extinguish the Awami League was followed by an announcement of by-elections for the vacant seats from 25 November to 9 December. These elections were closely controlled by the regime. The military adviser to the governor of East Pakistan was tasked with screening and handpicking the candidates. Yahya himself brought the various non-Awami League parties together and persuaded them to work together to ensure that the candidates in most constituencies were elected unchallenged.[9] These measures were designed to advertise the regime's readiness for a political solution and were overlaid with a veneer of civilian administration in East Pakistan. In mid-August, a senior civil servant was appointed chief secretary of the province. On 1 September, General Tikka Khan was replaced by Dr. Abdul M. Malik as governor of East Pakistan. A council of ten provincial ministers, inducted on 17 September, was composed of two renegade-elected Awami Leaguers and the rest from parties that had failed to win any seats in the elections of 1970.[10] To top it all off, Pakistan contested India's statements about the flow of refugees. In late August, Islamabad published a district-wise tally that put the total figure at just over 2 million—only a fourth of the numbers counted by India.[11]

These developments, alongside the continuing inflow of refugees, convinced New Delhi that the possibility of a political solution to the crisis was receding. Worse, the number of refugees cited by Pakistan was eerily close to the number of Muslims among the Bengali refugees. This suggested that the Pakistan government was not going to allow the Hindus to return to their homes. Until this point, the balance of influence within the Indian government had been tilted toward the advocates of a cautious approach in handling the crisis. The rationale for a shift toward a more proactive stance was laid out by K. Subrahmanyam, the preeminent civilian strategist in New Delhi. Subrahmanyam, we may recall, had advocated an early military intervention. Although his advice was then disregarded, he weighed in again in early August 1971 with a lengthy assessment that was circulated within the government.

Subrahmanyam conceded that "any action by India in regard to Bangla Desh is fraught with risk of escalation into full-scale war with Pakistan." Although going to war would undoubtedly impose costs on India, "cool and calm reflection will reveal that there are worse things than war." The policy of abstention from direct involvement "will only result in increased defence outlay for India, recurring expenditure on refugees, increased communal tension . . . erosion of the credibility of the Indian government . . . and [a] further sharply deteriorated security situation in eastern India and the likelihood of Pakistan creating trouble in Kashmir as a retaliation." Subrahmanyam argued that India could not only prevail in a military contest with Pakistan but also prevent intervention by the great powers. Even China, he held, could inflict little more than pinpricks on India. International opinion, especially at the United Nations, would oppose military intervention by India. "But the world public opinion is very much in advance of the opinions expressed by the national governments. This is a fact we must exploit." The political leadership, he emphasized, "has to weigh the likely consequences of different courses of action and adopt a solution which minimises the adverse impact on the country's interests."[12]

This time, Subrahmanyam's views had greater resonance with the Indian leadership. Toward the last week of August 1971, Indira Gandhi decided to adopt a coercive strategy toward Pakistan. By progressively increasing the military pressure on Pakistani forces in the east and by undermining their control over the province, she sought to convince the military regime that it would be better off seeking a negotiated settlement with Mujib than in persisting with its present course. In pursuit of this strategy, New Delhi stepped up its assistance to the Bengali fighters.[13]

II

The decision to increase support to the Bengali fighters was spurred by yet another consideration. New Delhi's relationship with the Bangladesh liberation movement had been far from cozy. Indeed, it was bedeviled by a host of problems. For a start, the Bangladesh leadership was vexed by India's refusal to accord recognition to the government-in-exile. The Bengalis felt that "they could not expect any other Government to recognise Bangla Desh unless [the] Government of India did so." Conversely, recognition by India would "enhance the prestige of [the] Bangla Desh Government." When told of India's concern that the act of recognition might trigger a war with Pakistan, they replied that "Pakistan was not in a position to take any action" owing to the difficulty of maintaining its forces in the east and concerns about Indian retaliation in the west.[14] The Indian government, however, continued on its cautious course. Mujibnagar's efforts to work with opposition parties and civil society groups to nudge the government only served to irk New Delhi. Indira Gandhi took particular umbrage at the efforts to convene an international conference and to form a "national front" aimed to "build up public pressure to favour recognition of the Bangla Desh Government."[15]

The second sore point pertained to India's support for the Bangladesh fighters. Until August 1971, India had extended limited assistance to the Mukti Fauj. India's military strategy since early May had been to train the Bangladesh fighters for guerrilla warfare and to prepare to employ them against the Pakistan army in stages. Commanders of the Mukti Fauj had insisted on raising in parallel a full division of regular army with all supporting elements, including artillery. The Indians had paid lip service to the idea but done nothing about it.[16] They had also kept tight control on military supplies for the liberation army. The commander in chief, Colonel Osmany, grumbled in early July that "adequate arms and ammunition are not being supplied to members of the BD [Bangladesh] Army."[17] In fact, the Mukti Fauj had largely been "fighting with arms they have captured from the Pakistan Army."[18] The secretary-general of the Awami League, Mizanur Rahman Choudhury, was not exaggerating much when he reported to the president of the exile government that "believe it or not, a soldier of the Mukti Fouz [sic] is not allotted more than 10 rounds of ammunition per day."[19] Osmany was also concerned that the Indian army was "trying to transform even the regular battalions of the East Bengal Regiment into guerrilla forces." The Indians, for their part, thought that the "Mukti Fauj was not paying enough attention to guerrilla operations." The eastern army commander, Lieutenant General Aurora, felt that "Col. Osmany was unsuited to lead the Mukti Fauj because he was too committed to regular warfare and was too old to learn."[20]

The Bengalis were further disappointed at New Delhi's evident lack of enthusiasm for their ambitious plans to train civilian volunteers for the liberation army. The Indian army had originally envisaged raising a guerrilla force of 20,000 fighters. There was no shortage of volunteers, but the quality of potential recruits was uneven. Hence, by the last week of June, only 6,000 irregulars had been trained for guerrilla activities. The Bangladesh commanders had initially wanted a force of 50,000 guerrillas and had settled for 30,000. They kept pressing their Indian counterparts to step up by training 5,000 guerrillas a month.[21] Osmany bitterly complained that "nothing so far has been about giving guerrilla training to the volunteers produced by the BD [Bangla Desh] Government." He had sent a proposal to Aurora in early June, "but there has been no response from the local Army authorities to this."[22]

A related issue was the operational subservience of the Mukti Fauj to the Indian army. A report prepared by the Indian external intelligence agency's Research & Analysis Wing (R&AW) noted that "this created a lot of subdued resentment. In certain places it was forcefully opposed and challenged by local commanders . . . it was felt that Mukti Fouj personnels [sic] were being used as cannon fodder."[23] Osmany claimed that there was "constant interference in the administration of the BD [Bangladesh] Army . . . the [Indian] Army is interfering in recruitment, postings and discharge of his men." He bluntly added that "there is a lot of dissatisfaction, discontent and misgivings in the BD [Bangladesh] Army."[24]

All this seeded doubt in the minds of at least some Bangladesh leaders about the wisdom of relying exclusively on India. "It is evident," wrote Mizanur Rahman, "that the Mukti Fouz [sic] has been badly neglected. We should not be lulled by soothing assurances only." He urged that the provisional government "should finally settle with the 'Friend Govt.' as to whether they will meet our total demand. If the 'Friend Govt.' expresses its inability, we should send competent persons abroad to procure weapons and other materials."[25]

New Delhi was aware of the simmering discontent in the liberation movement. A report sent to the Prime Minister's Secretariat underscored these problems and recommended that "the representatives of the Bangla Desh Government and Mukti Fouj [sic] High Command should also be given more freedom and scope to secure help and resources from appropriate quarters . . . otherwise they might feel that they are under too much control of Government of India—a feeling which is not conducive for promoting long-term friendly relations."[26] On receiving a copy of the report by the Awami League's secretary-general, the Indian home secretary wrote to Haksar that "our friends are already beginning to get estranged from us." New Delhi's liaison with them needed to be strengthened: "This serious lacuna must be removed quickly."[27] Following his meetings with the Bangladesh leadership, Jayaprakash Narayan wrote directly to the prime minister emphasizing "the danger of Big Brother behaviour on our part . . . The American behaviour in South Vietnam should be a lesson for us—do you remember the Ugly American?"[28]

Against this backdrop, the announcement of Mujib's trial and the other measures by the Yahya regime jolted the Indian government. The Mujibnagar government and the liberation army now despaired of attaining an independent Bangladesh and began chafing at the bit. New Delhi grew concerned not only about increasing the pressure on the Pakistan army, but also about maintaining its hold on the liberation movement. By increasing material support to the Bangladesh fighters and raising the tempo of their operations, Mrs. Gandhi sought at once to coerce Pakistan and to ensure that the liberation movement remained amenable to her control.

The Bangladesh forces were rapidly scaled up. The original target of training 20,000 guerrillas by the end of September was revised first to a monthly target of 12,000 and subsequently to 20,000 a month. By the end of October, the total strength of the liberation forces—now known as the Mukti Bahini, comprising the Mukti Fauj and the civilian freedom fighters—stood at nearly 80,000. As of 30 November, it was a little over 100,000.[29] The arms and matériel pipeline to the Mukti Bahini now began to flow. India also made strenuous efforts to procure more of the requisite equipment from abroad, including the heavy mortars from Israel.

Given the speed at which the Mukti Bahini was being raised and inducted into East Pakistan, it is not surprising that its guerrilla operations in September did not have the desired impact. Prime Minister Tajuddin Ahmad conceded to his Indian interlocutors that "over 30 per cent of guerrillas would run away in the face of Pakistani action, dumping even their arms right in the enemy's hand."[30] Nor were the operations against the Pakistan army along the borders particularly successful. This led the Indian army to assume a more active role. It not only provided increased fire support to the Mukti Bahini but also embedded some of its own troops, especially the commando units, to fight alongside it. Thereafter, the Mukti Bahini was able to inflict substantial damage on static installations and infrastructure in East Pakistan, including bridges, rail lines, roads, water transportation networks, power stations, communication systems, and ships in the Chittagong port.[31]

III

The operational efficacy of the Mukti Bahini was not the only worry for the Indian government. Rather more pressing were concerns about the friability of the Bangladesh movement. New Delhi was alert to the fact that the liberation movement was scored with several lines of tension. There was a fraught relationship between the army officers of the Mukti Fauj on the one hand, and Colonel Osmany and the Mujibnagar authorities on the other. The army officers had, of their own volition, pledged their allegiance to the Awami League and agreed to serve under the leadership of Osmany, but they soon became censorious of both.

This was partly because the commander in chief seemed more enthusiastic about administrative than operational issues and partly because the provisional government was unable to shape the strategy of the liberation war or meet the army officers' requirements. No sooner had he taken charge than Osmany settled down to draft a voluminous Army, Air Force, and Navy Act. "We wanted him to fight, but he is writing a book," exclaimed the finance minister, Mansoor Ali. "Who is going to read it?"[32] The sector commanders were incensed at Osmany's priorities.

They complained to their Indian colleagues that "no tactical plan was ever discussed in any sector . . . A strategical [sic] plan has never been thought of." When pressed by the army officers to procure equipment from abroad, the cabinet and Osmany apparently prepared a shopping list for "absurd things" such as vertical take-off and landing planes, surface-to-air missiles, and laser beams. All this led the army officers to conclude that "no one in the Bangladesh cabinet knows anything about war and its conduct" and that the liberation war was "being handled like [sic] a novice and non-professional way." Worse, some officers doubted "that the cabinet or the C in C [commander in chief] was not in favour of liberation war." A delegation of military officers met with Tajuddin Ahmad and asked him to create "a War Council to plan and execute the war."[33] This suggestion was turned down, resulting in continued tension between the politicians and the military officers.

A second axis of tension was between the Awami League and other political parties. New Delhi, it will be recalled, had been eager to ensure that the exile government was a big tent and that the liberation struggle involved diverse political forces. The Awami League's unwillingness to oblige had been noted with dissatisfaction in New Delhi. Officers of Mukti Fauj, too, had requested that Mujibnagar create "an all-party government enlisting support of all those who support Independent Bangladesh." Their principal concern was that "boys of only Awami League were recruited" for the Mukti Bahini.[34] As the crisis continued, the Indian government was increasingly convinced of the importance of a national unity government for Bangladesh, both to strengthen its case in the international arena and to undermine Pakistan's efforts to mask the problem with a façade of political settlement.

Groups other than the Awami League—particularly those on the left—were clamoring for representation in the government. A note sent to Haksar argued, for instance, that "it is necessary to reorganize the leadership of the Liberation war. The overall hegemony of the Awami League no doubt must remain but there is every need to organise a National Liberation Front," which would include "leaders like Maulana Bhashani, National Awami Party of Prof. Muzaffar Ahmed, and the Communist Party of East Bengal as well as some other left groups which have revolted against the Chinese leadership and are fighting the Pakistan Army." The radical elements suggested a further widening of the movement by raising an "International Brigade" of volunteers to support it. This brigade could receive the support of "students and youth organisations in different countries of Europe including U.K., France and West Germany as well as in North America. Some groups in Japan also are prepared to support the move, especially those groups which were associated with the anti-Vietnam war movement . . . The group of West Pakistani students led by Tariq Ali is also prepared to cooperate." The government of South Yemen was apparently "prepared to help in organizing the supply of arms and other material."[35]

The Indian government recoiled from the idea of resurrecting the specter of the Spanish Civil War. But it continued to impress upon Mujibnagar the need to bring in the other parties. Meeting with the Bangladesh cabinet in early July 1971, Jayaprakash Narayan said that "the Prime Minister of India had particularly desired him to discuss with them . . . the need for broad-basing the Bangla Desh movement." The cabinet resisted this suggestion. The Awami League "strongly feels" that to induct representatives of parties that had been defeated in the polls would "amount to doing what President Yahya Khan has been trying to do in Bangla Desh: that of trying to form a government by collecting defeated candidates and quislings." Narayan clarified that "Mrs. Gandhi herself had not at all suggested the inclusion of other party leaders in the Cabinet but their being associated in some way or the other with the freedom struggle." The cabinet shrugged it off, saying that "wherever possible offers of cooperation from such people were being availed of." The National Awami Party, they observed, "was already divided into small splinter groups . . . who have very little following," and Maulana Bhashani was "without any following whatsoever." The cabinet strongly felt that if widening the movement was "a pre-condition for Government of India giving them more help than is being given now, they should be clearly told so."[36]

Finally, New Delhi was also alert to the divisions within the Awami League leadership. For one thing, some senior Awami Leaguers resented Tajuddin Ahmad's assumption of the prime minister's office. Prominent among these were the foreign minister, Khandakar Moshtaque Ahmad and the Awami League's secretary-general, Mizanur Rahman Choudhury. They were also critical of the Bangladesh government's relationship with India and called for the diversification of its sources of dependence. Several other elected leaders took their cue from these Awami Leaguers and launched a virulent campaign against the Mujibnagar authorities. Tajuddin's secretary would recall that "cabinet meetings were often very stormy and the language used quite unsavoury." At one point, there was even a move within the Awami League to declare a lack of confidence in the prime minister's leadership.[37]

Moreover, a small group of influential young leaders refused to work with the Bangladesh government. Led by Mujib's nephew, Fazlul Haq Moni, this group, we may recall, had opposed the establishment of the government in exile. Moni claimed that before being arrested Mujib had entrusted him and four of his associates in the student movement with carrying on the struggle for the liberation of Bangladesh. His report was apparently corroborated by intelligence gathered by the R&AW. Moni quickly established a good relationship with the intelligence chief, R. N. Kao.

Owing to the lack of clarity about Mujib's intentions, Mrs. Gandhi allowed Kao to organize a separate militia under Moni's leadership—known as the Mujib Bahini—that would function independent of the Bangladesh government and the Mukti Fauj. The Mujib Bahini was also regarded as insurance against the possibility of the liberation movement being captured by the ultra-left Maoists. The militia was trained at two locations under the leadership of retired Major General Sujan Singh Uban, who had helped to raise the Special Frontier Force of Tibetan recruits in the wake of the 1962 war against China. The 10,000-strong Mujib Bahini was provided better training and equipment than the Mukti Bahini. It was also employed inside East Pakistan before the Mukti Bahini was inducted in August, though it appears that the Mujib Bahini was not used for direct attacks on the Pakistani forces.[38] Mujibnagar had reluctantly acquiesced in the formation of the Mujib Bahini and its operational independence; but Moni and his associates would continue to campaign against the government, and they presented a serious threat to Tajuddin's leadership.[39]

Managing these fault lines became all the more important after India decided to scale up its support for the liberation movement and push the crisis toward a desirable outcome. In early August, Indira Gandhi decided to appoint D. P. Dhar, who had just put the finishing touches to the Indo-Soviet treaty, as the chairman of policy planning committee in the Ministry of External Affairs. Dhar became New Delhi's point man for managing the relationship with the Bangladesh movement. Hitherto, the dealings with Mujibnagar had been handled by a midranking Ministry of External Affairs official. By contrast, Dhar was a political appointee with direct access to the prime minister. A man of considerable political acumen, experience, and charm, Dhar established a relationship of confidence and trust with Tajuddin. He also worked closely with the military chain of command in both India and Bangladesh, coordinating military operations with political moves, clearing bottlenecks in the supply chain, and patting egos all around.

In his initial meetings with the Mujibnagar authorities starting from 29 August, Dhar made it clear that New Delhi was prepared to move toward a resolution of the crisis within a definite time frame. More significantly, he gave a public statement that went beyond India's commitment to a "political solution" and affirmed its support for the exile government's resolution calling for "complete independence."[40] But there were two issues that demanded his immediate attention. First, the cabinet's unity had to be strengthened and its functioning improved. Dhar indicated that thenceforth New Delhi would respond only to those requests for assistance that had the approval of both the acting president and the prime minister of the Bangladesh government. Second, Dhar insisted the Bangladesh government had to bring in the other parties to support the liberation movement. He claimed that the involvement of the leftist groups—barring the Maoists, of course—was essential to secure external support, particularly from the Soviet Union. When the cabinet trotted out its well-rehearsed objections, Dhar told them that "the time has come when GOI [Government of India] must request BD [Bangla Desh] Govt. to form a broad national alliance . . . Otherwise the whole episode was fast becoming untenable for India."[41]

The Bangladesh cabinet had no option but to fall in line. On 8 September, the formation of a Five Party Consultative Committee was announced. This eight-member committee, including Bhashani, Muzaffar Ahmad, and a member from the Communist Party of Bangla Desh, would be chaired by Tajuddin and would "advise" the Mujibnagar government on the liberation struggle.[42] This fell short of the national front demanded by the smaller parties, but New Delhi hoped that it would impart credibility and cohesion to the liberation movement.

The Bangladesh government, in turn, requested that Dhar help rein in the Mujib Bahini. Dhar advised Tajuddin to send a representative to meet Kao and apprise him of the growing friction with the Mujib Bahini. Kao met with Mujibnagar's emissary on 13 September, but he declined to make any observations. At Dhar's suggestion, Tajuddin removed the restriction on the recruitment of leftist students for guerrilla training; this, he indicated, would swell the ranks of the Mukti Bahini and strike a balance with the Mujib Bahini.[43] By early October, Dhar had managed to get the prime minister's approval for instructing the Mujib Bahini to pledge its fealty to the Mujibnagar government and to cooperate with the Mukti Bahini. Notwithstanding these moves, Moni's militia continued to assert its operational independence.[44]

New Delhi, however, persisted in declining the exile government's requests for recognition. To mollify Mujibnagar's concerns, Dhar opened discussions with the cabinet on its long-standing demand for a friendship treaty between India and Bangladesh.[45] Even as these talks were under way, India learned of a development that could unravel all its efforts to shore up the liberation movement.

IV

On 30 July 1971, a member of the Awami League showed up at the US consulate in Calcutta seeking an appointment for Kazi Zahirul Qaiyum, a National Assembly member from the Awami League, to meet with the consul-general. Instead, the consulate arranged for Qaiyum to see a political officer the following day. Qaiyum said that he had come at the behest of Foreign Minister Khandakar Moshtaque Ahmad, who wished to reestablish the Awami League's contacts with the United States. He told the officer that the Awami League leadership feared the consequences of a war between India and Pakistan. Notwithstanding their declaration of independence, the Awami League desired a political settlement with Pakistan. The Awami League, he added, would be ready to retreat considerably from the positions it had hitherto taken. He even floated the possibility of a settlement that would allow elements of the Pakistan army to remain in East Bengal alongside a UN force. The best, perhaps only, way to resolve the crisis would be arranging a meeting between Richard Nixon, Yahya Khan, Indira Gandhi, and Mujibur Rahman. The American official remained noncommittal but agreed to meet with Qaiyum again.[46]

On 7 August, Qaiyum had another meeting with the American official. Reaffirming that he was contacting them under "specific instructions" from Khandakar Moshtaque, Qaiyum emphasized two points. One, the United States was the only country that could successfully arrange a settlement. Two, Mujib had to be a party to this settlement—if Mujib were executed, the prospects of a compromise "will be zero." Other Awami League leaders, including the cabinet members, had "no authority, no control over the masses." Conversely, any compromise negotiated by Mujib would be acceptable to the people, "even including a return to the status quo ante." Qaiyum urged the United States to convey the Awami League's desire for compromise to Yahya Khan. Khandakar was willing to travel to West Pakistan for negotiations, and he was also keen to confer with American officials but was unsure how to arrange such talks.[47]

The US embassy in Islamabad observed that even if Qaiyum's proposals represented those of the Bangladesh government, Yahya was unlikely to accept them. In serving as a conduit for these messages, the United States risked upsetting its relations with Pakistan. Nonetheless, in the interest of long-term relations with the Bangladesh leadership, the risk seemed worth running.[48] The White House had a rather different view. Kissinger insisted that asking Yahya to parley with the Awami Leaguers in Calcutta was "like asking Abraham Lincoln to deal with Jefferson Davis." Nixon agreed that "we can't ask Yahya to do that." Yet, he asked the State Department to sound out Ambassador Farland on this issue.[49] The consulate general in Calcutta was instructed to do nothing beyond probing the Awami League's willingness to negotiate for less than independence. In the next meeting with his American interlocutor, Qaiyum reiterated that he was acting under the instructions of the foreign minister and that the latter was willing to accept a negotiated settlement short of independence. He also emphasized that Mujib alone could negotiate on behalf of the Bengalis and get them to accept a settlement.[50]

On 19 August, Qaiyum sought an urgent meeting with his American contact. He claimed to have briefed the Bangladesh cabinet on 16 August about his discussions. The next day, Khandakar had informed him that the cabinet had decided that any agreement reached between Mujib and Yahya would be acceptable to them, provided it was arranged through the United States. The cabinet members, Qaiyum said, "believe that Mujib's life is more valuable than independence." Qaiyum claimed that he could get the signatures of 375 members of the provincial and national assemblies on a statement attesting to their agreement to seek a negotiated settlement. He also offered to have Khandakar prepare a document explaining his government's position to the United States.[51]

Encouraged by Qaiyum's avowals, Washington authorized the embassy in Islamabad to inform the Pakistan government about the contacts in Calcutta and to offer US assistance not as a mediator but as a "friend."[52] Farland mentioned to Yahya that a substantial number of elected Awami Leaguers were "seriously amenable" to a solution that preserved the unity of Pakistan, if such an agreement could be reached between him and Mujib. Yahya elided the question of negotiating with Mujib. He observed that he could not understand why the Awami Leaguers "who had been fully cleared did not come forward and take over the organization of a GOEP [Government of East Pakistan] so that he could transfer power soonest." Yahya's interest clearly lay not in an accord with Mujib but in finding collaborators in the ranks of the Awami League. Unsurprisingly, when Farland suggested quiet contacts between Pakistani officials and select Awami League leaders in a foreign country, Yahya supported the idea "wholeheartedly."[53]

Washington agreed with Farland's assessment that Yahya's reaction presented a "glimmer of hope." It was felt that the next step should be to establish direct contact with Khandakar and inform him that Pakistan was open to a meeting with representatives of Bangladesh.[54] Farland informed Yahya of Washington's thinking on 4 September. Yahya accepted the idea with alacrity, noting that Khandakar was one of the "true moderates" among Mujib's followers. He suggested that a meeting could be organized in East Pakistan. Farland, however, felt that London might be a more appropriate venue. Yahya did not disagree. At this point, Washington instructed the consulate in Calcutta to convey the message to the Bangladesh representative.[55] The US State Department thought that "the six points are within the ballpark." Kissinger agreed that this initiative could be "very helpful."[56]

These hopes were soon laid to rest. By the time the political officer in Calcutta contacted Qaiyum on 9 September, the situation on the ground had changed. D. P. Dhar's activism had started to buoy the sagging relationship between New Delhi and Mujibnagar. Tajuddin had confided to Dhar about Khandakar's clandestine contacts with the Americans and expressed concerns about his attempt to outflank the cabinet. Dhar advised Tajuddin to make it clear to his colleagues that there could be no negotiations with the Yahya regime under the prevailing conditions.[57] Qaiyum informed the Americans that Khandakar had told him "things have changed." No negotiations were possible while Mujib was in prison, for he was the only person who could negotiate with the Pakistan government. "We can't deliver the goods under the present circumstances," said Qaiyum. He observed that Yahya had to release Mujib and return him to Dhaka as well as declare amnesty for all those connected with the Bangladesh movement: "Then we can sit down and talk." When the American official pressed for a meeting with the foreign minister, Qaiyum hesitated. He warned that in any discussion with US officials Khandakar would take a "hard line," demanding the release of Mujib and complete independence for Bangladesh.[58]

True to form, Khandakar took a tough line when he sat down with the American officer on 29 September. Blaming American support to Pakistan for the continuation of the crisis, he asked the United States to lean on Yahya and ensure peaceful independence for Bangladesh. His list of demands included full independence for Bangladesh, the release of Mujib, and long-term economic assistance from the United States.[59] Khandakar's about-face was the measure of his prudence. By this time, his activities were under the surveillance of Indian intelligence agencies, and D. P. Dhar had advised Tajuddin to remove him from the cabinet. However, the acting president, Syed Nazrul Islam, was not in favor of such a drastic action that would showcase the differences within the cabinet. Instead, Khandakar was stripped of the foreign minister's portfolio, though he continued to remain in the cabinet.[60]

Of greater concern to India was the American role in this episode. New Delhi felt that instead of pressuring Yahya to negotiate with Mujib, the United States was helping him sow dissent in the Awami League's leadership. To smoke out the Americans, New Delhi instructed Ambassador Jha to encourage the United States to establish contact with the Mujibnagar government.[61] By bringing these contacts out in the open, India sought to monitor and regulate them. In his discussions with the State Department, Jha stressed that India's "principal concern was to see refugees go home." This could not come about merely by the cessation of conflict or the replacement of military rule with a civilian administration. Rather, it required the existence of a government in which the refugees had confidence. In India's judgment, "such a government must be Awami League government." Jha insisted that it was "not possible to have a dialogue which by-passed Mujib particularly when he is facing trial. Equally there can be no dialogue if [the] majority of elected people are disqualified." He argued that "only Yahya could make dialogue possible" and that the United States had greater influence on Yahya than India did on the Bangladesh leadership.[62]

When India's foreign minister traveled to the United Nations in early October, US Secretary of State William Rogers urged him to "initiate dialogue without insisting on Mujib's participation to see what could be accomplished." Swaran Singh replied that "the US has contacts with the Bangla Desh people. It has greater influence, it should try to bring about dialogue."[63] Yet India remained anxious about the susceptibility of members of the Bangladesh government to American influence and blandishments. Meeting an aide of Tajuddin on 16 October, D. P. Dhar expressed his concerns about the increasing factionalism within the exile government, in particular about the animosity toward the prime minister.[64] New Delhi was convinced that the crisis had to be steered to an end before the liberation movement began to flake.

V

Events on the ground increased New Delhi's sense of urgency. India's enhanced support to the Mukti Bahini and the accelerating tempo of military activity along the eastern borders made Pakistan apprehensive about the possibility of an Indian intervention in East Pakistan. Such an attack, the Pakistanis feared, would be aimed at carving out a "liberated zone" inside East Pakistan wherein the Bangladesh government could be installed. By the first week of September, Pakistan's Chief of General Staff, Gul Hassan Khan, had briefed Yahya on the plan for a massive Pakistani offensive in the western sector in the event of an Indian attack in the east. "We had to do something that would hurt India," he would write later. Yahya approved the plan, though he remained unsure of its details. At any rate, he ordered a full mobilization of Pakistani forces in the western sector.[65] To drive home the message to the Indians, Yahya stated in an interview that "if the Indians imagine they will be able to take one morsel of my territory without provoking war, they are making a serious mistake. Let me warn you and warn the world that it would mean war, out and out war."[66]

Until late September, the Indian government held back from mobilizing the armed forces, owing to concerns about maintaining secrecy and avoiding adverse international reactions. Thereafter, the army chief deemed it imprudent to accept the risk of a preemptive strike by Pakistan. In early October, Indian forces began trundling toward the borders in the east and west.[67]

By mid-October, the special unit in the Ministry of External Affairs dealing with the crisis prepared a detailed appraisal of the situation. The assessment concluded that the Indian forces would have to throw their weight fully behind the Mukti Bahini if the latter were to prevail against the Pakistan army. It also noted that the international community remained ambivalent about the emergence of an independent Bangladesh. If India moved toward a military conflict, the United States, China, and several other Western democracies would oppose India and support

Pakistan. This support, however, was likely to fall short of overt military involvement. Finally, it underscored the mounting domestic pressures on the government to take decisive action. The assessment was forwarded to the Political Affairs Committee of the cabinet. The prime minister and her colleagues decided that operational support for the Mukti Bahini would have to be qualitatively increased and that preparations needed to be made for the possibility of an open conflict with Pakistan.[68] Before the curtains could be raised for the final act, however, India sought to ensure that the international context would not impede the move toward imposing a solution of its own choosing.

VI

The country that mattered most for India's strategy was, of course, the Soviet Union. Despite the Indo-Soviet treaty, Moscow had been unwilling to fully support India's stance on the crisis. The Russians continued to believe that the refugee and political aspects of the crisis ought to be segregated. The Soviets also were eager to prevent another war on the subcontinent. Days after the treaty was signed, the Soviet ambassador in Washington, Anatoly Dobrynin, told Kissinger that Moscow was doing its best to restrain India. "They wanted peace in the subcontinent . . . their interest was stability." To maintain a balanced posture, they had invited Pakistan's foreign secretary to visit Moscow.[69] The Soviet foreign ministry told Pakistan's ambassador that in concluding the treaty their objectives "were not to encourage India but to restrain her." When Ambassador Marker observed that the Soviet Union was now the main arbiter of war and peace on the subcontinent, Fomin smiled broadly: "In that case, Mr. Ambassador, you can be sure there will be peace."[70]

In his meeting with Pakistan's foreign secretary on 6 September, Gromyko observed that Yahya had disregarded Soviet advice and "resorted to bloodshed and persecution." Although Yahya had spoken about a political settlement, "the situation has not improved substantially and the population of the area up to this moment is going through terrible deprivation, fear and uncertainty." The "only solution," he insisted, was "by political means." This would be possible only if the Pakistan government "stops its policy of repression and persecution. Only this will bring the refugees back, and other ways will fail." Alluding to Yahya's recent statement, he observed, "One gets the impression that certain circles in Pakistan are not against a military clash with India."[71]

"Please do not take any action," continued Gromyko, "that will oblige us to fulfil our obligations to a country with whom we have a Treaty of Friendship." Gromyko then paused and switched over to English: "The interpreter did not interpret me correctly. I did not use the word 'please.' I think you understand my meaning."[72] He went on to assure Sultan Khan that "we value relations with Pakistan and do not wish to experience a throwback." Sultan Khan replied that Pakistan would not take the initiative in starting hostilities against India. "But we will defend ourselves with all the strength at our command if we are subjected to an attack." Gromyko emphasized again that "the Pakistan Government and President should act with responsibility in the choice of methods." "Constraint, constraint, constraint! You must not yield to emotions."[73]

In public, the Soviet Union strove hard to take an even-handed stance on the crisis. At the Inter-Parliamentary Union Conference held in Paris on 10 September, the Soviet delegation voted for two resolutions that had been moved by Arab states which inclined toward Pakistan's position. The joint communiqué issued at the end of a visit to Moscow by the king of Afghanistan took an uncritical stance on the crisis. In his speech at the banquet, President Podgorny emphasized the need for a political settlement and the creation of conditions for the refugees to return. But he added that preservation of peace in the subcontinent depended "on the readiness of state leaders of that region to prevent their sliding down to a military conflict."[74]

None of this went down well with New Delhi. As India accelerated its military involvement in the crisis, it needed the Soviet Union's support both for supply of arms and for diplomatic cover on the international stage. On 27 September, Indira Gandhi reached Moscow for a crucial round of consultations. Brezhnev and Podgorny were in Bucharest when she landed in Moscow. Mrs. Gandhi put off her meeting scheduled for that evening because she wanted to speak to the troika of Soviet leadership in one meeting.[75]

The next day, Mrs. Gandhi assisted by D. P. Dhar held a marathon, six-hour meeting with Brezhnev, Podgorny, and Kosygin. She laid out at length the scale of the refugee problem, Pakistan's intransigence, and India's choice of building up military pressure while leaving the door ajar for a political solution. She also spoke of the gulf between West and East Pakistan, the quality of the liberation movement, the keenness of its desire for independence, the capacity of the liberation army to hold its own against the Pakistani forces, and the progressive program of Mujib, including his commitment to democracy, secularism, and socialism. After much discussion, Brezhnev observed that "there is an element of national liberation in the present situation." Podgorny agreed. Finally, the Soviet leaders asked what India expected of them. Mrs. Gandhi requested them to work for a political solution starting with Mujib's release and for military supplies to prepare for the contingency of war. The Soviet leadership agreed to consider these, but urged her to exercise restraint.[76]

Regardless of what was discussed behind closed doors, Moscow's public stance was slow in changing. Speaking to the Indian press that evening, Kosygin said that India's "problem is only refugees. The international community will help you get them back to East Pakistan." Foreign Secretary Kaul had to personally intervene and ensure that Kosygin's comments were not published. Later that night, Kosygin briefed the Indian journalists again, claiming that they had misunderstood his earlier remarks and that it was India's prerogative to deal with the crisis as it deemed fit.[77] Similarly, it was at India's insistence that the joint communiqué carried a line stating that "the Soviet side took into account the statement by the Prime Minister that the Government of India is fully determined to take all necessary measures to stop the inflow of refugees from East Bengal to India and to ensure that those refugees who are already in India return to their homeland without delay." As for the Soviet position, the communiqué merely read that the Soviet Union "reaffirmed its position" as laid down in Podgorny's appeal to Yahya of 2 April.[78]

In retrospect, it is clear that following Mrs. Gandhi's visit Moscow's stance began to shift in India's favor. Meeting with Nixon on 29 September, Gromyko observed that Moscow sought "to do everything possible to prevent a confrontation." Pakistan, he conceded, was the smaller country, but "to provoke a conflict one did not necessarily have to have superior size and strength." Indira Gandhi had assured them that she would not precipitate a clash with Pakistan. The Pakistanis had said the same to them, "but here the Soviets did not have as much confidence as in the case of the Indian leadership."[79]

An opportunity to ascertain Pakistan's position presented itself when Podgorny met Yahya at the extravaganza organized by the shah of Iran in Persepolis. The shah had already been in touch with the Russians, requesting that they exercise a restraining influence on India.[80] At his suggestion, a private meeting between Yahya and Podgorny was organized. On Podgorny's request, Yahya explained his plans for transferring power to elected civilian leaders. He insisted that it was India's interference that was complicating his efforts. So Podgorny asked Yahya, "Why don't you begin the process by starting talks with Sheikh Mujib? He is an essential factor in any peace process. If you can release him and secure his agreement to future plans, everything will fall into its proper place." Yahya irritably replied that he would never talk to "that traitor" and that his plans would produce a satisfactory result in a few months. Podgorny observed that with each passing day the crisis would become graver. "Please Mr. President," he said, "do not base your hopes on plans which may not materialize. You do not have unlimited time."[81]

The Soviet leadership concluded that Yahya was unwilling to work toward any reasonable solution, and Moscow decided to throw its weight behind India. Thus, when the US ambassador approached Gromyko to support a proposal—originally put forth by U Thant—for mutual withdrawal of Indian and Pakistan forces, the foreign minister told him that this would not help resolve the crisis. "The heart of the matter is that violence stems from the absence of political settlement. Yahya must be told that [the] only solution is political negotiations, discussion of freeing Mujibur Rahman, [and] negotiation with Mujib himself. Up to now nothing has been done to that end. Pakistan leaders must realize that they are on a very slippery road."[82] Four days later, Deputy Foreign Minister Firyubin landed in New Delhi for consultations under Article IX of the Indo-Soviet treaty. Over the next few days, the two sides reached complete accord in their assessment of the prevailing situation. On 28 October, Soviet Air Marshal P. S. Koutakhov reached New Delhi to negotiate the defense supplies urgently required by the Indian military. The same day, Swaran Singh informed the parliamentary consultative committee that India could count on "total support" from the Soviet Union.[83]

VII

Although Moscow's support was indispensable, Indira Gandhi was anxious that India should not be seen as supported solely by the Soviet Union. Given the public and official response to the crisis in Western Europe, she wanted to ensure that those countries—especially Britain and France, which were permanent members of the UN Security Council—did not hew to the American position by default.[84] From 25 October to 12 November, she toured a series of Western capitals: Brussels and Vienna, London and Washington, Paris and Bonn. On the eve of her departure, Mrs. Gandhi met the acting president and prime minister of Bangladesh and told them that she wished to make a final effort for a peaceful resolution of the crisis. She was, however, pessimistic about the prospects for success. If her efforts did fail, India would seriously consider launching a final offensive on her return.[85]

At each stop on the trip, the Indian prime minister interacted not only with her host government but also gave public addresses and interviews, and met intellectuals and artistes. With her acute antennae for cultural and political currents in Europe, she sought to shape the narrative of the crisis in ways that would speak to European public sensibilities. This was most evident in the way that she parried criticism of India's role in the crisis. On BBC television, for instance, she was asked if India was not contributing to the exodus of refugees by arming the Bengali guerrillas and if India should not cease supporting them to quieten the situation. Indira Gandhi tore into her interviewer: "Does that mean we allow the massacre to continue? . . . The massacre began long before there was a single guerrilla . . . What does quietening mean? Does it mean that we allow, we support the genocide? . . . May I ask you: when Hitler was on the rampage why didn't you say that let's keep quiet, and let's have peace in Germany, and let the Jews die, let Belgium die or let France die? . . . This would never have happened if the world community woke up to the fact when we first drew their attention to it."[86]

India's expectation of continued American antipathy was amply vindicated during her visit to Washington, DC. Nixon's objective was to buy time and deter India from embarking on war—at least until his own trip to Beijing had been completed. For Nixon and Kissinger believed that if they allowed India to humiliate Pakistan, their reputation in the eyes of China would suffer irreparable damage.

On the morning of 4 November, Nixon and Indira Gandhi, flanked by Kissinger and Haksar, met at the Oval Office in the White House. The president held forth on the steps taken by Yahya, including his willingness "to hold direct discussions with cleared Awami League leaders" and to meet a representative from the provisional government. He conceded the importance of Mujib, but he insisted that "the U.S. could not urge policies which would be tantamount to overthrowing President Yahya." The consequences of military action, Nixon warned, "were incalculably dangerous . . . The American people would not understand if India were to initiate military action against Pakistan." Mrs. Gandhi explained the Indian position at some length. The reality was that "it was no longer realistic to expect East and West Pakistan to remain together . . . The crucial issue remained the future of Mujib." When Nixon suggested withdrawal of troops from the borders and observed that Yahya had agreed to it, she did not respond. It was left to Haksar to point out that militarily this was not feasible for India.[87]

Nixon and Kissinger met in the Oval Office next morning to take stock of the previous day's meeting. When Nixon remarked that Indira Gandhi was being "a bitch," Kissinger observed that "the Indians are bastards anyway. They are starting a war there." Warming the president's cockles, he said, "While she was a bitch, we got what we wanted too . . . she will not be able to go home and say that the United States didn't give her a warm reception and therefore, in despair, she's got to go to war." "We really slobbered over the old witch," nodded Nixon. The fatuity of the assumption that Mrs. Gandhi had traveled all the way to Washington looking for an excuse to launch a war was matched by the overestimation of their impact on the prime minister. Turning to his aide Bob Haldeman, Nixon boasted, "You should have heard, Bob, the way we worked her around. I dropped stilettos all over her." It was decided that at their next meeting with Mrs. Gandhi the president would play it "cool."[88]

In the meeting that afternoon, it was Indira Gandhi who assumed her iciest air of aloofness. She made no reference at all to the subcontinental crisis, nor did she respond to Nixon's suggestion of the previous day. Instead, she took the initiative, quizzing Nixon about US foreign policy across the globe.[89] Mrs. Gandhi's attitude, Kissinger would later write, "brought out of all of Nixon's latent insecurities."[90] This was an astute observation. A month after this meeting—following the outbreak of war—Nixon would tell Kissinger that "what I'm concerned about, I really worry about, is whether or not I was too easy on the goddamn woman when she was here . . . She was playing us. And you know the cold way she was the next day . . . this woman suckered us."[91]

Mrs. Gandhi's meetings with the smaller European countries were equally unsuccessful. Belgium took a more activist stance than Austria, referring to India's assistance of the guerrillas and offering to mediate between India and Pakistan. When Mrs. Gandhi turned this down, Prime Minister Gaston Eyskens suggested mediation by the United Nations. Eventually the Indian prime minister took "a hard and uncompromising" stance, insisting that the only solution was for Mujib to be released and Bangladesh given its independence.[92]

The major European powers, however, were more tactful. The French envoy in New Delhi thought that Mrs. Gandhi was exercising considerable restraint. He argued that a premature attempt to counsel India about the dangers of war would be ineffective and harmful to Indo-French relations.[93] Paris also believed that Pakistan was "caught up with relatively short-range measures in [the] political area without needed focus on what really mattered, i.e. dealing with Mujib and [the] Awami League."[94]

In her meeting with President Pompidou, Mrs. Gandhi made it clear that India was opposed both to international mediation between India and Pakistan and to calls for withdrawal of troops from the borders. Underlining the dangers of a prolonged crisis, she observed that the liberation movement was likely to fall under the control of the extremists and that the possibility of Chinese involvement was likely to increase.[95] Pompidou assured her that he would weigh in with Yahya Khan. On 18 November, the French ambassador in Islamabad gave Yahya a letter from Pompidou urging him to release Mujib and commence negotiations with the Awami League leadership. An irate Yahya "shouted" at the French envoy that he would never negotiate with "miscreants" and people "guilty of crimes against the state."[96] Thereafter, French policy began to lean toward India. As a Belgian diplomat ruefully remarked, this shift was a "matter of realpolitik—they see nothing to be gained from staying with a sinking ship."[97]

France's position was moving in tandem with that of Britain. In the run-up to Mrs. Gandhi's visit, British officials wanted Prime Minister Heath to emphasize their desire for posting UN observers on both sides of the India-Pakistan border, for arranging troop withdrawals from the border areas, and for initiating talks between Yahya and Bangladesh representatives.[98] In the one-on-one meeting between the prime ministers on 31 October, Indira Gandhi said that "she did not see how to hold back the great pressures in India." "Mrs. Gandhi feared that this would lead to going to war with Pakistan." She was unsure if even Mujib could settle for something less than total independence. When Heath suggested mutual withdrawal of troops, Mrs. Gandhi replied that for military reasons Indian troops could not withdraw a short distance. "Any withdrawal would have to go a long way and this was not possible. She did not think the U.N. could help." Heath asked her to keep him informed if the situation deteriorated and suggested that she should publicly explain the reasons for India's refusal to consider proposals for troop withdrawal or posting of UN personnel.[99]

In parallel discussions at the level of officials, Haksar and Kaul stated that whatever might have been possible earlier, "the only outcome the Awami League could now be got to entertain was full independence." Further, for any negotiations to be effective and to command assent, it would "have to be achieved and blessed by Mujib himself." Yahya, they insisted, ought to directly negotiate with Mujib. "This should not be impossible." Alternatively, he could use an intermediary, though that would be less than satisfactory. "But Yahya was stupid, obstinate and drunk and they realised he might refuse to talk at all."[100]

Heath wrote to Yahya on 9 November urging him to consider releasing Mujib and negotiating with the Awami League's representatives.[101] Yahya responded by asking the British envoy to "report clearly to Mr. Heath that it was impossible for him to negotiate with Mujib." He told them that Britain was making a cardinal mistake in believing that Mujib represented the people of East Pakistan because he did not. The bulk of the people of East Pakistan were far more accurately represented by the cleared members of the Awami League. "You wait," said Yahya, "you will see that the prime minister will be from East Pakistan."[102] By the end of November, Heath was telling his colleagues on the cabinet's Defence and Oversea Policy Committee that "in the long run our interest probably lay more with India than Pakistan." He reminded them that "we should take care not to repeat our 1965 [India-Pakistan war] experience when . . . we had suffered maximum disadvantage without compensating benefit from either side."[103]

The shifting stance of Britain and France was mirrored in West Germany. On the eve of Prime Minister Gandhi's arrival, Chancellor Willy Brandt met the Pakistani envoy in Bonn. Challenging the latter's upbeat version of the measures taken by Yahya, Brandt said that "in all frankness he wished to point out the example of the British, who during the colonial period had never lost sight of who were the leaders of the masses in a particular country, e.g., Gandhi and Nehru. Therefore, perhaps there is a case for the government of Pakistan to hear out the advice of a man who had earlier aimed for only an autonomous status for East Pakistan." The ambassador interrupted to point out that Mujib "had gone too far in demanding a complete secession of East Pakistan." Brandt replied that "sometimes even seasoned politicians act irrationally in certain situations, but it is also possible that they again start thinking reasonably." Mujib, he averred, "seems to be important due to the huge number of followers he has. He [Brandt] will not, by the way, make any public statement to this effect; between countries with friendly relations, one must, however, be able to able to speak openly about such issues."[104]

Indira Gandhi and Brandt met thrice during her three-day visit. As in other capitals, the Indian prime minister stated that she was opposed to the stationing of UN observers on Indian soil, to the calls for mutual withdrawal, and to the idea of mediation between India and Pakistan. "The solution lies with Pakistan," she insisted: "the release of Mujibur Rahman and the resumption of negotiations with the representatives of the Awami League by the Pakistan central government."[105] Mrs. Gandhi admitted that India was supporting the Bangladesh guerrillas. "The support is restricted to just the bare minimum and has been effected only to prevent the East Bengalis from turning against the Indian government." The situation, she repeatedly observed, was extraordinarily serious and "akin to war." When asked what could be done to prevent further escalation, she "answered evasively or quite unconvincingly." West Germany concluded that "India no longer seems inclined to avoid the conflict with Pakistan."[106] Nevertheless, Brandt assured her that he would write to Yahya urging a political settlement.[107]

In their conversations with West German officials, Kaul and Haksar probed whether Bonn was continuing military supplies to Pakistan. They expressed particular concern about the recent supply of fighter aircraft to Iran, which might eventually end up in Pakistan.[108] The Indians had also been demanding that West Germany relax the arms embargo imposed in September and fulfill its previous commitments for the provision of chemicals and engines. In response to Mrs. Gandhi's visit, Brandt ordered the resumption of deliveries to India, though the embargo on Pakistan remained in place.[109] "So far as one could gauge," the West German foreign ministry observed, "the visit is being considered a success by the Indian side."[110] Indeed, India had precluded the possibility of an Atlantic entente on the Bangladesh crisis.

VIII

On returning to New Delhi, the prime minister ordered a further escalation of military action along the borders with East Pakistan. From early October, the Indian army had been supporting attacks by the Mukti Bahini on Pakistani border posts. This initially took the form of artillery fire on Pakistani positions and the participation of a small number of Indian troops in the offensives. In the second week of October, the army's eastern command ordered its formations not only to defend the border but also to carry out offensive operations up to ten miles inside East Pakistan. The idea was to capture important salients in East Pakistan that would assist in the eventual full-fledged military intervention. The captured territory was, however, held by the Mukti Bahini, with Indian troops retreating behind the borders.[111]

The scale and intensity of these operations rose sharply in mid-November. The fiercest of these preliminary operations took place at Boyra in the Jessore area. The Indian offensive started on the night of 12 November and made considerable headway. On 19 November, Pakistan launched a massive counterattack with armor and artillery supported by an air strike. Although the Indian forces eventually beat back the attack, downing three Pakistani aircraft in the process, it was clear by 21 November that the conflict had escalated to a new stage. In consequence, Indian troops were ordered to remain inside the captured territory all along the border.[112]

The prime minister claimed in parliament on 24 November that "it has never been our intention to escalate the situation" and that "we have instructed our troops not to cross the border except in self-defence." She dismissed as "propaganda" Pakistan's claims that India was "engaged in an undeclared war"—"This is wholly untrue."[113] The speech was, in fact, part of India's propaganda. Over two weeks back, Sydney Schanberg of the *New York Times* had filed a story quoting Indian officials as admitting that their troops had crossed into East Pakistan. Indira Gandhi had been in Paris when the piece was published, and she had been "deeply concerned at this leakage and desire[d] it to be thoroughly investigated." She instructed Indian officials "not to indulge in making statements which are politically damaging to our cause."[114] As the tempo of operations rose, it became increasingly difficult to deny Indian military involvement alongside the Mukti Bahini. In the last week of November, the prime minister gave the go-ahead for a full-scale attack on East Pakistan. The D-day was set for 4 December 1971.[115]

Meanwhile, the Pakistan army was watching the escalating conflict in the east with mounting disquiet. On the evening of 22 November, the chief of general staff briefed the president on the situation and urged him to order the attack on the western front. Yahya told Gul Hassan Khan that "serious negotiations are in progress at this time and if we opened a front in the West, these would be jeopardised."[116] Yahya was hoping that the UN Security Council would take cognizance of the fighting and intervene in the crisis. He had already written to the permanent members and the secretary-general. Yahya was also making frantic efforts to put a civilian government in place to provide a layer of legitimacy to his regime in the eyes of the international community. On 26 November, he briefed Bhutto on the outline of the new constitution designed by his experts, which would allow Yahya to remain president, supreme commander, and army commander in chief as well as retaining martial law powers. Four days later, he asked Bhutto to join a coalition government that would be headed by Nurul Amin, the old Bengali loyalist, who was one of only two non-Awami League members of the National Assembly elected from East Pakistan. Bhutto agreed to do so, provided he was designated deputy premier and foreign minister.[117]

By this time, Yahya's hopes for an intervention by the great powers had been deflated. The only major power that was inclined to raise the matter in the UN Security Council was the United States. The Soviet Union made it clear that it would block any move to prematurely summon the UN Security Council. Britain, too, conveyed to the United States that it wished to stand aloof. There were divisions within the Nixon administration as well. Nixon and Kissinger sought to come down heavily on India, but the State Department counseled against it. "It was a sad commentary on the state of the United Nations," Kissinger unctuously wrote in his memoirs, "when a full-scale invasion of a major country was treated by victim, ally, aggressor and other great powers as too dangerous to bring to the formal attention of the world body pledged by its charter to help preserve the peace."[118]

The full-scale invasion, however, was yet to come. On 29 November, Yahya made a tentative decision to open the western front, and the final decision was made the next day. The D-day originally chosen was 2 December, but it was postponed to 3 December 1971.[119] The decision was a compound of strategic and psychological considerations. By attacking in the west, the Pakistan army hoped to relieve pressure in the east and buy time for international action to damp down the conflict. The army's sense of vulnerability was coupled with a curious overconfidence about its superiority vis-à-vis India. The idea of the innate superiority of the Muslim soldier—the "one Muslim equal to ten Hindus" syndrome—had been bequeathed to Pakistan by the British Raj's theory of martial races, and it had been internalized by its military classes.

Added to this was the regime's pejorative view of the Indian prime minister, whom Yahya and his colleagues referred to as "that woman."

On the eve of war, writes a Pakistani historian, "private cars and public vehicles were plastered with 'Crush India' stickers. The radio was blaring martial music exhorting people to be ready for '*jehad*,' interspersed with vulgar parodies of Indian film songs about the person of Mrs. Gandhi."[120] When the preemptive strikes were launched on 3 December, the air chief told the military's public relations officer not to bother about conjuring up a justification. "Success is the biggest justification," he boasted. "My birds should be right over Agra by now, knocking the hell out of them. I am only waiting for the good news."[121]

The Pakistani attack was good news for India, too. After the clash of 21 November, Indian decision makers had been expecting an attack on the western front by Pakistan. The prime minister's secretary, P. N. Dhar, had argued that the military regime could not afford to let go of East Pakistan without inflicting some damage on India. He also believed that the Pakistanis might hope to trigger intervention by the United Nations and so stave off a military defeat in the east. India, he advised, should wait and allow Yahya to pick up the blame for starting the war. He reminded D. P. Dhar of Napoleon's advice: "never interrupt an enemy when he is making a mistake."[122]

D. P. Dhar was on the prime minister's plane traveling with her from Calcutta when the pilot informed them of the Pakistani air strikes. "The fool has done exactly what one had expected," he tersely remarked.[123] Indira Gandhi landed in New Delhi at around 10:45 PM and was received by the defense minister. She drove straight to the army headquarters where General Manekshaw briefed her on the actions taken on the western front and sought permission for launching the operations in the east. A little later the prime minister met with the rest of her cabinet. The decision was made to declare hostilities on Pakistan and to recognize Bangladesh. In the wee hours of 4 December 1971, the war for Bangladesh formally began.[124]

10

STRANGE VICTORY

As the sun went down in Dhaka, tens of thousands converged on the Race Course from all directions. Throughout the afternoon, the city had been humming with rumors of an impending surrender of the Pakistan army. At the ceremony, a small contingent of Pakistani and Indian soldiers presented an honor guard to Lieutenant General J. S. Aurora and Lieutenant General A. A. K Niazi. The surrender documents were signed by both commanders in front of a peering audience on that darkening evening. Niazi unbuttoned his epaulette, removed his revolver, and handed it to Aurora. The war for Bangladesh was at an end—just thirteen days after it had formally begun.

The speed and scale of the victory—India took around 93,000 prisoners of war—has led historians and chroniclers to assume that this outcome was a foregone conclusion. Sisson and Rose, to take but one example, argue that the result was "not in doubt, as the Indian military had all the advantages. Its force was considerably larger, much better armed, more mobile and had complete control of air and sea." India also had better logistics and excellent local intelligence owing to the Mukti Bahini. By contrast, the Pakistanis suffered from disadvantages on each score.[1] Add to this the claim that the Indian military had superb leadership while the lions of the Pakistan army were led by donkeys, and the outcome seems ineluctable.

To be sure, these factors did contribute to the Indian victory. But they did not make it inevitable. For the top Indian leadership had not conceived of such an outcome until well into the war, and then their strategy was shaped not just by operational considerations but wider political ones. Similarly, the eventual outcome was considerably influenced by chance and contingency. It was, in many ways, a strange victory.

I

What were India's political and military objectives on the eastern front? The conventional wisdom is that India sought to liberate East Pakistan by launching "an all-out offensive to capture Dhaka."[2] On the contrary, India's strategy was more modest. It aimed at capturing maximum possible territory, installing the government of Bangladesh, and thereafter securing the withdrawal of Pakistani forces, leading to eventual independence for Bangladesh. Indeed, from the outset, the contingency plan drawn up by the army headquarters did not specify the capture of Dhaka as the military aim, nor did the subsequent modifications to the war plan identify either Dhaka as the main objective or earmark resources for its capture.

The operational framework conceptualized by the director of military operations, Major General K. K. Singh, had three components. The first was to capture the two major ports of Chittagong and Khulna (a river port) and prevent further reinforcement of Pakistani forces in the region. The second was to secure such positions as would prevent the Pakistanis from switching their forces from one sector to another. These included key river crossings and airfields. The third was to split the Pakistani military formations within particular sectors into "penny packets" and thus enable their piecemeal destruction by the Indian army. The capture of Dhaka was considered—but deemed too ambitious. In the first place, reaching Dhaka would entail getting across at least one of the three massive rivers that traversed East Pakistan: the Padma, the Jamuna, and the Meghna. Crossing these rivers in the face of enemy opposition was seen as a tall order. In the second place, General Singh felt "rather strongly that the Indian Army, with its inherent inhibitions against anything unorthodox and a more speedy type of manoeuvre" was ill-suited for attempting the capture of Dhaka. In the third place, the military planners worked on the reasonable assumption that the operations would last no longer than three weeks. India's experience, especially during the 1965 war, was that international pressure for a ceasefire would not allow more prolonged operations. Owing to these considerations, the military task assigned to the army's eastern command was "limited to occupying the major portion of Bangladesh instead of the entire country." Both Major General Singh and General Manekshaw, the army chief, felt that this strategy would pave the way for the eventual collapse of the Pakistani resistance.[3]

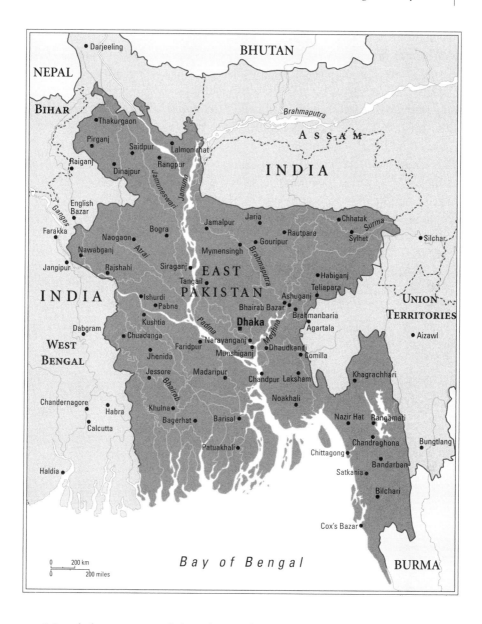

Manekshaw conveyed this plan to the eastern army commander, Lieutenant General Aurora, in early July 1971. Although Aurora agreed with the proposed plan, his chief of staff, Major General Jacob, demurred. Jacob felt that the plan should be designed with the deliberate aim of capturing Dhaka. A few months before, he had drawn up a draft sketch of operations premised on the idea of isolating and bypassing Pakistani strongholds and marching straight to Dhaka. These differences came to the fore at the beginning of August 1971, when Manekshaw and K. K. Singh visited the eastern command headquarters in Calcutta. After the director of military operations had spelled out the objectives and presented the plan, Jacob insisted that the "geopolitical heart" of East Pakistan was Dhaka and that its capture was imperative to ensuring control of East Pakistan. Manekshaw interjected and sought to defuse matters: "Don't you see if we take Khulna and Chittagong, Dacca will automatically fall?" Jacob replied that he did not agree, and he reiterated that Dhaka should be the key objective. Manekshaw, however, insisted that Dhaka was not a priority and that no troops would be allocated for its capture, and Aurora agreed.[4]

Enterprising commanders down the military chain bridled at the restricted aims of the plan. Lieutenant General Sagat Singh, commander of IV Corps based in Tripura, believed that his forces could swiftly advance to the Meghna River and thence to Dhaka. But the top brass remained unconvinced.[5] The commander of 301 Brigade, which stood within touching distance of Dhaka when the war ended, recalled that "at no stage . . . did I hear of Dacca being one of the objectives or the aim being the complete occupation of East Pakistan."[6]

By October 1971, the Indian plan was firmed up. In the eastern theater, the political objective was "to assist the Mukti Bahini in liberating *a part of Bangladesh,* where the refugees could be sent to live under their own Bangladesh Government."[7] The military strategy was "to capture sufficient area bordering the Brahmaputra and Meghna river lines." The theater was divided into four sectors. In the northwestern sector, which lay north of the Padma and west of the Jamuna, it was decided to advance up to the key communication center of Bogra and pin down the Pakistani forces. In the western sector, south and west of the Padma, the objective was to capture the main communication centers of Jessore and Jhenida. In the eastern sector, lying east of the Meghna, the plan was to occupy the Meghna bulge composed of three key towns along the river: Chandpur, Dhaudkandi, and Ashuganj. The Chittagong port would be dealt with by the Indian navy. In the northern sector, east of Jamuna and west of Meghna, a thrust would be made along the Jamalpur-Tangail axis to secure this area.[8]

These remained the objectives when the Indian offensive began on the night of 3 December. The air force chief, Air Chief Marshal P. C. Lal, would recall that the aims were "to gain as much ground as possible in the east, to neutralise the Pakistani forces there to the extent we could, and to establish a base as it were for a possible state of Bangladesh." This was because of the government's realization that the UN Security Council and the great powers were bound to intervene. The possibility of a complete collapse of Pakistani forces in East Pakistan and the fall of Dhaka were not regarded as likely outcomes. "Caution dictated," Lal observed, "that the [military] people commanding the East should work to limited objectives, but go about achieving them as rapidly as possible."[9]

The Indian offensive progressed broadly along the lines envisaged by the planners. In the western sector, Indian troops captured Jessore on 7 December, after the Pakistani garrison withdrew without a fight. The Pakistanis, however, put up a stern resistance in Khulna, a town that did not fall into Indian control until after the surrender of 16 December. In the northwestern sector, Indian forces were moving closer to the line of the Jamuna, though they frittered away precious resources and time in mounting set-piece attacks on well-prepared Pakistani positions. In the eastern sector, by contrast, the army made rapid progress, bypassing Pakistani strongholds and exploiting the gaps in their defenses. Lieutenant General Sagat Singh's assessment proved accurate: by 9 December, the city of Sylhet was surrounded and cut off from other Pakistani formations. His troops also had captured the three key towns on the banks of the Meghna—Ashuganj, Dhaudkandi, and Chandpur—and secured the Meghna bulge. The same evening, Indian forces in the northern sector were poised for an attack on Jamalpur following the garrison's refusal to surrender.

Even at this point, India's strategic aims had not expanded to include the capture of Dhaka. On 6 December, the Indian government announced its formal recognition of the government of Bangladesh.[10] Three days later, a note on India's objectives was prepared by the Prime Minister's Secretariat. This stated that India sought "a speedy return of 10 million refugees to their homeland" and that this was unlikely to happen "so long as the armies of West Pakistan continue to operate in Bangla Desh." The document did not state that India aimed to occupy Dhaka or to liberate all of East Pakistan; it only observed that "a mere cease-fire which does not simultaneously go into the basic causes of the conflict will prove . . . illusory."[11] New Delhi was evidently hoping that by the time a ceasefire was announced Indian forces would have made enough progress to render the Pakistani position politically untenable. Eventually, the scale of their victory just a few days later greatly exceeded their expectations. To understand this strange victory, we need to look beyond the battlefield.

II

"Pakistan thing makes your heart sick," said Nixon to Kissinger on learning of the war, "for them to be so done by the Indians and after we have warned the bitch." Kissinger's concerns were more practical. "If a major war [develops] without going to the Security Council it would be a confession of poverty."[12] At the Washington Special Actions Group (WSAG) meeting later that day, Kissinger said, "I've been catching unshirted hell every half-hour from the President ... He wants to tilt towards Pakistan."[13] This desire to tilt toward Pakistan, as noted earlier, stemmed from reputational concerns. Nixon and Kissinger believed that if they merely looked on while Pakistan was cut to size by India, their relationship with China would be nipped in the bud. As the war progressed, their concern with reputation would lead them to imagine that even greater interests were at stake and to take a series of steps that would profoundly, if unintentionally, influence the outcome of the conflict. The WSAG quickly concluded that the United States should call for a meeting of the UN Security Council and introduce a resolution.[14]

At the Security Council meeting the next day, the US permanent representative, George H. W. Bush, put forth a resolution calling for the cessation of hostilities, the withdrawal of the armed forces of India and Pakistan from each other's territories, and the use of the UN secretary-general's good offices to promote a settlement.[15] Because Pakistani troops on the western front had not yet broken through into Indian territory, the resolution was properly tilted toward Pakistan. In response, the Soviet Union tabled its own resolution, which tersely called "for a political settlement in East Pakistan which would inevitably result in a cessation of hostilities." This position, of course, sat well with India.[16] The Soviet proposal was a nonstarter, as only Poland supported it. When the American resolution was put to the vote, eleven member states of the Security Council voted for it and two against it. The Russians vetoed it.

Interestingly, Britain and France abstained on this vote. Even before the war formally began, the United Kingdom and France had begun adjusting their positions toward India. The British envoy had told the Indian government that if the crisis came up in the Security Council, they "would not find [the] British position in any way embarrassing to us on this matter."[17] When informed of the British and French abstentions, Nixon was peeved. "What do you think [is] the real game there," he asked Kissinger, "afraid to make Russia mad, isn't that it?" Kissinger concurred. "I am beginning to think," said Nixon, that "one of the worst mistakes we made was to push Britain onto the Common Market."[18] In any case, the Security Council carried on in its state of catatonia. Resolutions introduced by the smaller countries failed to take off. The People's Republic of China, which had recently entered the Security Council after having displaced Taiwan in October 1971, showed its evident inexperience; the resolution tabled by the Chinese representative "strongly condemning India" found no takers.[19]

The Security Council kept itself busy nitpicking innumerable amendments and hearing impassioned speeches. All this was music to Indian ears, as the Indian army continued to make steady inroads into East Pakistan. On 6 December—the day India formally recognized the Bangladesh government—the Soviets proposed a draft calling for an immediate ceasefire and calling upon Pakistan "simultaneously to take effective action towards a political settlement in East Pakistan, giving immediate effect to the Will of the East Pakistan population as expressed in the elections of December 1970."[20] In other words, the Soviets wanted a ceasefire accompanied by a transfer of power to the Bangladesh government while leaving the Indian forces in place. The resolution was vetoed by China. Eventually, the only resolution that was accepted by all members was to transfer the issue to the UN General Assembly.

In the Security Council debates, the Indian representative had initially sought to justify India's intervention on humanitarian grounds, arguing that "military repression" in East Pakistan was such as to "shock the conscience of mankind." "What has . . . happened," he asked, "to our conventions on genocide, human rights, self-determination, and so on?" India's motive was "to rescue the people of East Bengal from what they are suffering. If that is a crime, the Security Council should judge for itself." The Council was unmoved by such pleas, forcing the Indians to fall back on claims that they were acting in self-defense or—more imaginatively—that they were victims of "refugee aggression" by Pakistan.[21]

The issue was debated by the General Assembly in a marathon session that ran late into the night of 7 December. The resolution finally adopted by the General Assembly asked India and Pakistan to accept a ceasefire and withdraw their forces from each other's territory. It also urged the intensification of efforts "to create conditions necessary for the voluntary return of the East Pakistan refugees to their homes," but inserted the caveat that these efforts should be in accordance with "principles of the charter of the United Nations."[22] This was not surprising given that the General Assembly was dominated by champions of sovereignty from the Third World. All the same, it was a heavy blow for India when 104 countries voted in favor of the resolution and only eleven against it. The latter were the Soviet bloc (minus Romania), Bhutan, and India itself. There were ten abstentions, notably Britain and France. None of India's stalwart friends from the nonaligned world—Yugoslavia, Egypt, and Indonesia—had stood by it. The sole consolation lay in the fact that, unlike Security Council resolutions, the resolutions of the General Assembly were not binding on member states.

As the General Assembly debate wound down, both India and Pakistan sent their foreign ministers to New York for the next round of sparring at the United Nations.[23] In the meantime, Nixon and Kissinger were already focused elsewhere.

III

For several weeks, Kissinger had been working the back channel with the Soviets, emphasizing the need for Moscow to rein in India. In mid-November, he told the Soviet ambassador Anatoly Dobrynin that the United States was "extremely concerned" about the situation in the subcontinent: "We think India is determined to have a showdown . . . Sending arms to India is adding fuel." "I doubt that," Dobrynin told him. "I think it's publicity."[24] At a farewell dinner for Dobrynin, Kissinger again broached the issue of Soviet arms to India and the danger of war. According to Kissinger, the ambassador said he saw no reason why the United States and the Soviet Union should be "competitive" in South Asia. Moscow was "urging restraint on India." Dobrynin's account suggests that he did not take Kissinger's remarks too seriously.[25]

As the crisis escalated toward the end of November, Nixon wrote formally to Kosygin seeking support for the idea of withdrawing the troops of both sides to a limited distance and stationing UN observers.[26] Kosygin's reply was received on 3 December, after the war had begun. It claimed that Nixon's proposal was "scarcely feasible." The key to defusing the crisis lay in a political solution, which could only be initiated by the Pakistan government.[27]

Once the war was under way, Kissinger felt that "there's no way it [the crisis] could blow away without East Pakistan being separated from Pakistan." This did not, however, mean that the United States would acquiesce to a fait accompli. Kissinger held that American interests in one part of the world were tightly linked to those in others. Thus, adversaries and allies alike would observe US behavior and draw their conclusions about its resolve and reliability. Kissinger believed that "however this issue started and whatever the pros and cons of the local situation were, it's gone far beyond that."[28] "What we are seeing here," he told Nixon, "is a Soviet-India power play to humiliate the Chinese and also somewhat us." The dismembering of Pakistan would lead "all other countries watching it . . . [to conclude] that the friends of China and the United States have been clobbered by India and the Soviet Union."[29] Speaking to the treasury secretary, Kissinger outlined three concerns. First, "we have Indian-Soviet collusion, raping a friend of ours." Second, Beijing had reached out to the United States, concerned that the same situation might be visited on China. Hence, "some demonstration of our willingness to stand for some principles is important for that policy." Third, if the Soviets "get away with" this crisis, then "we have seen the dress rehearsal for a Middle Eastern war."[30]

Following the Soviet veto of the US resolution on 5 December, Kissinger was livid. The Russians, he insisted to Nixon, "are playing for big stakes here." "If the Chinese come out of this despising us, we lose that option." And "if the Russians think they backed us down," it would lead to a lot more trouble. Their "only hope," said Kissinger, was "to become very threatening to the Russians and tell them that if they are going to participate in the dismemberment of another country, that will affect their whole relationship to us." This sort of message could not be sent through the sedate diplomacy of the State Department; it needed an active back-channel effort.[31]

That afternoon, Kissinger met with the Soviet counselor Yuli Vorontsov to convey a message to Brezhnev. Nixon could not understand how the Soviet Union could seek a détente with the United States while "encouraging Indian military aggression against Pakistan." The United States and the Soviet Union, he warned, were "at a watershed in our relationship." If Moscow agreed to support a resolution for ceasefire and withdrawal, the United States would be prepared to work with them on a political solution.[32] Vorontsov expressed "surprise" and asked "why events between India and Pakistan are so insistently and obviously being extended to relations between our two countries." His assessment was that "the White House is nervous about the fairly complicated situation in which the U.S. has found itself" and that the message was an attempt to "transfer the dissatisfaction" over the situation "onto Soviet-U.S. relations."[33]

Clearly, the Russians did not regard the war as a crisis of high geopolitical stakes or linkages. Be that as it may, Nixon followed up with a written message to Brezhnev the next day. Nixon claimed the Soviet Union was backing India's quest to partition Pakistan, which ran counter to "recent encouraging trends" of cooperation between Washington and Moscow. It was in everyone's best interests, Nixon said, "if the territorial integrity of Pakistan were restored and military action were brought to an end." Nixon asked Brezhnev to use his "great influence" on India toward these ends.[34]

IV

On 6 December, the US Central Intelligence Agency (CIA) received intelligence from an Indian source that Prime Minister Gandhi had briefed her cabinet that day and emphasized that India had three aims in the war: quick liberation of Bangladesh, incorporation into India of the southern part of Azad Kashmir (Pakistan-administered Kashmir), and the destruction of Pakistan's military might so that it could never again attempt to challenge India.[35] Nixon and Kissinger seized upon this as firm evidence that India sought not only to liberate East Pakistan, but thereafter to launch a major attack on West Pakistan as well.

For one thing, it fit well their preconceptions about India's intentions. As far back as the summer of 1971, even before Kissinger's trip to the subcontinent, they had believed that "Mrs. Gandhi perceived a larger opportunity . . . perhaps trying to spread the centrifugal tendencies from East to West Pakistan."[36] In October, Kissinger told Zhou Enlai, "It is our judgment that the Indians see in this situation no longer a legal problem of East Pakistan but an opportunity to settle the whole problem of Pakistan which they have never accepted."[37] During Indira Gandhi's subsequent trip to Washington, Kissinger had strained to interpret her remarks about Balochistan along these lines. Further, because the intelligence had reached them in an unprocessed form, they were able to interpret and embellish it as they chose.

Not everyone gave it the same credence. When Kissinger raised the matter at a WSAG meeting, General John Ryan of the Joint Chiefs of Staff said, "We still think the Indians plan a holding action [in the west]—we don't think they will push very hard." He added that "it would take a long time for a transfer of all their divisions." Joseph Sisco of the State Department said, "Personally, I doubt that that is the Indian objective, but it may be."[38] Subsequent intelligence from the same source suggested that the Indian prime minister, unlike some of her colleagues, was not interested in attacking Azad Kashmir or West Pakistan.[39] But the inconsistency did not give pause to the White House. Indeed, Nixon wanted to leak the report to the press. Doing so he felt would "make her [Gandhi] look bad."[40] In the end, the report was not leaked; however, it was used by Nixon and Kissinger as the rationale to initiate a series of moves to which they already had been inclined.

First, Nixon decided to cut off economic aid to India. He had been threatening to do this all along. After 3 December 1971, Nixon believed that India would be discredited in the eyes of its Democratic supporters for having started the war. "We don't like this," he told Kissinger, "but you realize this is causing our liberal friends untold anguish."[41] Now this report would ensure that the State Department and the Congress could not oppose the suspension of aid to India.

Second, the White House sought to ensure the flow of arms to Pakistan. Because the Congress had imposed an embargo, the arms shipments had to be arranged through third parties. This, too, had been on their minds earlier. On 4 December, Yahya had told Ambassador Farland that his forces were in "desperate need of U.S. military supplies," and if the US administration was unable to provide them, "for God's sake don't hinder or impede the delivery of equipment from friendly third countries." On receiving this message, Nixon asked, "Can we help?" Kissinger replied, "I think if we tell the Iranians we will make it up to them we can do it." The shah of Iran was approached the next day and encouraged to transfer military equipment and munitions to Pakistan.[42]

After receiving the intelligence report, Kissinger took up the matter with the WSAG. The State Department looked into it and concluded that the president could not under law approve such transfers unless he took a policy stance that the United States was willing to supply this equipment directly to Pakistan. Kissinger denounced such reasoning as "doctrinaire." "The question is," he told the WSAG, "when an American ally is being raped, whether or not the U.S. should participate in enforcing a blockade of our ally, when the other side is getting Soviet aid."[43] Thereafter, the United States approached key Muslim countries—Jordan, Iran, Saudi Arabia, and Turkey—to supply weapons to Pakistan through an arms back-channel. Pakistan had independently approached these countries, but their willingness to accede to such requests was contingent on receiving assurance from the United States that the matériel sent to Pakistan would be made good. Even after Washington gave these transactions the go-ahead, things did not work out as planned by Kissinger and Nixon. The shah told the American envoy that he could not send Iranian aircraft and pilots to Pakistan because he was not prepared to risk a confrontation with the Soviets. Instead, the shah suggested that he could send his planes to Jordan, which in turn could send Jordanian plans to Pakistan.[44] Iran, in fact, had a secret agreement with Pakistan by which it would assume responsibility for the air defense of Karachi in the event of an India-Pakistan war. Yahya invoked the agreement, but the shah refused to observe the pact, claiming that it was no longer a purely bilateral conflict between Pakistan and India.[45]

Third, Nixon and Kissinger sought to draw China into the fray. They believed that this would not only rattle New Delhi, but also would underscore to Beijing the reliability of the United States. The White House had been eager to establish direct contact with China's representative at the United Nations to coordinate their moves, but the Chinese were not interested.[46] By the time the CIA input arrived, Nixon had begun to toy with the idea of getting the Chinese to intervene in the crisis. On the evening of 6 December, Nixon told Kissinger, "I think we've got to tell them [the Chinese] that some movement on their part we think toward the Indian border could be very significant." "Damnit," he exclaimed, "I am convinced that if the Chinese start moving the Indians will be petrified." Kissinger observed that the "weather is against them [the Chinese]." Nixon, however, believed that China still could make military moves against India. "The Chinese, you know, when they came across the Yalu [in the Korean War], we thought they were a bunch of goddamn fools in the heart of the winter, but they did it."[47]

Over the next two days, the CIA reviewed China's military posture along the Indian border and concluded that "the Chinese are not militarily prepared for major and sustained involvement in [the] Indo-Pak war." But China did retain "the option of a smaller scale effort, ranging from overt troop movements and publicized preparations to aggressive patrolling and harassment of Indian border outposts on a limited diversionary attack." The CIA, however, emphasized another aspect of their recent input regarding Gandhi's cabinet meeting. The prime minister had apparently told her colleagues that if China "rattled the sword," the Soviets had promised to "counter-balance" any such action.[48]

On the afternoon of 8 December, Nixon and Kissinger met in the Oval Office to take stock of the situation. Kissinger claimed that "the Indian plan is now clear. They're going to move their forces from East Pakistan to the west. They will then smash the Pakistan land forces and air forces, annex the part of Kashmir that is in Pakistan and then call it off." After this, he added, "the centrifugal forces in West Pakistan would be liberated. Baluchistan and the Northwest Frontier . . . will celebrate." West Pakistan would become like Afghanistan and East Pakistan—another Bhutan. And all of this would have been achieved by "Soviet support, Soviet arms, and Indian military force." Kissinger warned that "the impact of this on many countries threatened by the Soviet Union," particularly in the Middle East, would be grim. He also was worried that if the crisis ended in "complete dismemberment of Pakistan," the Chinese would conclude, "'All right. We [the United States] played it decently but we're just too weak.' And that they [the Chinese] have to break their encirclement, not by dealing with us, but by moving either [*transcription unclear*] or drop the whole idea."[49] In short, the grand design underpinning their opening with China could crumble in this crisis.

"Now what do we do?" asked Nixon. "We have got to convince the Indians now, we've got to scare them off from an attack on West Pakistan," replied Kissinger. He continued, "We could give a note to the Chinese and say, 'If you are ever going to move this is the time.'" Nixon agreed: "All right, that's what we'll do." Kissinger then added, "But the Russians I am afraid—but I must warn you, Mr. President, if our bluff is called, we'll be in trouble . . . we'll lose." He then claimed, "But . . . if we don't move, we'll certainly lose." Nixon said, "I'm for doing anything," but "we can't do this without the Chinese helping us. As I look at this thing, the Chinese have got to move to that damn border. The Indians have got to get a little scared." He instructed Kissinger to convey this message to the Chinese.[50]

Later that evening, Nixon reiterated his belief that China could exercise a restraining influence on India. "I tell you a movement of even some Chinese toward that border could scare those goddamn Indians to death."[51] The next morning, Kissinger grumbled to the president that the State Department was not sticking to the tough line coming out of the White House. For a moment, Nixon took off his blinkers: "Let's look . . . at what the realities are . . . The partition of Pakistan is a fact." Why, then, he asked, "are we going through all this agony?" Kissinger promptly stiffened the presidential spine: "We're going through this agony to prevent the West Pakistan army from being destroyed. Secondly, to maintain our Chinese arm. Thirdly, to prevent a complete collapse of the world's psychological balance of power, which will be produced if a combination of the Soviet Union and the Soviet armed client state can tackle a not so insignificant country without anybody doing anything."[52] It is evident that the notion of West Pakistan being destroyed was merely bolstering a position that stemmed from their wider, reputational concerns.

Kissinger sought and obtained a meeting with the Chinese representative to the United Nations, Huang Hua, on 10 December. He conveyed a message from Nixon that "if the People's Republic were to consider the situation on the Indian subcontinent a threat to its security, and if it took measures to protect its security, the US would oppose the efforts of others to interfere with the People's Republic." The "immediate objective" must be to prevent India from attacking West Pakistan. If nothing was done to stop this, "East Pakistan will become a Bhutan and West Pakistan will become a Nepal. And India with Soviet help would be free to turn its energies elsewhere."[53]

Huang's response was primly diplomatic. China's position, he said, was "not a secret." The stand taken by them in the United Nations was "the basic stand of our government." By contrast, the US stance was "a weak one." India and the Soviet Union were "on an extremely dangerous track." That said, Huang retreated to the fortress of philosophy and first principles. "We have an old proverb: 'If light does not come to the east it will come to the west. If the south darkens, the north must still have light.' And therefore if we meet with some defeats in certain places, we will win elsewhere." Kissinger grew impatient: "We agree with your theory, [but] we now have an immediate problem." When Huang refused to rise to bait, Kissinger bluntly said, "When I asked for this meeting, I did so to suggest Chinese military help, to be quite honest." But, he added, "This is for you to decide. You may have other problems on many other borders." Huang undertook to convey Nixon's message to Zhou Enlai.[54]

V

By the time Kissinger met Huang, the White House had set in motion two other consequential decisions. The first was to increase pressure on the

Soviet Union to lean on India. In response to Nixon's back-channel message and letter, the Soviets had maintained that it was imperative to obtain both a ceasefire and a political settlement that reflected the Bengalis' wishes. They had also criticized Nixon's insistence that the crisis represented a "watershed" in their relationship. Such an attitude would "hardly help" in finding a solution to the problem at hand.[55] This reply was received late on the night of 6 December, a few hours after the CIA had passed on its information on Indian plans. The day after, Kissinger's deputy, Alexander Haig, called Vorontsov and demanded a written reply to Nixon's letter. The president, he added, "wanted it understood that the 'watershed' term which he used was very, very pertinent, and he considers it a carefully thought-out and valid assessment on his part."[56]

In their meeting on 8 December—when Nixon asked Kissinger to approach the Chinese—Kissinger argued that militarily they "had only one hope now." This was "to convince the Indians the thing is going to escalate. And to convince the Russians that they are going to pay an enormous price." Aside from getting the Chinese to move, they could "take an aircraft carrier from Vietnam into the Bay of Bengal . . . We don't say they're there to—it would be a mistake. We just say we're moving them in, in order to evacuate American civilians." "I'd do it immediately," said Nixon; "I wouldn't wait 24 hours." Kissinger said that they should also send a "stem-winder of a note to the Russians to tell them that it will shoot everything, it will clearly jeopardize everything we have." He insisted that "we should do it all together." Pakistan, Nixon observed, was "going to lose anyway. At least we make an effort, and there is a chance to save it."[57]

That evening, Nixon reverted to the idea of tightening the screws on the Soviet Union and raising the stakes for Moscow. He felt that they should perhaps tell the Russians that "we feel that under the circumstances we have to cancel the summit [scheduled for 1972] . . . It's a tough goddamned decision." Kissinger felt that if they "play it out toughly" Nixon could "go to Moscow with [his] head up." But "if you just let it go down the drain, the Moscow summit may not be worth having." He argued that "if they maintain their respect for us even if you lose, we still will come out all right." "You mean, moving the carrier and letting the few planes [from Jordan] go in and that sort of thing[?]" Nixon asked. Kissinger maintained that it was a question of rescuing US credibility in a crisis "where a Soviet stooge, supported with Soviet arms, is overrunning a country that is an American ally."[58]

In the meantime, Brezhnev had sent a conciliatory reply to Nixon, saying that the Soviets were "profoundly concerned" about the situation in the subcontinent and reiterating that they wished to move toward a ceasefire and political negotiations between the Pakistan government and the Awami League leaders.[59] On the morning of 9 December, Vorontsov met with Kissinger to hand over this letter. Kissinger said that if India turned against West Pakistan "in the wake of East Pakistan" and tried "to secure a complete victory," then the US would prevent a crushing defeat of Pakistan and even be willing to take steps of a military nature. "The Indians must not forget," Kissinger said pointedly, "that the U.S. has allied commitments with respect to defending Pakistan."[60]

Later that day, Nixon met with the visiting Soviet agriculture minister, Vladimir Matskevich. He observed that "a great cloud" hung over the subcontinent and that it threatened to "poison this whole new relationship [between the United States and the Soviet Union] which has so much promise." He added, "If the Indians continue to wipe out resistance in East Pakistan and then move against West Pakistan, we then, inevitably, look to a confrontation. Because you see the Soviet Union has a treaty with India; we have one with Pakistan." He needed the urgency of obtaining a ceasefire to be understood in Moscow.[61]

Nixon and Kissinger's references to US treaty commitments were significant. The previous evening, Kissinger had urged Pakistan's ambassador to communicate with the State Department and formally invoke its "mutual security treaty."[62] But there was, in fact, no such treaty. The only extant agreement, which had been signed in March 1959 under the Eisenhower administration, pertained to commitments under Pakistan's membership in the Baghdad Pact and dealt with the contingency of aggression by a communist country. This agreement was never submitted to the Congress, let alone ratified. Kissinger frequently referred to a commitment made under the Kennedy administration, which was an assurance given (in an aide-mémoire) to Ayub Khan in late 1962 that the United States would come to Pakistan's aid if it was attacked by India. This had been extended to Ayub to assuage his concerns about the flow of US arms to India after the latter's war with China, but it certainly did not amount to a "treaty" of any kind.[63]

The White House could, however, count on Moscow being unable to parse such distinctions. When meeting with Vorontsov on the morning of 10 December, Kissinger claimed that there was "a secret protocol" in the US-Pakistan agreement, and he shared the aforementioned aide-mémoire with him. Kissinger said that the US military had already been ordered to begin preparations for possible military aid to Pakistan. These would be conducted in secret until 12 December under the pretext of "tactical redeployments" related to Vietnam. By Sunday, 12 December, the administration would have to make the final decision on whether to intervene in favor of Pakistan.

Kissinger's ploy had the desired effect of setting a cat among the Soviet pigeons. In a telegram to Moscow marked "Extremely Urgent," Vorontsov noted that from Kissinger's language he could infer that this military aid "involves moving U.S. aircraft carriers, and naval forces in general, closer to the subcontinent." The Americans, he wrote, "are only interested in the situation on the western border between Pakistan and India . . . Right now the White House clearly feels that the military aspect of the conflict in East Pakistan had already been decided in favor of India, and they are turning a blind eye to it."[64]

This was, of course, partially mistaken. Nixon and Kissinger believed that there was an outside chance for a ceasefire before the Pakistan army caved in on the eastern front. But Vorontsov's reference to the movement of the aircraft carrier was correct. That same day, Nixon instructed the chief of naval operations, Admiral Elmo Zumwalt, to assemble an impressive naval task force and move it off the coast of South Vietnam, into the Malacca Straits, and onward to the Bay of Bengal. Task Group 74 included the largest aircraft carrier in the US navy, the USS *Enterprise*.[65]

VI

No sooner had Moscow learned of Nixon and Kissinger's statements to Matskevich and Vorontsov than it began to lean on New Delhi.[66] Such was the urgency with which the Soviets conveyed their concerns that Indira Gandhi decided to send her trusted adviser D. P. Dhar to meet with the top Soviet leaders. Dhar left on the morning of 11 December carrying with him a missive from Mrs. Gandhi to Kosygin. "We have no design on the territory of others," she wrote, "nor do we have any desire to destroy Pakistan." As far as India was concerned, "we could cease fire tomorrow and even withdraw our forces to our own territory if the rulers of Pakistan would withdraw their forces from Bangla Desh and reach a peaceful settlement." For India now owed allegiance to the government of Bangladesh. "Without such a settlement," she insisted, "10 million refugees will not return to their homeland." A call to ceasefire "coupled with expressions of hope" about the return of refugees had "no purpose other than to cover up the annihilation of an entire nation." Indian forces fighting with the Mukti Bahini, she observed, had achieved "significant results."[67]

The Indian army had indeed made significant progress by this time. In particular, troops from the IV Corps stood on the eastern banks of the Meghna River on 9 December. Their commander had Dhaka in his sights, but had no firm orders to move ahead. Nor did he have the requisite river craft to attempt a crossing, the bridge having been blown up by the retreating Pakistani forces. General Sagat Singh liaised with the commander of the helicopter unit attached to his corps, and he arranged for an airlift of a sizable force. By the morning of 11 December, about 650 Indian troops were on the west bank of the Meghna.[68]

At this point, Dhaka came into the sights of the Indian leadership. The threat of an American intervention as well as Moscow's nervy reaction to it convinced New Delhi that its political aims could be only attained by a decisive military victory involving the capture of Dhaka and the surrender of Pakistani forces. This shift in objectives was also influenced by another development.

On the morning of 10 November, Governor A. M. Malik of East Pakistan sent a ceasefire proposal to the senior UN official in Dhaka, Paul Marc Henri. Over the previous few days, it had become increasingly clear that the defenses of the Pakistan army in East Pakistan were collapsing. The Pakistani military strategy in the eastern sector was to fight for territory at the border, fall back to fortified positions in the rear, and use these to interdict Indian maneuvers inside East Pakistan.[69] It has been frequently argued since then that the Pakistan army should have concentrated on the defense of Dhaka instead of spreading itself thin along the borders, but this perspective overlooks the point that the Pakistani strategy was premised on the expectation that India would aim to carve out territory in which to install the Bangladesh government—an assumption that was not far from reality. The problem lay in accomplishing staged, successful withdrawals—not an easy maneuver under the best of conditions.

On 7 December, Governor Malik had sent a telex message to Yahya suggesting that Pakistan should propose a political solution at the United Nations to obtain a ceasefire. The president's office had replied the next day asking the governor to continue the fight, informing him that a high-powered delegation was being "rushed" to the United Nations. However, the military position was worsening over time. On 9 December, General Niazi—the theater commander—sent a message to Rawalpindi painting a dismal military picture: "situation extremely critical . . . we will go on fighting and do our best." Niazi requested strikes on Indian air bases in the theater as well as airborne troops for the defense of Dhaka. In another message the following day, Niazi wrote, "orders to own troops issued to hold on [until the] last man last round which may not be too long . . . submitted for information and advice." In response, Yahya authorized the governor to take the necessary steps to prevent the destruction of civilians and to "ensure the safety of our armed forces by all political means that you will adopt with our opponent."[70]

After that, the military adviser to the governor, Major General Rao Farman Ali Khan, drafted the proposal that would be handed to Henri at 1:00 PM on 10 December. The proposal stated that the governor invited the elected representatives of East Pakistan to "arrange for the peaceful formation of the government in Dacca." Five requests were addressed to the United Nations: an immediate ceasefire, the repatriation of the armed forces to West Pakistan, the repatriation of all West Pakistan personnel, the safety of all persons settled in East Pakistan since 1947, and a guarantee of no reprisals. Although this was "a definite proposal" for a peaceful transfer of power, the "surrender of Armed Forces will not be considered and does not arise."[71]

When Yahya received a copy of the proposal, he was incensed. Reproving Malik for having "gone much beyond" his brief, Yahya observed that the proposal "virtually means the acceptance of an independent East Pakistan." The prevailing situation required only a "limited action by you [Malik] to end hostilities in East Pakistan."[72] Yahya quickly distanced himself from this proposal, but not before it had circulated in key chanceries, including among the Indians.[73] New Delhi now knew that the Pakistan army was on the brink of collapse in the eastern theater. This gave further impetus to the emerging decision to strike for Dhaka as well. At 4:00 PM on 11 December, an Indian parachute brigade was dropped at Tangail. The race for Dhaka had begun—but the road would turn out to be tortuous.

VII

On reaching Moscow, D. P. Dhar called on the Soviet premier to hand over the letter from Indira Gandhi. Alexei Kosygin was exceedingly

nervous, "shaking like a leaf." He asked Dhar about the progress of operations and about India's further intentions. "You must finish fast," he
insisted. Kosygin also informed Dhar that their first deputy foreign minister, Vasily Kuznetsov, was leaving for Delhi to consult with the Indian
leadership.[74] The Soviets had been tracking the movement of the US
naval task force sailing to the Bay of Bengal. They were deeply per-
turbed at the prospect of an escalation of the conflict and of their being
drawn into it.

In his meeting with Haksar on 12 December, Kuznetsov probed India's objectives on the western front. He emphasized that the US commitment to defending the territorial integrity of West Pakistan was "of a
nature and character that any provocation on our [India's] part that
might lead U.S.A. to conclude that we have territorial ambitions in west
Pakistan would enlarge the conflict."[75] New Delhi was already aware of
this possibility, as the foreign ministry had prepared an assessment of US
obligations to Pakistan. The note focused on the 1959 agreement and
concluded that the contents were "elastic enough" for Pakistan to invoke it. Whether the United States acceded to this request would depend
on "how far the U.S.A. will find it politically expedient" to interpret the
agreement in wide terms.[76] By the evening of 10 December, the Indian
navy was picking up signal intelligence about the impending move of
the US task force.[77] Two days later, the *New York Times* published the
news. The Indian embassy in Washington believed that three marine battalions had been "placed on the standby for emergency airlift" and that
a "bomber force aboard the 'Enterprise' had the US President's authority
to undertake bombing of Indian Army's communications, if necessary."[78]
New Delhi was anxious that the United States had a plan or an intention
to establish "a beachhead" in some part of East Pakistan to help with the
withdrawal and evacuation of Pakistan forces.[79]

The dispatch of USS *Enterprise* influenced Indian strategy in two different ways. As far as the eastern front was concerned, India decided to
accelerate the tempo of operations and conclude them before the task
force entered the waters of the Bay of Bengal. "Far from fraying our
nerves," Haksar conveyed to Kuznetsov, "it is promoting greater determination."[80] The army chief sent a succession of messages to General
Farman Ali in Dhaka urging him to surrender. "My forces are now closing in around Dacca and your garrisons there are within the range of my
artillery." Further resistance was "senseless," he stated. Manekshaw assured him of "complete protection and just treatment under Geneva

Convention" to all military and other personnel who surrendered to Indian forces.[81] At the same time, Manekshaw instructed the eastern army command to immediately capture all the towns in East Pakistan that Indian forces had bypassed: Dinajpur and Rangpur, Sylhet and Mynamati, Khulna and Chittagong. He was evidently concerned that if a ceasefire was declared soon, Indian troops would be in control of only two towns, Jessore and Comilla. The move to wind back and take control of the other locations would have entailed a significant—arguably fatal—diversion of resources from the drive toward Dhaka. However, fortunately for India, the commanders on the ground, instructed by General Jacob, disregarded the army chief's orders and maintained the momentum of the push to Dhaka.[82]

As far as the western front went, India exercised considerable circumspection to avoid giving any pretext to the United States for intervention. Haksar asked Mrs. Gandhi to convey to the army chief "that the complex political factors dominating our Western front with Pakistan require extreme care on our part."[83] He also wrote to the defense secretary that "anything that we may do or say which gives the impression that we have serious intentions, expressed through military actions or dispositions or propaganda, that we wish to detach parts of West Pakistan as well as that of Azad Kashmir would create a new situation."[84]

Furthermore, India reassured the Soviet leadership that "we have no repeat no territorial ambitions anywhere either in East or West Pakistan. Our recognition of Bangladesh is a guarantee against any territorial ambitions in the East and our position in the West is purely defensive." New Delhi also requested that Moscow "make a public announcement carrying the seal of the highest authorities in the Soviet Union that involvement or interference by third countries in the affairs of the subcontinent cannot but aggravate the situation in every way."[85] The Soviets welcomed the Indian assurance, but declined to make the announcement requested by India. They strongly felt that the longer the war dragged on, the higher was the possibility of US intervention.

Meanwhile, Nixon and Kissinger were anxiously awaiting Beijing's response to their request. "I am pretty sure," said Kissinger, "the Chinese are going to do something and I think that we'll soon see."[86] On the morning of 12 December, Nixon decided to send a message to Moscow that reiterated his stance. "We're not letting the Russians diddle us along," he said. Kissinger replied, "It's a typical Nixon plan. I mean it's bold. You're putting your chips into the pot again. But my view is that if we do nothing, there's a certainty of a disaster . . . at least we're coming off like men. And that's [*sic*] helps us with the Chinese." Kissinger informed Nixon that the task force would be in the Indian Ocean the next day.[87]

Haig interrupted the conversation and said that the Chinese wanted urgently to meet. Because Nixon and Kissinger were leaving for the Azores, they had suggested this meeting in New York with Haig. China's request for a meeting was "totally unprecedented," said Kissinger. It meant "they're going to move. No question they're going to move." A fantastic exchange ensued. "If the Soviets move against them [the Chinese]," said Kissinger, "and then we don't do anything, we'll be finished." Nixon asked, "So what do we do if the Soviets move against them? Start lobbing nuclear weapons in, is that what you mean?" Kissinger replied, "Well, if the Soviets move against them in these conditions and succeed, that will be the final showdown." He added, "If the Russians get away with facing down the Chinese, and if the Indians get away with licking the Pakistanis . . . we may be looking right down the gun barrel."[88]

This reckless web of geopolitical dreams rapidly unraveled. In the meeting with Haig, Huang Hua read out a message from Beijing. China "carefully studied the options" put forth by Kissinger. The Chinese leadership felt that the Security Council should reconvene and push for a resolution calling for ceasefire and mutual withdrawals. There was not a word about moving against India. Haig's recital of all the measures initiated by the administration failed to elicit anything more from Huang.[89] The gambit with China had come to naught.

Why did the Chinese refrain from acting as suggested by the White House? Even before the war broke out, China had not been inclined to militarily back Pakistan. One reason for this was its desire not to aggravate its problems with India, and so push India closer to the Soviet Union. This interest appears to have been buttressed by a message from Mrs. Gandhi to Zhou Enlai that had been sent the day before the meeting between Haig and Huang Hua. Mrs. Gandhi sought China's understanding for India's predicament and requested Zhou to "exercise your undoubted influence" on Yahya to acknowledge the will of the Bengalis. "We seek China's friendship," she said. "In my last letter I had indicated our readiness to discuss problems of mutual interest."[90]

A second reason was the strain between the political and military leaderships in China following the "Lin Biao affair." In the run-up to the India-Pakistan war, Mao Zedong was reasserting his control over the People's Liberation Army and had little interest in involving China in any military engagement. A third reason was Beijing's belief that any military move at this stage would be futile. As Zhou later told Kissinger, "By that time East Pakistan was already unable to be saved." China was not particularly impressed by the movement of the seventh fleet either. Zhou pointed out that Soviet submarines had "also closely followed you down into the Indian Ocean." When Kissinger boasted that the US force could take care of them "very easily," Zhou observed that "they [Soviets] could surface in such a way their [*sic*] support to East Bengal."[91]

VIII

As a result of China's refusal to become embroiled in the crisis, the Nixon administration shifted its attention to the Security Council. A resolution tabled by the United States on 13 November called for an immediate ceasefire and withdrawal as well as intensification of efforts to create conditions for the return of the refugees. It was vetoed by the Soviet Union. By this time, however, Moscow was eager both to secure an acceptable ceasefire at the earliest and to avoid wielding any further vetoes.

On 13 December, the Soviet ambassador in Delhi met Haksar and handed him a paper with certain principles for a Security Council resolution. Haksar countered by suggesting that they should start with the Farman Ali proposal about the transfer of power to elected representatives. The ambassador said that they only sought India's general approval at this stage and asked him to present the idea to Mrs. Gandhi before her meeting with First Deputy Foreign Minister Kuznetsov. Haksar parried by observing that he was not sure whether the prime minister would have enough time and that she would need to consult her cabinet colleagues. The ambassador pressed further and said that "time was the essence of the matter." Haksar advised the prime minister that "no harm would be done" if India agreed to consider these proposals, but they believed that it might be desirable for some country other than Soviet Union or Poland to take the initiative. "This would enable the Soviet Union to be free to resist amendments which would not be acceptable to us or even use [the] veto if the proposals take a shape which is unacceptable to us."[92] This was an erroneous reading of the Soviet stance, for Moscow wanted an early ceasefire.

On 14 December, the Soviet leadership sent a back-channel message to Nixon stating that "we have firm assurances by the Indian leadership that India has no plans of seizing West Pakistan territory." India had also expressed its willingness to stop fighting and pull back its forces if power was transferred to the elected representatives of East Pakistan. Thus, there was the "necessary basis for an immediate cessation of the conflict and this opportunity should be used." Referring to the US naval force powering toward the region, the Soviets asked, "Suppose the other side will also embark on the path of taking similar measures—what then will be the net result?" The message ended by reiterating that "now there is a basis for the solution and we must seize this opportunity."[93]

In the meantime, after obtaining Mrs. Gandhi's approval, Haksar drafted a note for the Political Affairs Committee of the cabinet. He observed that it was "clear that every day's delay in completing the military operations in Bangla Desh is playing into the hands of our opponents." In order to secure room for maneuver, India should agree to consider another draft resolution. "The political and tactical advantage of doing this need hardly be spelt out. We shall gain time. We would not appear negative and intransigent." The note set out a series of principles that could be incorporated into this draft resolution. First, there should be peaceful transfer of power in East Pakistan to elected representatives led by Mujibur Rahman, who should be immediately released. Second, there should be immediate cessation of military actions and a seventy-two-hour ceasefire initially. Third, on commencement of this period, Pakistani forces should begin withdrawal to designated places for the purpose of evacuation from East Pakistan. Fourth, all civilian personnel wishing to leave East Pakistan for West Pakistan and vice versa should be repatriated under UN supervision. Fifth, once the seventy-two-hour period was complete, the ceasefire should become permanent. Indian forces should withdraw from Bangladesh, but that withdrawal would begin only after consultations with the new government headed by Mujibur Rahman. Sixth, territorial gains should not be retained by either party in the western or eastern theater. These principles, Haksar pointed out, were "sufficiently elastic to generate discussion and give time." It was "well understood" that the resolution would not be introduced by the Soviet Union, Britain, France, or Poland, and that none of those countries or India would be "committed to these proposals."[94]

These hopes were soon belied. Although a draft resolution based on these proposals was indeed introduced in the Security Council on 14 December, to India's surprise and chagrin the resolution was tabled by Poland. This was an unambiguous indication that Moscow intended to back it because it was inconceivable that the Soviets would veto a resolution introduced by Poland. At this point, Dhaka had not yet fallen to Indian forces, so the Polish resolution had the potential to deprive India of the clear victory that was now sought. More worryingly, following discussions in the Security Council, Poland proposed a revised version on 15 December that omitted the original's reference to Mujibur Rahman.[95] This muddled the issue of the proposed transfer of power to elected representatives. In any event, India had not expected to be boxed into a corner by these proposals.

Worse yet was the introduction on 15 December of another draft resolution jointly sponsored by Britain and France. Hitherto, London and Paris had tilted toward New Delhi and abstained on crucial votes in the Security Council and the General Assembly. They had also impressed upon India the need to "finish the job as quickly as possible."[96] Faced with the prospect of an escalation of the war, Britain and France sponsored a resolution that they saw as offering a realistic chance for ceasefire. Their draft called for an immediate ceasefire and withdrawal of forces, and for "the urgent conclusion of a comprehensive political settlement in accordance with the wishes of the people concerned as declared through their elected and acknowledged representatives."[97] Prime Minister Heath also sent a message to Indira Gandhi commending this resolution.

At 7:00 PM (Indian Standard Time) on 15 December, the Political Affairs Committee of the Indian cabinet considered the resolution and Heath's message. The committee felt that "the Resolution puts us in an extremely disadvantageous, even critical, situation." It was "more retrograde than even [the] Farman Ali proposals." Although the ceasefire would come immediately into effect, "political negotiations are only in the nature of a pie in the sky." Even the "barest anatomy of the political settlement" was unspecified. Prime Minister Gandhi cabled Heath and President Pompidou urging them not to proceed with the resolution. The Indian delegation at the United Nations was instructed to "tell our British and French friends not to put us in an untenable situation."[98]

India's concerns over these draft resolutions were lent considerable urgency by the receipt earlier that day—at 2:20 PM (Indian Standard Time)—of another ceasefire proposal, this time from General Niazi in Dhaka. The previous afternoon, Niazi had received a message from Yahya that "further resistance is no longer humanly possible nor will it serve any useful purpose . . . You should now take all necessary measures to stop the fighting and preserve the lives of the armed forces personnel, all those from West Pakistan, and all loyal elements."[99] At 5:20 PM (Dhaka local time), Niazi and Farman Ali had approached the US consul general in Dhaka and asked him to transmit a proposal to New Delhi. This offered an immediate ceasefire on the condition that the regrouping of Pakistani forces would be mutually agreed upon by commanders of both sides; that India would guarantee the safety of all Pakistani military and paramilitary forces as well as all persons settled in East Pakistan since 1947; and that there would no reprisals against civilian collaborators of the administration. Niazi and Farman Ali wished to avoid using the word "surrender."[100]

Almost 19 hours passed before the proposal wended its way to New Delhi. The State Department asked Ambassador Farland to ascertain from the Pakistanis whether Niazi had the authority to advance such a proposal. On receiving confirmation from Foreign Secretary Sultan Khan, Farland reverted to Washington for instructions. The US State Department was chary of directly transmitting this proposal to India and thus inviting the wrath of the White House; instead, the US delegation at the United Nations was instructed to give it to Pakistan's foreign minister, Bhutto, with a hint that he might want to hand it to the Indian foreign minister in New York. Bhutto did not oblige. So the State Department instructed its UN representative to give it directly to the Indian delegation with the caveat that the United States took no position on its contents. Swaran Singh, however, was unable to get through to Haksar on the telephone, so he requested that the Americans pass on the message through their embassy in New Delhi.[101]

On seeing the message, New Delhi decided it was "misleading." "It does not talk of any surrender but assumes that the Pakistani military authorities will continue wherever they are with their arms."[102] The Indians, therefore, handed the US embassy a reply to Niazi from Manekshaw. The message repeated previous assurances of safety for all personnel and called on Niazi to order all forces in East Pakistan "to ceasefire immediately and surrender to my advancing forces." On receiving a positive reply, the message said, the eastern command would refrain from all ground and air attacks on Pakistani positions. As a token of good faith, India would desist from air action over Dhaka from 5:00 PM on 15 December. If Niazi failed to agree to this proposal, the Indian attacks would resume at 9:00 AM on 16 December.[103]

During these crucial hours, while New Delhi awaited Niazi's reply, the Security Council convened to consider the new proposals. The meeting began at 12:10 PM (US Eastern Standard Time) on 15 December. In the previous session, the British had sought a postponement to allow more time for consultation on their draft. This effectively ensured that the Anglo-French resolution was placed on the back burner. In this session, the Polish resolution came up for discussion. Before the meeting, Yahya had spoken with Bhutto on the telephone and told him that the Polish resolution looked good: "We should accept it." Bhutto had replied, "I can't hear you." When Yahya repeated himself several times, Bhutto only said, "What? What?" When the operator in New York intervened to inform them that the connection was fine, Bhutto told her to "shut up."[104] At the meeting, Bhutto said, "Let us face the stark truth. I have got no stakes left for the moment." He went on to make a moving speech denouncing the Security Council's failure to prevent the vivisection of Pakistan. In closing, Bhutto declared, "I will not be a party to the ignominious surrender of part of my country. You can take your Security Council. Here you are. I am going."[105] Bhutto tore up the resolution papers and stormed out of the meeting. The Polish resolution was buried.

Why did Bhutto not heed Yahya's advice and accept the resolution? Had it been passed in that session, it would have prevented the surrender of the Pakistani troops. Then again, that appears to be precisely why Bhutto scuttled the resolution. He seems to have been calculating that an ignominious defeat capped off by the surrender of tens of thousands of troops would deal such a blow to the Pakistan army as to shake its grip on the polity, which then would clear the ground for his own political ascendance. Singed by his dalliances with the military, both under Ayub and Yahya, Bhutto seems to have concluded that the new Pakistan must be built on the ash heap of the army's decisive defeat. He was not wrong.

Ultimately, Bhutto's decision to walk out on the Security Council saved the day for India. A few hours later, early in the morning of 16 December, Niazi's reply was received in New Delhi. Niazi sought an extension of the truce by six hours—up to 3:00 PM on 16 December—and suggested "a preliminary staff meeting" in Dhaka: "Meantime we are going ahead with ceasefire formalities." The Indian response made it clear that the Pakistanis would have to surrender, and Manekshaw agreed to extend the pause in fighting. He informed Niazi that General Jacob would arrive by helicopter in Dhaka at 12:30 PM the same day. "He will negotiate the terms of surrender. Your forces in Dacca must surrender at 1600 hours [4:00 PM] Indian Standard Time today."[106] Jacob reached Niazi's

headquarters at 1:00 PM, and soon after he read out the terms of the surrender to Niazi and his staff. A hush fell over the room as the Pakistanis
realized that this was an unconditional surrender. At 4:55 PM on 16 December 1971, Aurora and Niazi signed the Instrument of Surrender.[107]

IX

On the same day the Pakistan army surrendered in the east, New Delhi
announced a unilateral ceasefire on the western front that would come
into effect on 17 December. The decision was, of course, taken in the
context of the international developments over the preceding week. But
there were other, more immediate, strategic concerns that led Indira Gandhi to call for a ceasefire. For one thing, she was clear that a continuation
of the war "would not have produced a decisive military victory." For
another, it was "unthinkable" for India to enter West Pakistan as an occupying power. They would be in "a complete mess" with their garrisons
in the Punjab and elsewhere, for India had "no political base" in West
Pakistan as opposed to Bangladesh where it had "political allies."[108]

"It's the Russians working for us," said Nixon when he heard the news.
"We have to get the story out." "Congratulations, Mr. President," replied
Kissinger, "you have saved W[est] Pakistan."[109] Writing their memoirs
some years later, both men would claim success in their management of
the crisis. "By using diplomatic signals and behind-the-scenes pressures,"
wrote Nixon, "we had been able to save West Pakistan from the imminent threat of Indian aggression and domination."[110] "There is no doubt
in my mind," insisted Kissinger, "that it [the declaration of ceasefire] was
a reluctant decision resulting from Soviet pressure, which in turn grew
out of American insistence, including the fleet movement."[111]

However, as the foregoing account shows, India never had West Pakistan in its sights. Let us consider a final bit of evidence. In February
1972, Ambassador L K Jha wrote to Haksar about his efforts to track
down the alleged cabinet source for the intelligence report on the prime
minister's intention to attack West Pakistan. When Mrs. Gandhi read
this letter, she wrote on the margins: "Perhaps it is not necessary but we
should have then informed L K that at NO time have I ever made such a
statement. Besides even a discussion had not taken place at any Cabinet
Meeting."[112]

Nixon and Kissinger overplayed the importance of an intelligence
source, mainly because it helped them rationalize their desire to demon-

strate resolve to China and the Soviet Union. The problem was not merely deception but also self-deception. The only practical consequence of the aggressive US posturing was to spur the Indians to capture Dhaka and seal their victory—objectives that had not been on their strategic horizons when the war began. This was Nixon and Kissinger's war of illusions. In retrospect, they come across not as tough statesmen tilting toward their ally but as a picaresque pair tilting at windmills.

EPILOGUE:
THE GARDEN OF FORKING PATHS

Indira Gandhi was with a Swedish television crew when the red telephone on her table rang. She answered: "Yes," "yes," "thank you." The caller was General Manekshaw, giving her the news of the surrender in Dhaka. Mrs. Gandhi asked her Swedish interviewer to wait in her antechamber, then she briskly left for parliament. The House hung still with tension and anticipation, as she began reading out her statement: "The West Pakistan forces have unconditionally surrendered in Bangladesh . . . Dacca is now the free capital of a free country." The members of parliament erupted in acclamation and every line of her statement was cheered to the echo. In the days ahead, Indira Gandhi would be praised in parliament with awe and veneration. Even leaders of the opposition likened her to Durga, the martial goddess of the Hindu pantheon, and compared her to Shakti, the spiritual embodiment of energy and power. The *Economist,* capturing the mood of the times, crowned her the "Empress of India."[1]

In Pakistan, the effect of the war was equally electrifying. Yahya Khan and the military tamely handed over the levers of the state in West Pakistan to Zulfikar Ali Bhutto, who now assumed the office of the president and powers of the martial law administrator. On 7 January 1972, Bhutto went to the Islamabad airport to see off Sheikh Mujibur Rahman, who was flying to London and freedom. Three days later, Indira Gandhi stood on the tarmac of Delhi's airport to greet Mujib on his brief stopover. The two leaders addressed a huge rally pledging lasting friendship and fealty between their countries. That afternoon, Mujib landed in Dhaka. Standing atop an open Dodge truck, flanked by his lieutenants, Mujib was greeted by millions in a tumultuous and triumphal homecoming.

The groundswell of messianic emotions in India and Bangladesh was entirely understandable. India had not only won a decisive military victory, but had seemingly exorcised the specter of the "two-nation" theory that had haunted the subcontinent since 1947. Bangladesh had struggled against a murderous military regime and won its freedom. In some ways, this upsurge of emotion has yet to subside even today. It continues to suffuse popular memory and scholarly writing on the subject. In particular, the notion that the emergence of Bangladesh was inevitable is a product of the mood that followed the war. This apparently inexorable and teleological narrative would have found few takers before the fateful year of 1971. It is the glare of hindsight that distorts our understanding by portraying the eventual outcome in retrospect as somehow predestined.

In fact, there was nothing inevitable either about the breakup of united Pakistan or about the emergence of an independent Bangladesh. Rather, it was the product of historical currents and conjunctures that ranged far beyond South Asia. Furthermore, decolonization, the Cold War, and incipient globalization interacted with one another and intersected with the South Asian crisis in ways that were far from predictable. As countries of the Third World shook off the web of colonial control, they reinforced the principle of sovereignty in the international system and thwarted the extension of self-determination to groups within the new postcolonial states. This ensured that there was no clear divide between the global North and South on the Bangladesh crisis: the authoritarian states of the South were able to find common ground with countries of the North, such as the United States and Canada, in preventing international intervention to resolve the crisis short of war. Similarly, the Cold War context of the period blurred the divide between the West and the East. Initially both the United States and the Soviet Union were averse to the breakup of Pakistan. However, unlike the Soviet leadership, which viewed the crisis as regional, Nixon and Kissinger perceived great geopolitical interests at stake owing to their opening to China. Indeed, the main Cold War fault line of this crisis ran not between the West and East but within them. Thus, the clashes between the Soviet Union and the People's Republic of China in 1969 placed the erstwhile socialist allies at odds during the 1971 crisis. Similarly, the weakening bonds of the Western alliance led Britain, France, West Germany, and Japan to adopt positions at variance with that of the United States and closer to that of the

Soviet Union in the later stages of the crisis. The positions taken by these US allies were also in response to the pressure of public opinion, which in turn was shaped by various facets of the emerging globalization: new technologies of communication and transportation; new forms of humanitarian and human rights politics, stemming from the global protests of the 1960s; the widespread diffusion of the Sixties' counterculture, especially music; and the presence of diasporas owing to the movement of labor from the Third World to the First World. In the absence of these wider historical forces, the crisis of 1971 could have taken very different trajectories.

Without the global revolts of 1968, it is exceedingly unlikely that there would have been an uprising led by Pakistani students that not only deposed Ayub Khan but also radicalized the movement for autonomy in the eastern wing. This radical mobilization rendered it inconceivable for Mujibur Rahman and the Awami League to dilute their six-point program or to strive for accommodation with the ruling elites of West Pakistan as had happened in the past. Then, too, there was no smooth and straight highway that led to the destination of independence. It was, to invoke Jorge Luis Borges's striking image, a garden of forking paths.

To begin with, if Bhutto had not worked with the military regime in thwarting the Awami League's ascent to power, a united Pakistan could have been preserved, albeit as a looser federation. Without Bhutto's cooperation, the military would not have been as confident that West Pakistan would remain quiescent while the East was being suppressed. Ayub Khan's overthrow underlined the fact that the army could not realistically hope to crush an uprising in both wings. Had Bhutto joined forces with Mujib, as several contemporaries expected, the breakdown of Pakistan could have been averted.

Further, the breakdown of the Pakistani polity did not automatically imply its breakup. Different choices made by a range of actors could have taken events in rather different directions. This is not to conjure wishful "what if" scenarios but to consider the "embedded counterfactuals" that were either actively considered by these actors or were reasonably open to them.[2] If the Nixon administration had used its economic leverage on Pakistan in late April to early May 1971 and had clearly indicated to the Pakistani regime that it would soon be on the brink of pauperdom, it is highly probable that Yahya and his colleagues would have been forced to negotiate with Mujib and grant him his six points. By this time, the military crackdown had not yet assumed the proportions that made a loosely confederal arrangement entirely impossible for the Awami League to accept.

There were other plausible scenarios in which the Indian victory would have been limited and the independence of Bangladesh deferred, if not scuttled. If the Soviet Union had not switched its stance in late October 1971, it is unlikely that India would have planned to get as far as the lines of the major rivers in East Pakistan. Similarly, if British and French support—itself a product of the historical conjuncture—could not have been taken for granted, India would have had to plan for a shorter war. If the Chinese leadership had not been desirous of avoiding a complete break with India or been hamstrung by their internal politics, India could not have been confident of avoiding a limited Chinese intervention in support of Pakistan. This, too, would have affected India's military plans and restricted its political objectives. After the war began, if the United States had not made such threatening moves, it is quite possible that India might not have aimed at the capture of Dhaka and a complete victory. In each of these scenarios, India would have had to content itself with carving out a chunk of East Pakistan and therein installing the government of Bangladesh before withdrawing its own forces. The effect on the subsequent fate of "Bangladesh" would then have tenuously hung in the balance.

Up to the very end, this might well have been the situation. If Bhutto had not consigned the Polish resolution to the dustbin, it would almost certainly have passed, and Indian forces would have had to stop short of Dhaka. They would have obtained neither an unconditional surrender nor netted 93,000 prisoners of war. What's more, a quick withdrawal of India's forces would have rendered moot its ability to ensure a stable transition to an Awami League government. The Indians were well aware of the fact that there would be "complete civil chaos" in East Bengal after the fighting stopped.[3] Indeed, even after the decisive victory, the Indian leadership felt that "Bangladesh at present is, politically speaking, a primordial slime. Out of this chaos, cosmos has to be created."[4] This process may have been intractable, if the war had not ended the way it did. In particular, if various groups and factions in Bangladesh had continued to jockey for control, the stage might have been set for a civil war, with untold consequences for the country's political future. As late as 15 December 1971, the emergence of an independent Bangladesh with Mujibur Rahman at the helm was not a foregone conclusion.

I

Although the crisis of 1971 eventually reached a decisive denouement, its consequences for South Asia were far more complicated. Consider its impact on India-Pakistan relations. With the benefit of hindsight, it is frequently argued that Indira Gandhi won the war but lost the peace: that she failed to use the historic opportunity presented by the victory to impose a final settlement on Kashmir. Mrs. Gandhi, however, believed that a punitive settlement would only prepare the ground for further conflict with Pakistan. Such a settlement would not only stoke the re-vanchist tendencies in Pakistan but also destabilize its prospects for a democracy. Ultimately, she felt, the best hope for India lay in an internal transformation of Pakistan's polity and its attitude toward India.

In the run-up to the postwar conference held in Simla in the summer of 1972, Mrs. Gandhi was convinced by Haksar's observation that "historians now say that if those who sat around the table at Versailles to conclude a peace with Germany defeated during the First World War had acted with wisdom and not imposed upon Germany humiliating terms of peace, not only the rise of Nazism would have been avoided but also the seeds of the Second World War would not have been sown."[5] In negotiating the accord with Bhutto, she sought to treat defeated Pakistan on a footing of equality and respect. The accord not only laid the basis for a stable India-Pakistan relationship but also precluded the possibility of external intervention in bilateral disputes. More importantly, by converting the ceasefire line in Kashmir to a Line of Control that would gradually assume "the characteristics" of an international border, it held out the prospect of an eventual settlement of the Kashmir dispute. Bhutto agreed that "an agreement will emerge in the foreseeable future. It will evolve into a settlement. Let there be a line of peace; let people come and go; let us not fight over it."[6]

But it did not work out like that. Bhutto quickly retreated from their understanding and reverted to the traditional anti-India stance. By mid-1974, neither Bhutto nor Indira Gandhi had the political will or capital to forge a lasting settlement. Yet the assumption that Mrs. Gandhi could have forced a settlement on Pakistan overlooks her desire to avoid behaving in a manner that was "contrary to our interests, contrary to our traditions, contrary to our long devotion to international peace and cooperation."[7] More importantly, it discounts the weakness of Bhutto's own domestic position. Had India rammed through a final settlement on

Kashmir, it is quite likely that the Pakistan army would have deposed Bhutto even earlier than it did. The Simla accord gave Bhutto an opportunity to introduce a new constitution in 1973—a constitution that for all the tribulations visited upon it remains a beacon of hope for Pakistani democrats. Four decades on, it is not clear that Indira Gandhi was wrong.

The triangular relationship between India, Bangladesh, and Pakistan also evolved in ways that belied the decisive outcome of 1971. Following the Simla agreement, India was in principle open to repatriating the prisoners of war to Pakistan, but insisted that it could not be done without the concurrence of Bangladesh. Sheikh Mujib and his government were clear that this could happen only if Pakistan recognized the state of Bangladesh. Even then, those charged with war crimes would not be sent back.

As early as 1 January 1972, the interim government of Bangladesh decided to create the Genocide Investigation Commission. The Awami League repeatedly affirmed its intention of bringing to justice all individuals culpable of these crimes. As a first step, the Collaborators (Special Tribunal) Order of 1972 was promulgated. Under this order, over 37,000 individuals were arrested, and the trial of 2,842 was completed. Subsequently, as a measure to effect national reconciliation, Mujib proclaimed a general amnesty in November 1973. This acquitted those accused of petty crimes, but specifically excluded collaborators who were charged with serious offenses such as rape, murder, and arson.

During this period, the Bangladesh government was also preparing for the war crimes trials of Pakistani army officers. The initial list comprised 400 officers; it was subsequently reduced to 195 against whom irrefutable evidence had been collected. The possibility of these trials was naturally a major source of friction between Dhaka and Islamabad.

This issue was enmeshed with other outstanding disputes between the two countries. The tackling of these problems proved particularly difficult because Pakistan refused to recognize Bangladesh, so the negotiations had to be routed through India. In addition to the war crimes trials and the issue of recognition, the thicket of disputes also included the repatriation of the prisoners of war in Indian custody but held jointly by India and Bangladesh, and the repatriation of Bangladeshi civilians stranded in Pakistan and vice versa.

Bhutto played his cards carefully. From his standpoint, the delay in the repatriation of prisoners of war was not entirely a problem. It kept down the morale of the Pakistan army, and thus enabled him to strengthen his grip over the polity. But acquiescing in the trial of senior Pakistani officials in Bangladesh would be tantamount to signing a political suicide note. Bhutto responded by erecting obstacles in Bangladesh's road to seeking international recognition. He prevailed upon the Chinese to veto Bangladesh's entry to the United Nations, and upon important Muslim countries such as Iran, Turkey, and Saudi Arabia to withhold their recognition as well.

Faced with Pakistani intransigence on according recognition and civilian repatriation, Mujib decided to announce the trial of the 195 Pakistani army personnel. New Delhi took a pragmatic stance. It reminded Dhaka that the trials could further complicate its relations with Pakistan and would generate concern in the international community. To allay these fears, it was important that the Bangladesh government also announce the legal framework of the trial. As for civilian repatriation, India was of the view that Dhaka should set aside its precondition of official recognition and treat it as a humanitarian issue. The upshot of these consultations was twofold. Bangladesh brought into force the International War Crimes (Tribunals) Act in July 1973. It also reached an agreement with India that allowed the latter to negotiate on its behalf the exchange of civilians with Pakistan.

In the ensuing negotiations, Bhutto came out firmly against war crimes trials. "So far as prisoners of war are concerned," he told Haksar, "you can throw the whole lot in the Ganges, but I cannot agree to the trials." If Bangladesh did proceed with the trials, he would be forced to charge 203 Bengali civilian officials in Pakistan with espionage and high treason. If Mujib was reasonable, on the other hand, Bhutto might not only recognize Bangladesh but could "ask China to drop the veto."[8]

The Indians suggested to their Bangladeshi counterparts that the trials be postponed to facilitate the resolution of the other issues. By this time, the problem of international recognition, especially entry to the United Nations, was weighing heavily on Mujib's mind, and the possibility of reprisal trials by Pakistan was equally troubling. In August 1973, Mujibur Rahman assented to an agreement between India and Pakistan for repatriation of the prisoners of war and civilian internees, suspending the issue of trials. Eventually a tripartite agreement was concluded whereby those accused of war crimes were sent back to Pakistan with the understanding that these individuals would be tried in Pakistan. These trials, of course, never took place. But in February 1974, Pakistan accorded recognition to the People's Republic of Bangladesh.

In the meantime, India and Bangladesh signed a treaty of friendship in 1972, and the two countries began to negotiate outstanding problems over territorial enclaves and sharing of river waters. But Dhaka's attention was increasingly turned inward. The economy was a shambles, and reconstruction proved demanding. The overall economic productivity lagged well behind the prewar level, and the real income of agricultural and industrial workers sank to a lower level than in 1970. Economic management at all levels was rife with inefficiency and corruption. The global oil shock of 1973 sent the economy spiraling downward.

Further, Mujib's government was challenged by a plethora of left-leaning political groups—particularly after the elections of 1973, which they claimed had been heavily rigged. During these years, Bangladesh teemed with militias formed by the freedom fighters and was awash with weapons. In an attempt to put down these insurrectionary trends, Mujib arrogated to himself emergency powers that undermined democratic rights and civil liberties.

Finally, sections of the Bangladesh army were disgruntled by the government's creation and patronage of a paramilitary guard called the National Security Force. They were also peeved that their contribution to the liberation struggle was being downplayed. These perceptions were overlaid on an already problematic relationship between the army and the Awami League dating back to 1971. On 15 August 1975, a group of midranking army officers assassinated Mujib and several of his family members. A week later, four other members of the original Awami League high command—Tajuddin Ahmad, Syed Nazrul Islam, A. H. M. Kamruzzaman, and Mansoor Ali—were gunned down in their prison cells. The new president of Bangladesh, Khandakar Moshtaque Ahmad, granted amnesty to the killers. Soon, he was deposed in another coup by Major Ziaur Rahman. Bangladesh might have parted ways with Pakistan, but it continued to bear the mark of Cain in the form of military rule.

II

The tragic turn taken by Bangladesh soon after independence prompts a final counterfactual question. What if India had intervened early in the crisis of 1971? In his first meeting with D. P. Dhar in January 1972, Mujibur Rahman asked, "Why did India not intervene soon after the army crackdown in Bangla Desh?" Such an intervention, he observed "would have saved so much of suffering and valuable life."[9] Such an intervention had indeed been proposed, most forcefully by K. Subrahmanyam, and discussed. The reasons for India's reluctance have already been examined, but in retrospect the case for an early intervention—in May 1971—seems strong.

For one thing, the Pakistani military deployment in the eastern wing had not yet reached the levels that it eventually would. For another, the Pakistanis were still tied down and distracted by their operations against the Bengali units. In consequence, a swift intervention would not have been as arduous as the Indian political and military leadership assumed. Further, such an intervention could have presented a fait accompli to the great powers before they activated the UN machinery. Retrospective measures taken by the UN Security Council would not have undermined India's position a great deal.

Had such an intervention been successfully undertaken, it would have mitigated the brutalities visited upon the Bengalis, and the incalculable loss of life and violation of human dignity. It would also have limited the flow of refugees to India and the ensuing travails of displacement.

The obverse of this humanitarian tragedy was the cost imposed on Bangladesh by India's decision to support a liberation movement over many months. The strategy adopted by the Indian and Bengali forces of targeting roads and bridges, railroads and waterways, ports and power plants, dealt a deep blow to the economic prospects of independent Bangladesh—prospects that were already being undermined by Pakistani military operations. The prolonged liberation war also created the cauldron in which the witches' brew of post-independence politics came to a boil. The tensions between the army and the civilian leaders, between the Awami League and the leftist parties, between the variety of militias, and between the various factions of the Awami League all germinated during those nine months in 1971. In effect, the liberation war created the background conditions for the collapse of democracy in Bangladesh.

From this vantage point, the 1971 crisis seems to be not only the moment of India's greatest military triumph but also a grievous strategic error.

III

Four decades on, the history and memory of 1971 continue to shape the structure and texture of Bangladesh's politics and society. As of 2013, the government led by Mujibur Rahman's daughter Sheikh Hasina has commenced trials of those implicated in acts during the conflict that amount to crimes against humanity. Many of those standing trial were associated with the Jamaat-e-Islami (which opposed independence) and its affiliated paramilitary forces that aided the Pakistan army. The outcome of these trials remains uncertain, but it is clear that they are as much, if not more, about the present and future of Bangladesh as its past.

The 1971 crisis also has a contemporary resonance well beyond the confines of South Asia. For it proved to be a precursor of more recent conflicts in the Balkans, Africa, and the Middle East. The Bangladesh crisis prefigured many characteristic features of contemporary conflicts: the tension between the principles of sovereignty and human rights; the competing considerations of interests and norms; the virtues of unilateralism versus multilateralism; national lineups that blur the international divides of West and East, North and South; and the importance of international media and NGOs, diasporas and transnational public opinion. The Bangladesh crisis may have occurred during a watershed moment in the Cold War, but it was a harbinger of the post–Cold War world. Inasmuch as it turns the spotlight on these dilemmas and debates, this history of the 1971 crisis is not merely a narrative of the past but a tract for our times.

NOTES

Prologue

1. C. P. Shrivastava, *Lal Bahadur Shastri: A Life of Truth in Politics* (New Delhi: Oxford University Press, 1995), 391–94.

2. Srinath Raghavan, *War and Peace in Modern India: A Strategic History of the Nehru Years* (London: Palgrave Macmillan, 2010).

3. Jahan Dad Khan, *Pakistan Leadership Challenges* (Karachi: Oxford University Press, 1999), 51.

4. The best account is that of Robert McMahon, *Cold War on the Periphery: The United States, India, and Pakistan* (New York: Columbia University Press, 1994). Also see Anita Inder Singh, *The Limits of British Influence: South Asia and the Anglo-American Relationship 1947–56* (New York: St. Martin's Press, 1993).

5. Rudra Chaudhuri, *Forged in Crisis: India and the United States since 1947* (London: Hurst, 2013); Robert B. Rakove, *Kennedy, Johnson and the Nonaligned World* (Cambridge: Cambridge University Press, 2013).

6. For an important, if partial, new account, see Vojtech Mastny, "The Soviet Union's Partnership with India," *Journal of Cold War Studies* 12, no. 3 (2010): 52–56.

7. Record of conversation between Shastri and Brezhnev, 14 May 1965; record of conversation between Shastri and Kosygin, 15 May 1965, Subject File 15, T. N. Kaul Papers (I–III Installment), Nehru Memorial Museum and Library, New Delhi (hereafter NMML).

8. Memorandum for Politburo by Kosygin, 11 November 1965, Listy 45–54, Delo 489, Opis' 30, Fond 5, *Rossiskiy Gosudarstveniy Arkhiv Noveyshey Istorii,* Russian Government Archive of Contemporary History, Moscow (hereafter RGANI).

9. Record of conversation between T.T. Krishnamachari and Kosygin, 12 November 1965, Subject File 43, T.T. Krishnamachari Papers, NMML.

10. Soviet Report on the Tashkent Conference, February 1966, A18017, Politisches Archiv des uswärtigen Amtes, Bestand: Ministerium für Auswärtige Angelegenheiten (der ehemaligen DDR) [Political Archive of the Office for Foreign Affairs, Files: Ministry for Foreign Affairs of the Former GDR], Berlin (hereafter PAAA-MfAA).

11. Richard Sisson and Leo Rose, *War and Secession: Pakistan, India, and the Creation of Bangladesh* (Berkeley: University of California Press, 1990).

12. Yasmin Saikia, *Women, War and the Making of Bangladesh: Remembering 1971* (New Delhi: Women Unlimited, 2011); Antara Datta, *Refugees and Borders in South Asia: The Great Displacement of 1971* (London: Routledge, 2012); Sarmila Bose, *Dead Reckoning: Memories of the 1971 Bangladesh War* (London: Hurst, 2011); Nayanika Mookherjee, "The Absent Piece of Skin: Gendered, Racialized, and Territorial Inscriptions of Sexual Violence during the Bangladesh War." *Modern Asian Studies* 46, no. 6 (2012): 1572–1601.

13. For instance, L. Rushbrook Williams, *The East Pakistan Tragedy* (London: Tom Stacey, 1972); Safdar Mahmood, *Pakistan Divided* (New Delhi: Alpha Bravo, 1993), and *The Crisis in East Pakistan* (Islamabad: Government of Pakistan, 1971).

14. For instance, Rounaq Jahan, *Pakistan: Failure in National Integration* (New York: Columbia University Press, 1972); Badruddin Umar, *The Emergence of Bangladesh: Rise of Bengali Nationalism 1958–1971* (Karachi: Oxford University Press, 2006); A.M.A. Muhith, *Bangladesh: Emergence of a Nation*, 2nd ed. (Dhaka: University Press, 1994). A rare account written by a Pakistani that empathizes with the Bangladeshi narrative is Hasan Zaheer, *The Separation of East Pakistan: The Rise and Realization of Bengali Muslim Nationalism* (Dhaka: University Press, 2001).

15. For instance, Pran Chopra, *India's Second Liberation* (New Delhi: Vikas, 1974); G.S. Bhargava, *"Crush India" or Pakistan's Death Wish* (Delhi: Indian School Supply Depot, 1972); Mohammed Ayoob and K. Subrahmanyam, *The Liberation War* (New Delhi: S. Chand, 1972).

16. Badruddin Umar, *The Emergence of Bangladesh: Class Struggles in East Pakistan, 1947–1958* (Karachi: Oxford University Press, 2004), x (emphasis added).

17. Anatol Lieven, *Pakistan: A Hard Country* (London: Allen Lane, 2011), 10.

18. See, for instance, Sumit Ganguly, *Conflict Unending: India-Pakistan Tensions since 1947* (New Delhi: Oxford University Press, 2002), 52, which talks of the "Tenuous Bonds of Pakistan."

19. Willem Van Schendel, *A History of Bangladesh* (Cambridge: Cambridge University Press 2009), 114.

20. Figures from Ian Talbot, *Pakistan: A Modern History* (New Delhi: Oxford University Press, 1998), 170.

21. Ayesha Jalal, *Democracy and Authoritarianism in South Asia: A Comparative and Historical Perspective* (Cambridge: Cambridge University Press, 1995), 186–87; Talbot, *Pakistan,* 187.

22. Vijay Prashad, *The Darker Nations: A People's History of the Third World* (New York: New Press, 2007).

23. The pioneering and magisterial account is Odd Arne Westad, *The Global Cold War: Third World Interventions and the Making of Our Times* (Cambridge: Cambridge University Press, 2005). On the European dimension, see Marc Trachtenberg, *A Constructed Peace: The Making of the European Settlement, 1945–1963* (Princeton, NJ: Princeton University Press, 1999).

24. Akira Iriye, *Global Community: The Role of International Organizations in the Making of the Contemporary World* (Berkeley: University of California Press, 2002), 96–134.

25. Devesh Kapur, *Diaspora, Development, and Democracy: The Domestic Impact of International Migration from India* (Princeton, NJ: Princeton University Press, 2010), table 1.1, 3.

26. David Singh Grewal, *Network Power: The Social Dynamics of Globalization* (New Haven, CT: Yale University Press, 2008).

27. In particular, the brilliant, pathbreaking work of Jeremi Suri, *Power and Protest: Global Revolution and the Rise of the Détente* (Cambridge, MA: Harvard University Press, 2003), and Daniel J. Sargent, *A Superpower Adrift: History, Strategy and American Foreign Policy in the 1970s* (New York: Oxford University Press, forthcoming). Also see Matthew Connelly, *A Diplomatic Revolution: Algeria's Fight for Independence and the Origins of the Post–Cold War Era* (New York: Oxford University Press, 2002); Paul Thomas Chamberlin, *The Global Offensive: The United States, the Palestine Liberation Organization, and the Making of the Post–Cold War Order* (New York: Oxford University Press, 2012); Ryan M. Irwin, *Gordian Knot: Apartheid and the Unmaking of the Liberal World Order* (New York: Oxford University Press, 2012). Other works that emphasize the importance of this period are Eric Hobsbawm, *The Age of Extremes: 1914–1991* (London: Abacus, 1995); Niall Ferguson, Charles S. Maier, Erez Manela, and Daniel J. Sargent, eds., *The Shock of the Global: The 1970s in Perspective* (Cambridge, MA: Belknap Press, 2010); Thomas Borstelmann, *The 1970s: A New Global History from Civil Rights to Economic Inequality* (Princeton, NJ: Princeton University Press, 2010).

28. Bose, *Dead Reckoning,* 181.

1. The Turning Point

1. Altaf Gauhar, *Ayub Khan: Pakistan's First Military Ruler* (Karachi: Oxford University Press, 1996), 337–39.

2. Entry of 26 March 1969, Craig Baxter, ed., *Diaries of Field Marshal Mohammed Ayub Khan, 1966–1972* (Karachi: Oxford University Press, 2007), 309.

3. Samuel P. Huntington, *Political Order in Changing Societies* (New Haven, CT: Yale University Press, 1968), 250–51.

4. Figures from Ian Talbot, *Pakistan: A Modern History* (New Delhi: Oxford University Press, 1998), 171.

5. CIA Report, September 1968, in Jeremi Suri, ed., *The Global Revolutions of 1968* (New York: W.W. Norton, 2007), 217, 220.

6. Much of this writing is by participant observers. Todd Gitlin, *The Sixties: Years of Hope, Days of Rage,* rev. ed. (New York: Bantam, 1993); David Farber, *Chicago '68* (Chicago: University of Chicago Press, 1998); David Farber, ed., *The Sixties: From Memory to History* (Charlotte: University of North Carolina Press, 1994); Paul Berman, *A Tale of Two Utopias: The Political Journey of the Generation of 1968* (New York: W.W. Norton, 1996); Chris Harman, *The Fire Last Time: 1968 and After* (London: Bookmarks 1998); Kristin Ross, *May '68 and Its Afterlives* (Chicago: University of Chicago Press, 2002); Gerd Rainer-Horn, *The Spirit of '68: Rebellion in Western Europe and North America, 1956–1976* (New York: Oxford University Press, 2007).

7. Mark Kurlansky, *1968: The Year That Rocked the World* (London: Jonathan Cape, 2004); Arthur Marwick, *The Sixties: Cultural Revolution in Britain, France, Italy, and the United States, c.1958–c.1974* (New York: Oxford University Press, 1998); Martin Klimke and Joachim Scharloth, eds., *1968 in Europe: A History of Protest and Activism* (New York: Palgrave Macmillan, 2008); Martin Klimke, *Student Protests in West Germany and the United States in the Global Sixties* (Princeton, NJ: Princeton University Press, 2011). Volumes that do discuss Pakistan, albeit rather perfunctorily, are George Katsiaficas, *The Imagination of the New Left: A Global Analysis of 1968* (Cambridge, MA: South End Press, 1987); Phillip Gassert and Martin Klimke, eds., *Memories and Legacies of a Global Revolt* (Washington, DC: German Historical Institute Supplement, 2009).

8. Figures from "The Radical Wing in East Pakistan" by A. Halliley, 12 February 1969, FCO 37/468, The National Archives, Kew, London (hereafter TNA).

9. Badruddin Umar, *The Emergence of Bangladesh: Rise of Bengali Nationalism, 1958–1971* (Karachi: Oxford University Press, 2006), 64–73.

10. Speech on 7 March 1968, from Suri, *Global Revolutions,* 123.

11. Figures from Talbot, *Pakistan,* 171.

12. Ghazi Salahuddin, "Pakistan: The Year of Change," in Gassert and Klimke, *Memories and Legacies,* 95.

13. Sheila Rowbotham, *Promise of a Dream: Remembering the Sixties* (London: Verso, 2001), 118. More broadly, Jeremi Suri, "The Rise and Fall of an International Counterculture, 1960–1975," *American Historical Review* 144, no. 1 (2009): 45–68.

14. On the deep Cold War roots of 1968, see Jeremi Suri, *Power and Protest: Global Revolution and the Rise of the Détente* (Cambridge, MA: Harvard University Press, 2003).

15. Cited in Tariq Ali, *The Duel: Pakistan on the Flight Path of American Power* (London: Pocket Books, 2009), 68.

16. Cited in Lal Khan, *Pakistan's Other Story: The 1968–69 Revolution* (Delhi: Aakar Books, 2009), 140.

17. Salahuddin, "Pakistan: The Year of Change," 96.

18. Tariq Ali, *Street Fighting Years: An Autobiography of the Sixties* (Calcutta: Seagull, 2006), 308–9.

19. Minutes by F. A. Warner, 21 February 1969, FCO 37/468, TNA.

20. Eric Hobsbawm, *The Age of Extremes: The Short Twentieth Century, 1914–1991* (London: Abacus, 1995), 332–34. Also see Tony Judt, *Postwar: A History of Europe since 1945* (London: Pimlico, 2007), 412–13; Mark Mazower, *Dark Continent: Europe's Twentieth Century* (London: Allen Lane, 1998), 323–24.

21. UK High Commission (UKHC) Pakistan to Foreign and Commonwealth Office (FCO), 16 November 1968, FCO 37/466, TNA.

22. Entry of 28 November 1968, Baxter, *Diaries of Ayub Khan*, 287.

23. *Dawn* [Karachi], 30 November 1968.

24. Umar, *Rise of Bengali Nationalism*, 142–43.

25. "The Radical Wing in East Pakistan" by A. Halliley, 12 February 1969, FCO 37/468, TNA.

26. Tariq Ali, *Pakistan: Military Rule or People's Power?* (London: Jonathan Cape, 1970), 195–96.

27. Umar, *Rise of Bengali Nationalism*, 147–49.

28. Entries of 26 January 1969 and 8 February 1969, in Baxter, *Diaries of Ayub Khan*, 298–99.

29. Sheikh Mujibur Rahman, *The Unfinished Memoirs* (New Delhi: Viking, 2012).

30. Badruddin Umar, *The Emergence of Bangladesh: Class Struggles in East Pakistan, 1947–1958* (Karachi: Oxford University Press, 2004), 285–86.

31. Richard Sisson and Leo Rose, *War and Secession: Pakistan, India, and the Creation of Bangladesh* (Berkeley: University of California Press, 1990), 19–20.

32. Though Mujib was in touch with Indian officials, no evidence has yet emerged to suggest that he was conspiring with the Indians. Cf. Sisson and Rose, *War and Secession*, 42.

33. *Holiday* [Dhaka], 28 January 1969.

34. "The Radical Wing in East Pakistan" by A. Halliley, 12 February 1969, FCO 37/468, TNA.

35. Entry of 21 February 1969, in Baxter, *Diaries of Ayub Khan*, 301.

36. Entry of 26 February 1969, ibid., 302.

37. Entry of 16 February 1969, ibid., 300–1.

38. Entry of 23 February 1969, ibid., 301–2.

39. Gul Hassan Khan, *Memoirs of Lt. Gen. Gul Hassan Khan* (Karachi: Oxford University Press, 1993), 246–47.

40. Brigadier A.R. Siddiqi, *East Pakistan The Endgame: An Onlooker's Journal, 1969–1971* (Karachi: Oxford University Press, 2004) (hereafter *Onlooker's Journal*), 4; M. Attiqur Rahman, *Back to the Pavilion* (Karachi: Oxford University Press, 2005), 146–47.

41. Entry of 5 March 1969, in Baxter, *Diaries of Ayub Khan*, 304.

42. Gauhar, *Ayub Khan*, 323–24.

43. Entry of 21 March 1969, in Baxter, *Diaries of Ayub Khan*, 308. Also see Gohar Ayub Khan, *Glimpses into the Corridors of Power* (Karachi: Oxford University Press, 2007), 117.

44. *Dawn* [Karachi], 27 March 1969.

45. East Pakistani views were reflected in the writings of Rehman Sobhan, an influential intellectual. In particular, "What Follows Ayub's Abdication," *New Statesman* [London], 28 March 1969.

46. G.W. Choudhury, *Last Days of United Pakistan* (London: Hurst, 1974), 85.

47. Sisson and Rose, *War and Secession*, 25. Also see Sarmila Bose, *Dead Reckoning: Memories of the 1971 Bangladesh War* (London: Hurst, 2011), 19.

48. Rahman, *Back to the Pavilion*, 152.

49. Cited in Siddiqi, *Onlooker's Journal*, 25.

50. Hasan Zaheer, *The Separation of East Pakistan: The Rise and Realization of Bengali Muslim Nationalism* (Dhaka: University Press, 2001), 114–15; Choudhury, *Last Days*, 89.

51. On the last point, also see Sisson and Rose, *War and Secession*, 25.

52. Stanley Wolpert, *Zulfi Bhutto of Pakistan: His Life and Times* (New York: Oxford University Press, 1993), 132–33; Rafi Reza, *Zulfikar Ali Bhutto and Pakistan, 1967–1977* (Dhaka: University Press, 1997), 20; Zulfikar Ali Bhutto, *The Great Tragedy* (Karachi: Pakistan People's Party Publication, 1971), 75.

53. Choudhury, *Last Days*, 74–86; Zaheer, *Separation of East Pakistan*, 116; Reza, *Zulfikar Ali Bhutto*, 20; Hamoodur Rehman Commission, *Report of the Hamoodur Rehman Commission of Inquiry into the 1971 War, as Declassified by the Government of Pakistan* (Lahore: Vanguard, [2000?]), 73; six letters from P.R. Oliver to R.J. Stratton (British High Commission Pakistan), 4, 6, 9, and 10 June 1969, FCO 37/472, TNA.

54. *Dawn* [Karachi], 29 November 1969.

55. Choudhury, *Last Days*, 95.

56. *Dawn* [Karachi], 11 April 1970.

57. Reza, *Zulfikar Ali Bhutto*, 27–35; Anwar H. Syed, *The Discourse and Politics of Zulfikar Ali Bhutto* (New York: St. Martin's Press, 1992), 67–87; Hamid Jalal and Khalid Hasan, eds., *Politics of the People: Marching towards Democracy, January 1970–December 1971* (Rawalpindi: Pakistan Publications, [1972]), 3–156; memorandum of conversation with Bhutto, 23 February 1970, POL 12 PAK 1-1-70, Box 2524, US National Archives and Records Administration, College Park, MD (hereafter USNA).

58. Talukder Maniruzzaman, *Radical Politics and the Emergence of Bangladesh* (Dhaka: Bangladesh Books, 1975), 8–11; Umar, *Rise of Bengali Nationalism*, 82–83; Embassy in Pakistan to State, 4 June 1970, in Roedad Khan, ed., *American Papers: Secret and Confidential India-Pakistan-Bangladesh Documents 1965–1973* (Karachi: Oxford University Press, 1999), 368–69; Archer K. Blood, *The Cruel Birth of Bangladesh: Memoirs of an American Diplomat* (Dhaka: University Press, 2002), 59–60.

59. Maniruzzaman, *Radical Politics*, 3–30; Umar, *Rise of Bengali Nationalism*, 74–84, 124–33, 235–46.

60. Memorandum of conversation with Wali Khan, 23 February 1970, in Khan, *American Papers*, 353–54. Also see memorandum of conversation with Wali Khan, 25 June 1970, PAK 7-1-70, Box 2522, USNA.

61. Umar, *Rise of Bengali Nationalism;* Maniruzzaman, *Radical Politics;* Rangalal Sen, *Political Elites in Bangladesh* (Dhaka: University Press, 1986).

62. Muhammad Ghulam Kabir, *Minority Politics in Bangladesh* (New Delhi: Vikas, 1980).

63. Consul Dacca to State, 7 January 1970, in Khan, *American Papers*, 316; report on conversation with Mujibur Rahman, 22 October 1970, POL 14 PAK 1-1-70, Box 2526, USNA.

64. Talukder Maniruzzaman, *The Bangladesh Revolution and Its Aftermath* (Dhaka: University Press, 2003), 72–73.

65. *Dawn* [Karachi], 8 June 1970.

66. Personal interview with Kamal Hossain, Dhaka, 6 April 2010.

67. Consul Dacca to State, 7 January 1970, in Khan, *American Papers*, 317; report on conversation with Mujibur Rahman, 22 October 1970, POL 14 PAK 1-1-70, Box 2526, USNA.

68. *Interwing* [Dhaka], 6 April 1970.

69. *Dawn* [Karachi], 8 June 1970; *The People* [Dhaka], 21 October 1970, 18 October 1970.

70. Report on conversation with Mujib, Consul Dacca to Secretary of State (hereafter SS), 2 June 1970, POL 12 PAK ND, Box 2524, USNA.

71. Blood, *Cruel Birth,* 73–116; Siddiqi, *Onlooker's Journal,* 46; Herbert Feldman, *The End and the Beginning: Pakistan 1969–1971* (Karachi: Oxford University Press, 1975), 92.

72. *Morning News* [Dhaka], 27 November 1970.

2. Breakdown

1. Arshad Sami Khan, *Three Presidents and an Aide: Life, Power and Politics* (New Delhi: Pentagon Press, 2008), 130–31.

2. Brigadier A.R. Siddiqi, *East Pakistan The Endgame: An Onlooker's Journal, 1969–1971* (Karachi: Oxford University Press, 2004), 43, 45–46, 49–50.

3. Hamoodur Rehman Commission, *Report of the Hamoodur Rehman Commission of Inquiry into the 1971 War, as Declassified by the Government of Pakistan* (Lahore: Vanguard, [2000?]), 118, 124–25; Asghar Khan, *My Political Struggle* (Karachi: Oxford University Press, 2008), 19; M. Attiqur Rahman, *Back to the Pavilion* (Karachi: Oxford University Press, 2005), 170–71.

4. G.W. Choudhury, *Last Days of United Pakistan* (London: Hurst, 1974), 138–39; Shuja Nawaz, *Crossed Swords: Pakistan, Its Army, and the Wars Within* (Karachi: Oxford University Press, 2008), 260; Hasan Zaheer, *The Separation of East Pakistan: The Rise and Realization of Bengali Muslim Nationalism* (Dhaka: University Press, 2001), 146–47; Hamoodur Rahman Commission, *Report,* 77.

5. Choudhury, *Last Days,* 148.

6. Zaheer, *Separation of East Pakistan,* 130.

7. Siddiq Salik, *Witness to Surrender* (Dhaka: University Press, 1997), 29.

8. Siddiqi, *Onlooker's Journal,* 50–51.

9. Entry of 28 February 1970, in Craig Baxter, ed., *Diaries of Field Marshal Mohammed Ayub Khan, 1966–1972* (Karachi: Oxford University Press, 2007), 367.

10. Report on conversation with Yahya, Ambassador in Pakistan to Secretary of State (SS), 10 September 1970, Box 2525, POL 12 PAK 1-1-70, US National Archives and Records Administration, College Park, MD (hereafter USNA).

11. Memorandum of conversation between Bhutto and Consul General Karachi, 23 February 1970, POL 12 PAK 1-1-70, Box 2524; report on conversation with Bhutto, Consul General in Karachi to Embassy in Pakistan, 12 June 1970, POL 12-6 PAK 1-1-70, Box 2525, USNA; Ambassador in Pakistan to SS, 9 December 1970, in Roedad Khan, ed., *American Papers: Secret and Confidential India Pakistan Bangladesh Documents, 1965–1973* (Karachi: Oxford University Press, 1999), 432. Rafi Reza, a close political aide of Bhutto's, coyly confirms this in his memoir on Bhutto; see *Zulfikar Ali Bhutto and Pakistan, 1967–1977* (Dhaka: University Press, 1997), 21.

12. Mohammed Asghar Khan, *Generals in Politics: Pakistan 1958–1982* (New Delhi: Vikas, 1983), 28.

13. Stanley Wolpert, *Zulfi Bhutto of Pakistan: His Life and Times* (New York: Oxford University Press, 1993), 132–33; Reza, *Zulfikar Ali Bhutto*, 20; Zulfikar Ali Bhutto, *The Great Tragedy* (Karachi: Pakistan People's Party Publication, 1971), 75.

14. Richard Sisson and Leo Rose, *War and Secession: Pakistan, India, and the Creation of Bangladesh* (Berkeley: University of California Press, 1990), 57–58.

15. Reza, *Zulfikar Ali Bhutto*, 47.

16. *Pakistan Observer* [Dhaka], 21 December 1970.

17. *Pakistan Times* [Lahore], 22 December 1970; *Dawn* [Karachi], 25 December 1970.

18. Personal interview with Kamal Hossain, Dhaka, 6 April 2010; *Pakistan Observer* [Dhaka], 22 December 1970.

19. Reza, *Zulfikar Ali Bhutto*, 45.

20. Report on conversation with Mujib, 30 December 1970, Consul Dacca to SS, Box 2525, POL 12-6 PAK 1-1-70, USNA; Nurul Islam, *Making of Nation Bangladesh: An Economist's Tale* (Dhaka: University Press, 2003), 88, 93–97.

21. Zaheer, *Separation of East Pakistan*, 132–35; Hamoodur Rahman Commission, *Report*, 77–78; Salik, *Witness to Surrender*, 33–34.

22. Khan, *Three Presidents and an Aide*, 134–35; Sisson and Rose, *War and Secession*, 65–66.

23. *Dawn* [Karachi], 15 January 1971; *Pakistan Observer* [Dhaka], 15 January 1971.

24. Sisson and Rose, *War and Secession*, 67–68; Farida Aziz, "The Pakistan Crisis 1971" (PhD thesis, King's College London, 1988), 170–72; Bhutto, *Great Tragedy*, 20–21; Zaheer, *Separation of East Pakistan*, 136; Rao Farman Ali Khan, *How Pakistan Got Divided* (Lahore: Jang, 1992), 53; Khan, *Three Presidents and an Aide*, 149–50.

25. S.A. Karim, *Sheikh Mujib: Triumph and Tragedy* (Dhaka: University Press, 2005), 177; Rehman Sobhan "Negotiating for Bangladesh: A Participant's View," *South Asian Review* 4, no. 4 (1971): 315–26; Report on conversation with Bhutto, Ambassador in Pakistan to SS, 8 February 1971, POL 12-6 PAK 1-1-70, Box 2525, USNA; personal interview with Amirul Islam, Dhaka, 6 April 2010.

26. Khan, *How Pakistan Got Divided*, 56; Sisson and Rose, *War and Secession*, 74–75, 77; Safdar Mahmood, *Pakistan Divided* (New Delhi: Alpha Bravo, 1993), 103; Reza, *Zulfikar Ali Bhutto*, 54–56; Hamoodur Rahman Commission, *Report*, 79–80.

27. Archer K. Blood, *The Cruel Birth of Bangladesh: Memoirs of an American Diplomat* (Dhaka: University Press, 2002), 139; Khan, *Three Presidents and an Aide*, 142; *Pakistan Times* [Lahore], 14 February 1971.

28. Siddiqi, *Onlooker's Journal*, 57; Hamoodur Rahman Commission, *Report*, 80–81; Report on conversation with Daultana, 19 March 1971, Consul Lahore to State, POL 12 PAK 1-1-71, Box 2525, USNA.

29. *Dawn* [Karachi], 16 February 1971.

30. Reza, *Zulfikar Ali Bhutto*, 83.

31. Report on conversation with Alamgir Rahman, 24 February 1971, POL 12 PAK 1-1-71, Box 2525, USNA.

32. Mujib's statements in *Dawn* [Karachi], 20 February; *Pakistan Times* [Lahore], 25 February 1971; *Dawn* [Karachi], 1 March 1971.

33. Personal interview with Kamal Hossain, Dhaka, 6 April 2010.

34. State to Consul Dacca, 10 February 1971; Ambassador in Pakistan to SS, 12 February 1971, POL 12 PAK 1-1-71, Box 2525, USNA.

35. US ambassador's report on conversation with Mujib, 28 February 1971, reproduced in Blood, *Cruel Birth*, 150–52.

36. Khan, *How Pakistan Got Divided*, 55–56.

37. Hamoodur Rahman Commission, *Report*, 84; Zaheer, *Separation of East Pakistan*, 140–42; Sisson and Rose, *War and Secession*, 83–85; Aziz, "The Pakistan Crisis 1971," 181–83.

38. Nawaz, *Crossed Swords*, 264–66.

39. Gul Hassan Khan, *Memoirs of Lt. Gen. Gul Hassan Khan* (Karachi: Oxford University Press, 1993), 259–61; Aboobaker Osman Mitha, *Unlikely Beginnings: A Soldier's Life* (Oxford: Oxford University Press, 2003), 330–31; Salik, *Witness to Surrender*, 39–40.

40. Report on conversation with Yahya, 25 February 1971, POL 15-1 1-1-71, Box 2526, USNA.

41. Personal interview with Kamal Hossain, Dhaka, 6 April 2010; personal interview with Amirul Islam, Dhaka, 6 April 2010; Kamal Hossain's testimony in *Bangladesher Shadhinata Juddho: Dalil Patro* (Dhaka: Ministry of Information, Government of People's Republic of Bangladesh, 1985), 15:256–58; Khan, *How Pakistan Got Divided*, 60–61; Siddiqi, *Onlooker's Journal*, 63; Karim, *Sheikh Mujib*, 182; Salik, *Witness to Surrender*, 44; *Morning News* [Dhaka], 2 March 1971; *The People* [Dhaka], 2 March 1971.

42. Blood, *Cruel Birth*, 157–59, 165.

43. *Dawn* [Karachi], 4 March 1971.

44. Talukder Maniruzzaman, *The Bangladesh Revolution and Its Aftermath* (Dhaka: University Press, 2003), 76–77; Badruddin Umar, *The Emergence of Bangladesh: Rise of Bengali Nationalism, 1958–1971* (Karachi: Oxford University Press, 2006), 305–7.

45. *Dawn* [Karachi], 7 March 1971; Choudhury, *Last Days*, 158; Salik, *Witness to Surrender*, 52; personal interview with Dr. Kamal Hossain, Dhaka, 6 April 2010. Also see Kamal Hossain's testimony in *Bangladesher Shadhinata Juddho*, 15:264.

46. For US assessments of the military buildup, see Blood, *Cruel Birth*, 177–79; Sisco to SS, n.d., in Khan, *American Papers*, 498. On Bhutto's role, see Bhutto, *Great Tragedy*, 26–27; Reza, *Zulfikar Ali Bhutto*, 84.

47. Sisson and Rose, *War and Secession*, 98, 112.

48. Zaheer, *Separation of East Pakistan*, 148; Hamoodur Rehman Commission, *Report*, 93.

49. Personal interview with Kamal Hossain, Dhaka, 6 April 2010; personal interview with Amirul Islam, Dhaka, 6 April 2010; Kamal Hossain's testimony in *Bangladesher Shadhinata Juddho*, 15:261–64; Rehman Sobhan, "Negotiating for Bangladesh."

50. Umar, *Rise of Bengali Nationalism*, 297–98; *Dawn* [Karachi], 8 March 1971; *Pakistan Times* [Lahore], 8 March 1971; Blood, *Cruel Birth*, 175.

51. Consul Dacca to State, 11 March 1971, POL 12 PAK 1-1-71, Box 2525, USNA.

52. *Dawn* [Karachi], 10 March 1971; *Dawn* [Karachi], 14 March 1971; Sherbaz Khan Mazari, *A Journey to Disillusionment* (Karachi: Oxford University Press, 1999), 206; Shuakat Hayat Khan, *The Nation That Lost Its Soul: Memoirs of a Freedom Fighter* (Lahore: Jang, 1995), 309.

53. Bhutto, *Great Tragedy*, 29–30.

54. Reza, *Zulfikar Ali Bhutto*, 84; *Dawn* [Karachi], 15 March 1971.

55. Report on conversation with M.A. Qasuri of PPP, Consul Karachi to State, 11 March 1971, POL 12 PAK 1-1-71, Box 2525, USNA.

56. Report on conversation with Moinul Hossain, Consul Dacca to State, 16 March 1971, POL 12 PAK 1-1-71, Box 2525, USNA; personal interview with Kamal Hossain, Dhaka, 6 April 2010; personal interview with Amirul Islam, Dhaka, 6 April 2010; Kamal Hossain's testimony in *Bangladesher Shadhinata Juddho*, 15:265–66; Sobhan, "Negotiating for Bangladesh"; Hamoodur Rehman Commission, *Report*, 86; Sisson and Rose, *War and Secession*, 112–13.

57. Salik, *Witness to Surrender*, 62–63.

58. Personal interview with Kamal Hossain, Dhaka, 6 April 2010; personal interview with Amirul Islam, Dhaka, 6 April 2010; Kamal Hossain's testimony in *Bangladesher Shadhinata Juddho*, 15:266–67; Sisson and Rose, *War and Secession*, 113–17, 132; Zaheer, *Separation of East Pakistan*, 150; Sobhan, "Negotiating for Bangladesh."

59. Personal interview with Kamal Hossain, Dhaka, 6 April 2010; personal interview with Amirul Islam, Dhaka, 6 April 2010; Kamal Hossain's testimony in *Bangladesher Shadhinata Juddho*, 15:268–69; Zaheer, *Separation of East Pakistan*, 151.

60. Reza, *Zulfikar Ali Bhutto*, 72–73; Bhutto, *Great Tragedy*, 37.

61. Siddiqi, *Onlooker's Journal*, 73.

62. Personal interview with Kamal Hossain, Dhaka, 6 April 2010; Kamal Hossain's testimony in *Bangladesher Shadhinata Juddho*, 15:268–69.

63. Reza, *Zulfikar Ali Bhutto*, 75–77; Aziz, "The Pakistan Crisis 1971," 202–3; Bhutto, *Great Tragedy*, 34–36; Zaheer, *Separation of East Pakistan*, 153–54.

64. Personal interview with Kamal Hossain, Dhaka, 6 April 2010; personal interview, with Amirul Islam, Dhaka, 6 April 2010; Kamal Hossain's testimony in *Bangladesher Shadhinata Juddho*, 15:277–79; Islam, *Making of a Nation*, 99–100; Sobhan, "Negotiating for Bangladesh"; Sisson and Rose, *War and Secession*, 123–27; Zaheer, *Separation of East Pakistan*, 154–56.

65. Khan, *Nation That Lost Its Soul*, 313.

66. Sisson and Rose, *War and Secession*, 129–31; Zaheer, *Separation of East Pakistan*, 153; Hamoodur Rehman Commission, *Report*, 88; Reza, *Zulfikar Ali Bhutto*, 78.

67. Personal interview with Kamal Hossain, Dhaka, 6 April 2010; Kamal Hossain's testimony in *Bangladesher Shadhinata Juddho*, 15:279–80; Zaheer, *Separation of East Pakistan*, 157.

68. Consul Dacca to State, 24 March 1971, POL 12 PAK 1-1-71, Box 2525, USNA. Also see Blood, *Cruel Birth*, 193–94.

69. Salik, *Witness to Surrender*, 68–70; Khan, *How Pakistan Got Divided*, 83–85; Siddiqi, *Onlooker's Journal*, 85–88; Mitha, *Unlikely Beginnings*, 334–35.

70. *Dawn* [Karachi], 27 March 1971; *Pakistan Times* [Lahore], 27 March 1971.

71. Text of the plan is available in Salik, *Witness to Surrender*, 228–34.

72. Blood, *Cruel Birth*, 217–22.

73. Rafiqul Islam, *A Tale of Millions: Bangladesh Liberation War—1971*, 3rd ed. (Dhaka: Ananya, 2005); K.M. Safiullah, *Bangladesh at War*, 2nd ed. (Dhaka: Academic Publishers, 1995); Akhtar Ahmed, *Advance to Contact: A Soldier's Account of Bangladesh Liberation War* (Dhaka: University Press, 2000); A.S.M. Nasim, *Bangladesh Fights for Independence* (Dhaka: Columbia Prokashini, 2002).

74. Personal interview with Amirul Islam, Dhaka, 6 April 2010.

3. The Neighbor

1. Deputy High Commissioner Dhaka to Foreign Secretary, 14 March 1971, Subject File 90(a), P.N. Haksar Papers (III Installment), Nehru Memorial Museum and Library, New Delhi (hereafter NMML).

2. Muyeedul Hasan, *Muldhara '71* (Dhaka: University Press, 1986/2008), 10.

3. Deputy High Commissioner Dhaka to Foreign Secretary, 14 March 1971, Subject File 90(a), P.N. Haksar Papers (III Installment), NMML.

4. Hasan, *Muldhara '71*, 10.

5. Record of Foreign Minister's talk to Heads of Missions, London, 20 June 1971, Subject File 19, T.N. Kaul Papers (I, II, and III Installments), NMML.

6. P.N. Dhar, *Indira Gandhi, the "Emergency" and Indian Democracy* (New Delhi: Oxford University Press, 2000), 149–51.

7. Chandrashekar Dasgupta, "Was There an India Plot to Breakup Pakistan in 1971?" *The Hindu* [Madras], 17 December 2011.

8. Summary of the Consultative Committee Meeting held on 11.12.70, PI/125/82/70, National Archives of India, New Delhi (hereafter NAI).

9. Haksar to Indira Gandhi, 5 January 1971, Subject File 163, P.N. Haksar Papers (III Installment), NMML.

10. "Threat of a Military Attack or Infiltration Campaign by Pakistan," enclosed in Secretary R&AW to Cabinet Secretary, 14 January 1971, Subject File 220, P.N. Haksar Papers (III Installment), NMML.

11. Dasgupta, "Was There an India Plot?"

12. R&AW note for Haksar titled "PM's Instructions about Assessment of East Pakistan Affairs," n.d., Subject File 220, P.N. Haksar Papers (III Installment), NMML. The prime minister gave her instructions to Kao on 2 March 1971.

13. Ibid.

14. Dhar, *Indira Gandhi,* 151; Richard Sisson and Leo Rose, *War and Secession: Pakistan, India, and the Creation of Bangladesh* (Berkeley: University of California Press, 1990), 141.

15. Record of conversation with Mujibur Rahman prepared by D.P. Dhar, 29 January 1972, Subject File 233, P.N. Haksar Papers (III Installment), NMML.

16. Deputy High Commissioner Dhaka to Foreign Secretary, 14 March 1971, Subject File 90(a), P.N. Haksar Papers (III Installment), NMML.

17. Dhar, *Indira Gandhi,* 151–52; Sisson and Rose, *War and Secession,* 141–42; report on conversation with Secretary (East) in Ministry of External Affairs (MEA), 27 April, UKHC India to FCO, FCO 37/879, The National Archives, Kew, London (hereafter TNA).

18. Haksar to Indira Gandhi, 26 March 1971, Subject File 164, P.N. Haksar Papers (III Installment), NMML.

19. Statement by Swaran Singh, 27 March 1971, in *Bangladesh Documents* (New Delhi: Government of India, 1972), 1:671.

20. Interventions by Indira Gandhi, 27 March 1971, ibid., 1:669–70.

21. UKHC India to FCO, 28 March 1971, FCO 37/880, TNA; Text of Resolution, 31 March 1971, in *Bangladesh Documents,* 1:672.

22. Hasan, *Muldhara '71,* 10; P.V. Rajgopal, ed., *The British, the Bandits and the Bordermen: From the Diaries and Articles of K.F. Rustamji* (New Delhi: Wisdom Tree, 2009), 300–2; personal interview with Amirul Islam, Dhaka, 7 April 2010.

23. Hasan, *Muldhara '71,* 10–11; personal interview with Amirul Islam, Dhaka, 7 April 2010; Testimony of Rahman Sobhan in *Bangladesher Shadhinata Juddho: Dalil Patro* (Dhaka: Ministry of Information, Government of People's Republic of Bangladesh, 1985), 15: 397–98; Md Anisur Rahman, *My Story of 1971: Through the Holocaust That Created Bangladesh* (Dhaka: Liberation War Museum, 2001), 44–45. Also see Nurul Islam, *Making of Nation Bangladesh:*

An Economist's Tale (Dhaka: University Press, 2003), 112–15; Ashok Mitra, *A Prattler's Tale: Bengal, Marxism, Governance* (Kolkata: Samya, 2007), 244–49.

24. Haskar to Indira Gandhi, 1 April 1971, Subject File 227, P.N. Haksar Papers (III Installment), NMML.

25. Personal interview with P.N. Dhar, Delhi, 24 November 2009; Hasan, *Muldhara '71*, 11; personal interview with Amirul Islam, Dhaka, 7 April 2010.

26. Personal interview with Amirul Islam, Dhaka, 7 April 2010; Testimony of Rahman Sobhan in *Bangladesher Shadhinata Juddho*, 15:398–99. There have been other claimants to the paternity of this declaration including the BSF whose draft was apparently vetted by a lawyer in Calcutta (Rajgopal, *British, Bandits and Bordermen*, 305) and, more incredibly, the chief of staff of the Eastern Army Command, General Jacob, who also claims to have come up with the idea of a provisional government. J.F.R. Jacob, *Surrender at Dacca: Birth of a Nation* (Dhaka: University Press, 1991), 41.

27. "To the People of Bangla Desh," 11 April 1971, *Bangladesh Documents*, 1:282–86.

28. On the BSF's role, see Rajgopal, *British, Bandits and Bordermen*, 306–8. A television news clip of the ceremony can be seen at www.youtube.com/watch?v=Y4097iqHAYw.

29. Ministry of External Affairs (MEA) documents cited in S.N. Prasad, *The India-Pakistan War of 1971* (New Delhi: Ministry of Defence, 1992), 115. This important but unpublished official history is available in the public domain, http://www.bharat-rakshak.com/LAND-FORCES/Army/History/1971War/PDF/.

30. Prasad, *India-Pakistan War*, 109–14. The most prominent dissenting voice was that of Nirad Chaudhuri, the famous writer, who was a Hindu from preparatition East Bengal; he characteristically castigated the government's expressions of support as "opportunistic and a pettifogging exercise of chauvinism." See the article in *Hindustan Standard* [New Delhi], cited in ibid., 114.

31. Notes on discussions with M.C. Chagla, 3 April 1971; notes by Dr. Rahmatullah Khan and Dr. I.N. Tewari, n.d., Subject File 244, Jayaprakash Narayan Papers (III Installment), NMML.

32. Press statement, 2 April 1971, Subject File 251, Jayaprakash Narayan Papers (III Installment), NMML.

33. Note by T.N. Kaul, 1 May 1971, Subject File 227, P.N. Haksar (III Installment), NMML.

34. "Points for the Meeting" by Haksar, 6 May 1971, ibid.

35. Haksar's note to Indira Gandhi on meeting with opposition leaders on 7 May 1971, n.d. (ca. 6 May 1971), ibid.

36. Personal interview with Amirul Islam, Dhaka, 7 April 2010; Hasan, *Muldhara '71*, 14–15.

37. Record of conversation with Mujibur Rahman prepared by D.P. Dhar, 29 January 1972, Subject File 233, P.N. Haksar Papers (III Installment), NMML.

38. Quoted in Prasad, *India-Pakistan War,* 117–18.

39. Haksar's note to Indira Gandhi on meeting with opposition leaders on 7 May 1971, n.d. (ca. 6 May 1971), Subject File 227, P. N. Haksar (III Installment), NMML.

40. See, for instance, Pupul Jayakar, *Indira Gandhi: A Biography,* rev. ed. (New Delhi: Penguin, 1995), 223; Depinder Singh, *Field Marshal Sam Manekshaw: Soldiering with Dignity* (Dehradun: Natraj, 2002), 129.

41. Interview with Field Marshal Manekshaw, *Quarterdeck* (New Delhi, Naval Headquarters, 1996), reproduced as appendix 6 in Jacob, *Surrender at Dacca.*

42. Jacob, *Surrender at Dacca,* 35–36.

43. "Threat of a Military Attack or Infiltration Campaign by Pakistan," enclosed in Secretary R&AW to Cabinet Secretary, 14 January 1971, Subject File 220, P. N. Haksar Papers (III Installment), NMML.

44. Haksar to Indira Gandhi, 5 January 1971, Subject File 163, P. N. Haksar Papers (III Installment), NMML.

45. "Threat of a Military Attack or Infiltration Campaign by Pakistan," enclosed in Secretary R&AW to Cabinet Secretary, 14 January 1971, Subject File 220, P. N. Haksar Papers (III Installment), NMML.

46. Embassy in India to State, 27 March 1971, in US Department of State, *Foreign Relations of the United States, 1969–1976,* vol. 11: *South Asia Crisis, 1971* (hereafter *FRUS 1971*) (Washington, DC: United States Government Printing Office, 2005), 31–32; UKHC India to FCO, FCO 37/879, TNA.

47. Haksar's note to Indira Gandhi on meeting with opposition leaders on 7 May 1971, n.d. (ca. 6 May 1971), Subject File 227, P. N. Haksar (III Installment), NMML.

48. Haskar to Indira Gandhi, 1 April 1971, ibid.

49. D. P. Dhar to P. N. Haksar, 4 April 1971, Subject File 220, P. N. Haksar Papers (III Installment), NMML.

50. Sukhwant Singh, *India's Wars since Independence: The Liberation of Bangladesh* (New Delhi: Lancer, 1980), 18–20, 95–96. The author was deputy director of military operations at the army headquarters during the crisis. Also see Inder Malhotra, *Indira Gandhi: A Personal and Political Biography* (London: Hodder & Stoughton, 1989), 134–35; Katherine Frank, *Indira: The Life of India Nehru Gandhi* (London: HarperCollins, 2001), 333–34.

51. "Bangla Desh and Our Policy Options" by K. Subrahmanyam, Subject File 276, P. N. Haksar Papers (III Installment), NMML.

52. Ibid.

53. D. P. Dhar to Haksar, 18 April 1971, Subject File 220, P. N. Haksar Papers (III Installment), NMML.

54. Dhar, *Indira Gandhi,* 157; personal interview with P. N. Dhar, Delhi, 24 November 2009.

55. Haksar's note to Indira Gandhi on meeting with opposition leaders on 7 May 1971, n.d. (ca. 6 May 1971), Subject File 227, P.N. Haksar (III Installment), NMML.

56. Note on Jayaprakash Narayan's tour to Calcutta and border areas from 8–10 April 1971, n.d., Subject File 244, Jayaprakash Narayan Papers (III Installment), NMML.

57. Prasad, *India-Pakistan War,* 101–2; Rajgopal, *British, Bandits and Bordermen,* 303–4.

58. Rustamji to Narain, 14 April 1971, Subject File 227, P.N. Haksar (III Installment), NMML.

59. Prasad, *India-Pakistan War,* 102.

60. K.M. Safiullah, *Bangladesh at War,* 2nd ed. (Dhaka: Academic Publishers, 1995), 70–71; Hasan, *Muldhara '71,* 14–15. Also see Testimony of Rahman Sobhan in *Bangladesher Shadhinata Juddho,* 15:396.

61. Note on Jayaprakash Narayan's tour to Calcutta and border areas from 8–10 April 1971, n.d., Subject File 244, Jayaprakash Narayan Papers (III Installment), NMML.

62. Rajgopal, *British, Bandits and Bordermen,* 315–16.

63. "Points for the Meeting" by Haksar, 6 May 1971, Subject File 227, P.N. Haksar (III Installment), NMML.

64. Kao to Indira Gandhi, 13 April 1971, ibid.

65. "Current Pattern of the Pakistani Mil Ops, Appreciation of Pak Army's Strategic Objectives and Suggested Counteraction by the Mukti Fauj," 20 April 1971, Subject File 244, Jayaprakash Narayan Papers (III Installment), NMML.

66. Rustamji to Manekshaw, 23 April 1971, Subject File 258, P.N. Haksar Papers (III Installment), NMML.

67. Prasad, *India-Pakistan War,* 173–74.

68. Arun Bhattacharjee, *Dateline Mujibnagar* (Delhi: Vikas, 1973), 38.

69. "Points for the Meeting" by Haksar, 6 May 1971; "Note for the Meeting at 10 PM Tonight" by Haksar, 6 May 1971, Subject File 227, P.N. Haksar (III Installment), NMML.

70. Haksar to Indira Gandhi, 4 June 1971, Subject File 168, P.N. Haksar (III Installment), NMML.

71. Dhar, *Indira Gandhi,* 164, 172; personal interview with P.N. Dhar, Delhi, 24 November 2009.

72. Prasad, *India-Pakistan War,* 126.

73. Ibid., 122; J.N. Dixit, *Liberation and Beyond: Indo-Bangladesh Relations* (New Delhi: Konark, 1999), 49.

74. Haksar to S.M. Sikri (Chief Justice of India), 13 May 1971, Subject File 166, P.N. Haksar Papers (III Installment), NMML.

75. Sisson and Rose, *War and Secession,* 153.

76. Prasad, *India-Pakistan War,* 121.

77. Haksar to Sikri, 13 May 1971, Subject File 166, P.N. Haksar Papers (III Installment), NMML.

78. Record of Foreign Minister's talk to Heads of Missions, London, 20 June 1971, Subject File 19, T.N. Kaul Papers (I, II, and III Installments), NMML.

79. Personal interview with P.N. Dhar, Delhi, 24 November 2009.

80. Sisson and Rose, *War and Secession,* 152–53; Dhar, *Indira Gandhi,* 156; B.K. Nehru, *Nice Guys Finish Second: Memoirs* (New Delhi: Penguin, 1997), 545.

81. Prasad, *India-Pakistan War,* 124.

82. Dhar, *Indira Gandhi,* 154.

83. Haksar to Sikri, 13 May 1971, Subject File 166, P.N. Haksar Papers (III Installment), NMML.

84. Indira Gandhi's letter to heads of states/governments, 14 May 1971, ibid.

85. Dhar, *Indira Gandhi,* 156, 158.

86. Prime Minister's statement in Lok Sabha, 24 May 1971, in *Bangladesh Documents,* 1:672–75.

87. Record of Foreign Minister's talk to Heads of Missions, London, 20 June 1971, Subject File 19, T.N. Kaul Papers (I, II, and III Installments), NMML.

88. Kaul to D.P. Dhar, 7/8 May 1971, cited in Prasad, *India-Pakistan War,* 151n120.

89. Ibid., 106, 150n106.

90. Record of Foreign Minister's talk to Heads of Missions, London, 20 June 1971, Subject File 19, T.N. Kaul Papers (I, II, and III Installments), NMML.

91. Ibid.

4. The Grand Strategists

1. There are several biographies of Kissinger. See, especially, Walter Isaacson, *Kissinger: A Biography* (New York: Simon & Schuster, 2005). For a more wide-ranging and perceptive study, see Jeremi Suri, *Henry Kissinger and the American Century* (Cambridge, MA: Belknap Press, 2007).

2. Kissinger to Nixon, 28 April 1971, in US Department of State, *Foreign Relations of the United States, 1969–1976,* vol. 11: *South Asia Crisis, 1971* (hereafter *FRUS 1971*) (Washington, DC: United States Government Printing Office, 2005), 94–95.

3. Kissinger to Nixon, 28 April 1971, *FRUS 1971,* 95–97; note from Alexander Haig (Kissinger's deputy) to Nixon, 28 April 1971, and Nixon's handwritten note, ibid., 97n2 (emphases in original). Also see Henry Kissinger, *The White House Years* (London: George Weidenfeld & Nicolson, 1979), 855–56.

4. Christopher Van Hollen, "The Tilt Policy Revisited: Nixon-Kissinger Geopolitics and South Asia," *Asian Survey* 20, no. 4 (April 1980), 339; Robert Dallek, *Nixon and Kissinger: Partners in Power* (London: Allen Lane, 2007),

350–51. Also see Jack Anderson and George Clifford, *The Anderson Papers: From the Files of America's Most Famous Investigative Reporter* (New York: Random House, 1973).

5. Kissinger, *White House Years*, 842–918.

6. Van Hollen, "Tilt Policy Revisited," set the tone for much of the work that followed. Raymond Garthoff, *Détente and Confrontation: American-Soviet Relations from Nixon to Reagan,* rev. ed. (Washington DC: Brookings Press, 1994), 295–322; William Bundy, *A Tangled Web: The Making of Foreign Policy in the Nixon Presidency* (New York: Hill & Wang, 1998), 269–92; Jussi Hahnimaki, *The Flawed Architect: Henry Kissinger and American Foreign Policy* (New York: Oxford University Press, 2004), 154–84; Robert McMahon, "The Danger of Geopolitical Fantasies: Nixon, Kissinger and the South Asia Crisis of 1971," in *Nixon in the World: American Foreign Relations, 1969–1977,* ed. Fredrik Logevall and Andrew Preston (New York: Oxford University Press, 2008), 249–68; Gary Hess, "Grand Strategy and Regional Conflict: Nixon, Kissinger and the South Asia Crisis," *Diplomatic History* 31, no. 5 (2007): 959–63; Geoffrey Warner, "Nixon, Kissinger and the Breakup of Pakistan, 1971," *International Affairs* 81, no. 5 (2005): 1097–118. The sole exception to this is Richard Sisson and Leo Rose, *War and Secession: Pakistan, India, and the Creation of Bangladesh* (Berkeley: University of California Press, 1990), which adopts Kissinger's argument about an ostensible tilt to India.

7. Kissinger, *White House Years*, 848; Dennis Kux, *The United States and Pakistan, 1947–2000: Disenchanted Allies* (Washington, DC: Woodrow Wilson Center Press, 2001), 182.

8. Dennis Kux, *India and the United States: Estranged Democracies, 1941–1991* (Washington, DC: National Defense University Press, 1992), 279–80; Kux, *Disenchanted Allies,* 179; Kissinger, *White House Years,* 848.

9. McMahon, "Danger of Geopolitical Fantasies"; Hess, "Grand Strategy and Regional Conflict"; Warner, "Nixon, Kissinger and the Breakup of Pakistan"; Van Hollen, "Tilt Policy Revisited."

10. *FRUS 1971,* 264–67; US Department of State, *Foreign Relations of the United States, 1969–1976,* vol. E-7: *Documents on South Asia, 1969–1972* (hereafter *FRUS* E-7) (Washington, DC: United States Government Printing Office, 2005), docs. 146, 150.

11. Note on "India and the USA," n.d. [ca. summer 1969], WII 104/8/69, National Archives of India, New Delhi (hereafter NAI).

12. Haksar to Indira Gandhi, 30 July 1969, Subject File 42, Haksar Papers (I and II Installments), Nehru Memorial Museum and Library, New Delhi (hereafter NMML).

13. Record of conversation between Indira Gandhi and Nixon, 31 July 1969, Subject File 19, T.N. Kaul Papers (I, II, and III Installments), NMML; record of meeting between Indian and American delegations, 1 August 1969,

WII/121(31)/69, NAI. The American record of these conversations is found in *FRUS* E-7, doc. 29.

14. Haksar to Indira Gandhi, 30 July 1969, Subject File 42, Haksar Papers (I and II Installments), NMML.

15. National Security Study Memorandum 26, 21 February 1969, *FRUS* E-7, doc. 10; Kissinger, *White House Years,* 846.

16. Secretary of State (SS) to Department of State, 26 May 1969, *FRUS* E-7, doc. 23; Kux, *Disenchanted Allies,* 180.

17. Memorandum of conversation in New Delhi, 31 July 1969, *FRUS* E-7, doc. 29.

18. Memorandum of conversation in Lahore, 1 August 1969, ibid., doc. 32.

19. Jha to Kaul, 8 July 1970, and Jha to Swaran Singh, 29 June 1970, Subject File 277, P.N. Haksar Papers (III Installment), NMML.

20. Ambassador in India to SS, *FRUS* E-7, doc. 78.

21. Meeting of Secretary of State Rogers with Prime Minister and Foreign Minister, New York, 24 October 1970, Subject File 19, T.N. Kaul (I, II, and III Installments), NMML. For Rogers's account of the meeting, see the transcript of the telephone conversation between Rogers and Kissinger, 24 October 1970, *FRUS* E-7, doc. 89.

22. M.K. Rasgotra (Embassy in Washington) to A.K. Ray (Joint Secretary, Ministry of External Affairs [MEA]), 8 November 1970, WII/104(14)/70, NAI.

23. Department of State to Embassy in India, 27 October 1970, *FRUS* E-7, doc. 92; memorandum of conversation between Kissinger and Jha, 1 November 1970, ibid., doc. 94; Kissinger, *White House Years,* 849.

24. Note on "Political Implications of the United States military aid to Pakistan" by N.M. Khilnani (Joint Secretary, MEA), 5 December 1970, WII/109 (10)/70, NAI.

25. The most comprehensive account of the opening to China is Margaret Macmillan, *Nixon and Mao: The Week That Changed the World* (New York: Random House, 2007). Also see Hahnimaki, *Flawed Architect;* Dallek, *Nixon and Kissinger;* Jeffrey Kimball, *Nixon's Vietnam War* (Lawrence: University Press of Kansas, 1998). For Kissinger's most recent retrospective, see Henry Kissinger, *On China* (London: Allen Lane, 2011), 202–92.

26. Record of Foreign Minister's talk with President Nixon, 10 July 1969, Subject File 42, P.N. Haksar Papers (I and II Installments), NMML.

27. James Spain (Chargé d'Affaires in Pakistan) to Kissinger, 6 August 1969, in *The White House and Pakistan: Secret Declassified Documents, 1969–1974,* ed. F.S. Aijazuddin (Karachi: Oxford University Press, 2002) (hereafter *WHP*), 62–63. Also see the memorandum of conversation between Agha Hilaly and Harold Saunders, 28 August 1969, ibid., 67–68. To keep the initiative under wraps, there was no mention of this exchange in the American record of the

conversation prepared by Kissinger's aide. Spain stumbled upon it when he was comparing his transcripts with those of the Pakistanis, whereupon he wrote to Kissinger. The latter wrote a swift and stiff reply to Spain, asking him to keep his mouth shut. Kissinger also assured him that he would convey this matter to Secretary of State Rogers, which of course he had no intention of doing. Kissinger to Spain, 19 August 1969, ibid., 63–64.

28. Entry of 2 August 1969, in H.R. Haldeman, *The Haldeman Diaries: Inside the Nixon White House, The Complete Multimedia Edition* (Santa Monica, CA: Sony Electronic Publishing, 1994).

29. Memorandum of conversation between Agha Hilaly and Harold Saunders, 28 August 1969, *WHP*, 67–68; Kissinger to Nixon, 16 October 1969, ibid., 73; Sher Ali Khan Pataudi to Yahya, 10 October 1969, in F.S. Aijazuddin, *From a Head, through a Head, to a Head: The Secret Channel between the US and China through Pakistan* (Karachi: Oxford University Press, 2000), 27.

30. Hilaly to Yahya, 15 October 1969 in Aijazuddin, *From a Head*, 28–30.

31. Memorandum of conversation between Hilaly and Kissinger, 19 December 1969, *WHP*, 75–77; Kissinger to Nixon, 23 December 1969, ibid., 79–80.

32. Nixon to Yahya, 19 January 1970, enclosed in Kissinger to Nixon, 31 January 1970, *FRUS* E-7, doc. 46.

33. Messages of 14 February and 23 February 1970, in Aijazuddin, *From a Head*, 30–31.

34. Richardson to Nixon, 10 February 1970, *FRUS* E-7, doc. 47; Kissinger to Nixon, 16 March 1970, ibid., doc. 54; Kissinger to Nixon, 13 April 1970, ibid., doc. 57; Kissinger to Nixon, 11 June 1970, ibid., doc. 63.

35. Kissinger, *White House Years*, 849.

36. Memorandum of conversation between Nixon and Yahya, 25 October 1971, *FRUS* E-7, doc. 90.

37. Sultan Khan (Foreign Secretary) to Hilaly, 23 November 1971, in Aijazuddin, *From a Head*, 42–43; Sultan M. Khan, *Memories and Reflections of a Pakistani Diplomat* (London: Centre for Pakistan Studies, 1997), 246–47.

38. Kissinger to Nixon, 16 December 1970, enclosing text of note verbale, *WHP*, 115–16; Aijazuddin, *From a Head*, 50–53.

39. National Security Study Memorandum 118, 16 February 1971, *FRUS* E-7, doc. 115; Kissinger to Nixon, 22 February 1971, ibid., doc. 118.

40. Contingency Study on Pakistan—East Pakistan Secession, 3 March 1971, *FRUS* E-7, doc. 123.

41. Minutes of Senior Review Group Meeting, 6 March 1971, *FRUS 1971*, 8–16; Van Hollen, "Tilt Policy Revisited," 341; Nixon to Kissinger, 13 March 1971, *FRUS 1971*, 17–20.

42. Minutes of Washington Special Actions Group (hereafter WSAG) Meeting, 26 March 1971, *FRUS 1971*, 22–29.

43. Blood to SS, 28 March, 29 March, and 30 March 1971, *FRUS* E-7, docs. 125, 126, 127; Farland to SS, ibid., doc. 128.

44. Dhaka to State Department, 6 April 1971, *FRUS 1971,* 45–46. Also see Dhaka to State Department, 10 April, *FRUS* E-7, doc. 130.

45. Transcript of telephone conversation between Nixon and Kissinger, 30 March 1971, *FRUS 1971,* 37; transcript of telephone conversation between Rogers and Kissinger, 6 April 1971, ibid., 47–48; Archer Blood, *The Cruel Birth of Bangladesh: Memoirs of an American Diplomat* (Dhaka: University Press, 2002).

46. Excerpts from conversation with Kissinger and Haldeman, 12 April 1971, *FRUS 1971,* 65.

47. For a detailed examination of the links between the Biafran and East Pakistan crises, see Daniel J. Sargent, *A Superpower Adrift: History, Strategy, and American Foreign Policy in the 1970s* (New York: Oxford University Press, forthcoming), chap. 4.

48. Transcript of telephone conversation between Nixon and Kissinger, 29 March 1971, *FRUS 1971,* 35–36.

49. Jha to Kaul, 18 April 1971 (reporting conversation of 16 April), Subject File 277, P. N. Haksar Papers (III Installment), NMML.

50. Minutes of the Senior Review Group (SRG) Meeting, 9 April 1971, *FRUS 1971,* 59; Kissinger to Nixon (enclosing Rogers's memo), 13 April 1971, ibid., 66–67.

51. NSC Interdepartmental Group Paper, "Pakistan-American Relations: A Reassessment," n.d., *FRUS* E-7, doc. 132.

52. Kissinger, *White House Years,* 854.

53. Minutes of SRG Meeting, 19 April 1971, *FRUS 1971,* 76–84.

54. Saunders to Kissinger, 19 April 1971, ibid., 85–87 (emphasis in original). Also see Saunders to Kissinger, 16 April 1971, ibid., 69–72.

55. Message from Zhou to Nixon, 21 April 1971, in US Department of State, *Foreign Relations of the United States 1969–1976,* vol. 17: *China 1969–1972* (hereafter *FRUS China*) (Washington, DC: United States Government Printing Office), doc. 118.

56. Hilaly to Yahya, 28 April and 29 April 1971, in Aijazuddin, *From a Head,* 58–61. Also see Hilaly to Yahya, 4 May 1971, ibid., 63–64.

57. Memorandum of conversation between Farland and Kissinger, 7 May 1971, *FRUS 1971,* 108.

58. Report on conversation with General Akbar Khan, Embassy Pakistan to SS, 27 March 1971, Box 2530, POL 23-9 PAK, RG 59, US National Archives and Records Administration (hereafter USNA), College Park, MD.

59. Sisson and Rose, *War and Secession,* 166–68.

60. Minutes of the meeting of the Cornelius Committee held at the president's house on 26 May 1971, reproduced in Hasan Zaheer, *The Separation of East Pakistan: The Rise and Realization of Bengali Muslim Nationalism* (Dhaka:

University Press, 2001), 467–71 (also see 328–29); G.W. Choudhury, *Last Days of United Pakistan* (London: Hurst, 1974), 191–92. Choudhury coyly refrains from mentioning his own participation in this exercise.

61. Sisco to Rogers, 30 June 1971, *FRUS 1971*, 211–12; Nixon to Yahya, ibid., 213–14.

62. "Report of the Special Team on the Revival of Economic Activity in East Pakistan" is summarized in Zaheer, *Separation of East Pakistan*, 185–93. Hasan Zaheer was a member of the team and was able to access this and other documents in writing his account.

63. The next three paragraphs are drawn from Annexure I to "Pakistan: A note by Mr. Cargill on Recent Discussions with the Government and a Possible Course of Action for the Consortium," 21 May 1971, World Bank Papers, Center for the Advanced Study of India (hereafter CASI), University of Pennsylvania, Philadelphia; Zaheer, *Separation of East Pakistan*, 214–28.

64. The consortium for providing economic aid to Pakistan was led by the World Bank and consisted of Belgium, Canada, France, Germany, Italy, Japan, the Netherlands, the United Kingdom, and the United States.

65. UKHC Pakistan to Treasury, 3 May 1971, FCO 37/886, The National Archives, Kew, London (hereafter TNA); secret message from McNamara (President, World Bank) to Watanabe (President, Asian Development Bank) in G.B. Votaw to M.P.J. Lynch, 6 May 1971, World Bank Papers, CASI; Annex I to "Pakistan: A note by Mr. Cargill," 21 May 1971, ibid.; Zaheer, *Separation of East Pakistan*, 215–20.

66. Viqar Ahmed and Rashid Amjad, *The Management of Pakistan's Economy 1947–82* (Karachi: Oxford University Press, 1984), 302–03.

67. "Pakistan: A note by Mr. Cargill," 21 May 1971, World Bank Papers, CASI.

68. Ibid. Also see UKHC Pakistan to FCO, 4 May 1971, FCO 37/886, and "Brief for Secretary of State's use in the Cabinet: Pakistan," 5 May 1971, FCO 37/886, TNA.

69. Irwin to Nixon, 9 May 1971, POL-7 PAK, RG 59, USNA; High Commissioner in Pakistan to FCO, 6 May 1971, FCO 37/886, TNA.

70. Memorandum of conversation, 10 May 1971, *FRUS 1971*, 113.

71. "Pakistan—A Note on Discussions," 14 May 1971, World Bank Papers, CASI.

72. "The Situation in East Pakistan: A report by an IBRD/IMF Mission," 8 July 1971, World Bank Papers, CASI.

73. Cargill to McNamara, 26 June 1971, World Bank Papers, CASI.

74. Ibid.; "Pakistan: Paper for DOP," 23 July 1971, FCO 37/890, TNA.

75. Yahya to Nixon, 28 June 1971, *FRUS 1971*, 208–09; Nixon to Yahya, 1 July 1971, ibid., 213–14.

76. *Congressional Record*, 17 June 1971, 20702–704; Gallagher to McNamara, 12 July 1971, World Bank Papers, CASI.

77. Robert Jackson, *South Asian Crisis: India-Pakistan-Bangladesh* (London: Chatto & Windus, 1975), 63–64; Kissinger to Nixon, 3 August 1971, *FRUS 1971*, 306–7.

78. Cargill to McNamara, 26 June 1971, World Bank Papers, CASI.

79. Kissinger to Nixon, 28 April 1971, *FRUS 1971*, 95.

80. Record of 40 Committee Meeting, 9 April 1971, ibid., 63–65.

81. Memorandum of conversation between Kissinger and Jha, 21 May 1971, ibid., 129–32.

82. Transcript of telephone conversation between Nixon and Kissinger, 23 May 1971, ibid., 140. The contrast with their unwillingness to "politicize aid" for Pakistan was stark indeed.

83. Conversation between Nixon and Kissinger, 26 May 1971, *FRUS E-7*, doc. 135.

84. Memorandum for Kissinger from Hoskinson, 26 May 1971, ibid., doc. 134.

85. Minutes of WSAG meeting, 26 May 1971, *FRUS 1971*, 149–56.

86. Nixon's letter to Indira Gandhi, 28 May 1971, ibid., 160–61.

87. Conversation among Nixon, Kissinger and Swaran Singh, *FRUS E-7*, doc. 138.

88. Report on conversation between Jha and Irwin, State to Embassy in India, 24 June 1971, DEF 12-5 PAK, RG 59, USNA; Embassy in India to State, 23 June 1971, ibid.; State to Embassy in India, 27 June 1971, ibid.; report on conversation between Rasgotra and Van Hollen, in Roedad Khan, ed., *American Papers: Secret and Confidential India-Pakistan-Bangladesh Documents, 1965–1973* (Karachi: Oxford University Press, 1999), 609–10.

89. Record of conversation with Kissinger, 6 July 1971, enclosed in Haksar to Jha, 21 July 1971, Subject File 169, P.N. Haksar Papers (III Installment), NMML. Kissinger's much briefer, somewhat misleading description of this conversation is in Memorandum for the Record, 6 July 1971, *FRUS 1971*, 220–21.

90. Record of conversation with Kissinger, 6 July 1971, enclosed in Haksar to Jha, 21 July 1971, Subject File 169, P. N. Haksar Papers (III Installment), NMML.

91. Memorandum of conversation between Indira Gandhi and Kissinger, 7 July 1971, *FRUS 1971*, 221–25.

92. Record of conversation between Swaran Singh and Kissinger, 7 July 1971, Subject File 19, T.N. Kaul Papers (I, II, and III Installments), NMML. The American record is found in *FRUS 1971*, 226–31; also see Kissinger's Memorandum for the Record, n.d., ibid., 233.

93. Record of conversation between Jagjivan Ram and Kissinger, 7 July 1971, Subject File 229, P.N. Haksar Papers (III Installment), NMML. Also see the memorandum of conversation on 7 July, 12 July 1971, *FRUS E-7*, doc. 139; Kissinger's Memorandum for the Record, n.d., *FRUS 1971*, 234.

94. Memorandum for the Record, 6 July 1971, *FRUS 1971*, 220–21; Kissinger, *White House Years*, 861; Kissinger's Memorandum for the Record, n.d., *FRUS 1971*, 233.

95. Memorandum of conversation between Kissinger and Pakistani officials, 8 July 1971, *FRUS 1971*, 236–41; Kissinger to Haig, 9 July 1971, ibid., 242–43.

96. Memorandum on NSC Meeting, 16 July 1971, ibid., 264–67.

97. Minutes of Senior Review Group Meeting, 30 July 1971, ibid., 292–302.

98. Van Hollen, "Tilt Policy Revisited," 347.

99. Minutes of Senior Review Group Meeting, 30 July 1971, *FRUS 1971*, 292–302.

100. Memoranda of conversations on 10 & 11 July 1971, *FRUS China*, docs. 140, 143.

101. Kissinger, *White House Years*, 862.

102. Minutes of Senior Review Group Meeting, 23 July 1971, *FRUS 1971*, 271.

103. Cited in Seymour Hersh, *The Price of Power: Kissinger in the Nixon White House* (New York: Summit Books, 1983), 452. Also see Helms to Nixon, 29 July 1971, *FRUS 1971*, 291; Saunders to Kissinger, 7 September 1971, ibid., 391–93; memorandum of conversation between Jha and Kissinger, 11 September 1971, ibid., 407–8.

104. Note for Prime Minister and Foreign Minister by T.N. Kaul, 3 August 1971, Subject File 49, P.N. Haksar Papers (II Installment), NMML.

105. Note on "Sino-US Relations" by the Americas Division of MEA, 30 July 1971, WII/104/34/71, NAI.

5. The Reluctant Russians

1. Henry Kissinger, *The White House Years* (London: George Weidenfeld & Nicolson, 1979), 866–67.

2. Ashok Parthasarathi, "Forty Years of the Indo-Soviet Treaty: A Historic Landmark at the Global Level," *Mainstream* 49, no. 34 (13 August 2011), www.mainstreamweekly.net/article2951.html.

3. Indira Gandhi to Kosygin, 20 July 1968, Subject File 135, P.N. Haksar Papers (III Installment), Nehru Memorial Museum and Library, New Delhi (hereafter NMML).

4. Indira Gandhi to A.B. Vajpayee, n.d. (ca. 15 July 1968); Haksar's note for the Prime Minister, 13 July 1968, Subject File 135, P.N. Haksar Papers (III Installment), NMML.

5. Extracts from Romesh Bhandari to D.P. Dhar, 27 March 1969; note by T.N. Kaul, 7 April 1969, Subject File 203, P.N. Haksar Papers (III Installment), NMML. On Grechko's visit to India, also see A.G. Noorani, *Brezhnev Plan for Asian Security: Russia in Asia* (Bombay: Jaico, 1975), 60–61.

6. Haksar's minutes for the Prime Minister, 31 March 1969, on D.P. Dhar to Kewal Singh (Secretary, Ministry of External Affairs), 31 March 1969, Subject

File 203, P.N. Haksar Papers (III Installment), NMML. On the Soviet Union's role in the Sino-Indian conflict, see Srinath Raghavan, *War and Peace in Modern India: A Strategic History of the Nehru Years* (London: Palgrave Macmillan, 2010), 299–309.

7. Note by T.N. Kaul, 7 April 1969, Subject File 203, P.N. Haksar Papers (III Installment), NMML.

8. Haksar's note to the Prime Minister, 10 September 1969, ibid.

9. Indira Gandhi to Kosygin, n.d. (ca. 10 April 1969), ibid.

10. Record of conversation between Indira Gandhi and Kosygin, 6 May 1969, Subject File 140; "Soviet assessment of China and Chinese policies," note sent by Kaul to Haksar, n.d. (ca. June 1971), Subject File 258, P.N. Haksar Papers (III Installment), NMML.

11. Record of conversation between Indira Gandhi and Kosygin, 6 May 1969, Subject File 140, P.N. Haksar Papers (III Installment), NMML.

12. Model Draft of Treaty, n.d., Subject File 203, P.N. Haksar Papers (III Installment), NMML.

13. D.P. Dhar to Kaul, 9 October 1969, T.N. Kaul Papers (I, II, and III Installment), NMML.

14. "Soviet assessment of China and Chinese policies," note sent by Kaul to Haksar, n.d. (ca. June 1971), Subject File 258, P.N. Haksar Papers (III Installment), NMML.

15. Record of conversation between Kaul and Kosygin, 25 May 1970; record of conversation between D.P. Dhar and Kosygin, 23 March 1971; record of conversation between D.P. Dhar and Colonel General D.S. Sidorovich, 22 March 1971; D.P. Dhar to Kaul, 25 March 1971, Subject File 276, P.N. Haksar Papers (III Installment), NMML.

16. D.P. Dhar to Kaul, 3 March 1971, Subject File 203, P.N. Haksar Papers (III Installment), NMML.

17. Text of Nikolai Podgorny's letter to Yahya Khan, 2 April 1971, in *Bangladesh Documents* (New Delhi: Government of India, 1972), 1:510–11.

18. Kosygin's message cited in Jamsheed Marker, *Quiet Diplomacy: Memoirs of an Ambassador of Pakistan* (Karachi: Oxford University Press, 2010), 120–21.

19. "Guidelines for Consultation with the Communist Party of East Pakistan during the 9th Congress of the Communist Party of India," 30 September 1971, DY 30/IV A 2/20, no. 642, Archives of Parties and Mass Organizations of the Former German Democratic Republic in the Federal Archives, Berlin (hereafter SAPMO).

20. Mohit Sen, *A Traveller and the Road: The Journey of an Indian Communist* (New Delhi: Rupa, 2003), 314.

21. Yahya Khan to Podgorny, 5 April 1971, in R.K. Jain, ed., *Soviet South Asian Relations 1947–78* (New Delhi: Radiant, 1978), 106–8.

22. Two letters from D.P. Dhar to Haksar, 4 April 1971, Subject File 227, P.N. Haksar Papers (III Installment), NMML.

23. Record of Foreign Minister's conversation with USSR Chargé d'Affaires at 6 PM on 4 April 1971, 5 April 1971, Subject File 276, P. N. Haksar Papers (III Installment), NMML.

24. Ibid.; Prime Minister's comment on the same, 5 April 1971, Subject File 276, P. N. Haksar Papers (III Installment), NMML.

25. Top secret and personal letter from Dhar to Haksar, 4 April 1971, Subject File 227, P. N. Haksar Papers (III Installment), NMML; Sen, *Traveller and the Road*, 314, 319–20.

26. D. P. Dhar to Haksar, 18 April 1971, Subject File 89, P. N. Haksar Papers (III Installment), NMML.

27. Ibid.

28. Marker, *Quiet Diplomacy*, 121–22; Sultan M. Khan, *Memories and Reflections of a Pakistani Diplomat* (London: Centre for Pakistan Studies, 1997), 299–300.

29. Entry of 30 April 1971, in Craig Baxter, ed., *Diaries of Field Marshal Mohammed Ayub Khan, 1966–1972* (Karachi: Oxford University Press, 2007), 481.

30. Marker, *Quiet Diplomacy*, 121–22; Khan, *Memories and Reflections*, 299–300.

31. Indian Embassy Moscow to Foreign Ministry, 28 April 1971, Subject File 227, P. N. Haksar Papers (III Installment), NMML. The next paragraph draws on this document.

32. Two letters from D. P. Dhar to Haksar, 29 April 1971, Subject File 227, P. N. Haksar Papers (III Installment), NMML.

33. Ibid.

34. D. P. Dhar to Haksar, 29 April 1971, Subject File 227, P. N. Haksar Papers (III Installment), NMML.

35. Record of conversation between D. P. Dhar and Marshal Grechko, 5 June 1971, Subject File 258, P. N. Haksar Papers (III Installment), NMML. The next two paragraphs draw on this document.

36. D. P. Dhar to Kaul (copy to Haksar), 5 June 1971, Subject File 258, P. N. Haksar Papers (III Installment), NMML.

37. Record of conversation between Swaran Singh and Kosygin, 8 June 1971, Subject File 203, P. N. Haksar Papers (III Installment), NMML.

38. Ibid.

39. Records of conversations between Swaran Singh and Gromyko, 7–8 June 1971, Subject File 203, P. N. Haksar (III Installment), NMML.

40. Note to Prime Minister and Foreign Minister by Kaul, 15 June 1971, Subject File 89, P. N. Haksar Papers (III Installment), NMML.

41. Indira Gandhi to Kosygin, n.d. (ca. 12 June 1971), Subject File 169, P. N. Haksar Papers (III Installment), NMML.

42. Marker, *Quiet Diplomacy*, 123–30.

43. Ibid.

44. Handwritten note by Haksar on his meeting with Pegov, n.d. (ca. 25 June 1971), Subject File 229, P.N. Haksar Papers (III Installment), NMML.

45. Note to Prime Minister and Foreign Minister by T.N. Kaul, 3 August 1971, Subject File 49, P.N. Haksar Papers (II Installment), NMML. The next four paragraphs draw on this document.

46. Record of conversations between D.P. Dhar and Gromyko, 3 and 4 August 1971, Subject File 280, P.N. Haksar Papers (III Installment), NMML.

47. Record of conversation between D.P. Dhar and Kosygin, 5 August 1971, ibid.

48. "Discussion with Gromyko on 5/8/1971 at the luncheon," note by D.P. Dhar, 8 August 1971, ibid.

49. Record of conversation between Prime Minister and Gromyko, 10 August 1971, Subject File 19, T.N. Kaul Papers, NMML.

50. Ibid.

6. Poster Child and Pariah

1. Harold Evans, *My Paper Chase: True Stories of Vanished Times, An Autobiography* (London: Abacus, 2009), 354–57.

2. Roedad Khan, *Pakistan: A Dream Gone Sour* (Karachi: Oxford University Press, 1997), chap. 3.

3. Evans, *My Paper Chase*, 355.

4. Ibid., 356–57.

5. *Sunday Times* [London], 13 June 1971.

6. For instance, *New York Times*, 28 March 1971, 31 March 1971, 7 April 1971; *The Guardian*, 31 March 1971, 14 April 1971; *Times* [London], 3 April 1971; *New Statesman* [London], 16 April 1971.

7. *New Nation* [Singapore], 6 April 1971; *Saturday Review* (New York), 22 May 1971.

8. Harun-or Rashid, "British Perspectives, Pressures and Publicity Regarding Bangladesh, 1971," *Contemporary South Asia* 4, no. 2 (1995), 140–41.

9. Mohammed Delwar Hossain, "Framing the Liberation War of Bangladesh in the U.S. and the U.K. Media: A Content Analysis of *The New York Times* and *The Times* (London)" (MA thesis, Southern Illinois University, Carbondale, 2010).

10. Daniel J. Sargent, *A Superpower Adrift: History, Strategy, and American Foreign Policy in the 1970s* (New York: Oxford University Press, forthcoming), 134.

11. The best account of the evolution of humanitarian NGOs is Michael Barnett, *Empire of Humanity: A History of Humanitarianism* (Ithaca, NY: Cornell University Press, 2011), 37–38, 107–31.

12. Michael Cotey Morgan, "The Seventies and the Rebirth of Human Rights," in *The Shock of the Global: The 1970s in Perspective*, ed. Niall Ferguson, Charles S. Maier, Erez Manela, and Daniel J. Sargent (Cambridge, MA: Belknap Press, 2010), 242.

13. Richard Wolin, *The Wind from the East: French Intellectuals, the Cultural Revolution, and the Legacy of the 1960s* (Princeton, NJ: Princeton University Press, 2010). A more idiosyncratic account is Paul Berman, *Power and the Idealists: Or, the Passion of Joschka Fischer and Its Aftermath* (New York: Soft Skull Press, 2005).

14. Benjamin Nathans, "Soviet Rights-Talk in the Post-Stalin Era," in *Human Rights in the Twentieth Century*, ed. Stefan-Ludwig Hoffmann (New York: Cambridge University Press, 2011), 166–90. Also see Lyudmilla Alexeyeva, *Soviet Dissent: Contemporary Movements for National, Religious and Human Rights* (Middletown, CT: Wesleyan University Press, 1985).

15. Andreiĭ D. Sakharov, *Progress, Coexistence, and Intellectual Freedom,* (New York: Norton, [1968]), originally published in the *New York Times,* 22 July 1968.

16. Samuel Moyn, *The Last Utopia: Human Rights in History* (Cambridge, MA: Harvard University Press, 2010), 136–38.

17. Tom Buchanan, "'The Truth Will Set You Free': The Making of Amnesty International," *Journal of Contemporary History* 37, no. 4 (2002): 575–97; Barbara Keys, "Anti-Torture Politics: Amnesty International, the Greek Junta, and the Origins of the Human Rights 'Boom' in the United States," in *The Human Rights Revolution: An International History,* ed. Akira Iriye, Petra Goedde, and William I. Hitchcock (New York: Oxford University Press, 2012), 201–21.

18. Morgan, "Seventies and the Rebirth of Human Rights," 241; Daniel Levy and Natan Sznaider, "The Institutionalization of Cosmopolitan Morality: The Holocaust and Human Rights," *Journal of Human Rights* 3, no. 2 (2004): 143–57.

19. Tony Judt, *Postwar: A History of Europe since 1945* (London: Pimlico, 2007), 803–19; Peter Novick, *The Holocaust in American Life* (New York: Houghton Mifflin, 1999), 127–45.

20. Mark Mazower, *No Enchanted Palace: The End of Empire and the Ideological Origins of the United Nations* (Princeton, NJ: Princeton University Press, 2009), 28–65.

21. The treaty was ratified by President Ronald Reagan to deflect the criticism drawn by his ill-advised visit to a German cemetery where Nazi SS officers were buried. See Aryeh Neier, *The International Human Rights Movement: A History* (Princeton, NJ: Princeton University Press, 2012), 100–101.

22. Cited in Mark Mazower, *Governing the World: The History of an Idea* (London: Allen Lane, 2012), 318.

23. Moyn, *Last Utopia,* 84–119; Geoffrey Robertson, *Crimes against Humanity: The Struggle for Global Justice* (New York: New Press, 2000), 35–56.

24. Roland Burke, "From Individual Rights to National Development: The First UN International Conference on Human Rights, Tehran 1968," *Journal of World History* 19, no. 3 (2008): 283–84. For a more detailed treatment, see Burke's *Decolonization and the Evolution of International Human Rights* (Philadelphia: University of Pennsylvania Press, 2010).

25. Burke, "From Individual Rights," 288–89.

26. On Biafra, see Barnett, *Empire of Humanity,* 133–47; Sargent, *A Superpower Adrift*, chap. 4. For an important recent memoir, see Chinua Achebe, *There Was a Country: A Personal History of Biafra* (London: Allen Lane, 2012).

27. S. N. Prasad, *The India-Pakistan War of 1971* (New Delhi: Ministry of Defence, 1992), 101.

28. A. M. A. Muhith, *American Response to Bangladesh Liberation War* (Dhaka: University Press, 1996).

29. Rashid, "British Perspectives," 144.

30. Cited in Maggie Black, *A Cause for Our Times: Oxfam the First 50 Years* (Oxford: Oxfam Professional, 1992), 150.

31. Ibid., 150–51; Julian Francis, "Remembering the Month of March," *The Daily Star* [Dhaka], 26 March 2011.

32. Black, *Cause for Our Times*, 151–52.

33. Bengal Campaign Bulletin, 26 October 1971, Bengal Campaign File, Oxfam Archives, Oxford.

34. Richard Exley and Helen Exley, eds., *The Testimony of Sixty on the Crisis in Bengal* (Oxford: Oxfam, 1971). Also see Julian Francis, "Remembering 1971—'The Testimony of Sixty,'" *Daily Sun* [Dhaka], 19 October 2011.

35. Non-Governmental World Bodies' Appeal to the UN Sub-Commission, 20 July 1971, in *Bangladesh Documents* (New Delhi: Government of India, 1972), 1:660.

36. Statement on Pakistan by the Commission of Churches on International Affairs, 12 July 1971; text of appeal published in *La Religion,* 14 July 1971, in *Bangladesh Documents,* 1:608–11; Resolution of Latin American Parliament, 27 August 1971; Statement on East Pakistan at Pugwash Conference, 31 August 1971, in *Bangladesh Documents,* 2:179–81.

37. Ravi Shankar, *Raga Mala: An Autobiography* (New York: Welcome Rain, 1999), 217–18; Chris O'Dell, *Miss O'Dell: Hard Days and Long Nights with the Beatles, the Stones, Bob Dylan, and Eric Clapton* (New York: Touchstone, 2009), 195.

38. Interview with George Harrison in Claire Ferguson (director), *The Concert for Bangladesh Revisited* (Hollywood, CA: Apple Films/Rhino, 2005).

39. O'Dell, *Miss O'Dell*, 198.

40. Howard Sounes, *Down the Highway: The Life of Bob Dylan* (London: Blackswan Books, 2002), passim.

41. Cited in Shankar, *Raga Mala*, 220.

42. Clip from Channel 7 Eyewitness News in *Concert for Bangladesh Revisited*.

43. Nayanika Mookherjee, "Mobilising Images: Encounters of 'Forced' Migrants and the Bangladesh War of 1971," *Mobilities* 6, no. 3 (2011): 399–414.

44. George Harrison et al., *The Concert for Bangladesh* (Hollywood, CA: Apple Records, 1971).

45. Interview with Lord Puttnam in *Concert for Bangladesh Revisited*.

46. Pakistan Ministry of Foreign Affairs to All Missions, 30 September 1971, Avtar Singh Bhasin, *India-Pakistan Relations* (New Delhi: Geetika Publishers in cooperation with Public Diplomacy Division, Ministry of External Affairs, 2012), 3:1473.

47. For a fine and candid self-portrait, see Joan Baez, *And a Voice to Sing With: A Memoir* (New York: Simon & Schuster, 1987).

48. Muhith, *American Response*, 19.

49. Deborah Baker, *A Blue Hand: Allen Ginsberg and the Beats in India* (New Delhi: Penguin, 2008), 215, 223.

50. Allen Ginsberg, "On Jessore Road," *New York Times of the Web: Books,* 17 December 1971, www.nytimes.com/books/01/04/08/specials/ginsberg-jessore.html. The full poem is available in Allen Ginsberg, *Collected Poems 1947–1997* (New York: Harper Perennial Reprint edition, 2007).

51. Note from Permanent Representative India, 29 March 1971, S-0863-0001-01, UNSG U Thant Fonds, United Nations Archives, New York (hereafter UNA).

52. U Thant to Samar Sen, 30 March 1971, ibid.

53. Note Verbale from Pakistan, n.d. (ca. 8 April 1971), S-0863-0001-02, UNSG U Thant Fonds, UNA.

54. "The Crisis in East Pakistan March–April 1971," report submitted to Secretary-General by K. Wolff, 19 April 1971, S-0863-0001-03, UNSG U Thant Fonds, UNA.

55. Ibid.

56. C.A. Stavropoulos to U Thant, 21 April 1971, S-0863-0001-02, UNSG U Thant Fonds, UNA (emphasis added).

57. U Thant to Yahya, 22 April 1971; Yahya to U Thant, 29 April 1971, *Pakistan Horizon,* 24, no. 2 (1971): 140–41.

58. Kissinger to Nixon, 14 May 1971, and Consulate General Karachi to State, 22 May 1971, in US Department of State, *Foreign Relations of the United States, 1969–1976,* vol. 11: *South Asia Crisis, 1971* (hereafter *FRUS 1971*) (Washington, DC: United States Government Printing Office, 2005), 122, 138.

59. Aga Shahi (Permanent Representative of Pakistan) to U Thant, 22 May 1971, S-0863-0001-02, UNSG U Thant Fonds, UNA.

60. Two cables from Kittani to U Thant, 4 June 1971, S-0229-0001-15, UN East Pakistan Relief Operations (hereafter UNEPRO) Subject Files, UNA.

61. Mark Malloch-Brown, *The Unfinished Global Revolution: The Limits of Nations and the Pursuit of a New Politics* (London: Allen Lane, 2011), 60.

62. Record of press conference of UNHCR held at UN, 23 June 1971, *Bangladesh Documents*, 1:628–32.

63. J.N. Dixit, *Liberation and Beyond: Indo-Bangladesh Relations* (New Delhi: Konark, 1999), 77.

64. State to Embassy in India (reporting UNHCR's discussion with Rogers and Sisco on 24 June), 26 June 1971, *FRUS 1971*, 199–202.

65. Arnold Smith (Commonwealth Secretary-General) to Canadian High Commissioner in London, 19 July 1971, 20-INDIA-1-3-PAK Vol. 12, Library and Archives Canada (hereafter LAC).

66. U Thant's correspondence with Tunku is available in S-0863-0001-04, UNSG U Thant Fonds, UNA. Two letters are reproduced as appendixes in U Thant, *View from the UN* (New York: Doubleday, 1978), 496–97 (also see 424–25).

67. Brief for Prime Minister's Meeting with Arshad Husain, 26 April 1971, PREM 15/568, TNA.

68. Statements by Samar Sen at ECOSOC, 12 May, 17 May 1971, *Bangladesh Documents*, 1:618–25.

69. A. Dirk Moses, "The United Nations, Humanitarianism, and Human Rights: War Crimes/Genocide Trials for Pakistani Soldiers in Bangladesh, 1971–1974," in *Human Rights in the Twentieth Century*, ed. Stefan-Ludwig Hoffmann (New York: Cambridge University Press, 2011), 269; statement by New Zealand delegate at ECOSOC, 17 May 1971, *Bangladesh Documents*, 1:625.

70. Moses, "United Nations, Humanitarianism, and Human Rights," 269–71.

71. U Thant's Aide-Mémoire to Governments of India and Pakistan, 19 July 1971, *Bangladesh Documents*, 1:657.

72. U Thant's Memorandum to the President of the Security Council, 20 July 1971, ibid., 658–59.

73. India's reply to U Thant's Aide-Mémoire, 2 August 1971, ibid., 660–63.

74. Sadruddin to U Thant, 30 July 1971, S-0228-0002-08, East Pakistan Subject Files, UNA.

7. Power and Principle

1. Record of Foreign Minister's talk with Heads of Missions, London, 20 June 1971, Subject File 19, T.N. Kaul Papers (I, II, and III Installments), Nehru Memorial Museum and Library, New Delhi (hereafter NMML).

2. Ambassador in France to Joint Secretary (United Nations), Ministry of External Affairs (MEA), 6 July 1971, Subject File 171, P. N. Haksar Papers (III Installment), NMML.

3. Arnold Smith to High Commissioner for Canada, 19 July 1971, 20-Ind-1-3-Pak Vol. 12, RG 25, 8914, Library and Archives Canada, Ottawa (hereafter LAC).

4. Note on Indonesian Policy toward East Bengal, n.d. (ca. 25 June 1971); Response of N. P. Firyubin to the statement of Jayaprakash Narayan at their meeting on 25 May 1971, Subject File 36, Jayaprakash Narayan Papers (III Installment), NMML.

5. Response of N. P. Firyubin to the statement of Jayaprakash Narayan at their meeting on 25 May 1971, Subject File 236, Jayaprakash Narayan Papers (III Installment), NMML; personal interview with A. K. Damodaran, New Delhi, 6 April 2006.

6. Report on visit to Japan by S. S. Ray, 26 June 1971, Subject File 168, P. N. Haksar Papers (III Installment), NMML.

7. Report on visits to Malaysia and Thailand by S. S. Ray, 26 June 1971, ibid.

8. Haksar to Natwar Singh (Ambassador of India in Poland), 3 June 1971, ibid.; "Summary of Discussions of Pakistan Ambassadors Conference," 24–25 August 1971, ibid.

9. For a detailed account of West Germany–India relations during this period, see Johannes H. Voigt, *Die Indienpolitik der DDR: von den Anfängen bis zur Anerkennung (1952–1972)* (Cologne: Böhlau, 2008).

10. Report from GDR Consul General Calcutta, 13 April 1971, C 1762/76, Politisches Archiv des Auswärtigen Amtes, Bestand: Ministerium für Auswärtige Angelegenheiten (der ehemaligen DDR) [Political Archive of the Office for Foreign Affairs, Files: Ministry for Foreign Affairs (of the former GDR), Berlin, Germany] (hereafter PAAA-MfAA).

11. Minutes of meeting between Wintzer and Gromyko in East Berlin, 19 January 1972, DY 30/11654, Archives of Parties and Mass Organizations of the Former German Democratic Republic in the Federal Archives (SAPMO), Berlin (hereafter SAPMO).

12. Report from consulate general New Delhi, 28 July 1971, C 1044/77, PAAA-MfAA.

13. Note from Department of International Relations for the Politburo of the Central Committee of Socialist Unity Party, 19 June 1971, C814/75, PAAA-MfAA.

14. The best account is Amit Das Gupta, *Handel, Hilfe, Hallstein-Doktrin: die bundesdeutsche Süd asienpolitik unter Adenauer und Erhard 1949 bis 1966* (Husum, Germany: Matthieson, 2004). Also see Gupta's "Divided Nations: India and Germany" in *India in the World since 1947: National and Transnational*

Perspectives, ed. Andreas Hilger and Corinna R. Unger (Frankfurt: Peter Lang, 2012), 300–25.

15. Cited in Amit Das Gupta, "India and *Ostpolitik*," in *Ostpolitik, 1969–1974: European and Global Responses,* ed. Carole Fink and Bernd Schaeffer (New York: Cambridge University Press, 2009), 172.

16. Memorandum of meeting between Indian ambassador and Secretary of State, 26 May 1971, Band 595, B37, Politisches Archiv des Auswärtigen Amtes [Political Archive of the Office for Foreign Affairs, Berlin, Germany] (hereafter PAAA).

17. "India-Pakistan Relations," 7 June 1971, Band 596, B37, PAAA.

18. "The Indian Foreign Minister's visit to Bonn," 11 June 1971, Band 596, B37, PAAA.

19. Record of Foreign Minister's talk to Heads of Missions, London, 20 June 1971, Subject File 19, T.N. Kaul Papers (I, II, and III Installments), NMML.

20. A German consortium of nine leading NGOs had met with Swaran Singh during his visit and had been active in relief efforts. "Indian Foreign Minister's meeting with representatives of humanitarian organizations," 15 June 1971, Band 596, B37, PAAA.

21. Text of statement in *Pakistan Horizon* 24, no. 2 (1971), 154–55.

22. Statement made by French Foreign Ministry Spokesman, 12 June 1971, *Bangladesh Documents* (New Delhi: Government of India, 1972), 2:505.

23. Record of Foreign Minister's talk to Head of Missions, London, 20 June 1971, Subject File 19, T.N. Kaul Papers (I, II, and III Installments), NMML.

24. Editorial, *Combat* [Paris], 8 October 1971; *Bangladesh Documents,* 2:124.

25. Syed Muazzem Ali, "Remembering Andre Malraux and Peter Shore Who Stood by Us in 1971," *Daily Star* [Dhaka], 26 March 2007; *Le Figaro* [Paris], 8 October 1971, in *Bangladesh Documents,* 2:123–24.

26. Manifesto issued by the French Committee of Solidarity with Bangla Desh, *Bangladesh Documents,* 2:187.

27. Ambassador in France to Joint Secretary (United Nations) MEA, 6 July 1971, Subject File 171, P.N. Haksar Papers (III Installment), NMML

28. Sultan Khan to S.K Dehlavi (Ambassador of Pakistan, Paris), 2 October 1971, Subject File 220, P.N. Haksar Papers (III Installment), NMML. The letter appears to have been passed on to the Indians by a Bengali officer serving in the Pakistani mission in Paris.

29. Reproduced in Paris to FCO, 27 October 1971, FCO 37/909, The National Archives, Kew, London (hereafter TNA).

30. Reproduced in Paris to FCO, 30 October 1971, ibid.

31. Record of conversation with Mujibur Rahman prepared by D.P. Dhar, 29 January 1972, Subject File 233, P.N. Haksar Papers (III Installment), NMML.

32. "Summary of Discussions of Pakistan Ambassadors Conference," 24–25 August 1971, Subject File 168, P.N. Haksar Papers (III Installment), NMML.

33. R.J. Moore, *Escape from Empire: The Attlee Government and the Indian Problem* (Oxford: Clarendon Press, 1983); R.J. Moore, *Making the New Commonwealth* (Oxford: Clarendon Press, 1983); Anita Inder Singh, *The Limits of British Influence: South Asia and the Anglo-American Relationship, 1947–56* (New York: St. Martin's Press, 1993). Also see Robert McMahon, *Cold War on the Periphery: The United States, India, and Pakistan* (New York: Columbia University Press, 1994); Srinath Raghavan, *War and Peace in Modern India: A Strategic History of the Nehru Years* (London: Palgrave Macmillan, 2010).

34. Simon C. Smith, "Coming Down on the Winning Side: Britain and the South Asia Crisis, 1971," *Contemporary British History* 24, no. 4 (2010), 452.

35. Cited in John Darwin, *Britain and Decolonisation: The Retreat from Empire in the Post-War World* (Basingstoke, UK: Palgrave Macmillan, 1988), 324.

36. For an outstanding survey, see John Darwin, *The Empire Project: The Rise and Fall of the British World-System, 1830–1970* (Cambridge: Cambridge University Press, 2009), esp. 610–48. Also see Darwin, *Britain and Decolonisation*; Robert Holland, *The Pursuit of Greatness: Britain and the World Role, 1900–1970* (London: Fontana, 1991); David Reynolds, *Britannia Overruled: British Policy and World Power in the Twentieth Century,* 2nd ed. (London: Longman, 2000); Saki Dockrill, *Britain's Retreat from East of Suez: The Choice between Europe and the World?* (London: Palgrave, 2002); Philip Darby, *British Defence Policy East of Suez, 1947–1968* (Oxford: Oxford University Press, 1973); Matthew Jones, "A Decision Delayed: Britain's Withdrawal from South East Asia Reconsidered, 1961–1968," *English Historical Review* 117, no. 472 (2002), 569–95.

37. Sunanda Datta-Ray, *Looking East to Look West: Lee Kuan Yew's Mission India* (New Delhi: Viking, 2010).

38. UK High Commissioner (hereafter UKHC) Pakistan to Foreign and Commonwealth Office (hereafter FCO), 4 April 1971, FCO 37/881, TNA.

39. Statement reproduced in FCO to Islamabad, 5 April 1971, ibid.

40. J.A.N. Graham to I.J.M. Sutherland, 6 April 1971, ibid.

41. Record of meeting between Douglas-Home and Salman Ali, 6 April 1971, FCO 37/882, TNA.

42. Message from Prime Minister to President of Pakistan, n.d. [ca. 7 April 1971], ibid.

43. UKHC Pakistan to FCO, 9 April 1971, ibid.

44. Deputy High Commissioner Dhaka to I.J.M. Sutherland, 14 April 1971, ibid.

45. Report on call on Prime Minister by Arshad Husain, FCO to Islamabad, 27 April 1971, FCO 37/885, TNA.

46. Record of conversation between Douglas-Home and Arshad Husain, 3 May 1971, PREM 15/568, TNA.

47. Cited in Angela Debnath, "British Perceptions of the East Pakistan Crisis 1971: 'Hideous Atrocities on Both Sides'?" *Journal of Genocide Research* 13, no. 4 (2011), 435.

48. Prime Minister's message to President Yahya Khan, 11 June 1971, FCO 37/887, TNA.

49. Statement by Douglas-Home in House of Commons, 8 June 1971, ibid.

50. Notes for supplementary questions by I. J. M. Sutherland, 5 April 1971, FCO 37/881, TNA.

51. Douglas-Home to UKHC Pakistan, 17 April 1971, PREM 15/568, TNA.

52. "Arms supplies to India and Pakistan in the event of war," n.d. [ca. September 1971], FCO 37/910, TNA.

53. UKHC India to FCO, 28 June 1971, PREM 15/569, TNA.

54. Indira Gandhi to Heath, 13 May 1971; FCO to P. J. S. Moon, 25 May 1971, PREM 15/568, TNA.

55. FCO to New Delhi, enclosing message from Heath to Indira Gandhi, 11 June 1971, FCO 37/887 (emphasis added).

56. Note of the Prime Minister's meeting with Swaran Singh, 21 June 1971, PREM 15/569, TNA.

57. Report of meeting between Heath and Salman Ali, FCO to Islamabad, 23 June, FCO 37/887, TNA.

58. Cited in Debnath, "British Perceptions," 439; Smith, "Coming Down on the Winning Side," 455. Also see Yahya Khan to Heath, 29 June 1971; FCO to Islamabad, enclosing message from Heath to Yahya Khan, 29 June 1971, PREM 15/569, TNA.

59. Washington to FCO, 21 July 1971, PREM 15/445, TNA.

60. Memorandum for Prime Minister (DOP (71) 51), 28 July 1971, PREM 15/569, TNA.

61. Notes for Secretary of State's use in Cabinet by P. F. Walker, 2 August 1971, FCO 37/891, TNA.

62. R. J. A. Martin to P. F. Walker, 11 August 1971, ibid.

63. P. J. E. Male to I. J. M. Sutherland, 23 August 1971, ibid.

64. J. L. Pumphrey to Douglas-Home, 21 September 1971, FCO 37/893, TNA.

65. Record of conversation between Douglas-Home and Swaran Singh, 29 September 1971, FCO 37/909, TNA.

66. FCO to P. J. S. Moon, 4 October 1971, FCO 37/893, TNA.

67. "India/Pakistan: Policy Options for HMG in terms of British Interests," n.d. [ca. early October 1971], FCO 37/912, TNA.

68. "Pakistan: West without East," by I. J. M. Sutherland, 20 October 1971, FCO 37/894, TNA.

69. David Day, *The Great Betrayal: Britain, Australia and the Onset of the Pacific War, 1939–42* (Melbourne: Oxford University Press, 1992); Peter Edwards and Gregory Pemberton, *Crises and Commitments: The Politics and Diplomacy*

of *Australia's Involvement in Southeast Asian Conflicts, 1948–1965* (Sydney: Allen & Unwin, 1992); Karl Hack, *Defence and Decolonisation in Southeast Asia: Britain, Malaya and Singapore, 1941–1968* (London: Curzon, 2001).

70. Andrea Benvenuti, "Australian Reactions to Britain's Declining Presence in Southeast Asia, 1955–63," *Journal of Imperial and Commonwealth History* 34, no. 3 (2006): 407–29. Also see David Goldsworthy, *Losing the Blanket: Australia and the End of Britain's Empire* (Melbourne: Melbourne University Press, 2002).

71. Derek McDougall, "Australia and the British Military Withdrawal from East of Suez," *Australian Journal of International Affairs* 51, no. 2 (1997): 183–94; Gregory Pemberton, *All the Way: Australia's Road to Vietnam* (Sydney: Allen & Unwin, 1987).

72. Policy Planning Paper QP7, 9 March 1971; minutes on the paper by R.H. Robertson, 31 March 1971, A1838 625/14/19, National Archives of Australia (hereafter NAA).

73. Australian High Commissioner in Islamabad to Canberra, 8 April 1971, A1838 625/14/19 Part 1, NAA.

74. Australian High Commissioner in New Delhi to Canberra, 8 April 1971, 20-India-1-3-Pak Vol. 9, RG 25, 8914, LAC.

75. William McMahon to Indira Gandhi, 3 June 1971, Subject File 168, P.N. Haksar Papers (III Installment), NMML.

76. Minutes by K.M. Wilford, 9 June 1971, PREM 15/569, TNA.

77. Note on visit to Australia by Ray, 25 June 1971, Subject File 168, P.N. Haksar Papers (III Installment), NMML; record of conversation between S.S. Ray and L.H.E. Bury, 11 June 1971, 20-India-1-3-Pak Vol. 11, RG 25, 8914, LAC.

78. Australian High Commissioner in New Delhi to Canberra, 8 April 1971, A1209 1971/9230 Part 1, NAA.

79. "Agreed assessment between Australian High Commissioners in Pakistan and India," 22 July 1971, 20-India-1-3-Pak Vol. 14, RG 25, 8914, LAC.

80. Australian High Commissioner in London to Canberra, 24 November 1971, A1838 899/10/1 Part 2; Australian High Commissioner in London to Canberra, 30 November 1971, A1838 169/11/148 Part 48, NAA.

81. Omar Hayyat Khan, "Instruments of Influence: Canada and Arms Exports to South Asia, 1947–1971" (MA thesis, Carleton University, Ottawa), 2005.

82. Richard Pilkington, "In the National Interest? Canada and the East Pakistan Crisis of 1971," *Journal of Genocide Research* 13, no. 4 (2011), 458–59. Also see John Small, "From Pakistan to Bangladesh, 1969–1972: Perspective of a Canadian Envoy," in *"Special Trust and Confidence": Envoy Essays in Canadian Diplomacy,* ed. David Reece (Ottawa: Carlton University Press, 1996), 209–38.

83. Pilkington, "In the National Interest?," 454–55.

84. Memorandum for the Minister on Visit of Sardar Swaran Singh, 12 June 1971, 20-Ind-1-3-Pak Vol. 11, RG 25, 8914, LAC.

85. Record of Foreign Minister's talk to Head of Missions, London, 20 June 1971, Subject File 19, T. N. Kaul Papers (I, II, and III Installments), NMML.

86. High Commissioner in New Delhi to Ottawa, 14 June 1971, 20-Ind-1-3-Pak Vol. 11, RG 25, 8914, LAC.

87. India-Pakistan Task Force First Meeting, 30 June 1971, ibid. (emphasis added).

88. Trudeau to Indira Gandhi, 29 July 1971, 20-Ind-1-3-Pak Vol. 13, RG 25, 8914, LAC.

89. Trudeau to Yahya Khan, 5 August 1971, ibid.

90. Pilkington "In the National Interest?," 461.

91. "Summary of Recommendation of Parliamentarians," n.d., 20-Ind-1-3-Pak Vol. 13, RG 25, 8914, LAC.

92. Pilkington, "In the National Interest?," 462–63.

93. High Commissioner in Islamabad to Ottawa, 6 August 1971, 20-Ind-1-3-Pak Vol. 13, RG 25, 8914, LAC.

94. High Commissioner in Islamabad to Ottawa, 7 September 1971, ibid.

95. High Commissioner in New Delhi to Ottawa, 19 August 1971, ibid.

96. Proposed Canadian Position, October 1971, 20-1-2-Pak, RG 25, 10836, LAC.

97. Arnold Smith to High Commissioner for Canada, 19 July 1971, 20-Ind-1-3-Pak Vol. 12, RG 25, 8914, LAC.

98. Arnold Smith to High Commissioner for Canada, 19 July 1971; High Commissioner of Ceylon to Arnold Smith, 29 June 1971, ibid.

99. Heath to Russell Johnston, n.d. [ca. 7 April 1971], FCO 37/882, TNA.

100. Foreign Affairs Brief for Minister, 2 July 1971, A1838 899/10/1 Pt. 1, NAA.

101. Report of conversation between Canadian High Commissioner and Ceylon High Commissioner, Islamabad to Ottawa, 22 July 1971, 20-Ind-1-3-Pak Vol. 13, RG 25, 8914, LAC.

102. High Commissioner in New Delhi to Ottawa, 9 July 1971, 20-Ind-1-3-Pak Vol. 12, RG 25, 8914, LAC.

103. High Commissioner in New Delhi to Canberra, 5 July 1971, A1838 899/10/1 Pt. 1, NAA; Arnold Smith to High Commissioner for Canada, 19 July 1971, 20-Ind-1-3-Pak Vol. 12, RG 25, 8914, LAC.

104. Sirima Bandaranaike to Indira Gandhi, 25 May 1971, Subject File 168, P.N. Haksar Papers (III Installment), NMML; Dixit, *Liberation and Beyond*, 54–55.

105. Report on conversation with T.N. Kaul, High Commissioner in India to Ottawa, 21 May 1971, 20-Ind-1-3-Pak Vol. 10, RG 25, 8914, LAC.

106. Record of conversation between Shah and Bhutto, n.d. (ca. end December 1971), reproduced in Mohammed Yunus, *Bhutto and the Breakup of Pakistan* (Karachi: Oxford University Press, 2011), 46.

107. Haksar to Kaul, 25 June 1971, Subject File 168, P.N. Haksar Papers (III Installment), NMML.

108. Indira Gandhi to Mohammad Reza Shah Pahlavi, 25 June 1971, Subject File 168, P.N. Haksar Papers (III Installment), NMML.

109. Iqbal Akhund, *Memoirs of a Bystander: A Life in Diplomacy* (Karachi: Oxford University Press, 1998), 192.

110. Indira Gandhi to Tito, n.d. (ca. 4 September 1971), Subject File 172, P.N. Haksar Papers (III Installment), NMML.

111. Akhund, *Memoirs of a Bystander,* 192–93.

112. Indo-Yugoslav Joint Communiqué, 20 October 1971, in *Bangladesh Documents* 2:165.

113. President Tito's interview with CBS Television Network, 26 October 1971, in *Bangladesh Documents,* 2:169.

114. "Review of Indo-Egyptian relations in the context of the attitude adopted by Egypt during the Indo-Pakistan conflict in December 1971 and on Bangladesh," Embassy in Cairo to New Delhi, [?] February 1972, Subject File 220, P.N. Haksar Papers (III Installment), NMML.

115. Text in *Pakistan Horizon* 24, no. 2 (1971), 154–55.

116. "Review of Indo-Egyptian relations," Embassy in Cairo to New Delhi, [?] February 1972, Subject File 220, P.N. Haksar Papers (III Installment), NMML.

117. Entry of 2 July 1973, Israel Diary, in Sarvepalli Gopal, *Imperialists, Nationalist, Democrats: Collected Essays* (Ranikhet, India: Permanent Black, 2013), 415.

118. P.R. Kumaraswamy, *India's Israel Policy* (New York: Columbia University Press, 2010), 85–210.

119. Ambassador in Paris to Joint Secretary (UN) MEA, 6 July 1971, Subject File 171, P.N. Haksar Papers (III Installment), NMML.

120. R.N. Kao to Haksar, 4 August 1971, conveying message from Kaul to Haksar sent over R&AW channels on 3 August 1971, Subject File 220, P.N. Haksar Papers (III Installment), NMML (emphasis in original).

121. S.P. Chibber (Special Representative, Establissements Salgad) to G.L Sheth (Secretary Production, Ministry of Defence), 14 January 1973, ibid.

122. Golda Meir to Shlomo Zabludowicz [in Hebrew], 23 August 1971, ibid.

123. Handwritten note from D.N. Chatterjee to Haksar, 6 July 1971, Subject File 171, P.N. Haksar Papers (III Installment), NMML, cited in Ramachandra Guha, *India after Gandhi: The History of the World's Largest Democracy* (London: Macmillan, 2007), 771.

8. The Chinese Puzzle

1. Sultan M. Khan, *Memories and Reflections of a Pakistani Diplomat* (London: Centre for Pakistan Studies, 1997), 344.

2. Ibid., 344–45.

3. Ibid., 345; Gul Hassan Khan, *Memoirs of Lt. Gen. Gul Hassan Khan* (Karachi: Oxford University Press, 1993), 282; Shuja Nawaz, *Crossed Swords: Pakistan, Its Army, and the Wars Within* (Karachi: Oxford University Press, 2008), 294–95. Sisson and Rose claim that Zhou explicitly ruled out the possibility of a Chinese intervention in the event of war. See Richard Sisson and Leo Rose, *War and Secession: Pakistan, India, and the Creation of Bangladesh* (Berkeley: University of California Press, 1990), 251.

4. The full text of the speech was published in *Peking Review* 14, no. 49 (3 December 1971), 5.

5. Kalim Siddiqui, *Conflict, Crisis and War in Pakistan* (London: Macmillan, 1972), 14, cited in Iftekhar Ahmed Chowdhury, "Bangladesh: Opportunities and Challenges," in *A Resurgent China: South Asian Perspectives,* ed. S.D. Muni and Tan Tai Yong (New Delhi: Routledge, 2012), 55.

6. Record of conversation between Bhutto and Reza Pahlavi, cited in Mohammed Yunus, *Bhutto and the Breakup of Pakistan* (Karachi: Oxford University Press, 2011), 40.

7. G.W. Choudhury, *India, Pakistan, Bangladesh and the Major Powers* (New York: Free Press, 1975), 211.

8. Khan, *Memories and Reflections,* 243.

9. G. W. Choudhury, *Last Days of United Pakistan* (London: Hurst, 1974), 217.

10. Sisson and Rose, *War and Secession,* 250; Mizanur Rahman, *Emergence of a New Nation in a Multi-Polar World* (Seattle: University of Washington Press, 1978), 97–102; Chowdhury, "Bangladesh," 51–52.

11. Khan, *Memories and Reflections,* 303–5.

12. Zhou to Yahya, 11 April 1971, in J.A. Naik, *India, Russia, China, and Bangladesh* (New Delhi: S. Chand, 1972), 138 (emphasis added).

13. For a firsthand account of Pakistani creativity with the original letter, see "A Bengali's Grandstand View," *Far Eastern Economic Review* [Hong Kong], 11 October 1974.

14. Zhou to Yahya, 11 April 1971; Naik, *India, Russia, China, and Bangladesh,* 138.

15. Khan, *Memories and Reflections,* 305–8.

16. On China's attitudes to the world during the Cultural Revolution, see Ma Jisen, *The Cultural Revolution in the Foreign Ministry of China* (Hong Kong: Chinese University Press, 2004). For an excellent, synoptic account, see Odd

Arne Westad, *Restless Empire: China and the World Since 1750* (London: Bodley Head, 2012), 333–59.

17. John Garver, *Protracted Contest: Sino-Indian Rivalry in the Twentieth Century* (Seattle: University of Washington Press, 2001), 205.

18. Lorne Kavic, *India's Quest for Security: Defence Policies 1947–1965* (Berkeley: University of California Press, 1967); Raju G. C. Thomas, *Indian Security Policy* (Princeton, NJ: Princeton University Press, 1986).

19. Haksar to Indira Gandhi, 6 May 1969, cited in Tanvi Madan, "With an Eye to the East: The China Factor and the US-India Relationship, 1949–1979" (PhD diss., University of Texas at Austin, 2012), 425.

20. "Our China Policy: A Personal Assessment," 30 July 1968, R. K. Nehru Papers, Nehru Memorial Museum and Library, New Delhi (hereafter NMML).

21. "India and China: Policy Alternatives," n.d. [ca. late 1968], R. K. Nehru Papers, NMML.

22. Madan, "With an Eye to the East," 425–26.

23. On the Sino-Soviet split and its consequences, see the excellent books by Lorenz Luthi, *The Sino-Soviet Split: Cold War in the Communist World* (Princeton, NJ: Princeton University Press, 2008) and Sergey Radchenko, *Two Suns in the Heavens: The Sino-Soviet Struggle for Supremacy, 1962–1967* (Stanford, CA: Stanford University Press, 2009).

24. Roderick MacFarquhar and Michael Schoenhals, *Mao's Last Revolution* (Cambridge, MA: Harvard University Press, 2006), 308–10. Also see Lyle J. Goldstein, "Return to Zhenbao Island: Who Started Shooting and Why It Matters," *China Quarterly,* no. 168 (December 2001), 985–97.

25. "Soviet Report to GDR Leadership on 2 March 1969," *Cold War International History Project Bulletin* 6–7 (Winter 1995–96), 189–90.

26. MacFarquhar and Schoenhals, *Mao's Last Revolution*, 310–11.

27. Robert M. Gates, *From the Shadows: The Ultimate Insider's Story of Five Presidents and How They Won the Cold War* (New York: Simon & Schuster, 1996), 33–34.

28. Zhou Enlai's report to Mao Zedong, 22 March 1969, *Cold War International History Project Bulletin,* no. 11 (Winter 1998), 162.

29. Jian Chen, *Mao's China and the Cold War* (Chapel Hill: University of North Carolina Press, 2001), 239–40.

30. Chen, *Mao's China,* 248.

31. The Chinese Communist Party Central Committee's Order for General Mobilization in Border Provinces and Regions, 28 August 1969, *Cold War International History Project Bulletin,* no. 11 (Winter 1998), 168–69.

32. Cited in MacFarquhar and Schoenhals, *Mao's Last Revolution,* 314.

33. Ibid., 317; Westad, *Restless Empire,* 361.

34. Record of discussions between D. P. Dhar and Marshal Grechko, 5 June 1971, Subject File 229, P. N. Haksar Papers (III Installment), NMML.

35. Chen, *Mao's China*, 245–49; MacFarquhar and Schoenhals, *Mao's Last Revolution*, 315–16; Westad, *Restless Empire*, 362.

36. Chen, *Mao's China*, 240.

37. A. G. Noorani, *Brezhnev Plan for Asian Security: Russia in Asia* (Bombay: Jaico, 1975).

38. "China Offered a Place in Brezhnev's Asian Security System," report prepared for editors of Radio Free Europe, 24 September 1970, Open Society Archives, www.osaarchivum.org/files/holdings/300/8/3/text/98-3-224.shtml.

39. Chen Jian rightly underlines the importance of the waning of the Cultural Revolution for the opening to the United States (*Mao's China*, 242–45). It was important for the moves vis-à-vis India as well.

40. Li Danhui, "Mao Zedong's World Revolution Ideals and Sino-Indian Relations: Decoding Mao's Talk with the Delegation of the Communist Party of India (Leftists) on 13 December 1967," paper presented at the panel "The Sino-Indian Border Clashes and the Sino-Soviet Split: New Evidence from Chinese Archives," Cold War International History Project, Woodrow Wilson International Center for Scholars, Washington, DC, May 18, 2009.

41. Record of conversation between Indira Gandhi and Kosygin, 6 May 1969, Subject File 140, P. N. Haksar Papers (III Installment), NMML.

42. Draft for Prime Minister prepared by Haksar, 17 September 1969, Subject File 43, P. N. Haksar Papers (I and II Installments), NMML.

43. Draft of letter from Indira Gandhi to Tito, 8 September 1969, Subject File 43, P. N. Haksar Papers (I and II Installments), NMML. See also Indira Gandhi to Kosygin, 30 August 1969, ibid.

44. G. S. Iyer, "'Mao's Smile' Revisited," paper no. 413 (December 2009), Chennai Centre for China Studies, www.c3sindia.org/india/1068. The author was a junior official in the Indian embassy in Beijing at the time.

45. Embassy in Peking to Foreign New Delhi, 27 April 1970, Subject File 29, P. N. Haksar Papers (I Installment), NMML.

46. Iyer, "'Mao's Smile' Revisited."

47. Embassy in Peking to Foreign New Delhi, 1 May 1970, Subject File 29, P. N. Haksar Papers (I Installment), NMML.

48. Iyer, "'Mao's Smile' Revisited."

49. Haksar to Indira Gandhi enclosing draft telegram to Mishra, 6 May 1971, Subject File 153, P. N. Haksar Papers (III Installment), NMML.

50. For background, see Srinath Raghavan, *War and Peace in Modern India: A Strategic History of the Nehru Years* (London: Palgrave Macmillan, 2010), 264–66.

51. Mishra to Foreign Minister, 6 May 1971, Subject File 29, P. N. Haksar Papers (I Installment), NMML.

52. Haksar to Indira Gandhi enclosing draft telegram to Mishra, 25 May 1971, Subject File 153, P. N. Haksar Papers (III Installment), NMML.

53. Record of conversation between D. P. Dhar and Kosygin, 22 May 1970, Subject File 197, P. N. Haksar Papers (III Installment), NMML.

54. Mishra to Foreign Secretary, 13 August 1970, Subject File 29, P. N. Haksar Papers (I Installment), NMML.

55. Mishra to Prime Minister and Foreign Minister, 1 June 1971, ibid.

56. Mishra to Foreign Secretary, 5 June 1970, ibid.

57. Mishra to Foreign Secretary, 14 July 1970, ibid.

58. Two telegrams from Mishra to Foreign Secretary, 11 July 1970, ibid.

59. Mishra to Foreign Secretary, 13 August 1970, ibid.

60. Embassy in Belgrade to Foreign New Delhi, ibid.

61. Mishra to Paranjpe, 24 August 1970, ibid.

62. Memorandum of conversation, 10 July 1971, in US Department of State, *Foreign Relations of the United States, 1969–1976*, vol. 17: *China, 1969–1972* (hereafter *FRUS China*) (Washington, DC: United States Government Printing Office), doc. 140.

63. Ibid.

64. Memorandum of conversation, 11 July 1971, *FRUS China*, doc. 143.

65. Henry Kissinger, *White House Years* (London: George Weidenfeld & Nicolson, 1979), 862, 876, 886.

66. Personal interview with Brajesh Mishra, New Delhi, 8 January 2010.

67. Haksar to Indira Gandhi, 16 July 1971, enclosing draft letter to Zhou Enlai (sent on 18 July 1971), Subject File 169, P. N. Haksar Papers (III Installment), NMML.

68. Record of conversation between Indira Gandhi and Gromyko, 10 August 1971, Subject File 19, T. N. Kaul Papers (I, II, and III Installments), NMML.

69. Memorandum of conversation, 21 October 1971, in US Department of State, *Foreign Relations of the United States, 1969–1976*, vol. E-13: *Documents on China, 1969–1972* (hereafter *FRUS* E-13) (Washington, DC: United States Government Printing Office, 2005), doc. 41.

70. Memorandum of conversation, 22 October 1971, *FRUS* E-13, doc. 44.

71. Kissinger to Haig, 24 October 1971, *FRUS* E-13, doc. 50.

72. Mishra to Secretary (East) and Foreign Secretary, 29 October 1971, Subject File 220, P. N. Haksar Papers (III Installment), NMML.

73. Indira Gandhi to Haksar, 12 August 1971; Haksar to Indira Gandhi, 19 August 1971, Subject File 170, P. N. Haksar Papers (III Installment), NMML.

74. "Summary of Discussions of Pakistan's Ambassadors Conference," 24–25 August 1971, Geneva, ibid.

75. MacFarquhar and Schoenhals, *Mao's Last Revolution*, 292–300, 317–20. Also see Frederick C. Teiwes and Warren Sun, *The Tragedy of Lin Biao: Riding the Tiger during the Cultural Revolution 1966–1971* (London: Hurst, 1996), 111–15.

76. Jung Chang and Jon Halliday, *Mao: The Unknown Story* (London: Vintage, 2006), 671–77; Jin Qiu, *The Culture of Power: The Lin Biao Incident in*

the Cultural Revolution (Stanford, CA: Stanford University Press, 1999), 120–31; MacFarquhar and Schoenhals, *Mao's Last Revolution*, 324–28.

77. Cited in Qiu, *The Culture of Power*, 135.

78. Alexander V. Pantsov and Steven I. Levine, *Mao: The Real Story* (New York: Simon & Schuster, 2012), 550–51.

79. Cited in MacFarquhar and Schoenhals, *Mao's Last Revolution*, 335. On Zhou's role in this entire episode, see Gao Wenqian, *Zhou Enlai: The Last Perfect Revolutionary* (New York: Public Affairs, 2007), 201–26.

80. Chen, *Mao's China*, 269–71; MacFarquhar and Schoenhals, *Mao's Last Revolution*, 336–37.

81. Mishra to Secretary (East) and Foreign Secretary, 29 October 1971, Subject File 220, P.N. Haksar Papers (III Installment), NMML.

82. Mehta to Foreign Secretary, 6 November 1971, in Foreign New Delhi to Embassy in Paris, 8 November 1971, ibid.

83. High Commission in London to Foreign New Delhi, 12 November 1971, ibid.

84. Sisson and Rose, *War and Secession*, 252.

85. Mishra to Secretary (East), 8 November 1971, in Foreign New Delhi to Embassy in Bonn, 8 November 1971, Subject File 220, P.N. Haksar Papers (III Installment), NMML.

86. Mishra to Secretary (East), 8 November 1971, in Foreign New Delhi to Embassy in Bonn, 9 November 1971, ibid.

87. Memorandum on meeting between Indira Gandhi and the Federal Minister, 11 November 1971, Band 595, B37, Politisches Archiv des Auswärtigen Amtes [Political Archive of the Office for Foreign Affairs, Berlin, Germany] (hereafter PAAA).

9. Escalation

1. Depinder Singh, *Field Marshal Sam Manekshaw: Soldiering with Dignity* (Dehradun, India: Natraj, 2002), 158–59.

2. Henry Kissinger, *The White House Years* (London: George Weidenfeld & Nicolson, 1979), 880 (emphasis added).

3. The figures are from S.N. Prasad, *The India-Pakistan War of 1971* (New Delhi: Ministry of Defence, 1992), 194.

4. Ministry of Finance, *Economic Survey, 1971–72* (New Delhi: Government of India, 1972), 9–16; Prasad, *India-Pakistan War*, 195.

5. "Economy under Conditions of a Crisis" by P.N. Dhar, 21 July 1971, Subject File 260, P.N. Haksar Papers (III Installment), Nehru Memorial Museum and Library, New Delhi (hereafter NMML). Also see I.G. Patel, *Glimpses of Indian Economic Policy: An Insider's View* (New Delhi: Oxford University Press, 2002), 144–45.

6. *White Paper on the Crisis in East Pakistan* (Islamabad: Government of Pakistan, August 1971). On the drafting of the document, see Brigadier A.R. Siddiqi, *East Pakistan the Endgame: An Onlooker's Journal, 1969–1971* (Karachi: Oxford University Press, 2004), 159–61.

7. Richard Sisson and Leo Rose, *War and Secession: Pakistan, India, and the Creation of Bangladesh* (Berkeley: University of California Press, 1990), 172–73.

8. Rafi Reza, *Zulfikar Ali Bhutto and Pakistan, 1967–1977* (Dhaka: University Press, 1997), 99–112.

9. Hamoodur Rehman Commission, *Report of the Hamoodur Rehman Commission of Inquiry into the 1971 War, as Declassified by the Government of Pakistan* (Lahore: Vanguard, [2000?]), 385–87. Compare with Rao Farman Ali Khan, *How Pakistan Got Divided* (Lahore: Jang, 1992), 99–101.

10. Hasan Zaheer, *The Separation of East Pakistan: The Rise and Realization of Bengali Muslim Nationalism* (Dhaka: University Press, 2001), 334–42.

11. See Agha Shahi to U Thant, 2 September 1971, S-0863-0001-02, UNSG U Thant Fonds, United Nations Archives, New York City (hereafter UNA).

12. "Bangla Desh and India's National Security: The Options of India," n.d. [ca. first week of August 1971], in the author's possession. I am grateful to the late K. Subrahmanyam for a copy of this paper.

13. Personal interview with P.N. Dhar, Delhi, 24 November 2009; P.N. Dhar, *Indira Gandhi, the "Emergency" and Indian Democracy* (New Delhi: Oxford University Press, 2000), 175; J.N. Dixit, *Liberation and Beyond: Indo-Bangladesh Relations* (New Delhi: Konark, 1999), 64–65.

14. Note on Jayaprakash Narayan's meeting with Bangladesh Cabinet, 8–9 July 1971, Subject File 233, Jayaprakash Narayan Papers (III Installment), NMML.

15. Jayaprakash Narayan to Indira Gandhi, 15 September 1971, ibid.

16. Note on discussions held by Jayaprakash Narayan with Sector Commanders of Mukti Fauj (Major Ziaur Rahman and Major Khaled Mosharraf), 9 July 1971, ibid. Also see J.F.R. Jacob, *Surrender at Dacca: Birth of a Nation* (Dhaka: University Press, 1991), 90–91, 93.

17. Report of meeting between Joint Director (R&AW) and Prime Minister Tajuddin Ahmad and Colonel Osmany in Calcutta, 3 July 1971, Subject File 227, P.N. Haksar Papers (III Installment), NMML.

18. Note on discussions held by Jayaprakash Narayan with Sector Commanders of Mukti Fauj, 9 July 1971, Subject File 233, Jayaprakash Narayan Papers (III Installment), NMML.

19. Report by Secretary-General Awami League, 3 July 1971, Subject File 169, P.N. Haksar Papers (III Installment), NMML.

20. Note by Jayaprakash Narayan on meetings with Colonel Osmany and General Aurora, n.d. [ca. 9 July 1971], Subject File 233, Jayaprakash Narayan Papers (III Installment), NMML.

21. Note on discussions held by Jayaprakash Narayan with Sector Commanders of Mukti Fauj, 9 July 1971, ibid.

22. Report of meeting between Joint Director (R&AW) and Prime Minister Tajuddin Ahmad and Colonel Osmany in Calcutta, 3 July 1971, Subject File 227, P.N. Haksar Papers (III Installment), NMML.

23. Situational Report of Bangladesh Army, 5 July 1971, ibid.

24. Report of meeting between Joint Director (R&AW) and Prime Minister Tajuddin Ahmad and Colonel Osmany in Calcutta, 3 July 1971, ibid.

25. Report by Secretary-General Awami League, 3 July 1971, Subject File 169, P.N. Haksar Papers (III Installment), NMML.

26. Report on the visit of Border Areas of Assam, Meghalaya and Tripura (including a few pockets inside Bangla Desh) from 6–16 June 1971, ibid.

27. Note by Govind Narain, 13 July 1971, ibid.

28. Jayaprakash Narayan to Indira Gandhi, 20 July 1971, Subject File 233, Jayaprakash Narayan Papers, NMML.

29. The figures are from Prasad, *India-Pakistan War,* 203–4.

30. Report on discussions held with Bangla Desh leaders on 26 October 1971, n.d. [ca. 26 October 1971], Subject File 233, Jayaprakash Narayan Papers, NMML.

31. Prasad, *India-Pakistan War,* 203–14; Dixit, *Liberation and Beyond,* 88; Sisson and Rose, *War and Secession,* 210–11.

32. Faruq Aziz Khan, *Spring 1971: A Centre Stage Account of Bangladesh Liberation War,* 2nd ed. (Dhaka: University Press Ltd., 1998), 176.

33. Situational Report of Bangladesh Army, 5 July 1971, Subject File 227, P.N. Haksar Papers (III Installment), NMML.

34. Ibid.

35. "A note on How to Help the Mukti Fouj Win the Bangla Desh Liberation War," n.d. [ca. early September 1971], Subject File 227, P.N. Haksar Papers (III Installment), NMML.

36. Note on Jayaprakash Narayan's meeting with Bangla Desh Cabinet, 8–9 July 1971, Subject File 233, Jayaprakash Narayan Papers (III Installment), NMML.

37. Khan, *Spring 1971,* 183, 188–89.

38. Dhar, *Indira Gandhi,* 167–68; Prasad, *India-Pakistan War,* 214–15.

39. Muyeedul Hasan, *Muldhara '71* (Dhaka: University Press, 2008), 64–66; Khan, *Spring 1971,* 184–85.

40. *The Statesman* [Calcutta], 31 August 1971.

41. Note on discussion with D.P. Dhar, 31 August 1971, cited in Hasan, *Muldhara '71,* 72. Also see Arun Bhattacharjee, *Dateline Mujibnagar* (Delhi: Vikas, 1973), 43–44.

42. Robert Jackson, *South Asian Crisis: India-Pakistan-Bangladesh* (London: Chatto & Windus, 1975), 78–79; Khan, *Spring 1971,* 201; Embassy in New Delhi

to SS, 31 August 1971, POL 23-9 PAK, Central Files 1970–73, RG 59, US National Archives and Records Administration, College Park, MD (hereafter USNA).

43. Hasan, *Muldhara '71,* 87–88.

44. Note on conversation with Khandaker Moshtaq Ahmad and Tajuddin Ahmad, 26 October 1971, Subject File 233, Jayaprakash Narayan Papers (III Installment), NMML. Also see Hasan, *Muldhara '71,* 126.

45. Note on Jayaprakash Narayan's meeting with Bangla Desh Cabinet, 8–9 July 1971, Subject File 233, Jayaprakash Narayan Papers (III Installment), NMML; Hasan, *Muldhara '71,* 122–23.

46. Consulate General Calcutta to State, 1 July 1971, POL 23-9 PAK, Central Files 1970–73, RG 59, USNA.

47. Consulate General Calcutta to State, 7 August 1971, in US Department of State, *Foreign Relations of the United States, 1969–1976,* vol. 11: *South Asia Crisis, 1971* (hereafter *FRUS 1971*) (Washington, DC: United States Government Printing Office, 2005), 311–12.

48. Embassy in Islamabad to State, 9 August 1971, POL 23-9 PAK, Central Files 1970–73, RG 59, USNA.

49. Memorandum for the Record, Senior Review Group Meeting with President, 11 August 1971, *FRUS 1971,* 327.

50. State to Consulate General Calcutta, 14 August 1971; Consulate General Calcutta to State, 14 August 1971, POL 23-9 PAK, Central Files 1970–73, RG 59, USNA.

51. Consulate General Calcutta to State, 19 August 1971, ibid.

52. State to Embassy in Islamabad, 22 August 1971, ibid.

53. Embassy in Islamabad to State, 24 August 1971, *FRUS 1971,* 365–66.

54. State to Embassy in Islamabad, 31 August 1971, ibid., 371–72.

55. Embassy in Islamabad to State, 4 September 1971, POL 23-9 PAK, Central Files 1970–73, RG 59; State to Consulate General Calcutta, 4 September 1971, POL 17 INDIA-PAK, Central Files 1970–73, RG 59, USNA.

56. Minutes of WSAG, 8 September 1971, *FRUS 1971,* 399.

57. Dixit, *Liberation and Beyond,* 69; personal interview with P.N. Dhar, Delhi, 24 November 2009.

58. Consulate in Calcutta to State, 10 September 1971, POL 27 INDIA-PAK, Central Files 1970–73, RG 59, USNA.

59. Consulate in Calcutta to State, 29 September 1971, ibid.

60. Dixit, *Liberation War and Beyond,* 69–70; Hasan, *Muldhara '71,* 144.

61. Dhar, *Indira Gandhi,* 171–72; report of conversation with Jha in State to Embassy in New Delhi, 15 September 1971, *FRUS 1971,* 410.

62. State to Embassy in New Delhi, POL 27 INDIA-PAK, Central Files 1970–73, RG 59, USNA.

63. UN Mission to State, 2 October 1971, *FRUS 1971,* 429–30.

64. Hasan, *Muldhara '71,* 123–24.

65. Sisson and Rose, *War and Secession*, 211; Gul Hassan Khan, *Memoirs of Lt. Gen. Gul Hassan Khan* (Karachi: Oxford University Press, 1993), 306.

66. Yahya Khan's interview with *Le Figaro* [Paris], in *Bangladesh Documents* (New Delhi: Government of India, 1972), 2:136–37.

67. Sukhwant Singh, *India's Wars since Independence: The Liberation of Bangladesh* (New Delhi: Lancer, 1980), 49, 110.

68. Dixit, *Liberation and Beyond*, 78–81.

69. Memorandum of conversation between Dobrynin and Kissinger, 17 August 1971, *FRUS 1971*, 333.

70. Jamsheed Marker, *Quiet Diplomacy: Memoirs of an Ambassador of Pakistan* (Karachi: Oxford University Press, 2010), 132.

71. Cited in Sultan M. Khan, *Memories and Reflections of a Pakistani Diplomat* (London: Centre for Pakistan Studies, 1997), 319–21.

72. Cited in Marker, *Quiet Diplomacy*, 133.

73. Cited in Khan, *Memories and Reflections*, 322–32.

74. Sisson and Rose, *War and Secession*, 202; excerpts from Podgorny's speech on 14 September 1971 are found in *Bangladesh Documents*, 2:160–61.

75. Personal interview with A.K. Damodaran, New Delhi, 6 April 2006.

76. Record of conversation with Mujibur Rahman prepared by D.P. Dhar, 29 January 1972, Subject File 233, P.N. Haksar Papers (III Installment), NMML; personal interview with P.N. Dhar, Delhi, 24 November 2009; personal interview with A.K. Damodaran, New Delhi, 6 April 2006. D.P. Dhar's account is cited in Hasan, *Muldhara '71*, 90–91.

77. Personal interview with Subas Chakravarty (diplomatic correspondent, *Times of India*), New Delhi, 30 March 2010.

78. Indo-Soviet Joint Statement, 29 September 1971, *Bangladesh Documents*, 2:163.

79. Memorandum of Nixon's meeting with Gromyko, 29 September 1971, *FRUS 1971*, 425.

80. Embassy in Tehran to State, 6 October 1971, POL 27 INDIA-PAK, Central Files 1970–73, RG 59, USNA.

81. Cited in Khan, *Memories and Reflections*, 339–40.

82. Embassy in Moscow to State, 18 October 1971, POL 27 INDIA-PAK, Central Files 1970–73, RG 59, USNA.

83. Sisson and Rose, *War and Secession*, 202; A.G. Noorani, *Brezhnev Plan for Asian Security: Russia in Asia* (Bombay: Jaico, 1975), 145.

84. Personal interview with P.N. Dhar, Delhi, 24 November 2009; H.Y. Sharada Prasad, *The Book I Won't Be Writing and Other Essays* (New Delhi: Chronicle Books, 2003), 108–9.

85. Hasan, *Muldhara '71*, 126.

86. Transcript of interview with BBC, 1 November 1971 (from original video available on http://www.youtube.com/watch?v=fKiQboyDMUo). A slightly

different version is available in Government of India, *The Years of Endeavour: Selected Speeches of Indira Gandhi, August 1969–August 1972* (New Delhi: Publications Division, 1975), 541.

87. Memorandum on meeting between President Nixon and Prime Minister Indira Gandhi, *FRUS 1971*, 493–99.

88. Conversation among Nixon, Kissinger and Haldeman, 5 November 1971, in US Department of State, *Foreign Relations of the United States, 1969–1976*, vol. E-7: *Documents on South Asia, 1969–1972* (hereafter *FRUS* E-7) (Washington, DC: United States Government Printing Office, 2005), doc. 150.

89. Memorandum on meeting between Nixon and Indira Gandhi, 5 November 1971, *FRUS* E-7, doc. 151.

90. Kissinger, *White House Years*, 848.

91. Conversation between Nixon and Kissinger, 6 December 1971, *FRUS* E-7, doc. 162.

92. Report on meeting with Belgian Ministry of Foreign Affairs, Embassy in Brussels to Canberra, 26 October 1971, A1209 1971/9230 Part 1, National Archives of Australia, Canberra (hereafter NAA); "The Prime Minister's Talks with the Prime Minister of India on 31 October 1971: Additional Note by the FCO," n.d. [ca. 30 October 1971], PREM 15/960, The National Archives, Kew, London (hereafter TNA).

93. Report on conversation with French ambassador in Embassy in New Delhi to State, 12 October 1971, POL INDIA-PAK, Central Files 1970–73, RG 59, USNA.

94. Report on conversation with French first secretary in State to Embassy in Islamabad, 13 October 1971, ibid.

95. Report on meeting with French Ministry of Foreign Affairs, Embassy in Paris to Canberra, 12 November 1971, A1209 1971/9230 Part 1, NAA.

96. Report on conversation with French ambassador in Embassy in New Delhi to State, 1 December 1971, POL INDIA-PAK, Central Files 1970–73, RG 59, USNA.

97. Report on conversation with Belgian ambassador in Embassy in New Delhi to State, 29 November 1971, ibid.

98. Note for Prime Minister on Mrs. Gandhi's visit, 26 October 1971, PREM 15/960, TNA. Also see "Steering brief for the visit of the Indian Prime Minister," 29 October 1971, FCO 37/893, TNA.

99. Record of meeting between the Prime Minister and Mrs. Indira Gandhi at Chequers, 31 October 1971, PREM 15/960, TNA.

100. Record of conversation by Terence Garvey, 31 October 1971, FCO 37/909, TNA.

101. Message from Heath to Yahya Khan, FCO to UKHC Islamabad, 7 November 1971, PREM 15/569, TNA.

102. UKHC Islamabad to FCO, 18 November 1971, PREM 15/570, TNA.

103. Minutes of a meeting of Defence and Oversea Policy Committee, 30 November 1971, CAB 148/115, TNA.

104. Memorandum on conversation between Federal Chancellor and the Pakistan Ambassador, 8 November 1971, Band 478, B1, Political Archive of the Office for Foreign Affairs [Politisches Archiv des Auswärtigen Amtes], Berlin (hereafter PAAA).

105. "Reference Indira Gandhi's visit to Bonn," 12 November 1971; "Indian Prime Minister's Visit to Bonn," 12 November 1971, Band 595, B37, PAAA.

106. Memorandum on meeting between Indian Prime Minister and the Federal Minister, 11 November 1971, ibid.

107. "Indian Prime Minister's Visit to Bonn," 12 November 1971, ibid.

108. Memorandum on meeting between Indian Prime Minister and the Federal Minister, 11 November 1971, ibid.

109. Amit Das Gupta, "India and *Ostpolitik*," in *Ostpolitik, 1969–1974: European and Global Responses,* ed. Carole Fink and Bernd Schaeffer (New York: Cambridge University Press, 2009), 172–73.

110. "Indian Prime Minister's Visit to Bonn," 12 November 1971, Band 595, B37, PAAA.

111. Prasad, *India-Pakistan War,* 244; Jacob, *Surrender at Dacca,* 71; Singh, *India's Wars,* 123.

112. Sisson and Rose, *War and Secession,* 213.

113. Statement by Indira Gandhi, 24 November 1971, *Bangladesh Documents,* 2:141–42.

114. Message from Haksar to Defence Secretary in Indian Embassy in Paris to New Delhi, 8 November 1971, Subject File 235, P.N. Haksar (III Installment), NMML.

115. Personal interview with P.N. Dhar, Delhi, 24 November 2009; Katherine Frank, *Indira: The Life of India Nehru Gandhi* (London: HarperCollins, 2001), 338; Singh, *Field Marshal Sam Manekshaw*, 157; S. Muthiah, *Born to Dare: The Life of Lt Gen. Inderjit Singh Gill, PVSM, MC* (New Delhi: Penguin, 2008), 186.

116. Gul Hassan Khan, *Memoirs,* 322.

117. Zaheer, *Separation of East Pakistan,* 342–44; Reza, *Zulfikar Ali Bhutto,* 115–20.

118. Kissinger, *White House Years,* 894.

119. Shuja Nawaz, *Crossed Swords: Pakistan, Its Army, and the Wars Within* (Karachi: Oxford University Press, 2008), 295; Zaheer, *Separation of East Pakistan,* 360; Aboobaker Osman Mitha, *Unlikely Beginnings: A Soldier's Life* (Oxford: Oxford University Press, 2003), 353.

120. Zaheer, *Separation of East Pakistan,* 358.

121. Cited in Siddiqi, *Onlooker's Journal,* 199.

122. Dhar, *Indira Gandhi,* 179.

123. Cited in Dixit, *Liberation and Beyond*, 89.

124. Ibid., 89–90; P.C. Lal, *My Years with IAF* (New Delhi, Lancer International, 1986), 193.

10. Strange Victory

1. Richard Sisson and Leo Rose, *War and Secession: Pakistan, India, and the Creation of Bangladesh* (Berkeley: University of California Press, 1990), 214.

2. Ibid., 213–14.

3. Sukhwant Singh, *India's Wars since Independence: The Liberation of Bangladesh* (New Delhi: Lancer, 1980), 68–69, 72, 90–91. The author, Major General Sukhwant Singh, was the deputy director of military operations in 1971.

4. J.F.R. Jacob, *Surrender at Dacca: Birth of a Nation* (Dhaka: University Press, 1991), 60, 66–67.

5. Singh, *India's Wars*, 150–51.

6. H.S. Sodhi, *"Operation Windfall": Emergence of Bangladesh* (New Delhi: Allied Publishers, 1980), 110.

7. S.N. Prasad, *The India-Pakistan War of 1971* (New Delhi: Ministry of Defence, 1992), 279 (emphasis added).

8. Ibid., 280.

9. P.C. Lal, *My Years with IAF* (New Delhi, Lancer International, 1986), 171–72.

10. Indira Gandhi to Tajuddin Ahmad, 6 December 1971, Subject File 173, P.N. Haksar Papers (III Installment), Nehru Memorial Museum and Library, New Delhi (hereafter NMML).

11. "A note on India's objectives in the current conflict with Pakistan," 9 December 1971, ibid.

12. Telephone conversation between Nixon and Kissinger, 3 December 1971, in US Department of State, *Foreign Relations of the United States, 1969–1976*, vol. 11: *South Asia Crisis, 1971* (hereafter *FRUS 1971*) (Washington, DC: United States Government Printing Office, 2005), 593–94.

13. Minutes of WSAG Meeting, 3 December 1971, ibid., 597.

14. Minutes of WSAG Meeting, 4 December 1971, ibid., 624.

15. Draft resolution by the US, 4 December 1971, *Bangladesh Documents* (New Delhi: Government of India, 1972), 2:334–35.

16. Draft resolution by the USSR, 4 December 1971, ibid., 336.

17. Secretary (East), MEA to High Commissioner in London, 27 November 1971, in Avtar Singh Bhasin, ed., *India-Pakistan Relations, 1947–2007: A Documentary Study* (New Delhi: Geetika Publishers in cooperation with Public Diplomacy Division, Ministry of External Affairs, 2012), 3:1520–21.

18. Telephone conversation between Nixon and Kissinger, 5 December 1971, *FRUS 1971,* 639.

19. For texts of these resolutions introduced on 5 December 1971, see *Bangladesh Documents,* 2:336–38.

20. Draft resolution by the USSR, 4 December 1971, ibid., 339.

21. Nicholas Wheeler, *Saving Strangers: Humanitarian Intervention in International Society* (Oxford: Oxford University Press, 2000), 60–64.

22. Resolution adopted by the General Assembly, 7 December 1971, *Bangladesh Documents,* 2:342–43.

23. Haksar to Indira Gandhi, 7 December 1971, Subject File 173, P.N. Haksar Papers (III Installment), NMML.

24. Telephone conversation between Kissinger and Dobrynin, 15 November 1971 in David C. Geyer and Douglas E. Selvage, eds., *Soviet-American Relations: The Détente Years, 1969–1972* (Washington, DC: United States Government Printing Office, 2007), 519.

25. Memorandum of conversation (US), 18 November 1971, in Geyer and Selvage, *Soviet-American Relations,* 523; Memorandum of conversation (USSR), 18 November, ibid., 527.

26. Nixon to Kosygin in State to Ambassador in Moscow, *FRUS 1971,* 568–69.

27. Kosygin to Nixon in Embassy in Moscow to State, 3 December 1971, POL 27 INDIA-PAK, US National Archives and Records Administration, College Park, MD (hereafter USNA).

28. Telephone conversation between Kissinger and Rogers, 5 December 1971, *FRUS 1971,* 634.

29. Telephone conversation between Nixon and Kissinger, 5 December 1971, ibid., 637–38.

30. Telephone conversation between Kissinger and Connally, 5 December 1971, in US Department of State, *Foreign Relations of the United States, 1969–1976,* vol. E-7: *Documents on South Asia, 1969–1972* (hereafter *FRUS E-7*) (Washington, DC: United States Government Printing Office, 2005), doc. 159.

31. Telephone conversation between Kissinger and Rogers, 5 December 1971, *FRUS 1971,* 641–42.

32. Memorandum of conversation (US), 5 December 1971, in Geyer and Selvage, *Soviet-American Relations,* 529–30.

33. Memorandum of conversation (USSR), 5 December 1971, ibid., 530–32.

34. Nixon to Brezhnev, 6 December 1971, *FRUS 1971,* 667–68.

35. CIA Intelligence Information Cable, 7 December 1971, ibid., 686–87.

36. Henry Kissinger, *The White House Years* (London: George Weidenfeld & Nicolson, 1979), 856.

37. Memorandum of conversation 22 October 1971, in US Department of State, *Foreign Relations of the United States, 1969–1976*, vol. E-13: *Documents on China, 1969–1972* (hereafter *FRUS* E-13) (Washington, DC: United States Government Printing Office, 2005), doc. 44.

38. Minutes of WSAG meeting, 8 December 1971, *FRUS 1971*, 691, 694.

39. CIA Intelligence Information Cable, 13 December 1971, *FRUS* E-7, doc. 183.

40. Conversation between Nixon and Kissinger, 6 December 1971, *FRUS* E-7, doc. 162.

41. Conversation between Nixon and Kissinger, 4 December 1971, *FRUS 1971*, 612.

42. Farland to Kissinger, 4 December 1971; conversation between Nixon and Kissinger, 4 December 1971; report on meeting with Shah of Iran, 5 December 1971, ibid., 610n3, 610n4, 610.

43. Minutes of WSAG meeting 8 December 1971, ibid., 694.

44. Report from embassy in Tehran, 8 December 1971, Box 643, NSC Files, Nixon Presidential Materials, USNA.

45. Mohammed Yunus, *Bhutto and the Breakup of Pakistan* (Karachi: Oxford University Press, 2011), 36.

46. Telephone conversation between Nixon and Kissinger, 4 December 1971, *FRUS 1971*, 612.

47. Conversation between Nixon and Kissinger, 6 December 1971, *FRUS* E-7, doc. 162.

48. Nixon to Kissinger, 8 December 1971, *FRUS 1971*, 689.

49. Conversation between Nixon, Kissinger, and Attorney General Mitchell, 8 December 1971, *FRUS* E-7, doc. 165.

50. Ibid.

51. Telephone conversation between Nixon and Kissinger, 8 December 1971, *FRUS* E-7, doc. 166.

52. Conversation between Nixon and Kissinger, 9 December 1971, ibid., doc. 168.

53. Memorandum of conversation, 10 December 1971, *FRUS 1971*, 755–56.

54. Ibid., 757–63.

55. Message from the USSR to the US, 6 December 1971, ibid., 677–78.

56. Telephone conversation between Haig and Vorontsov, 8 December 1971, ibid., 700.

57. Conversation between Nixon, Kissinger, and Attorney General Mitchell, 8 December 1971, *FRUS* E-7, doc. 165.

58. Telephone conversation between Nixon and Kissinger, 8 December 1971, ibid., doc. 166.

59. Brezhnev to Nixon, 8 December 1971, *FRUS 1971*, 706–8.

60. Vorontsov to Soviet Foreign Ministry, 9 December 1971, in Geyer and Selvage, *Soviet-American Relations,* 535–36.

61. Conversation between Nixon and Matskevich, 9 December 1971, *FRUS* E-7, doc. 169.

62. Telephone conversation between Kissinger and Ambassador Raza, 8 December 1971, ibid., doc. 166.

63. William Bundy, *A Tangled Web: The Making of Foreign Policy in the Nixon Presidency* (New York: Hill & Wang, 1998), 276; footnote in *FRUS* E-7, doc. 164.

64. Vorontsov to Soviet Foreign Ministry, 10 December 1971, in Geyer and Selvage, *Soviet-American Relations,* 538.

65. Elmo Zumwalt, *On Watch: A Memoir* (New York: Quadrangle, 1976), 367–68.

66. For a short account by Brezhnev's aide, see Alexander M. Alexandrov-Argentov, *Ot Kollontai do Gorbacheva: Vospominaniia* (Moscow: Mezhdunarodniie otnosheniia, 1994), 218–20, 242.

67. Indira Gandhi to Kosygin, 10 December 1971, with covering note from Haksar, Subject File 173, P. N. Haksar Papers (III Installment), NMML.

68. Prasad, *India-Pakistan War,* 566–67; Lal, *My Years with the IAF,* 212–14. Also see Ashok Kalyan Verma, *Bridge on the River Meghna: The Dash to Dhaka* (New Delhi: Knowledge World Publishers, 2009).

69. Shuja Nawaz, *Crossed Swords: Pakistan, Its Army, and the Wars Within* (Karachi: Oxford University Press, 2008), 300.

70. Rao Farman Ali Khan, *How Pakistan Got Divided* (Lahore: Jang, 1992), 124–27.

71. Siddiq Salik, *Witness to Surrender* (Dhaka: University Press, 1997), 198.

72. Yahya to Malik, 10 December 1971, reproduced in Hamoodur Rehman Commission, *Report of the Hamoodur Rehman Commission of Inquiry into the 1971 War, as Declassified by the Government of Pakistan* (Lahore: Vanguard, [2000?]), 257.

73. Text of message from Marc Henri to U Thant; Haksar to Kaul, 11 December 1971, Subject File 174, P. N. Haksar Papers (III Installment), NMML.

74. Personal interview with A.K. Damodaran, New Delhi, 6 April 2006. Damodaran had accompanied Dhar to this meeting.

75. Personal interview with P.N. Dhar, New Delhi, 24 November 2009; Haksar to Indira Gandhi, 13 December 1971, Subject File 174, P. N. Haksar Papers (III Installment), NMML.

76. Note on "Mutual defence assistance obligations under treaties between Pakistan and U.S.A." by Historical Division, Ministry of External Affairs (MEA), 11 December 1971; forwarded to Haksar by Secretary (East) on 12 December 1971, Subject File 87, P. N. Haksar Papers (III Installment), NMML.

77. S.M. Nanda, *The Man Who Bombed Karachi: A Memoir* (New Delhi: HarperCollins, 2004), 239; N. Krishnan, *No Way But Surrender: An Account of the Indo-Pakistan War in the Bay of Bengal, 1971* (New Delhi: Vikas, 1980), 52.

78. Note by AMS Division, January 1972, MEA, WII/109/1/72, National Archives of India, New Delhi (hereafter NAI).

79. Report on conversation between Jha and Sisco in State to Embassy in New Delhi, 14 December 1971, *FRUS 1971*, 816.

80. Haksar to D.P. Dhar, 14 December 1971, Subject File 174, P.N. Haksar Papers (III Installment), NMML.

81. Text of message from Manekshaw to Farman Ali in Haksar to Kaul, 13 December 1971, Subject File 173, P.N. Haksar Papers (III Installment), NMML.

82. Jacob, *Surrender at Dacca*, 129–30.

83. Haksar to Indira Gandhi, 13 December 1971, Subject File 174, P.N. Haksar Papers (III Installment), NMML.

84. Haksar to K.B. Lall and R.C. Dutt, 14 December 1971, ibid.

85. Haksar to D.P. Dhar, 14 December 1971, ibid.

86. Telephone conversation between Nixon and Kissinger, 11 December 1971, *FRUS 1971*, 769.

87. Conversation between Nixon, Kissinger and Haig, 12 December 1971, *FRUS* E-7, doc. 177.

88. Ibid.

89. Memorandum of conversation, 12 December 1971, in US Department of State, *Foreign Relations of the United States, 1969–1976*, vol. 17: *China, 1969–1972* (hereafter *FRUS China*) (Washington, DC: United States Government Printing Office), doc. 177.

90. Haksar to Mishra enclosing message from Indira Gandhi to Zhou, 11 December 1971, Subject File 174, P.N. Haksar Papers (III Installment), NMML.

91. Memorandum of conversation, 20 June 1972, *FRUS* E-7, doc. 267.

92. Ibid.

93. Message from Soviet leadership to Nixon, 14 December 1971, *FRUS 1971*, 801–2.

94. Note for the Political Affairs Committee of the Cabinet, 13 December 1971 (presented to the committee on 14 December), Subject File 174, P.N. Haksar Papers (III Installment), NMML.

95. Text of Polish resolutions in *Bangladesh Documents*, 2:353–55.

96. Apa Pant (High Commissioner in London) to Haksar, 15 December 1971, Subject File 233, P.N. Haksar Papers (III Installment), NMML.

97. Text of UK-France resolution in *Bangladesh Documents*, 2:356.

98. Haksar to Kaul, 15 December 1971, Subject File 173, P.N. Haksar Papers (III Installment), NMML.

99. Reproduced in Salik, *Witness to Surrender*, 207.

100. Consulate General Dacca to State, 14 December 1971, *FRUS 1971,* 808–10.

101. State to Islamabad, 14 December 1971; Islamabad to State, 14 December 1971; State to New Delhi, 14 December 1971; State to New Delhi, 15 December 1971; New Delhi to State, 15 December 1971, POL 27 INDIA-PAK, USNA. Also see Haksar to Indira Gandhi, 15 December 1971, Subject File 173, P. N. Haksar Papers (III Installment), NMML.

102. Message from Indira Gandhi to Pompidou, 15 December 1971, Subject File 173, P. N. Haksar Papers (III Installment), NMML.

103. Message from Manekshaw to Niazi, 15 December 1971, ibid.

104. Cited in Sisson and Rose, *War and Secession,* 306–7.

105. 1614th Meeting of the UN Security Council, 14/15 December 1971, S/PV. 1614, UN Archives.

106. Exchange of messages in Haksar to Kaul, 16 December 1971, Subject File 173, P. N. Haksar Papers (III Installment), NMML.

107. Jacob, *Surrender at Dacca,* 141–47.

108. Haksar to Indira Gandhi, 1 April 1972, Subject File 180, P. N. Haksar Papers (III Installment), NMML.

109. Transcript of telephone conversation between Nixon and Kissinger, 16 December 1971, *FRUS* E-7, doc. 191.

110. Richard Nixon, *RN: The Memoirs of Richard Nixon* (New York: Grosset & Dunlap, 1978), 530.

111. Kissinger, *White House Years,* 913.

112. Jha to Haksar, 17 February 1972; Indira Gandhi's handwritten comments (emphasis in original), 2 March 1972, Subject File 243, P. N. Haksar Papers (III Installment), NMML.

Epilogue

1. Inder Malhotra, *Indira Gandhi: A Personal and Political Biography* (London: Hodder & Stoughton, 1989), 139–41.

2. Paul W. Schroeder, *Systems, Stability and Statecraft: Essays on the International History of Modern Europe* (New York: Palgrave Macmillan, 2004), 157–60.

3. Haksar to Kaul, 15 December 1971, Subject File 173, P. N. Haksar Papers (III Installment), Nehru Memorial Museum and Library, New Delhi (hereafter NMML).

4. Haksar to Indira Gandhi, 18 December 1971, Subject File 174, P. N. Haksar Papers (III Installment), NMML.

5. Comments on Simla Conference by Haksar, n.d., Subject File 181, Haskar Papers (III Installment), NMML.

6. Cited in P. N. Dhar, *Indira Gandhi, the "Emergency" and Indian Democracy* (New Delhi: Oxford University Press, 2000), 192.

7. Comments on Simla Conference by Haksar, n.d., Subject File 181, P. N. Haskar Papers (III Installment), NMML.

8. Record of conversation, 27 July 1973, Subject File 97, P. N. Haksar Papers (III Installment), NMML.

9. Record of conversation with Mujibur Rahman prepared by D. P. Dhar, 29 January 1972, Subject File 233, P. N. Haksar Papers (III Installment), NMML.

BIBLIOGRAPHY

Manuscript Sources

Nehru Memorial Museum and Library, New Delhi (NMML)

Jayaprakash Narayan Papers
P. N. Haksar Papers
R. K. Nehru Papers
T. N. Kaul Papers
T. T. Krishnamachari Papers

Official Records

Archives of Parties and Mass Organizations of the Former German Democratic Republic in the Federal Archives [Stiftung Archiv der Parteien und Massenorganisationen der DDR im Bundesarchiv] (SAPMO), Berlin.

Library and Archives Canada (LAC), Ottawa.

National Archives of Australia (NAA), Canberra.

National Archives of India (NAI), New Delhi

Nixon Presidential Materials, Yorba Linda, California.

Oxfam Archives, Oxford.

Political Archive of the Office for Foreign Affairs [Politisches Archiv des Auswärtigen Amtes] (PAAA), Berlin.

Political Archive of the Office for Foreign Affairs Ministry for Foreign Affairs of the Former GDR [Politisches Archiv des Auswärtigen Amtes, Bestand: Ministerium für Auswärtige Angelegenheiten (der ehemaligen DDR)], (PAAA-MfAA), Berlin.

Russian Government Archive of Contemporary History [Rossiiskii Arkhiv Sotsialno-politicheskoi Istorii] (RGANI), Moscow.

The National Archives (TNA), Kew, London.

United Nations Archives (UNA), New York City.

US National Archives and Records Administration (USNA), College Park, Maryland.

World Bank Papers, Center for the Advanced Study of India (CASI), University of Pennsylvania, Philadelphia.

Interviews

Subas Chakravarty, New Delhi
A. K. Damodaran, New Delhi
P. N. Dhar, New Delhi
Kamal Hossain, Dhaka
Amirul Islam, Dhaka
Brajesh Mishra, New Delhi
K. Subrahmanyam, New Delhi

Newspapers and Periodicals

Daily Star (Dhaka)
Dawn (Karachi)
Far Eastern Economic Review (Hong Kong)
Guardian (London)
Hindu (Madras)
Holiday (Dhaka)
Interwing (Dhaka)
Morning News (Dhaka)
New Nation (Singapore)
New Statesman (London)
New York Times
Pakistan Observer (Dhaka)
Pakistan Times (Dhaka)
People (Dhaka)
Saturday Review (New York)
Statesman (Calcutta)
Sunday Times (London)
Times (London)
Times of India (Bombay)

Works Cited

Achebe, Chinua. *There Was a Country: A Personal History of Biafra*. London: Allen Lane, 2012.

Ahmed, Akhtar. *Advance to Contact: A Soldier's Account of Bangladesh Liberation War*. Dhaka: University Press, 2000.

Ahmed, Viqar, and Rashid Amjad. *The Management of Pakistan's Economy 1947–82*. Karachi: Oxford University Press, 1984.

Aijazuddin, F. S. *From a Head, through a Head, to a Head: The Secret Channel between the US and China through Pakistan*. Karachi: Oxford University Press, 2000.

———, ed. *The White House and Pakistan: Secret Declassified Documents, 1969–1974*. Karachi: Oxford University Press, 2002.

Akhund, Iqbal. *Memoirs of a Bystander: A Life in Diplomacy*. Karachi: Oxford University Press, 1998.

Alexandrov-Argentov, Alexander M. *Ot Kollontai do Gorbacheva: Vospominaniia*. Moscow: Mezhdunarodniie otnosheniia, 1994.

Alexeyeva, Lyudmilla. *Soviet Dissent: Contemporary Movements for National, Religious and Human Rights*. Middletown, CT: Wesleyan University Press, 1985.

Ali, Tariq. *The Duel: Pakistan on the Flight Path of American Power*. London: Pocket Books, 2009.

———. *Pakistan: Military Rule or People's Power?* London: Jonathan Cape, 1970.

———. *Street Fighting Years: An Autobiography of the Sixties*. Calcutta: Seagull, 2006.

Anderson, Jack, and George Clifford. *The Anderson Papers: From the Files of America's Most Famous Investigative Reporter*. New York: Random House, 1973.

Ayoob, Mohammed, and K. Subrahmanyam. *The Liberation War*. New Delhi: S. Chand, 1972.

Aziz, Farida. "The Pakistan Crisis 1971." PhD diss., King's College London, 1988.

Baez, Joan. *And a Voice to Sing With: A Memoir*. New York: Simon & Schuster, 1987.

Baker, Deborah. *A Blue Hand: Allen Ginsberg and the Beats in India*. New Delhi: Penguin, 2008.

Bangladesh Documents. 2 vols. New Delhi: Government of India, 1972.

Bangladesher Shadhinata Juddho: Dalil Patro. 15 vols. Dhaka: Ministry of Information, Government of People's Republic of Bangladesh, 1985.

Barnett, Michael. *Empire of Humanity: A History of Humanitarianism*. Ithaca, NY: Cornell University Press, 2011.

Baxter, Craig, ed. *Diaries of Field Marshal Mohammed Ayub Khan, 1966–1972*. Karachi: Oxford University Press, 2007.

Benvenuti, Andrea. "Australian Reactions to Britain's Declining Presence in Southeast Asia, 1955–63." *Journal of Imperial and Commonwealth History* 34, no. 3 (2006): 407–29.

Berman, Paul. *Power and the Idealists: Or, the Passion of Joschka Fischer and Its Aftermath*. New York: Soft Skull Press, 2005.

———. *A Tale of Two Utopias: The Political Journey of the Generation of 1968*. New York: W. W. Norton, 1996.

Bhargava, G. S. *"Crush India" or Pakistan's Death Wish*. Delhi: Indian School Supply Depot, 1972.

Bhasin, Avtar Singh, ed. *India-Pakistan Relations, 1947–2007: A Documentary Study*. 10 vols. New Delhi: Geetika Publishers in cooperation with Public Diplomacy Division, Ministry of External Affairs, 2012.

Bhattacharjee, Arun. *Dateline Mujibnagar*. Delhi: Vikas, 1973.

Bhutto, Zulfikar Ali. *The Great Tragedy*. Karachi: Pakistan People's Party Publication, 1971.

Black, Maggie. *A Cause for Our Times: Oxfam the First 50 Years*. Oxford: Oxfam Professional, 1992.

Blood, Archer K. *The Cruel Birth of Bangladesh: Memoirs of an American Diplomat*. Dhaka: University Press, 2002.

Borstelmann, Thomas. *The 1970s: A New Global History from Civil Rights to Economic Inequality*. Princeton, NJ: Princeton University Press, 2010.

Bose, Sarmila. *Dead Reckoning: Memories of the 1971 Bangladesh War*. London: Hurst, 2011.

Buchanan, Tom. "'The Truth Will Set You Free': The Making of Amnesty International." *Journal of Contemporary History* 37, no. 4 (2002): 575–97.

Bundy, William. *A Tangled Web: The Making of Foreign Policy in the Nixon Presidency*. New York: Hill & Wang, 1998.

Burke, Roland. *Decolonization and the Evolution of International Human Rights*. Philadelphia: University of Pennsylvania Press, 2010.

———. "From Individual Rights to National Development: The First UN International Conference on Human Rights, Tehran 1968." *Journal of World History* 19, no. 3 (2008): 283–84.

Chamberlin, Paul Thomas. *The Global Offensive: The United States, the Palestine Liberation Organization, and the Making of the Post–Cold War Order*. New York: Oxford University Press, 2012.

Chang, Jung, and Jon Halliday. *Mao: The Unknown Story*. London: Vintage, 2006.

Chaudhuri, Rudra. *Forged in Crisis: India and the United States since 1947*. London: Hurst, 2013.

Chen, Jian. *Mao's China and the Cold War*. Chapel Hill: University of North Carolina Press, 2001.

Chopra, Pran. *India's Second Liberation*. New Delhi: Vikas, 1974.

Choudhury, G. W. *India, Pakistan, Bangladesh and the Major Powers*. New York: Free Press, 1975.

————. *Last Days of United Pakistan*. London: Hurst, 1974.

Chowdhury, Iftekhar Ahmed. "Bangladesh: Opportunities and Challenges." In *A Resurgent China: South Asian Perspectives,* edited by S. D. Muni and Tan Tai Yong, chapter 3. New Delhi: Routledge India, 2012.

Cold War International History Project Bulletin. Washington, DC: Woodrow Wilson International Center for Scholars, 1992–.

Connelly, Matthew. *A Diplomatic Revolution: Algeria's Fight for Independence and the Origins of the Post–Cold War Era*. New York: Oxford University Press, 2002.

Dallek, Robert. *Nixon and Kissinger: Partners in Power*. London: Allen Lane, 2007.

Danhui, Li. "Mao Zedong's World Revolution Ideals and Sino-Indian Relations: Decoding Mao's Talk with the Delegation of the Communist Party of India (Leftists) on 13 December 1967." Paper presented at the panel "The Sino-Indian Border Clashes and the Sino-Soviet Split: New Evidence from Chinese Archives," Cold War International History Project, Woodrow Wilson International Center for Scholars, Washington, DC, May 18, 2009.

Darby, Philip. *British Defence Policy East of Suez, 1947–1968*. Oxford: Oxford University Press, 1973.

Darwin, John. *Britain and Decolonisation: The Retreat from Empire in the Post-War World*. Basingstoke, UK: Palgrave Macmillan, 1988.

————. *The Empire Project: The Rise and Fall of the British World-System, 1830–1970*. Cambridge: Cambridge University Press, 2009.

Datta, Antara. *Refugees and Borders in South Asia: The Great Displacement of 1971*. London: Routledge, 2012.

Datta-Ray, Sunanda. *Looking East to Look West: Lee Kuan Yew's Mission India*. New Delhi: Viking, 2010.

Day, David. *The Great Betrayal: Britain, Australia and the Onset of the Pacific War, 1939–42*. Melbourne: Oxford University Press, 1992.

Debnath, Angela. "British Perceptions of the East Pakistan Crisis 1971: 'Hideous Atrocities on Both Sides'?" *Journal of Genocide Research* 13, no. 4 (2011): 421–50.

Dhar, P. N. *Indira Gandhi, the "Emergency" and Indian Democracy*. New Delhi: Oxford University Press, 2000.

Dixit, J. N. *Liberation and Beyond: Indo-Bangladesh Relations*. New Delhi: Konark, 1999.

Dockrill, Saki. *Britain's Retreat from East of Suez: The Choice between Europe and the World?* London: Palgrave, 2002.

Edwards, Peter, and Gregory Pemberton. *Crises and Commitments: The Politics and Diplomacy of Australia's Involvement in Southeast Asian Conflicts, 1948–1965*. Sydney: Allen & Unwin, 1992.

Evans, Harold. *My Paper Chase: True Stories of Vanished Times, An Autobiography.* London: Abacus, 2009.

Exley, Richard, and Helen Exley, eds. *The Testimony of Sixty on the Crisis in Bengal.* Oxford: Oxfam, 1971.

Farber, David. *Chicago '68.* Chicago: University of Chicago Press, 1998.

———, ed. *The Sixties: From Memory to History.* Charlotte: University of North Carolina Press, 1994.

Feldman, Herbert. *The End and the Beginning: Pakistan 1969–1971.* Karachi: Oxford University Press, 1975.

Ferguson, Niall, Charles S. Maier, Erez Manela, and Daniel J. Sargent, eds. *The Shock of the Global: The 1970s in Perspective.* Cambridge, MA: Belknap Press, 2010.

Frank, Katherine. *Indira: The Life of India Nehru Gandhi.* London: HarperCollins, 2001.

Ganguly, Sumit. *Conflict Unending: India-Pakistan Tensions since 1947.* New Delhi: Oxford University Press, 2002.

Garthoff, Raymond. *Détente and Confrontation: American-Soviet Relations from Nixon to Reagan.* Rev. ed. Washington, DC: Brookings Press, 1994.

Garver, John. *Protracted Contest: Sino-Indian Rivalry in the Twentieth Century.* Seattle: University of Washington Press, 2001.

Gassert, Phillip, and Martin Klimke, eds. *Memories and Legacies of a Global Revolt.* Washington, DC: German Historical Institute Supplement, 2009.

Gates, Robert M. *From the Shadows: The Ultimate Insider's Story of Five Presidents and How They Won the Cold War.* New York: Simon & Schuster, 1996.

Gauhar, Altaf. *Ayub Khan: Pakistan's First Military Ruler.* Karachi: Oxford University Press, 1996.

Geyer, David C., and Douglas E. Selvage, eds. *Soviet-American Relations: The Détente Years, 1969–1972.* Washington, DC: United States Government Printing Office, 2007.

Ginsberg, Allen. *Collected Poems 1947–1997.* Reprint ed. New York: Harper Perennial, 2007.

———. "On Jessore Road." *New York Times of the Web: Books,* 17 December 1971, www.nytimes.com/books/01/04/08/specials/ginsberg-jessore.html.

Gitlin, Todd. *The Sixties: Years of Hope, Days of Rage.* Rev. ed. New York: Bantam, 1993.

Goldstein, Lyle J. "Return to Zhenbao Island: Who Started Shooting and Why It Matters." *China Quarterly,* no. 168 (2001): 985–97.

Goldsworthy, David. *Losing the Blanket: Australia and the End of Britain's Empire.* Melbourne: Melbourne University Press, 2002.

Gopal, Sarvepalli. *Imperialists, Nationalist, Democrats: Collected Essays.* Ranikhet, India: Permanent Black, 2013.

Government of India. *The Years of Endeavour: Selected Speeches of Indira Gandhi, August 1969–August 1972.* New Delhi: Publications Division, 1975.

Guha, Ramachandra. *India after Gandhi: The History of the World's Largest Democracy.* London: Macmillan, 2007.

Gupta, Amit Das. "Divided Nations: India and Germany." In *India in the World since 1947: National and Transnational Perspectives,* edited by Andreas Hilger and Corinna R. Unger, 300–25. Frankfurt: Peter Lang, 2012.

———. *Handel, Hilfe, Hallstein-Doktrin: die bundesdeutsche Süd asienpolitik unter Adenauer und Erhard 1949 bis 1966.* Husum, Germany: Matthieson, 2004.

———. "India and *Ostpolitik.*" In *Ostpolitik, 1969–1974: European and Global Responses,* edited by Carole Fink and Bernd Schaeffer, chapter 8. New York: Cambridge University Press, 2009.

Hack, Karl. *Defence and Decolonisation in Southeast Asia: Britain, Malaya and Singapore, 1941–1968.* London: Curzon, 2001.

Hahnimaki, Jussi. *The Flawed Architect: Henry Kissinger and American Foreign Policy.* New York: Oxford University Press, 2004.

Haldeman, H. R. *The Haldeman Diaries: Inside the Nixon White House, the Complete Multimedia Edition.* Santa Monica, CA: Sony Electronic, 1994.

Hamoodur Rehman Commission. *Report of the Hamoodur Rehman Commission of Inquiry into the 1971 War, as Declassified by the Government of Pakistan.* Lahore: Vanguard, [2000?].

Harman, Chris. *The Fire Last Time: 1968 and After.* London: Bookmarks, 1998.

Harrison, George, Eric Clapton, Bob Dylan, Jim Keltner, Ustad Ali Akbar Khan, Billy Preston, Ustad Alla Rakha, Leon Russell, Ravi Shankar, Ringo Starr, and Klaus Voormann. *The Concert for Bangladesh.* Hollywood, CA: Apple, 1971. LP.

———. *The Concert for Bangladesh Revisited.* Directed by Claire Ferguson. Hollywood, CA: Apple Films/Rhino, 2005. DVD, two discs. Concert originally recorded live August 1, 1971, Madison Square Garden, New York.

Hasan, Muyeedul. *Muldhara '71.* Dhaka: University Press, 2008. Originally published in 1986.

Hersh, Seymour. *The Price of Power: Kissinger in the Nixon White House.* New York: Summit Books, 1983.

Hess, Gary. "Grand Strategy and Regional Conflict: Nixon, Kissinger and the South Asia Crisis." *Diplomatic History* 31, no. 5 (2007): 959–63.

Hobsbawm, Eric. *The Age of Extremes: The Short Twentieth Century, 1914–1991.* London: Abacus, 1995.

Holland, Robert. *The Pursuit of Greatness: Britain and the World Role, 1900–1970*. London: Fontana, 1991.

Hossain, Mohammed Delwar. "Framing the Liberation War of Bangladesh in the U.S. and the U.K. Media: A Content Analysis of *The New York Times* and *The Times* (London)." MA thesis, Southern Illinois University, Carbondale, 2010.

Huntington, Samuel P. *Political Order in Changing Societies*. New Haven, CT: Yale University Press, 1968.

Iriye, Akira. *Global Community: The Role of International Organizations in the Making of the Contemporary World*. Berkeley: University of California Press, 2002.

Irwin, Ryan M. *Gordian Knot: Apartheid and the Unmaking of the Liberal World Order*. New York: Oxford University Press, 2012.

Isaacson, Walter. *Kissinger: A Biography*. New York: Simon & Schuster, 2005.

Islam, Nurul. *Making of Nation Bangladesh: An Economist's Tale*. Dhaka: University Press, 2003.

Islam, Rafiqul. *A Tale of Millions: Bangladesh Liberation War—1971*. 3rd ed. Dhaka: Ananya, 2005.

Iyer, G. S. "'Mao's Smile' Revisited: Some Observations." Paper no. 413 (December 2009), Chennai Centre for China Studies, www.c3sindia.org /india/1068.

Jackson, Robert. *South Asian Crisis: India-Pakistan-Bangladesh*. London: Chatto & Windus, 1975.

Jacob, J. F. R. *Surrender at Dacca: Birth of a Nation*. Dhaka: University Press, 1997.

Jahan, Rounaq. *Pakistan: Failure in National Integration*. New York: Columbia University Press, 1972.

Jain, R. K., ed. *Soviet South Asian Relations 1947–78*. New Delhi: Radiant, 1978.

Jalal, Ayesha. *Democracy and Authoritarianism in South Asia: A Comparative and Historical Perspective*. Cambridge: Cambridge University Press, 1995.

Jalal, Hamid, and Khalid Hasan, eds. *Politics of the People: Marching towards Democracy, January 1970–December 1971*. Rawalpindi: Pakistan Publications, [1972].

Jayakar, Pupul. *Indira Gandhi: A Biography*. Rev. ed. New Delhi: Penguin, 1995.

Jisen, Ma. *The Cultural Revolution in the Foreign Ministry of China*. Hong Kong: Chinese University Press, 2004.

Jones, Matthew. "A Decision Delayed: Britain's Withdrawal from South East Asia Reconsidered, 1961–1968." *English Historical Review* 117, no. 472 (2002): 569–95.

Judt, Tony. *Postwar: A History of Europe since 1945*. London: Pimlico, 2007.

Kabir, Muhammad Ghulam. *Minority Politics in Bangladesh*. New Delhi: Vikas, 1980.

Kapur, Devesh. *Diaspora, Development, and Democracy: The Domestic Impact of International Migration from India*. Princeton, NJ: Princeton University Press, 2010.

Karim, S. A. *Sheikh Mujib: Triumph and Tragedy*. Dhaka: University Press, 2005.

Katsiaficas, George. *The Imagination of the New Left: A Global Analysis of 1968*. Cambridge, MA: South End Press, 1987.

Kavic, Lorne. *India's Quest for Security: Defence Policies, 1947–1965*. Berkeley: University of California Press, 1967.

Keys, Barbara. "Anti-Torture Politics: Amnesty International, the Greek Junta, and the Origins of the Human Rights 'Boom' in the United States." In *The Human Rights Revolution: An International History*, edited by Akira Iriye, Petra Goedde, and William I. Hitchcock, 201–21. New York: Oxford University Press, 2012.

Khan, Arshad Sami. *Three Presidents and an Aide: Life, Power and Politics*. New Delhi: Pentagon Press, 2008.

Khan, Asghar. *My Political Struggle*. Karachi: Oxford University Press, 2008.

Khan, Faruq Aziz. *Spring 1971: A Centre Stage Account of Bangladesh Liberation War*. 2nd ed. Dhaka: University Press, 1998.

Khan, Gohar Ayub. *Glimpses into the Corridors of Power*. Karachi: Oxford University Press, 2007.

Khan, Gul Hassan. *Memoirs of Lt. Gen. Gul Hassan Khan*. Karachi: Oxford University Press, 1993.

Khan, Jahan Dad. *Pakistan Leadership Challenges*. Karachi: Oxford University Press, 1999.

Khan, Lal. *Pakistan's Other Story: The 1968–69 Revolution*. Delhi: Aakar Books, 2009.

Khan, Mohammed Asghar. *Generals in Politics: Pakistan, 1958–1982*. New Delhi: Vikas, 1983.

Khan, Omar Hayyat. "Instruments of Influence: Canada and Arms Exports to South Asia, 1947–1971." MA thesis, Carleton University, Ottawa, 2005.

Khan, Rao Farman Ali. *How Pakistan Got Divided*. Lahore: Jang, 1992.

Khan, Roedad, ed. *American Papers: Secret and Confidential India-Pakistan-Bangladesh Documents 1965–1973*. Karachi: Oxford University Press, 1999.

———. *Pakistan: A Dream Gone Sour*. Karachi: Oxford University Press, 1997.

Khan, Shuakat Hayat. *The Nation That Lost Its Soul: Memoirs of a Freedom Fighter*. Lahore: Jang, 1995.

Khan, Sultan M. *Memories and Reflections of a Pakistani Diplomat*. London: Centre for Pakistan Studies, 1997.

Kimball, Jeffrey. *Nixon's Vietnam War.* Lawrence: University Press of Kansas, 1998.

Kissinger, Henry. *On China.* London: Allen Lane, 2011.

———. *The White House Years.* London: George Weidenfeld & Nicolson, 1979.

Klimke, Martin. *Student Protests in West Germany and the United States in the Global Sixties.* Princeton, NJ: Princeton University Press, 2011.

Klimke, Martin, and Joachim Scharloth, eds. *1968 in Europe: A History of Protest and Activism.* New York: Palgrave Macmillan, 2008.

Krishnan, N. *No Way But Surrender: An Account of the Indo-Pakistan War in the Bay of Bengal, 1971.* New Delhi: Vikas, 1980.

Kumaraswamy, P. R. *India's Israel Policy.* New York: Columbia University Press, 2010.

Kurlansky, Mark. *1968: The Year That Rocked the World.* London: Jonathan Cape, 2004.

Kux, Dennis. *India and the United States: Estranged Democracies, 1941–1991.* Washington, DC: National Defense University Press, 1992.

———. *The United States and Pakistan, 1947–2000: Disenchanted Allies.* Washington, DC: Woodrow Wilson Center Press, 2001.

Lal, P. C. *My Years with IAF.* New Delhi: Lancer International, 1986.

Levy, Daniel, and Natan Sznaider. "The Institutionalization of Cosmopolitan Morality: The Holocaust and Human Rights." *Journal of Human Rights* 3, no. 2 (2004): 143–57.

Lieven, Anatol. *Pakistan: A Hard Country.* London: Allen Lane, 2011.

Luthi, Lorenz. *The Sino-Soviet Split: Cold War in the Communist World.* Princeton, NJ: Princeton University Press, 2008.

MacFarquhar, Roderick, and Michael Schoenhals. *Mao's Last Revolution.* Cambridge, MA: Harvard University Press, 2006.

Macmillan, Margaret. *Nixon and Mao: The Week That Changed the World.* New York: Random House, 2007.

Madan, Tanvi. "With an Eye to the East: The China Factor and the US–India Relationship, 1949–1979." PhD diss., University of Texas, Austin, 2012.

Mahmood, Safdar. *The Crisis in East Pakistan.* Islamabad: Government of Pakistan, 1971.

———. *Pakistan Divided.* New Delhi: Alpha Bravo, 1993.

Malhotra, Inder. *Indira Gandhi: A Personal and Political Biography.* London: Hodder & Stoughton, 1989.

Malloch-Brown, Mark. *The Unfinished Global Revolution: The Limits of Nations and the Pursuit of a New Politics.* London: Allen Lane, 2011.

Maniruzzaman, Talukder. *The Bangladesh Revolution and Its Aftermath.* Dhaka: University Press, 2003.

———. *Radical Politics and the Emergence of Bangladesh.* Dhaka: Bangladesh Books, 1975.

Marker, Jamsheed. *Quiet Diplomacy: Memoirs of an Ambassador of Pakistan.* Karachi: Oxford University Press, 2010.

Marwick, Arthur. *The Sixties: Cultural Revolution in Britain, France, Italy, and the United States, c.1958–c.1974.* New York: Oxford University Press, 1998.

Mastny, Vojtech. "The Soviet Union's Partnership with India." *Journal of Cold War Studies* 12, no. 3 (2010): 52–56.

Mazari, Sherbaz Khan. *A Journey to Disillusionment.* Karachi: Oxford University Press, 1999.

Mazower, Mark. *Dark Continent: Europe's Twentieth Century.* London: Allen Lane, 1998.

———. *Governing the World: The History of an Idea.* London: Allen Lane, 2012.

———. *No Enchanted Palace: The End of Empire and the Ideological Origins of the United Nations.* Princeton, NJ: Princeton University Press, 2009.

McDougall, Derek. "Australia and the British Military Withdrawal from East of Suez." *Australian Journal of International Affairs* 51, no. 2 (1997): 183–94.

McMahon, Robert. *Cold War on the Periphery: The United States, India, and Pakistan.* New York: Columbia University Press, 1994.

———. "The Danger of Geopolitical Fantasies: Nixon, Kissinger and the South Asia Crisis of 1971." In *Nixon in the World: American Foreign Relations, 1969–1977,* edited by Fredrik Logevall and Andrew Preston, 249–68. New York: Oxford University Press, 2008.

Ministry of Finance. *Economic Survey 1971–72.* New Delhi: Government of India, 1972.

Mitha, Aboobaker Osman. *Unlikely Beginnings: A Soldier's Life.* Oxford: Oxford University Press, 2003.

Mitra, Ashok. *A Prattler's Tale: Bengal, Marxism, Governance.* Kolkata: Samya, 2007.

Mookherjee, Nayanika. "The Absent Piece of Skin: Gendered, Racialized, and Territorial Inscriptions of Sexual Violence during the Bangladesh War." *Modern Asian Studies* 46, no. 6 (2012): 1572–1601.

———. "Mobilising Images: Encounters of 'Forced' Migrants and the Bangladesh War of 1971." *Mobilities* 6, no. 3 (2011): 399–414.

Moore, R. J. *Escape from Empire: The Attlee Government and the Indian Problem.* Oxford: Clarendon Press, 1983.

———. *Making the New Commonwealth.* Oxford: Clarendon Press, 1983.

Morgan, Michael Cotey. "The Seventies and the Rebirth of Human Rights." In *The Shock of the Global: The 1970s in Perspective,* edited by Niall Ferguson, Charles S. Maier, Erez Manela, and Daniel J. Sargent, 237–50. Cambridge, MA: Belknap Press, 2010.

Moses, A. Dirk. "The United Nations, Humanitarianism, and Human Rights: War Crimes/Genocide Trials for Pakistani Soldiers in Bangladesh, 1971–1974." In *Human Rights in the Twentieth Century*, edited by Stefan-Ludwig Hoffmann, 258–79. New York: Cambridge University Press, 2011.

Moyn, Samuel. *The Last Utopia: Human Rights in History*. Cambridge, MA: Harvard University Press, 2010.

Muhith, A. M. A. *American Response to Bangladesh Liberation War*. Dhaka: University Press, 1996.

———. *Bangladesh: Emergence of a Nation*. 2nd ed. Dhaka: University Press, 1994.

Muthiah, S. *Born to Dare: The Life of Lt. Gen. Inderjit Singh Gill, PVSM, MC*. New Delhi: Penguin, 2008.

Naik, J. A. *India, Russia, China, and Bangladesh*. New Delhi: S. Chand, 1972.

Nanda, S. M. *The Man Who Bombed Karachi: A Memoir*. New Delhi: Harper-Collins, 2004.

Nasim, A. S. M. *Bangladesh Fights for Independence*. Dhaka: Columbia Prokashini, 2002.

Nathans, Benjamin. "Soviet Rights-Talk in the Post-Stalin Era." In *Human Rights in the Twentieth Century*, edited by Stefan-Ludwig Hoffmann, 166–90. New York: Cambridge University Press, 2011.

Nawaz, Shuja. *Crossed Swords: Pakistan, Its Army, and the Wars Within*. Karachi: Oxford University Press, 2008.

Nehru, B. K. *Nice Guys Finish Second: Memoirs*. New Delhi: Penguin, 1997.

Neier, Aryeh. *The International Human Rights Movement: A History*. Princeton, NJ: Princeton University Press, 2012.

Nixon, Richard. *RN: The Memoirs of Richard Nixon*. New York: Grosset & Dunlap, 1978.

Noorani, A. G. *Brezhnev Plan for Asian Security: Russia in Asia*. Bombay: Jaico, 1975.

Novick, Peter. *The Holocaust in American Life*. New York: Houghton Mifflin, 1999.

O'Dell, Chris. *Miss O'Dell: Hard Days and Long Nights with the Beatles, the Stones, Bob Dylan, and Eric Clapton*. New York: Touchstone, 2009.

Pantsov, Alexander V., and Steven I. Levine. *Mao: The Real Story*. New York: Simon & Schuster, 2012.

Parthasarathi, Ashok. "Forty Years of the Indo-Soviet Treaty: A Historic Landmark at the Global Level." *Mainstream* 49, no. 34 (August 13, 2011), www.mainstreamweekly.net/article2951.html.

Patel, I. G. *Glimpses of Indian Economic Policy: An Insider's View*. New Delhi: Oxford University Press, 2002.

Pemberton, Gregory. *All the Way: Australia's Road to Vietnam*. Sydney: Allen & Unwin, 1987.

Pilkington, Richard. "In the National Interest? Canada and the East Pakistan Crisis of 1971." *Journal of Genocide Research* 13, no. 4 (2011): 451–74.

Prasad, H. Y. Sharada. *The Book I Won't Be Writing and Other Essays.* New Delhi: Chronicle Books, 2003.

Prasad, S. N. *The India-Pakistan War of 1971.* New Delhi: Ministry of Defence, 1992.

Prashad, Vijay. *The Darker Nations: A People's History of the Third World.* New York: New Press, 2007.

Qiu, Jin. *The Culture of Power: The Lin Biao Incident in the Cultural Revolution.* Stanford, CA: Stanford University Press, 1999.

Radchenko, Sergey. *Two Suns in the Heavens: The Sino-Soviet Struggle for Supremacy, 1962–1967.* Stanford, CA: Stanford University Press, 2009.

Raghavan, Srinath. *War and Peace in Modern India: A Strategic History of the Nehru Years.* London: Palgrave Macmillan, 2010.

Rahman, M. Attiqur. *Back to the Pavilion.* Karachi: Oxford University Press, 2005.

Rahman, Muhammad Anisur. *My Story of 1971: Through the Holocaust That Created Bangladesh.* Dhaka: Liberation War Museum, 2001.

Rahman, Mizanur. *Emergence of a New Nation in a Multi-Polar World.* Seattle: University of Washington Press, 1978.

Rahman, Sheikh Mujibur. *The Unfinished Memoirs.* New Delhi: Viking, 2012.

Rainer-Horn, Gerd. *The Spirit of '68: Rebellion in Western Europe and North America, 1956–1976.* New York: Oxford University Press, 2007.

Rajgopal, P. V., ed. *The British, the Bandits and the Bordermen: From the Diaries and Articles of K. F. Rustamji.* New Delhi: Wisdom Tree, 2009.

Rakove, Robert B. *Kennedy, Johnson and the Nonaligned World.* Cambridge: Cambridge University Press, 2013.

Rashid, Harun-or. "British Perspectives, Pressures and Publicity Regarding Bangladesh, 1971." *Contemporary South Asia* 4, no. 2 (1995): 139–49.

Reynolds, David. *Britannia Overruled: British Policy and World Power in the Twentieth Century.* 2nd ed. London: Longman, 2000.

Reza, Rafi. *Zulfikar Ali Bhutto and Pakistan, 1967–1977.* Dhaka: University Press, 1997.

Robertson, Geoffrey. *Crimes against Humanity: The Struggle for Global Justice.* New York: New Press, 2000.

Ross, Kristin. *May '68 and Its Afterlives.* Chicago: University of Chicago Press, 2002.

Rowbotham, Sheila. *Promise of a Dream: Remembering the Sixties.* London: Verso, 2001.

Safiullah, K. M. *Bangladesh at War.* 2nd ed. Dhaka: Academic Publishers, 1995.

Saikia, Yasmin. *Women, War and the Making of Bangladesh: Remembering 1971.* New Delhi: Women Unlimited, 2011.

Sakharov, Andreiĭ D. *Progress, Coexistence, and Intellectual Freedom.* New York: Norton, [1968]. Originally published in the *New York Times,* 22 July 1968.

Salahuddin, Ghazi. "Pakistan: The Year of Change." In *Memories and Legacies of a Global Revolt,* edited by Phillip Gassert and Martin Klimke, 95–98. Washington, DC: German Historical Institute Supplement, 2009.

Salik, Siddiq. *Witness to Surrender.* Dhaka: University Press, 1997.

Sargent, Daniel J. *A Superpower Adrift: History, Strategy, and American Foreign Policy in the 1970s.* New York: Oxford University Press, forthcoming.

Schroeder, Paul W. *Systems, Stability and Statecraft: Essays on the International History of Modern Europe.* New York: Palgrave Macmillan, 2004.

Sen, Mohit. *A Traveller and the Road: The Journey of an Indian Communist.* New Delhi: Rupa, 2003.

Sen, Rangalal. *Political Elites in Bangladesh.* Dhaka: University Press, 1986.

Shankar, Ravi. *Raga Mala: An Autobiography.* New York: Welcome Rain, 1999.

Shrivastava, C. P. *Lal Bahadur Shastri: A Life of Truth in Politics.* New Delhi: Oxford University Press, 1995.

Siddiqi, Brigadier A. R. *East Pakistan the Endgame: An Onlooker's Journal, 1969–1971.* Karachi: Oxford University Press, 2004.

Siddiqui, Kalim. *Conflict, Crisis and War in Pakistan.* London: Macmillan, 1972.

Singh, Anita Inder. *The Limits of British Influence: South Asia and the Anglo-American Relationship 1947–56.* New York: St. Martin's Press, 1993.

Singh, Depinder. *Field Marshal Sam Manekshaw: Soldiering with Dignity.* Dehradun, India: Natraj, 2002.

Singh, Sukhwant. *India's Wars since Independence: The Liberation of Bangladesh.* New Delhi: Lancer, 1980.

Sisson, Richard, and Leo Rose. *War and Secession: Pakistan, India, and the Creation of Bangladesh.* Berkeley: University of California Press, 1990.

Small, John. "From Pakistan to Bangladesh, 1969–1972: Perspective of a Canadian Envoy." In *"Special Trust and Confidence": Envoy Essays in Canadian Diplomacy,* edited by David Reece, 209–38. Ottawa: Carlton University Press, 1996.

Smith, Simon C. "Coming Down on the Winning Side: Britain and the South Asia Crisis, 1971." *Contemporary British History* 24, no. 4 (2010): 451–70.

Sobhan, Rehman. "Negotiating for Bangladesh: A Participant's View." *South Asian Review* 4, no. 4 (1971): 315–26.

Sodhi, H. S. *"Operation Windfall": Emergence of Bangladesh*. New Delhi: Allied Publishers, 1980.

Sounes, Howard. *Down the Highway: The Life of Bob Dylan*. London: Blackswan Books, 2002.

Suri, Jeremi, ed. *The Global Revolutions of 1968*. New York: W. W. Norton, 2007.

———. *Henry Kissinger and the American Century*. Cambridge, MA: Belknap Press, 2007.

———. *Power and Protest: Global Revolution and the Rise of the Détente*. Cambridge, MA: Harvard University Press, 2003.

———. "The Rise and Fall of an International Counterculture, 1960–1975." *American Historical Review* 114, no. 1 (2009): 45–68.

Syed, Anwar H. *The Discourse and Politics of Zulfikar Ali Bhutto*. New York: St. Martin's Press, 1992.

Talbot, Ian. *Pakistan: A Modern History*. New Delhi: Oxford University Press, 1998.

Teiwes, Frederick C., and Warren Sun. *The Tragedy of Lin Biao: Riding the Tiger during the Cultural Revolution, 1966–1971*. London: Hurst, 1996.

Thant, U. *View from the UN*. New York: Doubleday, 1978.

Thomas, Raju G. C. *Indian Security Policy*. Princeton, NJ: Princeton University Press, 1986.

Trachtenberg, Marc. *A Constructed Peace: The Making of the European Settlement, 1945–1963*. Princeton, NJ: Princeton University Press, 1999.

Umar, Badruddin. *The Emergence of Bangladesh: Class Struggles in East Pakistan, 1947–1958*. Karachi: Oxford University Press, 2004.

———. *The Emergence of Bangladesh: Rise of Bengali Nationalism, 1958–1971*. Karachi: Oxford University Press, 2006.

US Department of State. *Foreign Relations of the United States, 1969–1976*. Vol. 11: *South Asia Crisis, 1971*. Washington, DC: United States Government Printing Office, 2005. http://history.state.gov/historicaldocuments/frus1969-76v11.

———. *Foreign Relations of the United States, 1969–1976*. Vol. E-7: *Documents on South Asia, 1969–1972*. Washington, DC: United States Government Printing Office, 2005. http://history.state.gov/historicaldocuments/frus1969-76ve07.

———. *Foreign Relations of the United States, 1969–1976*. Vol. E-13: *Documents on China, 1969–1972*. Washington, DC: United States Government Printing Office, 2005. http://history.state.gov/historicaldocuments/frus1969-76ve13.

———. *Foreign Relations of the United States 1969–1976*. Vol. 17: *China 1969–1972*. Washington, DC: United States Government Printing Office, 2005. http://history.state.gov/historicaldocuments/frus1969-76v17.

Van Hollen, Christopher. "The Tilt Policy Revisited: Nixon-Kissinger Geopolitics and South Asia." *Asian Survey* 20, no. 4 (1980): 339–61.

Van Schendel, Willem. *A History of Bangladesh*. Cambridge: Cambridge University Press, 2009.

Verma, Ashok Kalyan. *Bridge on the River Meghna: The Dash to Dhaka*. New Delhi: Knowledge World Publishers, 2009.

Voigt, Johannes H. *Die Indienpolitik der DDR: von den Anfängen bis zur Anerkennung (1952–1972)*. Cologne: Böhlau, 2008.

Warner, Geoffrey. "Nixon, Kissinger and the Breakup of Pakistan, 1971." *International Affairs* 81, no. 5 (2005): 1097–118.

Wenqian, Gao. *Zhou Enlai: The Last Perfect Revolutionary*. New York: Public Affairs, 2007.

Westad, Odd Arne. *The Global Cold War: Third World Interventions and the Making of Our Times*. Cambridge: Cambridge University Press, 2005.

———. *Restless Empire: China and the World since 1750*. London: Bodley Head, 2012.

Wheeler, Nicholas. *Saving Strangers: Humanitarian Intervention in International Society*. Oxford: Oxford University Press, 2000.

White Paper on the Crisis in East Pakistan. Islamabad: Government of Pakistan, August 1971.

Williams, L. Rushbrook. *The East Pakistan Tragedy*. London: Tom Stacey, 1972.

Wolin, Richard. *The Wind from the East: French Intellectuals, the Cultural Revolution, and the Legacy of the 1960s*. Princeton, NJ: Princeton University Press, 2010.

Wolpert, Stanley. *Zulfi Bhutto of Pakistan: His Life and Times*. New York: Oxford University Press, 1993.

Yunus, Mohammed. *Bhutto and the Breakup of Pakistan*. Karachi: Oxford University Press, 2011.

Zaheer, Hasan. *The Separation of East Pakistan: The Rise and Realization of Bengali Muslim Nationalism*. Dhaka: University Press, 2001.

Zumwalt, Elmo. *On Watch: A Memoir*. New York: Quadrangle, 1976.

ACKNOWLEDGMENTS

This book has been at least seven years in the making, and several hands have contributed to the work. I should like to begin by thanking the staff at the following archives and libraries: Nehru Memorial Museum and Library, New Delhi; National Archives of India, New Delhi; Centre for Policy Research, New Delhi; US National Archives and Records Administration, College Park, Maryland; Nixon Presidential Materials, Yorba Linda, California; United Nations Archives, New York City; Van-Pelt Dietrich Library Center, University of Pennsylvania, Philadelphia; Lamont Library, Harvard University, Cambridge; The National Archives, Kew, London; Oxfam Archives, Oxford; Maughan Library, King's College London, London; Joint Services Command and Staff College Library, Shrivenham; Stiftung Archiv der Parteien und Massenorganisationen der DDR im Bundesarchiv [Archives of Parties and Mass Organizations of the Former German Democratic Republic in the Federal Archives], Berlin; Politisches Archiv des Auswärtigen Amtes [Political Archive of the Office for Foreign Affairs], Berlin; Rossiiskii Arkhiv Sotsialno-politicheskoi Istorii [Russian Government Archive of Contemporary History], Moscow; Library and Archives Canada, Ottawa; National Archives of Australia, Canberra.

My research in Dhaka would not have been possible without the help of Shapar Selim, Mahmud Rahman, and Akku Chowdhury. For sharing their perspectives on the 1971 crisis, I am grateful to Akhtar Ahmad, Habibul Alam, Sarwar Ali, Haroon Habib, Syed Sadrud Jaman Halal, and Sajjad Zaheer. I have also had the pleasure and honor of meeting and interviewing some exceptional individuals who were involved in the events that I have chronicled in this book. Kamal Hossain and Amirul Islam gave generously of their time. I deeply regret the fact that I cannot place this volume in the hands of other protagonists who shared their insights with me: A. K. Damodaran, P. N. Dhar, Brajesh Mishra, and K. Subrahmanyam. This book owes them a great deal, and so does history.

In researching this book, I was fortunate to be assisted at various points by Rakesh Ankit, Sandeep Bhardwaj, and Swapna Nayudu. Sandeep deserves special thanks for being much more than a "research assistant." He managed my office while I disappeared for a long spell of writing and, more generally, humored my obsession with the 1971 crisis. Anirban Bandhyopadhyay helped translate the Bengali sources. I also owe a debt of gratitude to friends who went out of their way in providing me with various materials that were not easy to access: Rohit Chandra, Josie Joseph, Madhav Khosla, Bill Reid, and Lorenz Luthi.

The manuscript was read at short notice by Ramachandra Guha, Daniel Sargent, and Jeremi Suri. Their detailed and perceptive comments helped me tighten the book and sharpen its arguments: I am profoundly grateful. Devesh Kapur and Partha Mukhopadhyay tried their best to remedy my ignorance of public finance and international economics. My conversations on the history and politics of this period with Rudra Chaudhuri, Mahesh Rangarajan, and Pranay Sharma have been very illuminating, for me at any rate. Needless to say, all remaining errors of fact and interpretation are mine alone.

A number of institutions and individuals have supported me while I researched and wrote this book. Defence Studies Department, King's College London, granted me an extended leave of absence. Devesh Kapur not only invited me to spend a month at the Center for the Advanced Study of India, University of Pennsylvania, but generously placed at my disposal documents from the World Bank that he had procured as that institution's official historian. David Malone invited me to Ottawa for a conference and arranged for me to stay on to consult the Canadian archives. Sunil Khilnani appointed me to a senior research fellowship at King's India Institute, King's College London, and has been a great source of encouragement. I began seriously working on this book only after I joined the Centre for Policy Research in 2009. Few places can provide a more congenial perch from which to observe contemporary Indian foreign policy as well as write international history. I am most grateful to Pratap Bhanu Mehta and other colleagues for their support and encouragement over the years.

The ideas and arguments in this book were presented at several settings and were, in consequence, refined and improved. For these opportunities I am grateful to K. Sivaramakrishnan at Yale University; Mahesh Rangarajan at Nehru Memorial Museum and Library; Ashutosh Varshney, Prerna Singh, and Vipin Narang at the Brown-M.I.T.-Harvard Seminar on South Asian Politics; and Kriti Kapila at King's India Institute, King's College London.

While writing this book, I was fortunate to be invited to join a remarkable group that met over a couple of years to think about India's strategic choices and produced the document *NonAlignment 2.0*. I have learned immensely from these wide-ranging discussions, and I would like to thank Lieutenant General (Retd.) Prakash Menon, Nandan Nilekani, Shyam Saran, Siddharth Varadarajan, as well as Latha Reddy and Shivshankar Menon.

I am grateful—for their patience, encouragement, and advice—to my editors, Sharmila Sen of Harvard University Press, and Anuradha Roy and Rukun Advani of Permanent Black. Heather Hughes at Harvard University Press and Melody Negron at Westchester Publishing Services worked under an extremely pressing deadline to convert my raw manuscript into a finished book. Vickie West did a superb job as copyeditor. Isabelle Lewis drew the maps.

Without my agent, Gill Coleridge, this book might not have seen the light of day. Her wisdom and tact have been crucial throughout. My thanks also go to Cara Jones of Rogers, Coleridge & White Agency.

My largest debt is to my family. My wife, Pritha, remains my greatest inspiration. Our children, Kavya and Dhruv, were born during the course of finishing the book. Kavya is two years old as it goes into press and is delighted that I have finally obeyed her injunction to "close the laptop." My mother-in-law, Sukanya Venkatachalam, has been a pillar of support. My parents, Geetha and K. S. Raghavan, have kindly overlooked my neglect of filial responsibilities while I wrote this book. For their love, support, and encouragement, no mere acknowledgment can suffice. This book is for them.

INDEX